Trade Unions and European Integration

T0382728

Trade Unions and European Integration brings together pessimists and optimists on trade unionism under the contemporary pressures of European integration. The Great Recession has brought new attention to structural problems of the European integration process, specifically monetary integration, holding the potential to disable any transnational co-ordination. Other authors argue that the current crisis also poses the chance for mobilization and new impulses for European trade unionism. This is discussed in the volume alongside a variety of topics including bargaining coordination, co-determination, European governance regimes, and European wide mobilization.

While the importance of the question of how trade unionism and wage policy can, will, and should develop under the conditions of European integration seems widely shared, the polarization of the debate itself deserves our attention to learn about the opposing arguments and points of view, and to enhance academic discussion as well as consultancy to policy makers. This volume addresses this debate by bringing together the most distinguished voices and searching for common ground as well as new perspectives on European trade unionism and collective bargaining. The chapters of the volume, organized topically, are each accompanied by a comment from a distinguished scholar, highlighting the divisions of the debate. With this innovative approach, this book advances the dialogue between what have become openly opposed camps of optimists and pessimists on the future of European integration, trade unionism, and its future chances.

Trade Unions and European Integration will appeal to students and researchers interested in fields such as European Studies, Industrial Relations, Political Economics, Social Movements, and Sociology of Work.

Johannes M. Kiess is a post-doctoral researcher at Siegen University, Germany.

Martin Seeliger is an assistant professor at the Europa-Universität Flensburg, Germany.

Routledge Advances in Sociology

For more information about this series, please visit: www.routledge.com/ Routledge-Advances-in-Sociology/book-series/SE0511

Trade Unions and European Integration

A Question of Optimism and Pessimism?

Edited by
Johannes M. Kiess and
Martin Seeliger

LONDON AND NEW YORK

First published 2019
by Routledge
2 Park Square, Milton Park, Abingdon, Oxon OX14 4RN

and by Routledge
605 Third Avenue, New York, NY 10017

First issued in paperback 2020

Routledge is an imprint of the Taylor & Francis Group, an informa business

British Library Cataloguing-in-Publication Data
A catalogue record for this book is available from the British Library

Library of Congress Cataloging-in-Publication Data
A catalog record has been requested for this book

ISBN 13: 978-0-367-72816-8 (pbk)
ISBN 13: 978-0-367-18885-6 (hbk)

Typeset in Times New Roman
by codeMantra

CV 01.08.2021 0420

Contents

List of figures

List of tables

List of contributors

Andreas Bieler, University of Nottingham

Hans-Jürgen Bieling, Eberhard Karls University Tübingen

Donatella della Porta, Scuola Normale Superiore (Florence)

Anne Engelhardt, Kassel University

Roland Erne, UCD Michael Smurfit Graduate Business School (Dublin)

Vera Glassner, Johannes-Kepler-University (Linz)

Sara Lafuente Hernández, Researcher, European Trade Union Institute

Martin Höpner, Max Planck Institute for the Study of Society (Cologne)

Stefanie Hürtgen, University of Salzburg

Johannes Kiess, University of Siegen

Guglielmo Meardi, University of Warwick

Madelaine Moore, Kassel University

Oliver Nachtwey, University of Basel

Susanne Pernicka, Johannes-Kepler-University Linz

Ludger Pries, Ruhr-Universität Bochum

Martin Seeliger, Europa-Universität Flensburg

Daniel Seikel, Institute for Economic and Social Research (WSI) in the Hans-Böckler-Foundation (Düsseldorf)

Wolfgang Streeck, Max Planck Institute for the Study of Society (Cologne)

Georg Vobruba, University of Leipzig

Benjamin Werner, University of Bremen

Preface

This book is the result of lively – sometimes nightly – discussions between us editors about the deficits of sociological research on trade unions in Europe. We both have written our PhDs in the field and ever since enjoy engaging in controversial discussions about the different – pessimistic and optimistic – perspectives on central issues. These issues include but are not limited to wage bargaining coordination, codetermination, mobilization, and European governance, including the respective social preconditions. One central observation was that some of the research perspectives did talk about common phenomena – but not to each other. This may be a result of differentiation processes within academia; nevertheless it is a fact that obstructs controversial discussions and balanced accounts on a topic too important to play only a niche role in the scholarship on European integration. Hence, we decided with this volume to go beyond complaining and private discussions.

The thoughts presented in the introduction represent our cooperation, which benefitted over the last few years from institutional bases in Cologne, Jena, Flensburg, and Siegen. The Max Planck Institute for the Study of Societies in Cologne was not only inspirational in its often critical assessment of integration but, in the form of Martin Höpner's research group on the Political Economy of the European Integration, also provided us with a logistic base to start the editing of this volume. The focus of the Jena power resources approach, in contrast, opened insights into the potentials and capacities of trade union action. In Siegen, several projects focussing on European sociological research questions complemented these perspectives with a micro-sociological one. In Flensburg, too, the focus on European sociology adds a contrasting perspective to those of Cologne and Jena.

Chapter 1

Introduction

Trade unions under the pressure of European integration. A question of optimism and pessimism?

Martin Seeliger and Johannes Kiess

What role do trade unions play in the European integration process? Ten years after the European Court of Justice called into question basic tenets of the European "social model" (Höpner 2013) with its decisions on the free movement of services and the institutionalised right to strike, and with the crisis of globalised financial capitalism forcing the so-called "debt countries" into austerity by political mandate, putting Southern Europe's working class under distress, this issue – the "trade unions under the great transformation", as Deppe (2012) put it – is more pressing than ever (Seeliger 2019).

The integration of ever more European countries into an ever-institutionally deepening common market has always been the cornerstone of European integration, famously coined by the heads of states and government in 1981[1] as a "commitment to progress towards an ever closer union". However, contrary to the neo-functionalist hope for spillover effects and as the deepening inequalities within the common currency area have shown, strengthening economic interdependencies has by no means led to the kind of social cohesion that social scientists often think is a necessity for a somewhat fair and just coexistence (Polanyi 1957). While from a neo-classical point of view, the integration of a common labour market allows for a more efficient division of labour and thus more effective means of production (Smith 1904), capitalist means of organisation[2] also require some collective form of organisation of labour interests. Under current conditions, we would still think of trade unions first to offer this kind of collective mobilisation.

The deepening of European integration has institutionalised several mechanisms within the Eurozone, most importantly through the abolition of tariff and trade barriers as well as the linking of labour market and social policy to the macroeconomic benchmark management of the Economic and Monetary Union (EMU). These mechanisms implicate regime competition regarding national-level labour and employment regulations. Therefore, the coincidental and systematic deficit of European integration is that this "negative integration" (Scharpf 1999) has – up until now – not been sufficiently accompanied by measures of "positive integration", i.e., the establishment of meaningful institutionalised social policy at the European level. Precisely because of the ever-advancing integration of the European Single Market, any European trade union strategy would have to focus on the stabilisation or expansion of national-level labour markets and social policies, and/or their supplementation at the European level.

Thus, for national-level trade unions and labour organisations, the biggest challenge lies in the necessity to formulate a concerted political strategy to influence the process of integration. However, specifically against the backdrop of the European Union's (EU's) Eastern enlargement in 2004 and 2007, we can identify a threefold problem of heterogeneity in the field of trade union politics: first, European Member States differ widely regarding institutional settings like labour law or national modes of wage bargaining. Second, on the organisational level, we can also find national evolutionary paths that shaped the structure, scope, and ideological orientation of the respective trade union movements. Third, especially between Eastern and Northern European trade unions, the gap in terms of power resources continues to be challenging, resulting in asymmetric coordination between them (see Seeliger 2017 and this volume). Developing common political positions thus happens under conditions of inequality within these (at least) three dimensions. We can therefore assume that the establishment of common positions is becoming not only more important but also more difficult.

Most recently, the difficulties have increased in the wake of the cascade of crises that have shaken up the EU. If we indeed see ourselves in the middle of an open-ended process of politicisation of the EU (Zürn 2013: 413), then, we would argue, this diagnosis is most important for trade unions as organisations representing European wage earners. "Hard times may result in strategic paralysis, but can also stimulate the framing of new objectives, new levels of intervention, and new forms of action" (Gumbrell-McCormick/ Hyman 2013: 192) – it is probably hard to find a more precise assessment of the state of European trade union politics and its perspectives.

As the contemporary debate shows, assessments of what role European trade unions are able to fulfil within this constellation vary a great deal, even among the most prominent representatives of political sociology of industrial relations. While Jelle Visser (2012: 130) thinks it is more likely that "21st century capitalism will be shaken up by banks rather than by trade unions", others, like Klaus Dörre, read the wage conflicts of the "strike year" 2015 as new tailwind for the renewal of trade union power resources in the structural conflict between capital and labour, with hope for European mobilisation in particular (Dörre et al. 2016).

Against this backdrop, two questions arise: do trade unions (because of their resources and, in connection with these, their positions within the political system) have the ability to emerge as agents of a new form of social integration in the EU? And, second, would such strategic orientation even be in accordance with the often quite specific interests of diverse organisations, which vary not only because of national settings or in terms of sectoral affinity and industry interests but also because of ideological orientation? This volume addresses this constellation, for which the academic literature on the EU offers so many differing assessments (for a general overview see Rüb/Müller 2013; Streeck 2013; Seeliger 2017).[3] In this introductory chapter, we will first discuss the possibilities and limits of trade union politics under the pressure of European integration more generally before we go on to distinguish between four perspectives discussed in the literature. Our aim is to introduce the different sub-disciplines and literatures to each other and facilitate discussion between opposing "camps"; between theoretical and empirical perspectives; and between more optimistic, pro-integrationist and more pessimistic, integration-sceptical assessments.

Possibilities and limits of trade union policy in the process of European integration

Summarising the classic literature on industrial relations in the European context, Marginson and Sisson (2004: XVI) criticise a strong focus on structural issues. While the work on European trade unions since the turn of the century also included some attention to trade unions' potential for action, most studies interested in the political importance of national trade union organisations at the European level can still today be seen as mostly comparative work in a traditional sense. These static perspectives on national circumstances, however, neglect initiatives that provoke conflicts, have a clear potential for politicisation, and imply the potential for institutional change (Kowalsky 2010: 139).

After a first phase of classic studies, a second phase of trade union politics and trade union research started with the founding of the European Trade Union Congress (ETUC) in 1973. On the occasion of the enlargement of the European Economic Community of Great Britain, Denmark, and Ireland, 167 trade unions from 15 Western European countries joined the new European-level umbrella organisation. In addition to descriptive (Niethammer 1977) and field-specific contributions (Köpper 1982), the number of ideological publications in this phase rose as well. To give just one example, Gorz (1974: 224) refers in his work to the "problem of the international strategy of the workers' movement in the face of European integration". The need for transnational organisation and compromise on political strategies had become an important normative question.

At the beginning of the 1990s, the institutionalisation of the common market again marked the entry into a new phase – one that was once more characterised by an even stronger European orientation, also with regard to trade unions themselves. This came with new political salience, which, among other things, was evident in higher membership fees as well as in the transfer of qualified secretaries to Brussels (Schmitter/Streeck 1991: 136f). For example, Dolvik (1999: 16) observed that "European unions wanted to develop a coherent response and to change the rules of the game". At this point, the contours of a powerful concept, which since then has served as a vehicle of political mobilisation, became apparent within the discourse on European integration: the concept of a "Social Europe". Formed and publicised by the then-President of the European Commission Jacques Delors, the idea of a "European Social Model" is based on the assumption that market integration can only develop the desired economic impulses if it is flanked by the establishment of social policy hedges.[4] As the most prominent achievement of this phase, experts particularly emphasise the establishment of the "social dialogue" between European social partners (Weinert 2009). The spirit of optimism that the corresponding establishment of labour market policy institutions at the European level produced at this time – also amongst academic observers – is not least reflected in the hopeful diagnosis of an emerging "Euro-corporatism" (Falkner 1998).

Given the deepening of European competencies in the context of the monetary union and market integration as well as in the context of the various enlargements since 2004, the last 20 years can again be considered a qualitatively new phase of European integration (Mittag 2009). However, while the economic policy measures for the integration of the common market are reflected in a general trend of liberalisation in the Organisation for Economic Co-operation and Development (OECD) countries (Höpner et al. 2011), the establishment of EU-wide standards for the preservation of national minimum standards in social and labour market policy legislation has for the most part remained meaningless (Scharpf 2012). Moreover, a sequence of market-constituting jurisprudence by the European Court of Justice has further encouraged the trend towards the abolition of national labour market institutions with an additional "trend towards successive acceptance of national legislation" (Höpner/Schäfer 2010: 9; Höpner 2011). In light of the most recent economic and social developments in Europe, a growing number of scholars are voicing critical opinions. For example, representatives of the research group "State Project Europe" (2011: 7) recognise a dominance of neo-liberalism in the EU institutions, which Streeck (2013) labels a "liberalization machine" and Deppe (2013) calls out as "authoritarian capitalism".

As Haas (1958: 215) already described in the 1950s, the attitudes of national trade union organisations towards the implications and consequences of European integration emerge from the political heterogeneity of the Union and thus before country-specific backgrounds: "The attitude of labour towards integration depends on the economic and political conditions under which the unions of the ECSC countries live and operate". This assessment has become much more important following the Eastern enlargement of the EU in 2004 (Estonia, Latvia, Lithuania, Malta, Poland, Slovakia, Slovenia, the Czech Republic, Hungary, and Cyprus) and 2007 (Bulgaria and Romania). Inequalities within European countries – but also between them – have since gained interest within the field of European sociology (e.g., Heidenreich 2003; Delhey/Kohler 2006; Heidenreich/Wunder 2008), as have comparative assessments of life satisfaction (Delhey/Kohler 2006; Lahusen/Kiess 2018), transnational solidarity (e.g., Lahusen/Grasso 2018), and identity or EU support (e.g., Mau 2005; Gerhards/Lengfeld 2015). The pace and already achieved depth of integration, we may conclude from this wide field of research, has effects on the people in Europe, and this again affects the process of European integration.

In one way or another, as shown in this brief historical reconstruction, the negotiation of cross-border cooperation between trade unions in the EU takes place under the umbrella of a "European Social Model" or "Social Europe". However, due to the widely differing meanings of the concept, there is no agreement whatsoever about exactly what is meant by the term. According to Hyman (2006: 121), "Social Europe" is an analytical category, an ideological construct, as well as a controversy. The multiple uses of the term follow from its conceptual history. The original introduction can be traced back to the political discussion of the early 1970s (Pierson/Leibfried 1998; Streeck 1998a). With the first "Social Action Plan" of the European Community in 1974 and the European Regional Development Fund established one year later, the Member States presented a supranational initiative to extend the activities of the community into the area of social policy for the first time (Rhodes 1998: 330). In the course of the 1980s and 1990s, the term became increasingly important in the context of the discussion about "(neo-)corporatism", and it gains importance today against the background of recent liberalisation developments (not least because of the low practical importance of any form of "Euro-corporatism").

Even considering the fuzziness of this "European Social Model", it appears to be a significant trait of this debate that the content of any existing or desired "European Social Model" follows the Western (!) European concept of welfare capitalism, i.e., a specific "'historical compromise' between capital and labour" (Streeck 2003: 93). Thus, the European trade unions and the parliamentary left in Europe link to this concept the hope of "preserving that 'European Social Model'; which is characterised by a socially regulated variant of capitalism, that aims at a combination of economic efficiency and (relative) social equality" (Schulten 2005: 15; our translation).

As a point of reference for concrete political positions, demands, and measures, the application of the concept in political practice is subject to constant and fundamental negotiation within the left as well as within and among trade unions. As a "socio-political formula of the future", the concept of a "European Social Model" "is a political-ideological construct [...] which defines and propagates European similarities which should be realised" (Aust et al. 2002: 273; our translation). The discussion about the meaning of the symbolic framework "Social Europe" is thus not least a framing process: the aim of establishing a specific understanding of the concept is also to find "a shared interpretative framework that facilitates coordination, exchange, and ultimately commitment" (Ansell 1997: 360).

Against the backdrop of the negative impact of European integration on trade unions within the member countries over the past years (especially in Southern Europe), it seems remarkable that the belief in the fundamental possibility of a "European Social Model" has survived the turmoil of the crisis, at least among European trade union officials. Despite and because of the obvious adversities and distortions that the process has brought to European workers (Stützle 2014), basic support for integration comes from the belief that the strengthening of the European level of regulation will counter the recent liberalisation trend. In general, scholars such as Streeck (2015) and Wagner (2013) see a particular preference for the transnational regulatory arena among representatives at the European level. Höpner (2015: 30) argues that a normative paradigm exists in which any problem of European integration seems to be solvable by even "more of Europe", that is, by shifting political competences and democratic processes towards the political system of the EU and thus beyond the status quo. Apart from such criticism of "normative integrationism", Vobruba (2015, 2017) argues – from an actor-centred institutionalist perspective – that actors in once established institutional settings have the tendency to react with further institution building when confronted with problematic situations. While we can assume quite generally that the goal of European trade union cooperation is social progress, integrationist measures in this sense are means to an end. If, on the other hand, a "more of Europe" becomes a general instrument, which is used to solve all sorts of political problems or even to an ideological purpose that compromises social goals, such strategies are referred to as "normative integrationist".

In order to differentiate positions in the literature on the possibilities and limits of European trade unionism under the pressure of advancing integration, in the following section, we describe four principal perspectives. We are, by no means, claiming, however, that these can always be clearly separated, and we do not wish to push any individual researcher into a specific "camp". We simply aim to sketch out the debate and analytically distinguish different perspectives in order to facilitate a more fruitful and interdisciplinary discussion.

Perspectives on European integration between optimism and pessimism

With the liberalisation processes discussed earlier in mind, Meardi (2012: 156), too, sees the enlarged Union as an "initial test for union capacities". If trade unions do fail in establishing joint positions on a cross-border scale, corresponding internationalist efforts on an even larger, or global, scale are in vain. Looking at this starting question, and considering the political status quo as well as contemporary developments, we can identify a continuum of positions within the literature.

On the one hand, "optimistic" contributions emphasise – based on empirical and (often only) conceptual findings – the possibility and – based on the identification of push and pull factors – the necessity of international cooperation (Kowalsky 2010). On the other hand, "pessimistic" contributions point to the obstacles of international trade union representation, identifying the causes particularly in the threefold heterogeneity problem discussed earlier, a general loss of influence at the national level, and the lack of the commitment of European associations to their member organisations. Against this backdrop, according to Mittag (2010: 44), trade unions are hardly succeeding in reaching unanimous positions in the debate over a "European Social Model" that has been fading for years or in the even more conceptual debate over a "Social Europe".

We have differentiated the following presentation of these two "broad – albeit somewhat oversimplified – camps of 'Euro-optimists' and 'Euro-pessimists'" (Platzer 1997: 68) further into four important but not exhaustive categories. We have also included different epistemological perspectives as this, in our view, more adequately represents the scholarship relevant to the question posed in the beginning. Once again, however, we do not seek to give a thorough overview of the literature but simply aim to present an analytical distinction on the basis of which this important debate can thrive. Some scholars will appear in more than one category; from others we may only cite one study to exemplify one category, thus oversimplifying research agendas. We argue, however, that a reflection on different perspectives can nevertheless stimulate fruitful discussions in an academic world where research tends to speak to one specific literature, ignoring debates in other contexts.

The (pessimist) perspective of comparative political economy

A first perspective we want to highlight takes as its analytical starting point the assumption that unions, in their role as wage cartels and authorities of the political representation of the interests of wage earners, face the task of integrating various and partly competing individual interests. This is the somewhat universal problem of all trade unions (Dribbusch 2014; cf. Zeuner 2004; Hyman 2003). Historically, the nation-state has offered the most important framework for this exercise. According to Mittag (2010: 42), trade unions are therefore primarily concerned with national-level institutions and conflicts, including national communications structures.

At the same time, according to the Commission, the panorama of national industrial relations within the EU is "one of diversity", and thus there is no "general EU model of trade unionism" apparent (European Commission

2011: 8). In the context of the Eastern enlargement Meardi (2012: 16) polemicises against this reading and points at its implications: "The EU's motto unitas in pluralitate ('United in Diversity') sounds increasingly like meaning unitas in inaequalitate ('United in Unequality')". Most importantly, against the backdrop of the post-Soviet privatisation waves, new business start-ups, and a general decline in full-time employment, the bargaining capability of Eastern European trade unions does not match that of their Western European sister organisations (Deppe/Tatur 2002; Galgoczi 2014). To cut a long story short, in order to establish common political positions between trade unions from the old and the new member countries, a key challenge arises particularly from the weak *wage bargaining structures* in Eastern European countries (with the exception of Slovenia).

A further complication arises from the fact that many Eastern European trade unions have *low resources* due to their comparatively low mobilisation rates and small membership. With regard to their negotiating status at the European level, this weakness translates into a weak position against the strong trade unions in Western Europe (Hoffmann 2010: 152). The effects of the financial crisis on Eastern European countries have even worsened these inequalities (Bernaciak et al. 2014: 44), and we can expect long-term consequences for the weakened Southern European trade unions as well, enforcing a second geographical divide.

In addition to the scarcity of financial resources among the national associations, *intercultural differences* can ultimately be the cause of misunderstandings regarding the establishment of common political positions between Eastern and Western European representatives at the EU level (Klemm et al. 2011). And, of course, added to this East-West divide comes the North-South divide, which can be expected to increase due to the long-term effects of the Euro-crisis.

Against the backdrop of structural heterogeneity between trade union organisations at the meso and national frameworks at the macro level, contributions from the field of comparative political economics reach the conclusion that a "European Social Model" that would harmonise labour and employment standards at the level of Western European welfare states is highly unlikely (see Höpner/Schäfer 2010, 2012a, 2012b; Chapter 7 in this volume).

While the emphasis on restrictions that oppose a transnational organisation of trade unions is without question an important aspect and should definitely be included in any empirical assessment, the emphasis solely on institutional conditions established by work in this field raises questions about the possible creative potentials of political actors. Thus, against such a structuralist or deterministic view, Kowalsky (2010: 139) argues, it should also be noted that European initiatives that provoke conflicts clearly have potential for politicisation, and thus a potential for change.

The perspective of (calculated) Euro-optimism

While the comparative political economy perspective's emphasis on structural heterogeneity focusses epistemologically on the obstacles of cross-border institution formation, a second perspective takes as a starting point of its considerations the challenges that are motivating unions to pursue transnational organisation in the first place. In this respect, Ebbinghaus and Visser (1994: 250) distinguish between push and pull factors: while a loss of influence and wage pressure at the national level increases the need for international cooperation, the idea of a strong European level of regulation, from this perspective, promises new potentials for political influence.

An important – if not the most important – assumption of such "optimistic" contributions is the notion that trade unions have, under conditions of European integration (and globalisation as a whole), no other option than representing their interests collectively and on an international scale. Only if they overcome national egoisms (for example, in terms of wage restraint) could new foundations of political power be established. According to Ulrich Beck (2000), one of the most prominent representatives of such an internationalisation-optimistic position, trade unions, like other organisations, have to re-invent themselves transnationally. Because of such (perceived) necessities, representatives of this perspective are often quite positive about the assessment of the sensitivity of trade unionism towards Europe: today, the European agenda, they claim, is well represented across departments of trade unions' bureaucracies, and the topic is reported to be firmly anchored within trade union education (Hoffmann 2011: 149).

In addition to the perceived necessity for international cooperation, there is also a normative attitude at the core of this "calculated-optimistic" perspective. Following not least Marx's ideal of the worldwide unity of all proletarians, the action of the labour movement should be directed (at least nominally) at the largest possible version of a solidarity community. It is in this context that the political thrust of proletarian "inter"-nationalism (Lenin 1969) gains its contours. Bormann and Jungehülsing (2016: 58) sum up the basic idea of this political orientation: "The interests of those exploited by capital are basically the same worldwide, and the indignation about the injustice involved should also be spread throughout the world" (our translation).

A similar assumption leads Brunkhorst (2014: 167) to recognise a "transnational class situation" (our translation) among European wage earners, which, through well-organised forms of discussion among national trade union representatives, can turn into shared "class consciousness". Indeed, if we look at the strike statistics of the crisis years, we see that in 2010 alone, 24 general strikes were held in Europe – more than in a whole decade in the 1980s and 1990s, respectively (Gallas/Nowak 2012). As a consequence, Brunkhorst (2014: 166) concludes that there is a "transnationalisation of the class struggle" as an "alternative to the retreat into the fortress of the national welfare state" (again our translation). Because of the continued austerity policies across the continent, this crisis is now for the first time perceived as a common European problem. At the same time, Brunkhorst goes on to suggest that global capitalism has made the already pacified class conflict between labour and capital manifest again, even in the richer countries that can (still) rely on the decommodification capacity of the welfare state. Thus, national class struggles become increasingly meaningless because the long-term unemployed German shares far more material and ideological interests with his Greek colleague than with his respective wealthy countrymen. Trans- or inter-national mobilisation against an equally transnationalised enemy should be the consequence.

Loh and Skupien (2016: 594) make a complementary claim by highlighting the potentials of a European trade union movement: "A strong and functioning European trade union movement, institutionalised, for example, in the form of the European Trade Union Confederation, can serve as a central – or at least a complementary – actor for other European public and transnational parties" (our translation). With their proposal of strong European wage coordination to prevent internal competition, as well as the introduction of a European minimum wage, the authors also use two frequently found reference points of Euro-optimist reasoning in support of their proposal (cf. Schroeder/Weinert 2004; Schulten et al. 2005). They top their proposal off with the idea of introducing a European unemployment insurance scheme in order to "backhandedly" (sic!) allow for social transfers within the EU to tackle growing inequalities.

Contributions from this end of the spectrum, we can conclude, do not lack ideas by any means. Rather, their lack of an empirical basis of such claims stands out (see Chapter 6 in this volume for the problems of establishing meaningful wage coordination). The fact that representatives of a certain perspective or political argument consider certain measures to be necessary does not mean that such proposals can actually be realised. However, true to the proverb "hope is a rope", assessments of the potential of international organisation also (or even above all) serve their enablement in the first place. Thus, we opted to characterise this perspective as one of "calculated Euro-optimism".

The Euro-sceptic perspective

While the comparative political-economic perspective emphasises institutional heterogeneity, and purpose-oriented contributions justify the possibility of European organisation out of necessity, a third perspective on European trade unionism is highly sceptical of any integrationist development based on an action-theoretical point of view. In this sense, scholars such as Hoffmann (2010: 100) identify multiple problems for trade union activities at the European level, which can be disentangled as follows.[5]

As indicated earlier (see "Perspectives on European integration between optimism and pessimism"), the contemporary framework of trade union action in the context of European integration is one of continued liberalisation and deregulation. From this point of view, the market-based restructuring of the EU places national settings in systematic regime competition (Streeck 1998a). In the literature on welfare state research, this has been thoroughly discussed as a possible trend of convergence towards a neoliberal paradigm (Fehmel 2012; Hermann 2014; Elsässer et al. 2015). For trade unions, most prominently and already towards the end of the 1990s, Streeck described this shift as one to "competitive solidarity" (1998b: 252):

> In trying to adapt to the new economic circumstances, national communities seek to defend their solidarity, less through protection and redistribution than through joint competitive and productive success – through politics, not against markets, but within and with them, gradually replacing protective and redistributive with competitive and productive solidarity.

Under given conditions, a number of reasons within the federation itself speak against an effective organisation of trade union power at the European level. With regard to the material resources of European trade unions, Platzer (2010) recognises three deficits of organisational transnationalisation. First, "serious asymmetries" have always existed between the corporate structures of representation at the European level, which (second) reflected the low level of staffing and (third) the "structural underfinancing" of European associations in general and trade unions in particular – whose budget was between 20% and 60% dependent on EU Commission subsidies (our translations: see also Martin/Ross 2001).

Koch-Baumgarten (2006: 219) furthermore recognises important content-related dysfunctions within the internal structure of the associations: "Elite communication, informal procedures, long legitimation chains, unequal participatory opportunities, as well as unequal influence for regional, sectoral, and gender groups, remain fundamental obstacles to the internal decision-making processes" (our translation). In addition to the international heterogeneity that is emphasised by the perspective of comparative political economy, Seeliger and Wagner (2016) recognise a cleavage between the European industry associations and the ETUC, resulting from the increasingly integrationist orientation of the ETUC's representatives. The ETUC's ability to "aggregate the different national trade union objectives into enforceable programs" (Armingeon 1994: 209, our translation) in such a constellation is seriously put into question. At the same time, Dribbusch (2014: 343) sees strong, persistent effects of the national member organisations of the European associations: "European trade union policy plays only a marginal role in the everyday life of trade unions, with only few exceptions.

Apart from a few small working groups, there is no internationalism at the member's level, at least not in Germany". European politics, according to the author (ibid.), is "primarily a matter of full-time specialists within the trade unions' bureaucracy".

Beyond the labour movement's own organisational and structural limitations, potential partners of trade unions at the European level, most notably employer's organisations, have shown little interest in collective bargaining – even though European social dialogue is institutionalised and could produce legally binding agreements (Branch/Greenwood 2001) – that goes beyond the coordination of policies under the "shadow of law" (Falkner 2000). Observers conclude that the European social dialogue "does not constitute a system of industrial relations on the European level" (de Boer et al. 2005) but rather forms a lobbying channel. At the same time, the European institutions themselves may welcome trade unions as well as social movement actors at the European level not least because of their own lack of legitimacy, but in fact are not the right address for labour claims as long as the Member States are the ones in charge of any meaningful policy decision (see Chapter 3 in this volume).

From this perspective, and in the face of the frequently rigid organisational structures, it is at least questionable to what extent – and if at all – one can hope for a timely (re)vitalisation of the European trade union movement (Voss/Sherman 2001). However, there are some important arguments against the rigorous notion of the "substantial lack of success of symbolic euro-corporatism" (Schulten 2000: 238).

Reflexive optimism

A fourth perspective to be found in the literature on European trade unions takes as its starting point the empirically ascertainable intensification of cross-border activities (Weinert 2001: 336). In this sense, Dörre (2010: 900), too, describes "first attempts to the formation of transnational bargaining systems [...] as well as international interests". We shall refer to this position as reflexive optimism.[6] From this perspective, objections raised by comparative political economy towards the establishment of common trade union positions at the EU level are by no means obsolete. However, the "transnational exchange relations between labour-political actors", as Pernicka (2015: 16) criticises, "remain underexposed".

In order not to have to remain at an appellative level, work in this area is often characterised by a specific methodology that allows for a research-based framework beyond the deterministic bias of comparative political economy. For example, we can identify an action-theoretic-constructivist approach, from which the preferences and interests of political actors appear to be by no means fixed but seem to be subject to constant negotiation (Lewis 2005, Seeliger 2017; Kiess in this volume, Chapter 16). A second major difference is that, in this perspective, the nation-state is by no means the primary reference unit. Starting with the assumption "that the variation in industrial relations arrangements within countries and *within* industrial sectors is probably as large as that *between* industries and countries" (Hyman 2001a: 221), at least case study-based research, often referred to as "Global Labour Studies", puts local initiatives at centre stage and points to them as possible breeding grounds for international solidarity (Webster et al. 2008).

Another reversal of sceptical axioms is the re-interpretation of internationalisation as an opportunity. For example, Evans (2010: 353) emphasises that precisely the neoliberal internationalisation of value creation in disembedded labour markets creates opportunities for the establishment of workers' power: "[R]ather than assuming the global level is labour's Achilles heel, it makes sense to explore how mobilisation at the global level can contribute to contestation at the local and national level". Can the supposed crisis of labour politics thus be understood as an opportunity (see also Chapter 2 in this volume)? The difference from the aforementioned "calculated Euro-optimism" of "reflexive optimists" lies in the empirical openness of the latter (see the comment by Kiess in this volume, Chapter 15).

A similar assessment can be found with Gumbrell-McCormick and Hyman (2013: 193), who see the heterogeneity between organisations from different countries by no means as a hurdle, but as an opportunity to expand their own action repertoire. Organisational learning, according to the authors (ibid.),

> is most likely when there is a leadership team from diverse backgrounds and with a range of organizational experiences, and is least likely when there is a homogeneous leadership group deeply embedded in bureaucratic routines.

An emergent structure of different EU-wide regulatory initiatives, whose interdependence could gradually converge into an EU-wide structure, is also described by Turner (1996, 2005) as well as by Pries (2010). Further empirical examples can be found in the mobilisation against the country of origin principle in the Services Directive (Arnold 2008), in the initiatives on wage coordination (Glassner/Pernicka 2014a, 2014b), or in the moderating activities of European Works Councils (EWCs) under conditions of EU-wide location competition (Hertwig et al. 2009).

Another important point of reference for the perspective of reflexive optimism is, finally, the potential of significant symbols and discourses that can develop among political actors in the course of European integration. While Kowalsky (2010: 87) identifies the "real problem of Europe" in the "far-reaching lack of debates and political alternatives to European issues", Preunkert and Vobruba (2015) recognise – especially against the backdrop of the Euro-crisis – the (at least potentially) productive importance of conflicts for the establishment and implementation of a European bargaining arena. A similar argument is also brought forward by Platzer (2010), who considers the European trade union federations to be "social laboratories" that could develop new reference systems of trade union action in the medium term as starting points of "New Utopias" (Hyman 2001b: 173; see also Chapter 10 in this volume).

Concluding remarks and outlook

In this introduction we set out to analytically distinguish four perspectives in the literature on the possibilities and limits of European trade unionism under the pressure of advancing integration. Strict assessments from a comparative political-economic perspective emphasise the heterogeneity of the European Member States and thus the structural differences between national trade union movements. The calculated optimist perspective points at the necessity of transnational organisations and concludes its feasibility from this necessity. Here we find the most advanced ideas of how Europe could be developed. We contrasted this with what we called the Euro-sceptic perspective arguing that the possibilities of organisation and meaningful policy-making for trade unions at the European level are, at best, restricted. Finally, we identified the perspective of reflexive optimism, which apparently holds some optimism towards integration, but carefully investigates the actual development of mobilisation in this respect. We by no means claim that these perspectives alone capture the wide range of scholarship or that scholarly work can always be separated clearly into such categories. And of course, we do not wish to push any individual researcher to identify with a specific perspective or even into a specific "camp". Rather, we have shown that some authors (including ourselves) appear in several of the four subsections as they already draw on different perspectives in order to reach well-informed assessments.

However, our starting point was that the academic knowledge production relevant to pressing contemporary questions is divided between sub-disciplines or specific "literatures" (one of the downsides of over-specialisation in academia) while, as the following chapters will show, questions like transnational coordination are addressed by most of them in one way or another. We aimed to sketch out the debate to facilitate a more fruitful and interdisciplinary discussion, as this topic will gain further centrality in the near future. And we aimed to collect multiple perspectives in this volume in order to contribute to the search for trade union strategies at the European level as well as their critical assessment by social scientists. To underline the diversity of approaches, we invited scholars from various fields of research to present their expertise in a full chapter. For each chapter we then asked another scholar for a critical comment providing critique, complementing perspectives, or contradicting expertise. In the following we will sketch out the content of the volume in order of appearance.

In Chapter 2, *Donatella della Porta* looks at the intersection of social movement studies and trade union studies, taking the (mutual) disinterest as a starting point. Moreover, a large part of social movement studies since the 1990s has systematically excluded capitalism and related research questions from their portfolio. Especially in what she identifies as the contemporary era of "late neo-liberalism" and with the Euro-crisis fuelling new protest dynamics, social movement studies need to refocus attention towards class issues. In fact, they already have and della Porta finds both "optimistic" (or anti-systemic, Wallerstein-oriented) and "pessimistic" (or defensive, Polanyi-oriented) assessments in the literature and in her own observation of new formations of class-based social movements. Whether hopes or fears are justified, however, is hard to say as of today. The crisis of labour mobilisation today in a long-term perspective may turn out to be only a silent phase before a new uprising.

Wolfgang Streeck comments on *Donatella della Porta* by pointing out structural characteristics of the European "fake polity" which fundamentally "lacks sovereignty" while being, in fact, governed by national governments. Because of this, any hopes of social movement actors to impact on European institutions and their policy-making in any meaningful way seem unrealistic. Also, European solidarity between trade unions, e.g., between Northern and Southern workers, is structurally limited to lip services since the wage regimes of the European Member States co-governed (at least still to some extent) by trade unions stand in competition with each other. Rather than "framing" such views on European integration optimistic or pessimistic, Streeck argues to be realistic about their constraining characteristics.

The fourth chapter by *Andreas Bieler* and *Hans-Jürgen Bieling* aims "to explore the partially diverging strategic choices by European trade unions and their impact on the development of industrial relations". The authors do so against the backdrop of neo-Gramscian theory, which emphasises the hegemony of neo-liberalism, backed by social classes across countries benefitting from the current arrangements. In this situation, strategic choice for trade unions is not only limited but also, again across countries, potentially contradicting. Consequently, to escape from the deadlock of institutionalised and further progressing neoliberal restructuring, trade unions and their (political) allies need to develop counter-hegemonic projects, the authors argue.

In his comment *Georg Vobruba* challenges this analysis for epistemological reasons but also points at its self-intimidating effect. If "neo-liberalism" is hegemonic and thus potentially subverting every policy field and social actor, the agency of trade unions is already limited to this hegemonic order. Against this reading, the author points at the ambivalent character of European integration and emphasises that even the crisis policies were not all "neo-liberal". Also, the role of trade unions within national contexts but also within the European integration process is ambivalent. Here the two chapters find some common ground. However, Vobruba would prefer future research to concentrate on the complex conflict constellations that trade unions are involved in.

Susanne Pernicka and *Vera Glassner* are concerned with the development and status quo of European wage coordination (Chapter 6). While in the 1990s trade unions themselves tried to establish coordination following principles like social protection and solidarity, since the Euro-crisis a new supranational economic governance regime "includes authoritative forms of wage coordination across different national fields". This governance seeks to transform national industrial relations towards market liberalism. The authors analyse these transformations from a field theoretical and power sensitive theoretical perspective. Because earlier ideas of solidarity are not dominant in the policy discourse, any "reorientation of supranational policy actors towards a wage policy that names and shames strategies of wage undercutting and forming policy coalitions against the dismantling of collective wage setting institutions" seems unlikely.

In the following comment *Martin Höpner* adds to this pessimistic assessment from a comparative political economy perspective, but his critique is even more fundamental: because the exchange rates within the common currency area are fixed, unit labour costs can only be adjusted through internal devaluation effectively throwing out attempts to coordinate wages. The author argues that European wage policy, moreover, faces a coordination paradox because of the heterogeneity of European wage bargaining institutions: while internal coordination is the structural precondition for supranational wage coordination, it is actually countries with coordinated wage regimes that are practising "beggar their neighbours" politics, because they are able to control their wages more effectively. Against this backdrop, there seems only be the alternative wage bargaining autonomy *or* common currency area.

In Chapter 8, *Martin Seeliger* investigates the heterogeneity of national contexts or, more precisely, the differing role trade unions are able to play in the development of policy positions at the European level. This is the case in particular with Eastern European trade unions which have differing interests but also very different resources when it comes to negotiating with their Northern European counterparts. Seeliger exemplifies this with empirical material from the discussions about a European minimum wage and on the Freedom of Services. The chapter points at the instrumental meaning of social Europe and at the important role of social skills among European-level trade unionists. This leads third to a rather ambiguous assessment of the possibilities for European trade unionism. While the heterogeneity and power disparity are underlined, there is also fruitful cooperation which could possibly be enhanced by adopting more democratic decision-making processes and enabling financial support of weaker member organisations.

Guglielmo Meardi in his comment largely agrees with Seeliger's assessment and asks for further attention to the central concepts of power, international integration, and skills. Like Vobruba before, Meardi assumes that the power relations are more complex than they appear and how current research conceptualises them. Distinctions like East West or North South are in most cases not adequate to a reality where also weaker organisations enter coalitions, employ concepts like "Social Europe", and lobby for their interests. Moreover, Europeanisation has already had an impact on the different actors; thus social skills and ideas have spread, although some of these ideas take time to flourish.

Ludger Pries investigates in Chapter 10 whether EWCs are effective institutions in providing consultation, information, and interest exchange for both management and employees. The author argues that with the EWCs *"a European body of interest mediation and regulation"* is being institutionalised. This could form one crucial cornerstone of the emergence of European societal integration, thus going beyond the field of industrial relations. Analysing EWCs as "potentialities", Pries argues, reveals a dynamic of Europeanisation of labour relations, the growing legal negotiation potential of EWCs, and leverage effects between countries and actors. In a very optimistic reading, EWCs could also inform the global establishment of interest representation and labour regulation.

Stefanie Hürtgen criticises the majority of the literature on EWCs as well as Pries's chapter for not asking consequently about the effects of EWCs on social protection. The emergence of a "Social Europe" and, alongside, European standards of social protection that would stop any races to the bottom would, however, form the main reference frame to evaluate EWCs. In order to employ such an evaluation, Hürtgen refers to further disciplines, namely sociology of work and industry, debates from the Global Production Network literature, and Critical European Political Economy. Against this backdrop, the author emphasises the structurally limited impact of EWCs on the social dimension of European integration. For one, work site competition across Europe needs to be read as multidimensional and multiscalar and EWCs with its limitation on information and consultation are not adequately organised. Thus, EWCs are to be analysed as genuine European institutions, yes, but until now they are almost insignificant in their impact on social regulation.

In Chapter 12, *Sara Lafuente Hernández* focusses on the development of pan-European co-determination rights dissecting the current institutional anchorage of co-determination in EU law. Based in part on regulatory analysis but more importantly an analysis of the recent Erzberger case and its political implications, the chapter argues that the Court of Justice of the European Union (CJEU) withdrew from a catalyst role in furthering EU protection of co-determination rights. Moreover, the law is not neutral; in that it is often impacting negatively on co-determination within the Member States. In order to be effective in securing national level co-determination,

European level co-determination rights need to be incorporated within the broader EU law. This implicates a call for political action at the European level, since, as Lafuente Hernández emphasises, national power balances have shifted and stand under the pressures of the internal market.

In the following comment (Chapter 13), *Benjamin Werner* takes a much more pessimistic perspective, arguing that Europe "is not the answer" to the erosion of co-determination (while both authors share the assessment that, so far, European integration is undermining it). Going beyond this, Werner emphasises the role and case law of the CJEU. Its interpretations of the freedom of establishment have made regime-shopping easier for companies. Similarly, free movement of capital as interpreted by the CJEU so far but more critically in its likely consequence is a direct threat to more sophisticated national co-determination rights. Crucially, CJEU case law is part of the primary law of the Treaties and cannot be changed by EU legislation, but only by changing the Treaties itself. For Werner, in light of the already lacking minimum baseline for any co-determination at the European level this is not very likely. Thus, instead of European level action, national measures (if possible coordinated and by learning from each other) to protect co-determination are most advisable.

Chapter 14 by *Daniel Seikel* takes a closer look at European economic governance, its implications for bargaining autonomy, and democratic capitalism more generally. Quite obviously, the new economic governance established in the wake of the Euro-crisis includes direct attacks on collective bargaining and thus on trade unions themselves, aiming at lowering and generally monitoring unit labour costs in the Member States. As emphasised already in the beginning of this introduction, trade unions' ability to engage in collective bargaining is a corner stone of organised, democratically domesticated, and socially embedded capitalism. Recent developments are thus not only a threat to trade unions and shift the power balance towards capital, but also put into question the European Social Model – on the European as well as on the national level – entirely.

The following comment (Chapter 15) by *Johannes Kiess* attempts to broaden the focus by arguing that the drivers and origins of the new authoritarian European economic governance are by no means a European level invention. Rather, the international competition and the structural weakness of trade unions around the world as well as the dominance of neo-liberal economic ideas make an "unfriendly environment" for trade unions. More so, capitalism is always an "unfriendly environment" and singling out European integration may lead to wrong conclusions, endangering the political integration project without helping national labour movements much at all. Instead, this European economic governance is a result or consequence of the restructuring of contemporary capitalism. Trade unions can only tackle it by learning about this situation, developing new strategies and alliances, and thus consequently shape national and European institutions in their favour.

In Chapter 16, *Johannes Kiess* analyses how British and German social actors framed the crisis (or rather the cascade of crises following the US real estate bubble). In the wake of the crisis and its framing by trade unions and their counterparts, the more general conflict about the "right" form of capitalism as well as the strong similarities between the cases of (liberal) UK and (coordinated) Germany became visible; despite institutional differences between the UK and Germany, the basic conflicts and main narratives of the actors were very similar. For trade unions, learning more about the quite similar struggles of their sister organisations could be one cornerstone for transnational cooperation and mutual support. This ideational perspective thus adds to dominant rational choice and institutional approaches by offering insights into what social partners are actually trying to say and how they say it. Moreover, by advocating specific frames and readings of the crisis, including which way of capitalist development is to favour, social actors articulate strategic choices aimed not least at challenging or reinforcing hegemonic readings.

Oliver Nachtwey in his comment holds against this emphasis of the social construction of crisis the materiality of the Euro-crisis. Moreover, he criticises that constructivist approaches can only unfold their potential if they can be strictly connected to a materialistic perspective and concrete policy analysis showing how the framing of specific issues is related to actual politics and policies. That is, what is also important for the room of manoeuvre of trade unions is the specific context, for example the government in power. The comment also points at potential further research hypotheses, particularly on how framings emerge within organisations.

Madelaine Moore and *Anne Engelhardt* in Chapter 18 show in a comparative analysis how in Ireland and Portugal the push towards authoritarian neo-liberalism has not only created political instability but also "space for social movements and trade unions to push back". Conceptually, the chapter informs top-down comparative political-economic perspective on neoliberal hegemony with insights towards the disruptive and challenging developments on the ground. The state theoretical departure point conceptualises the state as *"the material condensation of power relations"*. Empirically, the authors show that in both countries trade unions and social movement actors were able to form wider alliances that were successful in challenging (some of) the austerity policies. However, the "relationship between the state, trade unions, and movements is more of a tug of war" than being finalised, as trade unions continue to "reflect and respond to the environmental and institutional dynamics or context they find themselves in".

In the final comment, Roland Erne argues for a more nuanced perspective on trade unions and their strategies that may change over time and depending on circumstances, asking for caution for the use of typologies. In other words, and against Moore and Engelhardt's strict reading, the same trade union may act as part of the state apparatus, but then change to social movement strategies depending on its power resources vis-à-vis employers and political leaders. Regarding the pressures of Europeanisation, Erne argues that the question at hand is not "*if* there will be any European coordination of national wage and social policies" as there already is one, although not a labour-friendly one. However, contradictions in this new governance regime also open up opportunities that can be exploited by trade unions and their allies. Uncovering the success or failure of their strategies must build on multi-sited fieldwork.

We thank all authors for their valuable contributions and hope that this volume is the contribution to on-going academic debates as well as the political discussion about the pressures, chances, and pitfalls of European integration that we envisaged two years ago.

Notes

1 Solemn Declaration on European Union. European Council, Stuttgart 19 June 1983, p. 25.
2 To us this includes in a wider sense (the organisation of) the production and distribution of economic goods under the terms and conditions of a market economy and of capital concentration.
3 The thoughts presented in this introduction represent the authors' cooperation that has benefited over the last couple of years from their institutional bases in Cologne, Jena, Flensburg, and Siegen. The Max Planck Institute for the Study of Societies in Cologne was not only inspirational in its often-critical assessment of integration but, in the form of Martin Höpner's research group on the Political Economy of the European Integration, also provided us with a logistic base to start of the editing of this volume. The focus of the Jena power resources approach, in contrast, opened insights into the potentials and capacities of trade union action. In Siegen, several projects with focus on European sociological research questions complemented these perspectives with a micro-sociological one. In Flensburg, too, the focus on European sociology adds a contrasting perspective to Cologne and Jena.
4 In view of the creation of the common market and the forthcoming monetary union, the Maastricht Treaty (1992) and Amsterdam (1997) were pointing in the same direction.
5 Similar typologies can be found across the literature – e.g. in the works of Platzer (1997), Bernaciak (2010), and Ramsay (1999).
6 We borrow here from Ulrich Beck's concept of reflexive modernity, pointing at the contemporary focus on re-evaluation of the bases of modernity (Beck et al. 2003).

Literature

Ansell, Chris (1997): Symbolic Networks: The Realignment of the French Working Class, 1887–1894. *American Journal of Sociology* 103 (2): 359–390.
Armingeon, Klaus (1994): Die Regulierung der kollektiven Arbeitsbeziehungen in der Europäischen Union. In: Streeck, Wolfgang (ed.): *Staat und Verbände. PVS-Sonderheft*. Opladen: Westdeutscher Verlag, 207–222.

Arnold, Lisa Maria (2008): Die Entstehung der europäischen Dienstleistungsricht-linie im Spannungsfeld organisierter Interessen: Eine Fallstudie zum Einfluss von Gewerkschaften und Unternehmerverbänden im Europäischen Parlament. Hertie School of Governance – working papers, No. 36.

Aust, Andreas et al. (2002): Konjunktur und Krise des Europäischen Sozialmodells. Ein Beitrag zur politische Präexplanationsdiagnostik. *Politische Vierteljahreszeitschrift* 43 (2): 272–301.

Beck, Ulrich (2000): "Freiheit statt Kapitalismus, ein Gespräch mit Richard Sennet und Ulrich Beck". www.zeit.de/2000/15/200015.beck_sennett.xml.

Beck, Ulrich; Giddens, Anthony; Lash, Scott (2003): *Reflexive Modernisierung. Eine Kontroverse*. Frankfurt am Main: Suhrkamp.

Bernaciak, Magdalena (2010): Cross-Border Competition and Trade Union Responses in the Enlarged EU: Evidence from the Automotive Industry in Germany and Poland. European Journal of Industrial Relations 16 (2): 119–135.

Bernaciak, Magdalena et al. (2014): *European Trade Unionism: From Crisis to Renewal?* Brussels: ETUI Report 133.

Bormann, Sarah; Jungehülsing, Jenny (2016): Einleitung. In: Bormann, Sarah et al. (eds.): *Last Call for Solidarity: Perspektiven grenzüberschreitenden Handelns von Gewerkschaften*. Hamburg: VSA, 15–39.

Branch, Ann; Greenwood, Justin (2001): European Employers: Social Partners? In: Compston, Hugh; Greenwood Justin (eds.): *Social Partnership in the European Union*. London: Palgrave Macmillan, 41.70.

Brunkhorst, Hauke (2014): Das doppelte Gesicht Europas – Zwischen Kapitalismus und Demokratie. Berlin: Suhrkamp.

De Boer, Rob; Benedictus, Hester; van der Meer, Marc (2005): Broadening without Intensification: The Added Value of the European Social and Sectoral Dialogue. *European Journal of Industrial Relations* 11 (1): 51–70.

Delhey, Jan; Kohler, Ulrich (2006): From Nationally Bounded to Pan-European Inequalities? On the Importance of Foreign Countries as Reference Groups. *European Sociological Review* 22 (2): 125–140.

Deppe, Frank (2012): *Gewerkschaften in der Großen Transformation. Von den 1970er Jahren bis heute*. Köln: PapyRossa.

Deppe, Frank (2013): *Autoritärer Kapitalismus. Demokratie auf dem Prüfstand*. Hamburg: VSA.

Deppe, Rainer; Tatur, Melanie (2002): *Rekonstitution und Marginalisierung. Transformationsprozesse und Gewerkschaften in Polen und Ungarn*. Frankfurt a.M./ New York: Campus.

Dolvik, Jon Erik (1999): *Die Spitze des Eisbergs. Der EGB und die Entwicklung eines Euro-Korporatismus*. Münster: Westfälisches Dampfboot.

Dörre, Klaus (2010): Überbetriebliche Regulierung von Arbeitsbeziehungen. In: Böhle, Fritz (Hg.): *Handbuch Arbeitssoziologie*. Wiesbaden: VS, 873–912.

Dörre, Klaus et al. (2016): *Streikrepublik Deutschland? Die Erneuerung der Gewerkschaften in Ost und West*. Frankfurt a.M./New York: Campus.Dribbusch, Heiner (2014): Voraussetzungen internationaler Solidarität: zur Diskussion um einen europäischen Generalstreik. *WSI Mitteilungen* 5/2014: 337–344.

Ebbinghaus, Bernhard; Visser, Jelle (1994): Gewerkschaften und Europäische Integration Barrieren und Wege 'grenzenloser' Solidarität. In: Streeck, Wolfgang (ed.): *Staat und Verbände*. Wiesbaden: Westdeutscher Verlag, 223–255.

Elsässer, Lea; Rademacher, Inga; Schäfer, Armin (2015): Cracks in the Foundations: Retrenchment in Advanced Welfare States. *Economic Sociology: The European Electronic Newsletter* 16 (3): 4–16.

European Commission (2011): *Industrial Relations in Europe 2010.* http://ec.europa. eu/social/BlobServlet?docId=6607&langId=en.

Evans, Peter (2010): Is It Labor's Turn to Globalize? Twenty-First Century Opportunities and Strategic Responses. *Global Labour Journal* 1 (3): 352–379.

Falkner, Gerda (1998): *EU Social Policy in the 1990s: Towards a Corporatist Policy Community.* London: Routledge.

Falkner, Gerda (2000): The Council or the Social Partners? EC Social Policy between Diplomacy and Collective Bargaining. *Journal of European Public Policy* 7 (5): 705–724.

Fehmel, Thilo (2012): Welfare State Convergence in Europe: On the Structural Approximation of European Social Security Systems. *European Journal of Transnational Studies* 4 (2): 54–80.

Galgoczi, Bela (2014): *Wage Developments and Wage Setting in Central Europe. Draft.* Brussels: ETUI.

Gallas, Alexander; Nowak, Jörg (2012): Agieren aus der Defensive. Ein Überblick zu politischen Streiks in Europa mit Fallstudien zu Frankreich und Großbritannien. In: Gallas et al. (eds.): *Politische Streiks im Europa der Krise.* Hamburg: VSA, 24–106.

Gerhards, Jürgen; Lengfeld, Holger (2015): *European Citizenship and Social Integration in the European Union.* London: Routledge.

Glassner, Vera; Pernicka, Susanne (2014a): Transnational Trade Union Strategies Towards European Wage Policy: A Neo-Institutional Framework. *European Journal of Industrial Relations* 20 (1): 1–18.

Glassner, Vera; Pernicka, Susanne (2014b): Transnationale Strategien der Gewerkschaften im europäischen Metallsektor: Ansätze zur Europäisierung der Lohnpolitik. *Industrielle Beziehungen* 21 (3): 277–299.

Gorz, André (1974): *Zur Strategie der Arbeiterbewegung im Neokapitalismus.* Frankfurt a.M.: Europäische Verlagsanstalt.

Gumbrell-McCormick, Rebecca; Hyman, Richard (2013): *Trade Unions in Western Europe. Hard Times, Hard Choices.* Oxford: Oxford University Press.

Haas, Ernst B. (1958): *The Uniting of Europe.* Stanford: Stanford University Press.

Heidenreich, Martin (2003): Regional Inequalities in the Enlarged Europe. *Journal of European Social Policy* 13 (4): 313–333.

Heidenreich, Martin; Wunder, Christoph (2008): Patterns of Regional Inequality in the Enlarged Europe. *European Sociological Review* 24 (1): 19–36.

Hermann, Christoph (2014): Structural Adjustment and Neoliberal Convergence in Labour Markets and Welfare: The Impact of the Crisis and Austerity Measures on European Economic and Social Models. *Competition & Change* 18(2): 111–130.

Hertwig, Markus et al. (eds.) (2009): *European Works Councils in Complementary Perspectives.* Brussels: ETUI.

Hoffmann, Jürgen (2010): Perspektiven der europäischen Arbeitsbeziehungen und Gewerkschaften zwischen Modernisierung, Europäisierung und Globalisierung. *Leviathan* 38 (1): 89–102.

Hoffmann, Reiner (2011): Offensiv die Europäisierung der Arbeitsbeziehungen und der Gewerkschaften voranbringen. In: Kowalsky, Wolfgang; Scherrer, Peter (eds.): *Gewerkschaften für einen europäischen Kurswechsel. Das Ende der europäischen Gemütlichkeit.* Münster: Westfälisches Dampfboot, 131–155.

Höpner, Martin (2011): Der europäische Gerichtshof als Motor der europäischen Integration: Eine akteursbezogene Erklärung. *Berliner Journal für Soziologie* 21 (2): 203–229.

Höpner, Martin (2013): Soziale Demokratie? Die politökonomische Heterogenität Europas als Determinante des demokratischen und sozialen Potenzials der Europäischen Union. *Europarecht Beiheft* 1/2013: 69–89.

Höpner, Martin (2015): Der integrationistische Fehlschluss. *Leviathan* 43 (1): 29–42.

Höpner, Martin et al. (2011): Liberalisierungspolitik. Eine Bestandsaufnahme der Rückführung wirtschafts- und sozialpolitischer Interventionen in entwickelten Industrieländern. *Kölner Zeitschrift für Soziologie und Sozialpsychologie* 63 (1): 1–32.

Höpner, Martin; Schäfer, Armin (2010): Grenzen der Integration – Wie die Intensivierung der Wirtschaftsintegration zur Gefahr für die politische Integration wird. *Integration* 33 (1): 3–20.

Höpner, Martin; Schäfer, Armin (2012a): Embeddedness and Regional Integration. Waiting for Polanyi in a Hayekian Setting. *International Organization* 66 (3): 429–455.

Höpner, Martin; Schäfer, Armin (2012b): *Integration among Unequals.* MPIfG Discussion Paper 12/5.

Hyman, Richard (2001a): Trade Union Research and Cross-National Comparison. *European Journal of Industrial Relations* 7(2): 203–223.

Hyman, Richard (2001b): *Understanding Trade Union Identities. Between Market, Class and Society.* London: Sage.

Hyman, Richard (2003): *Trade unions and the ambiguities of social Europe*, Paper presented at the IIRA Conference, Berlin, 7–12 September.

Hyman, Richard (2006): Strukturierung des transnationalen Raumes. Kann Europa dem multinationalen Kapital die Stirn bieten? In: Brinkmann, Ulrich et al. (eds.): *Endspiel des kooperativen Kapitalismus? Institutioneller Wandel unter den Bedingungen des marktzentrierten Paradigmas.* Wiesbaden: VS, 121–168.

Klemm, Matthias et al. (2011): *"Das Umfeld ist bei ihnen völlig anders". Kulturelle Grundlagen der europäischen betrieblichen Mitbestimmung.* Berlin: Sigma.

Koch-Baumgarten, Sigrid (2006): Globale Gewerkschaften und Industrielle Beziehungen in der Global Governance. *Industrielle Beziehungen* 13 (3): 205–222.

Köpper, Ernst-Dieter (1982): *Gewerkschaften und Außenpolitik. Die Stellung der westdeutschen Gewerkschaften zur wirtschaftlichen und militärischen Integration der Bundesrepublik in die Europäische Gemeinschaft und in die NATO.* Frankfurt a.M./New York: Campus.

Kowalsky, Wolfgang (2010): Gewerkschaften und Europa. *IPG* 3/2010: 128–144.

Lahusen, Christian; Grasso, Maria (2018): *Solidarity in Europe – Citizens' Responses in Times of Crisis.* Basingstoke: Palgrave Macmillan.

Lahusen, Christian; Kiess, Johannes (2018): 'Subjective Europeanization': Do Inner-European Comparisons Affect Life Satisfaction? *European Societies.* Online first. https://www.tandfonline.com/doi/abs/10.1080/14616696.2018.1438638?needAccess=true#aHR0cHM6Ly93d3cudGFuZGZvbmxpbmUuY29tL2RvaS9hYnMvMTAuMTA4MC8xNDYxNjY5Ni4yMDE4LjE0Mzg2Mzg/bmVlZEFjYmY2Vzcz10cnVlQBAMA==

Lenin, Wladmir Iljitsch (1969): *Über die Nationalitätenpolitik und den proletarischen Internationalismus.* Moskau: APN.

Lewis, Jeffrey (2005): The Janus Face of Brussels. Socialization and Everyday Decision Making in the European Union. *International Organization* 59 (4): 937–971.

Loh, Wulf; Skupien, Stephan (2016): Die EU als Solidargemeinschaft. *Leviathan* 44 (4): 578–603.

Marginson, Paul; Sisson, Keith (2004): *European Integration and Industrial Relations. Multi-Level Governance in the Making.* New York: Palgrave Macmillan.

Martin, Andrew; Ross, George (2001): Trade Union Organizing at the European Level: The Dilemma of Borrowed Resources. In: Imig, Dough; Tarrow, Sidney (eds.): *Contentious Europeans: Protest and Politics in an Emerging Polity.* Lanham: Rowman & Littlefield, 53–76.

Mau, Steffen (2005): Europe from the Bottom: Assessing Personal Gains and Losses and Its Effects on EU Support. *Journal of Public Policy* 25 (3): 289–311.

Meardi, Guglielmo (2012): *Social Failures of EU Enlargement. A Case of Workers Voting with Their Feet.* London: Routledge.

Mittag, Jürgen (2009): Deutsche Gewerkschaften und europäische Integration: Forschungsphasen, Desiderate und Perspektiven aus historischer Sicht. In: Mittag (ed.): *Deutsche Gewerkschaften und europäische Integration im 20. Jahrhundert.* Bochum: Institut für soziale Bewegungen, 5–24.

Mittag, Jürgen (2010): Gewerkschaften zwischen struktureller Europäisierung und sozialpolitischer Stagnation. *Aus Politik und Zeitgeschichte* 13/14: 40–46.

Niethammer, Lutz (1977): Defensive Integration – Der Weg zum EGB und die Perspektive einer westeuropäischen Einheitsgewerkschaft. In: Bordors et al. (Hg.): *Gewerkschaftliche Politik: Reform aus Solidarität. Zum 60. Geburtstag von Heinz O. Vetter.* Köln: Bund, 567–596.

Pernicka, Susanne (2015): Einleitung. In: Pernicka, Susanne (ed.): *Horizontale Europäisierung im Feld der Arbeitsbeziehungen.* Wiesbaden: Springer, 1–16.

Pierson, Paul; Leibfried Stephan (1998): Mehreebenen-Politik und die Entwicklung des 'Sozialen Europa'. In: Dies (ed.): *Standort Europa. Sozialpolitik zwischen Nationalstaat und europäischer Integration.* Frankfurt a.M.: Suhrkamp, 11–57.

Platzer, Hans-Wolfgang (1997): The Europeanisation of Industrial Relations – State and Perspectives of the Academic Debate. In: *Forschungsgruppe Europäische Gemeinschaften (FEG)*, Studie Nr. 10. Marburg.

Platzer, Hans-Wolfgang (2010): *Europäisierung der Gewerkschaften. Gewerkschaftspolitische Herausforderungen und Handlungsoptionen auf europäischer Ebene.* Bonn: Friedrich-Ebert-Stiftung.

Polanyi, Karl (1957): *The Great Transformation. Political and Economic Origins of Our Time.* Boston: Beacon Press.

Pries, Ludger (2010): *Erwerbsregulierung in einer globalisierten. Welt.* Wiesbaden: VS.

Preunkert, Jenny; Vobruba, Georg (eds.) (2015): *Krise und Integration. Gesellschaftsbildung in der Eurokrise.* Wiesbaden: Springer.

Ramsay, Harvie (1999): In Search of International Union Theory. In: Waddington, Jeremy (ed.): *Globalization and Patterns of Labour Resistance.* London: Macmillan, 192–239.

Rhodes, Martin (1998): Das Verwirrspiel der, Regulierung: 'Industrielle Beziehungen und ‚soziale Dimension'. In: Leibfried, Stephan; Pierson, Paul (eds.): *Standort Europa. Sozialpolitik zwischen Nationalstaat und europäischer Integration.* Frankfurt a.M.: Suhrkamp, 100–154.

Rüb, Stefan; Müller, Torsten (2013): *Arbeitsbeziehungen im Prozess der Globalisierung und Europäischen Integration. Ökonomische und soziale Herausforderungen im Zeichen der Euro-Krise.* Baden-Baden: Nomos.

Scharpf, Fritz W. (1999): *Governing in Europe: Effective and Democratic?* Oxford: Oxford University Press.

Scharpf, Fritz W. (2012): Was soll und kann die Europäische Union? *Zeitschrift für Staats- und Europawissenschaften* 10 (4): 540–550.

Schmitter, Philippe C.; Streeck, Wolfgang (1999): *The Organization of Business Interests: Studying the Associative Action of Business in Advanced Industrial Societies.* MPIFG Discussion Paper 99/1.

Schroeder, Wolfgang; Weinert, Rainer (2004): Designing Institutions in European Industrial Relations: A Strong Commission Versus Weak Trade Unions? *European Journal of Industrial Relations* 10 (2): 199–217.

Schulten, Thorsten (2000): Zwischen nationalem Wettbewerbskorporatismus und symbolischen Euro-Korporatismus – zur Einbindung der Gewerkschaften in die neoliberale Restrukturierung Europas. In: Bieling, Hans-Jürgen; Steinhilber, Jochen (eds.): *Die Konfiguration Europas. Dimensionen einer kritischen Integrationstheorie.* Münster: Westfälisches Dampfboot, 222–242.

Schulten, Thorsten (2005): Gewerkschaften und europäische Integration. Aktuelle Facetten eines ambivalenten Verhältnisses. In: Beerhorst, Joachim; Urban, Hans-Jürgen (eds.): *Handlungsfeld europäische Integration. Gewerkschaftspolitik in und für Europa.* Hamburg: VSA, 14–36.

Schulten, Thorsten et al. (2005): Thesen für eine europäische Mindestlohnpolitik. In: Schulten, Thorsten et al. (eds.): *Mindestlöhne in Europa.* Hamburg: VSA, 301–306.

Seeliger, Martin (2017): *Die soziale Konstruktion organisierter Interessen. Gewerkschaftliche Positionsbildung im Zuge der europäischen Integration.* Frankfurt a.M./New York: Campus.

Seeliger, Martin (2019): *Trade Unions in the Course of European Integration. The Social Construction of Organized Interest.* London: Routledge

Seeliger, Martin; Wagner, Ines (2016): *Workers United? Political Preference Formation among European Trade Unions.* Köln: Discussion Paper Reihe des Max-Planck-Institut für Gesellschaftsforschung.

Smith, Adam (1904): *An Inquiry into the Nature and Causes of the Wealth of Nations.* London: Methuen & Co.

Staatsprojekt Europa (2011): *Die EU in der Krise - Zwischen autoritärem Etatismus und europäischem Frühling.* Münster: Westfälisches Dampfboot.

Streeck, Wolfgang (1998a): Vom Binnenmarkt zum Bundesstaat? Überlegungen zur politischen Ökonomie der europäischen Sozialpolitik. In: Leibfried, Stephan; Pierson, Paul (eds.): *Standort Europa. Sozialpolitik zwischen Nationalstaat und europäischer Integration.* Frankfurt a.M.: Suhrkamp, 369–421.

Streeck, Wolfgang (1998b): The Internationalization of Industrial Relations in Europe: Prospects and Problems. *Politics and Society* 26 (4), 429–459.

Streeck, Wolfgang (2003): Gewerkschaften in Westeuropa. In: Schroeder, Wolfgang; Wessels, Bernhard (Hg.): *Die Gewerkschaften in Politik und Gesellschaft der Bundesrepublik Deutschland.* Wiesbaden: Westdeutscher Verlag, 86–100.

Streeck, Wolfgang (2013): *Gekaufte Zeit. Die vertagte Krise des demokratischen Kapitalismus.* Berlin: Suhrkamp.

Streeck, Wolfgang (2015): Heller, Schmitt and the Euro. *European Law Journal* 21 (3): 361–370.

Stützle, Ingo (2014): *Austerität als politisches Projekt. Von der monetären Integration Europas zur Eurokrise.* Münster: Westfälisches Dampfboot.

Turner, Lowell (1996): The Europeanization of Labour: Structure Before Action. *European Journal of Industrial Relations* 2 (3): 325–344.

Turner, Lowell (2005): From Transformation to Revitalization: A New Research Agenda for a Contested Global Economy. *Journal of Industrial Relations* 32 (4): 383–399.

Visser, Jelle (2012): The Rise and Fall of Industrial Unionism. *Transfer* 18: 129–141.

Vobruba, Georg (2015): Europasoziologie – Institutionen und Leute in der Europäischen Integration. *Zeitschrift für Staats- und Europawissenschaften* 13 (3): 374–369.

Vobruba, Georg (2017): *Krisendiskurs: Die nächste Zukunft Europas.* Weinheim: Beltz Juventa.

Wagner, Anne-Catherine (2013): The Personnel of the European Trade Union Confederation: Specifically European Types of Capital? In: Georgakakis, Didier; Rowell, Jay (eds.): *The Field of Eurocracy: Mapping EU Actors and Professionals.* New York: Palgrave Macmillan, 188–201.

Webster, Eddie; Lambert, Robert; Bezuidenhout, Andries (2008): *Grounding Globalization: Labour in the Age of Insecurity.* Malden: Blackwell.

Weinert, Rainer (2001): Zur Zwangseuropäisierung nationaler Gewerkschaften. *Soziale Welt* 52 (3): 323–339.

Weinert, Rainer (2009): *Die Rolle der Gewerkschaften in der europäischen Sozialpolitik. Was die offene Methode der Koordinierung bedeutet.* Berlin: Sigma.

Zeuner Bodo (2004): Widerspruch, Widerstand, Solidarität und Entgrenzung – neue und alte Probleme der Gewerkschaften. In: Beerhorst Joachim et al. (eds.): *Kritische Theorie im gesellschaftlichen Strukturwandel.* Frankfurt a. M.: Suhrkamp, 318–353.

Zürn, Michael (2013): Nachwort: die Finanz- und Schuldenkrise. In: Zürn, Michael; Ecker-Erhardt, Matthias (ed.): *Die Politisierung der Weltpolitik. Umkämpfte internationale Institutionen.* Berlin: Suhrkamp, 413–425.

Chapter 2

Trade unions in the European crisis

A social movement perspective

Donatella della Porta

Introduction

Trade unions and European integration have been, for long, silent in social movement studies. Research on Europeanisation and social movements was late to develop and remained split between analyses of social movements lobbying in Brussels and those contesting European Union (EU) summits in the street. Research on trade unions has been even more marginal as the main assumption has been that the industrial conflicts had been institutionalised, and the working class co-opted. As Fantasia and Stephan Norris (2004) noted, what made also difficult for social movement studies to study unions was that, indeed, for a long time, unions did not function as social movements.

What is more, social movement studies paid little attention to the structural conditions for the development of fundamental conflicts in our society. As Beverly Silver and Şahan Savaş Karataşlı (2016) recently noted, "The mainstream of the social movement literature since the 1990s has in large measure dismissed the concept of 'capitalism' from its toolkit for understanding social movements, while at the same time placing 'labour movements' outside its field of inquiry". This gap is all the more perplexing "during an era in which global capitalism became ever more powerful" (Hetland/Goodwin 2013: 90; also della Porta 2015).

With now growing conceptual tools and empirical evidences, in parallel to the debate on unions and European integration sketched in the introductory chapter to this volume, also in social movement studies there have been split between "optimistic" and "pessimistic" positions on the role of unions face to both Europeanisation processes, and therefore decline of nation-state centrality, and the neoliberal development in capitalism, with the related retrenchment of the welfare state.

In what follows, after reviewing some main contributions on social movements (with particular attention to the labour movement) which address the potential impact of both structural transformations, I will present some of the challenges for class conflicts in what I called "late neo-liberalism", marked by the financial crisis in its European dimension (della Porta 2015, 2017a, b).

European integration and social movement studies

Protest usually addresses the national level of government. Historically, a new repertoire of collective action – whose main features survived until today – developed together with the nation-state, contributing to the rise of citizenship rights (Marshall 1950; Bendix 1964; Tilly 1984). Even though the nation-state is no longer the exclusive point of reference for social movements, research on protests noted that it remains the target of most of them (Imig/Tarrow 2002; della Porta/Tarrow 2004). The costs of mobilising at international level as well as the reduced opportunities offered by international organisations, including the EU, are mentioned in order to explain pessimist expectation about the capacity of civil society actors to address EU institutions. More optimistic about the potential for social movements – including unions – to address the EU level, research on international civil society organisations points, however, at their steep growth. Resembling what the introduction to this volume calls "reflexive optimism", research, however, also pointed at the growth of symbolic and material resources for transnational mobilisation (della Porta 2009a, b).

Europeanisation and the domestication of protests

Research on the EU singled out strategies of "crossed influence", with mobilisation at the national level to change decisions at the European level as well as the use of the European level as a source of resources for modifying national decisions. This path, defined as *domestication* of protests, has been followed by movements that found little opportunities within EU institutions. Given a limited electoral accountability and the difficulty in building a European public sphere (della Porta/Caiani 2004), movements that want to influence the EU tend to put pressure on their national governments that, at their turn, are expected to negotiate better arrangements at supranational levels. In their analysis of protest in Europe, Doug Imig and Sidney Tarrow (2002) find out in fact that most EU-related events (406 out of 490) were cases of domestication, which characterises in particular mobilisations of European farmers (Bush/Imi 2001), but also of trade unions that have historically developed channels of access to national institutions.

If such path of mobilisations might be seen as being proof of the dominant position of the nation-state, empirical investigations, however, also pointed at the emergence, in the course of these campaigns, of innovations both in the organisational structure and in the frames of the protest (della Porta 2007). National diversity tends therefore to enrich strategically the actors that engage in transnational collective action.

Europeanisation and the externalisation of protests

In some cases, social movement organisations have, however, also looked at the EU as an additional arena for the mobilisation of resources that may then be used at the national level. Through a path of *externalisation* (Chabanet 2002), national organisations target the EU in attempts to put pressure on their own governments. This path characterised movements that tend to ally transnationally, and have in fact appealed to the kinds of discourse and identity legitimised at the European level. On this, more structured social movement organisations can exploit a search for the legitimisation of EU institutions which has opened some consultation channels, even if in a quite selective way. This is the case, for instance, of environmental campaigns (Rootes 2002) but also of the Euro-strike in 1997 (Lefébure/ Lagneau 2002). Social movement organisations need, however, to adapt to the rules of the game (Marks/McAdam 1999; Guiraudon 2002). Feminists, environmentalists and unions have also been able to obtain some (rather limited) favourable decisions from the Court of Justice, especially with the increasing competence of the EU on environmental and social policies (Balme/Chabanet 2002; Mazey 2002; Rootes 2002). The debate about good governance and the democratic deficit had raised hopes for a growing involvement of civil society (starting with Delors and the "Social Dialogue"). Given the support of the EU (especially the former DG V, now DG EMPL), the Europeanisation of trade unions, with the creation of the European Trade Union Confederation, has been described as "a story of interactions between European institutions seeking to stimulate Euro-level interest representation, a small number of unionists who perceived Europe as important, and the growing significance of European integration itself" (Martin/Ross 2001: 57; see also Branch 2002). Feminists, environmentalists and unions have also been able to obtain some favourable decisions from the Court of Justice, especially with the increasing competence of the EU on environmental and social policies (Balme/Chabanet 2002; Mazey 2002). In general, however, some groups – especially, business associations and private corporations – emerge as more effective than others in organising and influencing EU institutions. Moreover, the more important EU institutions become, the more structured and less accessible they seem to be for weakly organised interests (Rootes 2002).

Although access remained unequal, some formal and informal opportunities for influencing the EU institutions have been opening up and tested by social movement organisations. Beyond their varying degrees of success, initiatives at the EU level have facilitated networking among social movement organisations of different countries, focussing their attention on the European dimension of multilevel governance. Even with these limits, one effect of "externalisation" has been the creation of supranational organisational structures and identities. The European arenas offered in fact to representatives of different social movement organisations of all EU countries the opportunity to meet each other, build organisational networks, co-ordinate activity and construct supranational discourses. Growing interaction facilitates the development of common, more or less European, identity.

Europeanisation and the transnationalisation of protests

The Europeanisation of protest also followed a third, broader trend of *transnationalisation* that contributed to the development of the global justice movement. Domestication and externalisation of protest seem to have facilitated the rise of a type of conflict directly linked to the characteristics of the EU that is expressed increasingly through unconventional forms involving loosely structured networks of European activists. The aim of these protests tends to be more and more general, with the participation of national and supranational actors that turn simultaneously to various governmental levels. More and more, Europeanised protest addresses the lack of concerns at the EU level for problems of social equality. It is precisely against European economic and social policies that mobilisations developed since the end of the 1990s, with some early protests that, though rare, represent neverthe-less an important occasion for transnational encounters (on the European Marches against unemployment in 1997 and 1999, Chabanet 2002). The search for "another Europe" is most in evidence in protest demonstrations against EU summits, but also organised the European Social Forums (ESFs). Expressing strong criticism of the forms of European integration, but no hostility to the building of European identities and institution, this movement can be seen as a critical social capital for the emerging of a European polity. Since Amsterdam and Cologne, counter-summits have contested all of the main EU summits: in Nice, Gothenburg, Barcelona and Copenhagen, tens of thousands marched during EU summits to protest EU decisions. Since 2002, social movement activists – including unionists from Southern but also Central and Northern Europe, and more recently also from the East (della Porta 2009a, 2009b) – have also met yearly in EFSs to debate Europeanisation and its limits (della Porta/Diani 2006). The platform of the first ESF presented it as the first step in the construction of a critical public sphere for the discussion of the European Convention and its limits. The policies of the EU are criticised as essentially neoliberal, advocating the privatisation of public services and the flexibility of the work market, with resulting increases in work insecurity. Together with the democratisation of the European institutions, under the banner "another Europe is possible", social policies are demanded, including taxation of capital and of financial transactions. There are also claims for the reduction of indirect taxes and public intervention to help the weakest social groups as well as for the strengthening of public services like school and health. Of the activists interviewed at ESF events, only a few express support for a strengthening of national governments (19% agree much or very much), while 33% support a strengthening of the EU and macro-regional institutions and as many as 70% would welcome the building of new institutions of world governance. A 2005 survey carried out at a demonstration in Rome against the EU Bolkestein Directive found that although only 11% of the activists disagreed with the statement that the EU constitutional treaty would endanger the national welfare state and social policies, as many as 80% agreed (64% of them strongly) that "an alternative model of European integration is necessary in order to resist neoliberal globalization". In this sense, these social movement activists represent a "social capital" of committed citizens that, although critical, might represent an important source for the building of a European citizenship. As with the construction of the nation-state, for European institution-building the presence of a critical social capital works as a challenge and a resource (della Porta 2007). As in the formation of the nation-state, the territorial issue is articulated alongside others: support for Europe is linked to different images of Europe as built by different actors. A complex process of symbolic appropriation of Europe as a theme has also brought about an extension of the definition of the "conflict over Europe", layering various other cleavages over the original territorial ones (concerned with the boundaries of the *polity*).

Capitalist development and social movement studies

While the analyses of the effects of European integration on social movements focussed especially on the organisational characteristics of EU institutions, a second relevant question to assess the challenges and opportunities of European integration for labour refers to the specific neoliberal policies that have characterised EU institutions (Streeck 2011; Joerges 2015). Social movements of the 2000s develop within an EU dominated by neoliberalism. To use Harvey's categories (2005: 11), in "embedded liberalism",

> market processes and entrepreneurial and corporate activities were surrounded by a web of social and political constraints and a regulatory environment that sometimes restrained but in other instances led the way in economic and industrial strategy... The business cycle was successfully controlled through the application of Keynesian fiscal and monetary policies. A social and moral economy (sometimes supported by a strong sense of national identity) was fostered through the activities of an interventionist state. The state in effect became a force field that internalised class relations. Working-class institutions such as labour unions and political parties of the left had a very real influence within the state apparatus.

To the contrary, neoliberalism, as a theory of political economic practices, postulates that

> human well-being can best be advanced by liberating individual en-
> trepreneurial freedoms and skills within an institutional framework
> characterized by strong private property rights, free markets, and free
> trade. The role of the state is to create and preserve an institutional
> framework appropriate to such practices.
>
> (ibid.: 11)

Also on this issue, social movement studies might be seen as split between pessimistic and optimistic views, broadly reflecting the positions presented in the introduction to this volume. While the New Social Movement perspective had assumed an institutionalisation of labour and the emergence of new conflicts, with rather cosmopolitan outlook, collective action in the neoliberal crisis has been rather seen as defensive Polanyi-like counter-movements, and instead as proactive anti-systemic movements within World System type of approaches.

The New Social Movement perspective

It is in "embedded liberalism", and especially the forms it took at the core of capitalism, that the social movement scholars who analyse the big trans-formations in the societal systems had in mind when theorising about "New Social Movements" in the 1970s. In particular, in Alain Touraine's work, social movements are considered as a driving force in societal develop-ments as the functioning of each society reflects the struggle between two antagonistic actors that fight over the control of the type of transforming action which a society exercises upon itself (Touraine 1977: 95–96). The historicity of each societal formation is defined by the intertwining of a system of knowledge, a type of accumulation and a cultural model – that different types of society can be identified, along with the social classes which accompany them. Classes are defined by "cultural orientations and set within social relations defined by an unequal connection with the so-cial control of these orientations" (Touraine 1981: 61). Touraine singled out four types of society: agrarian, mercantile, industrial and "programmed". The "programmed society", which is emerging after the industrial society, is characterised by the "production of symbolic goods which model or trans-form our representation of human nature and the external world" (Touraine 1987, 1985). The central actors in social conflicts are therefore no longer classes linked to industrial production but rather groups that fight about the use and destination of cognitive and symbolic resources.

With a pessimist view about the capacity of the labour movement to sur-vive as relevant societal actor, research in social movements addressed the spreading of cleavages outside of the factories, the forging of new collective identities, and the resistance to the hierarchical work of society and the market. As the Fordist large factory, with workers performing similar tasks, as well as their concentration in urban areas – both conditions facilitating dense networks in which a class identity could develop (Thompson 1963; Tilly 1978; Fantasia 1988) – were fading away, the social bases of the industrial conflict were seen as weakened by the changes in the organisation of industrial work with new automated technologies, the decentralisation and the growth of informal economy, urban restructuring, as well as the decline of the importance of the industrial sector face to administrative and service occupations (Castells 1996).

Neoliberalism, with the deregulation of the labour market and ensuing precarisation of workers' condition, further challenged the role of labour in general and of trade unions in particular. However, it also "brought back" awareness of the importance of conflicts around material inequalities that the New Social Movement scholars had seen as weakening. While some researchers noted that protests of labour issues had always remained central, others pointed at their increasingly dominant role in the years 2010s (della Porta et al. 2015).

Movements and counter-movements

When looking at the industrial conflicts, a perspective, which re-emerged in the crisis, has referred to Karl Polanyi's (1957/1944) double movement, with the shift, in capitalist development, between social protection and free market, through the action movements and counter-movement. This type of view would bring to rather pessimist assessment of the potential to develop a proactive and transnational oriented European labour movement, rather expecting increasing competition within labour at national level and among labour from different countries, differently affected by neoliberal developments. What Polanyi deals with as counter-movement is the mobilisation of those who feel betrayed by changes like those produced in neoliberalism and who react by trying to go back to the old system. As in the first wave of liberalism, deep-rooted rights are challenged as taken away and this produced a rebellion not only against the poverty but also against a betrayal of their rights. Also cuts in welfare, e.g. in the subsidies for unemployed, are cynically justified in the name of a necessity to make some victims for the sake of profit and economic growth. The separation between the state and the market is here as well an illusion, because the state creates the legal conditions for those developments through a growing contamination, with elites in business and politics overlapping in different institutional settings.

Polanyi's approach has been criticised as relying too much on the ideological pressure of the free-market doctrine, on the one hand, and, on the other hand, on a rather spontaneous counter-movement, prompted by a sort of functionalist logic. Moving beyond Polanyi, Burawoy singles out a sequence of three successive counter-movements: for labour rights, for social rights, for human rights. Referring to the latter, as opposing contemporary moves towards free market, he notes its fragmentation:

> There have been national reactions to market expansion – whether in the form of Islamic nationalism or shades of socialism in Latin America – but they cannot reverse third-wave marketization as this requires a planetary response to the global reach of finance capital and the looming environmental catastrophe that threatens the whole earth. Indeed, finance capital is the force behind the precariatization of labor – both its recommodification and, correlatively, its excommodification ... – as well as the rising levels of debt, not just at the level of the individual but also of the community, the city, the state, and even the region. .... A countermovement will have to assume a global character, couched in terms of human rights since the survival of the human species is at stake.

At least in part, social movements – and in particular, the labour movement in late neoliberalism – have mobilised in the defence of those rights, which had developed in the 1960s and 1970s in the first world with democracies but also in the third world with the developmental states, or in the second world with the really existing socialism being an ideology of rights – rights to housing, health, education, jobs. Anti-austerity protests are recognised as empowering capacity, which remains, however, defensive and national in scope (Burawoy 2015). The search is still open for new forms of organisation as

> the forms of left-wing political organization established in the period 1945–73, when expanded reproduction was in the ascendant, were inappropriate to the post-1973 world, where accumulation by dispossession moved to the fore as the primary contradiction within the imperialist organization of capital accumulation.
>
> (ibid.: 172)

Connecting fragmented struggles would require to "rise above nostalgia for that which has been lost" (ibid.: 178).

The world system approach and anti-systemic movements

A more optimistic view on the capacity of labour unions to fight for workers' rights is proposed by the world system approach. According to scholars such as Immanuel Wallerstein, Giovanni Arrighi and Beverly Silver, anti-systemic movements have resisted capitalism, opposing its logic as, "to be antisystemic is to argue that neither liberty nor equality is possible under the existing system and that both are possible only in a transformed world" (Wallerstein 1990: 36). While recognising transnational differences, world system theorists expect increasing protests as exploitation grows as "When oppression becomes particularly acute, or expectations particularly deceived or the power of the ruling stratum falters, people have risen up in an almost spontaneous manner to cry a halt" (Arrighi et al. 1989: 29). While resistance to capitalism was initially expressed through riots and revolts, later challengers began organised in anti-systemic movements, becoming more effective. Anti-systemic movements were particularly successful after the Second World War in the form of social democratic movements in core countries, communist ones in the semiperiphery and peripheries, national liberation in the periphery. Unable to end inequality, those regimes continued, however, to work as "part of the social division of labour of historical capitalism" (Wallerstein 2004: 71). The movement of 1968, then, represented a revolt not only against capitalism, but also against the perceived failure of the previous anti-systemic movements.

In this vision, the capitalist oppression is, therefore, expected to result in the revolt of the oppressed, with different dynamics at the core, the semi-periphery and the periphery. In a system far from equilibrium, "small social mobilizations can have very great repercussions" (Wallerstein 2010: 141). If the counter-movements in Polanyi's type of explanations are backward looking, anti-systemic movements rather challenge the existing order. In particular, following Marx analysis, rebellion is expected against attempts to commodify labour power, which "is embodied in human beings who complain and resist if they are made to work too long, too hard or too fast" (Silver/Karatasli 2016: 137). In particular, protests tend to spread in the periphery and labour organises even under very difficult type of conditions, even under totalitarian regimes (Silver 2003).

Empirical evidences in comparative perspective

Empirical evidences are, as often happens, mixed, providing no definitive answers to the question of the capacity of labour as a movement to address the challenges of European integration in the European crisis. We can see this on two main related issues: the class basis of anti-austerity protests and the role that trade unions have played in them.

The class basis in anti-austerity protests

Anti-austerity protests brought back concern with the class dimension of contentious politics that mainstream social movement studies had long forgotten. In 2011, protesters were considered mostly as members of a new precarious class that had been dramatically hit by the austerity policies.

Differently, the protests in 2013 have been interpreted as "middle class" phenomena, with cosmopolitan identities. According to Fukuyama (2013),

> The theme that connects recent events in Turkey and Brazil to each other, as well as to the 2011 Arab Spring and continuing protests in China, is the rise of a new global middle class. In Turkey and Brazil, as in Tunisia and Egypt before them, political protest has been led not by the poor but by young people with higher-than-average levels of education and income.

With the support of statistical definitions of middle classes as encompassing those above the poverty line – in part manipulated to push forward an image of globalisation as successful in modernising backward countries – the 2013 protests in countries such as Turkey or Brazil have been described as an emerging middle class, impatient with neoliberal forms of authoritarianism and manifesting this dissatisfaction in the streets (Yörük/Yüksel 2014).

This vision has been challenged, however. As Therborn (2013: 16) noted, the critique to neoliberalism came from varying combinations of pre-capitalist groups (as indigenous people), extra-capitalist "wretched of the earth" (as casual labourers, landless peasants and street vendors), but also workers and emerging middle-class layers. As he summarised,

> pre-capitalist populations, fighting to retain their territory and means of subsistence; 'surplus' masses, excluded from formal employment in the circuits of capitalist production; exploited manufacturing workers across rustbelt and sunbelt zones; new and old middle classes, increasingly encumbered with debt payments to the financial corporations – these constitute the potential social bases for contemporary critiques of the ruling capitalist order. Advance will almost certainly require alliances between them, and therefore the inter-articulation of their concerns.
>
> (ibid.)

Empirical research confirmed indeed the mobilisations against austerity of various social classes, with complex processes of proletarisation of former middle classes as well as precarisation of labour. So, "social movements may be a response to the lifting of protections won against commodification, what we might call recommodification – as when welfare benefits are reduced, trade unions are decertified, labor laws violated or withdrawn" (Burawoy 2015). Besides processes of recommodification, there is, however, also resistance to excommodification, defined as

> the expulsion of entities from the market, entities that were formerly commodities ... Ex-commodification captures the expanded production

of waste – the idea that there are lots of useful things that, to their detriment, are expelled from the market. …In relation to *labor*, the source of
precarity is, indeed, exclusion from the labor market. …In many places,
and increasingly all over the world, expanding reservoirs of surplus labor make it a privilege to be exploited.

(Burawoy 2015)

Protests are frequently called by those that Guy Standing called as *precariat*, composed of people

> who have minimal trust relations with capitalism or the state, making it
> quite different from the salariat. And it has none of the social contract
> relationship of the proletariat, whereby labour securities were provided
> in exchange for subordination and contingent loyalty, the unwritten
> deal underpinning welfare state.

(Standing 2011: 9)

As Silver and Karatasly (2016: 139) noted, there are two types of working-
class protest. First, there is the

> protest by new working classes being 'made' in areas where capital is
> expanding … and protest by established working classes being 'un-
> made' in areas where capital is disinvesting (the post-2009 wave of anti-
> austerity protests in Europe is a paradigmatic example).

But there are also protests against the destruction of established liveli-
hoods, which proceed faster than the development of new ones related to
the growing mass of unemployed, underemployed and precariously employed. Here, resistance emerges from "those *segments of the working class
who are deprived of the means of livelihood but who have not been absorbed
into stable wage employment—those whom capital has essentially 'bypassed'*"
(ibid.: 139).

Data from surveys, which we made at demonstrations that took places
in times of crisis, confirms cross-national differences among countries that
were hit differently by the austerity. In all countries, the young people, who
were most hit by the crisis, mobilised more – especially the highly educated young people with very low chances to enter into the protected labour market and enjoy welfare state's entitlements. Young people, without
a possibility of security in the labour market, precarious and unemployed,
constituted the large part of the movement. They were, however, joined also
by groups that are undergoing precarisation processes, among which are
those employed in public sector, the blue-collar workers in the big factories,
and retired people.

The organisational dimension

Also in terms of organisational forms, contentious politics in times of austerity has reflected these contextual characteristics, trying to change them but also being forced to adapt to them. In particular, the forms of participation of labour and trade unions varied. Research comparing various European cases in which the financial crisis has hit most has noted that, while Polanyi's type of counter-movements mobilised everywhere, movements of anti-systemic character have emerged especially where the socioeconomic crisis had more disruptive effects on citizens' everyday lives. In fact, it was especially in Iceland, Greece and Spain, where disruption of the quotidian was most dramatic, that the agentic power of the contentious citizens has fuelled discontent with political authorities, entangled in a strong crisis of responsibility, testified by the fall of trust and legitimacy indicators as well as by the (unexpected) emergence of new parties.

In *Spain*, the protest on 15 May 2011 started a long and strong wave of contention that innovated within both social movements and more traditional political actors. Although including some more traditional forms of contention (among them, prominently, strikes and marches), the protest repertoire was largely transformed by the emergence of new forms, such as the *acampadas* (camps), but also by the re-emergence of old forms of contention, similar to charivari, which singled out alleged perpetrators for public shaming rituals. The organisational forms within the social movement arena were also influenced by the wave of protest, with the strengthening of a horizontal, inclusive, assembly-based model that had already spread during the global justice movement (della Porta 2007). The youth played a particularly important role in the mobilisations. The contentious framing included a defence of citizenship rights, but also proactive visions of progressive transformations of the welfare system towards conceptions and practices of the commons. Strongly oriented to denounce the immorality of the degenerated system, protestors also imagined ways to transcend existing state and market institutions. Experimenting with different strategies and playing within different arenas, the Spanish cycle of anti-austerity protests empowered the citizens, also having transformative effects on the party system (della Porta et al. 2016). While unions organised several strikes, their interactions with the social movement organisations of the "horizontal" sector remained tense. The movement's ideas and practices, nurtured within local assemblies and self-managed collectives, also influenced labour conflicts through the so-called "waves" (*mareas*) in the public sector.

Similarly, as the square camps spread to *Greece*, anti-austerity protests also acquired very innovative characteristics, mobilising as much as one-third of the population in multi-class and multi-actor coalitions (Rüdig/ Karyotis 2013). The well-established horizontal tradition that characterised the Greek social movement culture was reflected in the organisational structure as well as in the repertoire of action of the protest cycle. The protests mobilised, however, also many previously uncommitted citizens who had been directly hit by the crisis. Claims in defence of social rights were accompanied by proposals for reinventing democracy. Unions of various forms, sizes, and persuasions mobilised the workers in numerous strikes (Diani/Kousis 2014). Met at times with brutal repression and developing within an already radicalised milieu, the protests occasionally escalated into violence. Outrage at political scandals fed mistrust in the political class, as well as in calls against the immorality of the institutional system, accused of betraying the citizens and discharging their rights (Sergi/Vogiatzoglou 2013). Massive participation in anti-austerity also empowered the citizens towards the development of various self-help and direct actions, including the occupation and self-management of factories or the organisation of grassroots activities against the suffering and deprivation produced by the crisis. While alternative forms of self-organisation were experimented with, the electoral arena was also affected by the protests, with the strengthening of the radical left, culminating in Syriza's conquering of the government in 2015.

In *Iceland*, as well, the protests erupted unexpectedly, involving a large part of a population whose experience with contentious politics was extremely limited. Against the government, who blamed the global crisis, protestors spread a moral frame stigmatising the political corruption of an octopus-like elite, made up of businesspeople and politicians, which had acted out of greed against the tradition of solidarity of Icelanders. While the traditional role of the state was reclaimed, protests also empowered new visions within the very horizontal organisational format of a citizens' movement. The mobilisations that started – with a rock concert – by the agency of a tiny and unpolitical group spread quickly and massively as public protest meetings in downtown Reykjavík became a regular occurrence (Bernburg 2015: 13). While remaining mainly peaceful, the protest forms included several innovations, from the pots and pans demonstrations to the bottom up process of constitution writing. In a virtuous circle, the massive response increased the sense of efficacy by participants, fuelling further participation. Organised horizontally, the protest activities were capable of empowering the Icelandic people, producing innovative ideas.

In Portugal, Ireland, Italy and Cyprus, protests, even when strong, remained more bounded to traditional contentious traditions and actors, putting forward claims of defence of previous conditions (della Porta 2017).

In *Portugal*, protests increased steadily during austerity times, but this took especially more traditional forms such as strikes (including five general strikes), marches (almost 600 protests were registered in Lisbon in 2012 alone), and petitions, but with less success for *acampadas*. Contentious politics remained peaceful and very much targeting the national institutions (Accornero/Pinto 2014). With large participation of traditional actors, including trade unions, political parties and even police and military personnel organisations, protestors advocated the defence of labour and citizens' rights. While new actors were also present, mobilising especially the young precarious generation, they tended to adapt their organisational forms to open channels of access to institutions. Symbols, such as slogans and music, were used to root the protest within the glorious past of the carnage revolution of 1974 (Baumgarten 2013). While some innovative conceptions of democracy emerged, with appeals to citizens' participation, contentious politics remained rooted in more conventional visions, with requests for "more" and "better quality" democracy. Coordinatory committees for anti-austerity protests included new and old organisations, with the left in Parliament increasing its support throughout the protests.

As in Portugal, in *Italy* there was also a growth in protests in defence of challenged citizens' rights, but overall contentious politics was more reactive than proactive. In fact, anti-austerity protests were often carried out by more traditional collective actors (della Porta/Reiter 2012; della Porta/Andretta 2013; della Porta et al. 2015). While labour conflict was sustained, it was not systematically linked to other types of mobilisation that emerged on public education or the right to the city. Also the repertoire of protest, which remained in part, anchored in the past, with attempts to build camps in the city squares encountering very little success. Main unions called for strikes, but they were not only divided among themselves but also without connections to the social movement organisations that had emerged in the global justice movement as well as in successive waves of protest. Innovative forms, such as social strikes, were invented, but without sustained empowering capacity. No strong social or political coalitions formed to challenge neoliberal reforms. In a situation traditionally characterised by a large but not autonomous civil society, rather accustomed to search for support in the centre-left parties and their collateral organisations, social movements had weak capacity to mobilise against governments that were supported by the main centre-left party. As for framing, the reconquering of lost rights dominated, with only limited attempts to single out proposals for the building of participatory forms of democracy and a practice of commons. While achieving an important victory in the referendum against the privatisation of water supply (della Porta et al. 2017), and notwithstanding the electoral punishment of the two main parties in the 2013 general elections, no alternative vision of justice and democracy spread during the protests. Parliamentary opposition to austerity policies was in fact carried out by the M5S, which had a tense relationship with social movements on the left (della Porta et al. 2016).

Also in *Ireland*, protest was certainly not absent, but here as well it took more traditional forms in defence of established rights. While there were, especially at the beginning of the crisis (2008 and 2009), strikes and mass demonstrations organised especially by the unions, rooted in particular in the public sector, protests then subsided when the unions accepted austerity policies, in the hope of some future rewards. In particular, in March 2010, the *Public Service Agreement 2010–2014* "copper-fastens previous unilateral pay reductions while containing a tentative commitment to avoid additional pay cutting measures, unless faced with a further economic crisis" (McDonough/Dundon 2010: 558). Some protest camps were organised in 2011, but with very limited capacity for mobilisation, while discontent with the government was instead channelled into the electoral arena. The most innovative protests have developed since 2014, with the emergence of social movement organisations after the peak of the crisis – for example, with the Right2Water campaign.

Finally, in Cyprus, negotiations with the Troika, initiated by the left-wing governments in 2012 and continuing after the change in government by the right-wing party in 2013, brought about opposition both in the streets and in parliament. Two intense but short waves of protest developed in the most important moments of negotiation with the EU, European Central Bank (ECB) and International Monetary Fund (IMF) in the fall of 2012 and the spring of 2013. The protestors took up frames of defence of national sovereignty, sometimes revisiting the anti-neo-colonialism discourse developed during the struggle for independence from the United Kingdom. As in Ireland, contentious politics was mainly moved by more traditional actors, such as the public sector trade unions that were at the core of the "Alliance against the Memorandum". They also took the more traditional forms of strikes and demonstrations, often in front of parliament, although with some use of social media campaigning as well. As the bail-in hit especially foreign (Russian) investors and the sum gathered from the bail-in (rather than state funds) was used for recapitalising the banking sector, the potential for building up a broad social coalition was limited. Weak traditions of protest but high degrees of control of civil society by the main party of the left also explain the weakness of autonomous mobilisation of the society.

Conclusion

In conclusion, social movement studies present optimistic and pessimistic views on both the capacity of social movements to mobilise (and be successful) at EU level and the space for a "return of class conflict" in the neoliberal crisis. In parallel with the debate between optimist and pessimist views sketched out in the introductory chapter, social movement studies are torn between a normative optimism, which sees transnationalisation as a necessary step in order to affect the institutions where power moved, and the empirical pessimism based upon the observation of close (and closer and closer) political opportunities for challengers in neoliberal Europe as well as of the costs of mobilising transnationally. While the great recession – in what I defined as late neoliberalism (della Porta 2015; della Porta 2017b) – has certainly produced a return of the movements in the streets and the squares of most European countries, the labour has mobilised in very different forms in different countries. The balance between defensive Polanyi-like moves and offensive, anti-systemic moves has varied much cross-nationally with a search for appropriate organisational structures and, what is more, collective identity, which is still on the making.

As recent attempts by labour to mobilise transnationally against neoliberalism in Europe – such as the Day of Action and Solidarity, across Europe on 14 November 2012, called by the European Trade Union Confederation (ETUC) to promote a social compact and oppose austerity – have shown, the potential that comes from the internal diversities in the unions field, but also the risks that being "unite in diversities" strengthen internal inequalities (della Porta/Park 2016). To which extent the EU can work as a coral reef triggering a revival of trade unions and class struggle is a very open question.

Nevertheless, we also observed that labour is still mobilised in different forms. We can agree that "the image of a disappearing working class" (and class movement) came from the misleading generalisation to the all world of trend relevant for its core, as well as from the error of mistaking short-term developments for long-term ones – so that "once we *lengthen the time horizon of our analysis* what looks like a terminal crisis of labor movements—the end of history—may turn out to be another lull between recurrent major labor movement upsurges" (Silver/Karatasli 2016: 136). Polanyi-like defensive counter-movements and Wallerstein-like anti-systemic movements see the involvement of labour and the unions, even if in different forms and with different strength.

Literature

Accornero, Guya; Pinto, Pedro Ramos (2014): "Mild Mannered"? Protest and Mobilisation in Portugal under Austerity. 2010–2013. *Western European Politics* 38 (3): 1–25.

Arrighi, Giovanni; Hopkins, Terence K.; Wallerstein, Immanuel (1989): *Antisystemic Movements.* London: Verso.

Balme, Richard; Chabanet, Didier (2002): *Introduction. Action collective et gouvernance de l'Union Européenne.* In: Balme, Richard; Chabanet, Didier (eds.): *L'action collective en Europe.* Paris: Presses de Sciences Po, 21–120.

Baumgarten, Britta (2013): Geração à Rasca and Beyond: Mobilizations in Portugal after 12 March 2011. *Current Sociology* 61 (4): 457–473.

Bendix, Ralph (1964): *Nation Building and Citizenship.* New York: Wiley and Son.

Bernburg, Jon G. (2015): *Economic Crisis and Mass Protest: The Pots and Pans Revolution in Iceland.* Farnham: Ashgate.

Branch, Ann P. (2002): The Impact of the European Union on the Trade Union Movement. In: Balme, Richard; Chabanet, Didier (eds.): *L'action collective en Europe.* Paris: Presses de Sciences Po, 279–312.

Burawoy, Michael (2015): Facing an Unequal World. *Current Sociology* 63 (1): 5–34.

Bush, Evelyn; Imi, Pete (2001): European Farmers and Their protests. In: Imig, Doug; Tarrow, Sidney (eds.): *Contentious Europeans. Protest and Politics in an Emerging Polity.* Lanham: Rowman & Littlefield, 97–121.

Castells, Manuel (1996): *The Information Age. Vol. I: The Rise of the Network Society.* Oxford/Cambridge: Blackwell.

Chabanet, Didier (2002): *Les marches européennes contre le chômage, la précarité et les exclusions.* In: Balme, Richard; Chabanet, Didier (eds.): *L'action collective en Europe.* Paris: Presses de Sciences Po, 461–494.

della Porta, Donatella (2007): *The Global Justice Movement in Cross-National and Transnational Perspective.* Boulder: Paradigm.

della Porta, Donatella (ed.) (2009a): *Democracy in Social Movements.* London: Palgrave.

della Porta, Donatella (ed.) (2009b): *Another Europe.* London: Routledge.

della Porta, Donatella (2015): *Social Movements in Times of Austerity.* Cambridge: Polity.

della Porta, Donatella (2017a): Neoliberalism and Its Discontents: An Introduction. In della Porta, Donatella; Andretta, Massimiliano; Fernandes, Tiago; O'Connor, Francis; Romanos, Eduardo; Vogiatzoglou, Markos (eds.): *Neoliberalism and its Discontents.* London: Palgrave, 1–38.

della Porta, Donatella (2017b): *Riding the Wave.* Amsterdam: Amsterdam University Press.

della Porta, Donatella; Caiani, Manuela (2004): *Europeanization and Social Movements.* Oxford: Oxford University Press.

della Porta, Donatella; Tarrow, Sidney (2004): Transnational Movements and Global Activism: An Introduction. In: della Porta, Donatella; Tarrow, Sidney (eds.): *Transnational Movements and Global Activism: An Introduction.* New York: Rowman and Littlefield, 1–17.

della Porta, Donatella; Diani, Mario (2006): *Social Movements: An Introduction.* Oxford: Blackwell.

della Porta, Donatella; Reiter, Herbert (2012): Desperately Seeking Politics. *Mobilization: An International Quarterly* 17 (3): 349–361.

della Porta, Donatella; Andretta, Massimiliano (2013): Protesting for Justice and Democracy. *Contemporary Italian Politics* 5 (1): 23–37.

della Porta, Donatella; Mosca, Lotenzo; Parks, Luisa (2015): Subterranean Politics and Visible Protest in Italy. In: Kaldor, Mary; Selchow, Sabine (eds.): *Subterranean Politics in Europe.* London: Palgrave, 60–93.

della Porta, Donatella; Parks, Luisa (2016): Social Movements, the European Crisis, and EU Political Opportunities. *Comparative European Politics* 16 (1): 85–102

della Porta, Donatella; Fernandez, Joseba; Kouki, Hara; Mosca, Lorenzo (2016): *Movement Parties in Times of Austerity.* Cambridge: Polity.

della Porta, Donatella; O'Connor, Francis; Portos, Martin; Subirats Ribas, Anna (2017): *Referendums from Below.* Bristol: Policy Press.

Diani, Mario; Kousis, Maria (2014): The Duality of Claims and Events: The Greek Campaign against Troika's Memoranda and Austerity, 2010–2012. *Mobilization: An International Quarterly* 19 (4): 387–404.

Fantasia, Rick; Stepan-Norris, Judith (2004): The Labor Movement in Motion. In: Snow, David A.; Soule Sarah H.; Kriesi, Hanspeter (eds.): *The Blackwell Companion to Social Movements.* Oxford: Blackwell, 555–575.

Fantasia, Rick (1988): *Cultures of Solidarity. Consciousness, Action, and Contemporary American Workers.* Berkeley: University of California Press.

Fukuyama, Francis (2013): "The Middle Class Revolution." *The Wall Street Journal*, June 28. www.wsj.com/articles/SB10001424127887323873904578571472700348086.

Guiraudon, Virginie (2002): Weak Weapons of the Weak? Transnational Mobilization around Migration in the European Union. In: Imig, Doug; Tarrow, Sidney (eds.): *Contentious Europeans. Protest and Politics in an Emerging Polity.* Lanham: Rowman & Littlefield, 163–183.

Harvey, David (2005): *A Brief History of Neoliberalism.* Oxford: Oxford University Press.

Hetland, Gabriel; Goodwin, Jeff (2013): The Strange Disappearance of Capitalism from Social Movement Studies. In: Barker, Colin; Cox, Laurence; Krinski, John; Nilsen, Alf Gunvald (eds.): *Marxism and Social Movements.* Leiden: Brill, 83–102.

Imig, Doug; Tarrow, Sidney (1999): The Europeanization of Movements? Contentious Politics and the European Union. October 1983–March 1995. In: Della Porta, Donatella; Kriesi, Hanspeter; Rucht, Dieter (eds.): *Social Movements in a Globalizing World.* New York: Macmillan, 112–133.

Imig, Doug; Tarrow, Sidney (2002): La contestation politique dans l'Europe en formation. In: Balme, Richard; Chabanet, Didier (eds.): *L'action collective en Europe.* Paris: Presses de Sciences Po, 195–223.

Joerges, Christian (2015): The Legitimacy Problématique of Economic Governance in the EU. In: Hertie School of Governance (ed.): *Governance Report 2015.* Oxford: Oxford University Press, 69–94.

Lefébure, Pierre; Lagneau, Eric (2002): Le moment Volvorde: action protestataire et espace publique européen. In: Balme, Richard; Chabanet, Didier (eds.): *L'action collective en Europe.* Paris: Presses de Sciences Po, 495–529.

Marks, Gary; McAdam, Doug (1999): On the Relationship of the Political Opportunities to the Form of Collective Action. In: Della Porta, Donatella; Kriesi, Hanspeter; Rucht, Dieter (eds.): *Social Movements in a Globalizing World.* New York: Macmillan, 97–111.

Martin, Andrew; Ross, George (2001): Trade Union Organizing at the European Level: The Dilemma of Borrowed Resources. In: Imig, Doug; Tarrow, Sidney (eds.): *Contentious Europeans. Protest and Politics in an Emerging Polity.* Lanham: Rowman & Littlefield, 53–76.

Marshall, Thomas H. (1992 [1950]): Citizenship and Social Class. In: Marshall, Thomas H.; Bottomore, Tom B. (eds.): *Citizenship and Social Class.* London: Pluto Press, 3–51.

Mazey, Sonia (2002): L'Union Européenne et les droits des femmes: de l'européanisation des agendas nationaux à la nationalisation d'un agenda européen? In: Balme, Richard; Chabanet, Didier (eds.): *L'action collective en Europe.* Paris: Presses de Sciences Po, 405–432.

McDonough, Terrence; Dundon, Tony (2010): *Thatcherism Delayed? The Irish Crisis and the Paradox of Social Partnership.* SSRN Scholarly Paper ID 1702602. Rochester: Social Science Research Network. http://papers.ssrn.com/abstract=1702602.

Polanyi, Karl (1957/1944): *The Great Transformation: The Political and Economic Origins of Our Time.* London: Beacon Press.

Rootes, Christopher A. (2002): The Europeanization of Environmentalism. In: Balme, Richard; Chabanet, Didier (eds.): *L'action collective en Europe.* Paris: Presses de Sciences Po, 377–404.

Rüdig, Wolfgang; Karyotis, Georgios (2014): Who Protests in Greece? Mass Opposition to Austerity. *British Journal of Political Science* 44 (3): 487–513.

Sergi, Vittorio; Vogiatzoglou, Markos (2013): Think Globally, Act Locally? Symbolic Memory and Global Repertoires in the Tunisian Uprising and the Greek Anti-Austerity Mobilizations. In: Fominaya, Christina F.; Cox, Laurence (eds.): *Understanding European Movements: New Social Movements, Global Justice Struggles, Anti-Austerity Protest.* London: Routledge, 220–235.

Silver, Beverly (2003): *Forces of Labor. Workers' Movements and Globalization since 1870.* Cambridge: Cambridge University Press.

Silver, Beverly; Karataşlı, Şahan Savaş (2016): Historical Dynamics of Capitalism and the Labour Movement. In: della Porta, Donatella; Diani, Mario (eds.): *Oxford Handbook on Social Movements.* Oxford: Oxford University Press, 133–145.

Standing, Guy (2011) *The Precariat.* London: Bloomsbury.

Streeck, Wolfgang (2011): *The crisis in contest. Democratic capitalism and its contradictions.* MPIfG, Discussion Paper 11/15.

Therborn, Göran (2013): *The Killing Fields of Inequality.* Cambridge: Polity.

Thompson, Edward H. (1963): *The Making of the English Working Class.* London: Penguin.

Tilly, Charles (1978): *From Mobilization to Revolution.* Reading: Addison-Wesley.

Tilly, Charles (1984): Social Movements and National Politics. In: Bright, Charles; Harding, Susan (eds.): *Statemaking and Social Movements: Essays in History and Theory.* Ann Arbor: University of Michigan Press, 297–317.

Touraine, Alain (1977): *The Self-Production of Society.* Chicago: University of Chicago Press.

Touraine, Alain (1981): *The Voice and the Eye. An Analysis of Social Movements.* Cambridge: Cambridge University Press.

Touraine, Alain (1985): An Introduction to the Study of Social Movements. *Social Research* 52: 749–788.

Touraine, Alain (1987): *The Workers' Movement.* Cambridge: Cambridge University Press.

Wallerstein, Imannuel (1990): Antisystemic Movements: History and Dilemma. In: Amin, Samir; Arrighi, Giovanni; Frank, Andre G.; Wallerstein, Imannuel (eds.): *Transforming the Revolution.* New York: Monthly Review Press, 13–52.

Wallerstein, Immanuel (2004): *World Systems Analysis: An Introduction.* Durham: Duke University Press.

Wallerstein, Immanuel (2010): Structural Crises. *New Left Review* 62: 133–142.

Yörük, Erdem; Yüksel, Murat (2014): Class and Politics in Turkey's Gezi Protests. *New Left Review* 89 (Sept.–Oct.): 103–123.

Chapter 3

Comment on della Porta

Wolfgang Streeck

This is a useful chapter. It summarises the state of the art on an often-overlooked subject, listing the relevant literature in case readers want to explore the matter further. And it supplements this with concise case accounts of recent developments in the relationship between social movements and trade unions in a number of countries. I have nothing to hold against or add to Donatella's piece. So I will limit myself to one specific aspect of what now tends to be called the "framing" of an issue before I proceed to several, more or less related general remarks on social movement and trade union politics in, and in relation to, the European Union (EU). The intention here is to sketch out a baseline for research and theory on this subject, in the sense of a list of fundamental conditions underneath whatever conjunctural, sectoral, topical, etc., modulations may be observable on top of them. I am doing this because I suspect that much of the work on and discussion of "European integration" is far too occupied with minor fluctuations in current events, to the neglect of deeply rooted priors that remain importantly in force regardless of what happens on the surface.

First on "framing". When it comes to the EU in particular, most consumers and too many producers of "Europe"-related social science sooner or later categorise arguments and conclusions in terms of whether they are "optimistic" or "pessimistic". I note in passing that such distinction is meaningless unless one specifies what side one is on. For example, concerning the time-honoured idea of a "social dimension" of the EU "optimism" may mean that one expects it to come about, in which case one is very likely a trade union sympathiser, or alternatively that one expects it *not* to come about, which would be the optimism of a neoliberal economist or, which is by and large the same, of a friend of capital – a *Kapitalversteher*. Symmetrically, of course, on "pessimism", which for a trade unionist means the "social dimension" won't come while for an employer it means it will. More important, optimism and pessimism are psychological categories that characterise persons or their general outlook on life; in social science, one should think, it is realism that counts, not whether its producer is or is not a happy-go-lucky type. I am not saying this for nothing. I have for more than two decades pointed out that the idea of a "Social Europa" had basically turned into an illusion propagated by national governments and a Brussels bureaucracy that had very different things on their agenda. I claim that most of my occasional, always carefully calibrated predictions on where the EU was about to go next were right, at least pointed in the right direction. (So austerity and "structural reforms" under EMU did not come as a surprise to me, nor should they have to my readers.) All too often, however, I had to observe that colleagues and users of my work got around the facts and logical arguments that I had so painstakingly put together by declaring Streeck to be a "pessimist". In their eyes this rendered my assembled evidence irrelevant, entitling them, upon having declared themselves "optimists", not to weigh my evidence against theirs with the only justification that they were, unlike me, nice and pleasant people. Let me assure you that this is not what Gramsci had in mind when he spoke of the "optimism of the will": will includes action not just wish; political struggle not just article-writing and certainly more than a personal determination to produce good news.

On to a few baseline facts on social movements, trade unions and the EU. First, social movements cannot govern; they depend on an addressee willing, for whatever reason, to listen to them and act on their demands. This is unlike trade unions, which, where there (still) is collective bargaining, do co-govern the wage relationship together with employers, ideally on equal terms. (Without collective bargaining trade unions turn into social movements pure and simple.) For social movements to be effective their addressee must be receptive to them, meaning in simple English weak enough to be vulnerable to their pressure. This condition is far from always present. Moreover, trade unions tend to be relatively well resourced while most social movements are not. This may make them liable to accepting material support from addresses, substituting for such support from their constituents. The result may be more or less pervasive collusion resulting in co-optation of the movement into the institutions that it tries to influence ("yellow movements", in parallel to "yellow unions").

Second, "Brussels" is not a good addressee for social movements. It is, essentially, a fake polity, one that lacks sovereignty – which does not prevent it from pretending the opposite. Again as a "baseline", Brussels is run by national governments which are the only players in town to command that most precious political resource, state sovereignty; never was this more obvious than during the years of crisis management after 2008. Only an addressee with some sort of sovereignty, however, can be responsive to social movement demands. Moreover, the Brussels institutional setup is such that the power of its component elements varies inversely with their accessibility to movement-type mobilisation. The Parliament is the most accessible Brussels institution, but it is largely powerless: it cannot appoint or de-elect a government, nor can it initiate legislation. The Commission, for its part, pretends to be a government, but it is no more than a bureaucracy; it would like to change this and will therefore try to be receptive to "European" political mobilisation, but it cannot make concessions that the Council won't condone. As to the Council, it is an intergovernmental body *par excellence*, and what happens there are international power games and diplomatic negotiations impenetrable to outsiders. Next, the European Court of Justice (ECJ) is a court, powerful as such, but as courts are these days it has little taste for collective rights and collective action, especially in the labour market (also because its charter is essentially competition law and the enforcement of the "four freedoms" of the internal market). As to, finally, the European Central Bank (ECB), it is safely shielded from public scrutiny and public pressure; in fact its entire structure is designed from the beginning to immunise monetary policy against electoral, let alone social movement politics.[1]

Third, as indicated, not only the Commission but also other EU institutions like to pretend that they are more than they are, and they spend a great deal of effort on creating and sustaining a myth – or as one puts it today, a "narrative" – of their power and importance. On this, enormous resources are being spent. The matter is complicated by the fact that national governments do not object to the Union's symbolic self-aggrandisement; in fact, since their neoliberal turn in the 1990s, they are happy to help Brussels make people believe that it is Brussels, not the national governments, that is calling the shots in Europe. Blame is shifted upwards, allowing national governments to defend neoliberal policies at home by pointing to Brussels and referring opponents to "Europe". (One result is right-wing populist movements and parties turning "anti-European" where in fact the problems their clients want addressed are problems that national capitals have created and refuse to deal with.)[2]

Fourth, as in particular the Commission works to keep the European myth alive and make itself appear as a big political player, it is only too willing to help European-level trade unions and, to a lesser extent, social movement organisations to build a presence in Brussels, by funding offices, officials, research institutes, conferences, interpreters, etc. The idea here is to cultivate a "corporatist" infrastructure for the Commission of intermediary organisations obliged to the Commission and the Parliament for the access and material support provided to them. Such organisations are effectively subject to what Schmitter and I have once called a "logic of influence" – governing the give-and-take between interest groups and their institutional interlocutors – while they are much less controlled by their "logic of membership", i.e., their relationship to their social base (Schmitter/Streeck 1999 [1982]). This is so because in Europe, social movements and trade unions are, for cultural, political and practical reasons, nationally based and organised, nested in inherited, nationally specific structures linking them to their members on the one hand and their national political systems on the other. While they can and do meet at European level, indeed increasingly so and typically funded by the EU in its effort to build legitimacy through a supranational constituency of intermediary organisations of its own, substantive interests and procedural routines and preferences are too different from country to country to make for more than very general common policies that are from the beginning understood to have little operational meaning if at all.

Fifth, one can illustrate this with reference to the demands of trade unions and social movements for European-international "solidarity" in relation to austerity, low growth, low investment, indebtedness, unemployment, regional and national economic disparities and the like. Organisation matters – meaning that the way polities are constituted and political actors organised affects the substance of their interests and the demands they are willing and able to make in the political arena. We have learned this in the past when comparing the labour market interests of workers in craft unions to those of workers in industrial unions (Streeck 2005). In Europe it is the specifically European configuration of nation-states and supranational institutions that shapes what workers and citizens on the ground perceive to be their interests and where they can and cannot unite in supranational collective action.

Very fundamentally, again, workers in European industrial relations, including social and labour market policy, are not just workers but also taxpayers. While as workers they may perhaps feel to be in the same boat as their fellow-workers in other countries, as taxpayers they find themselves in conflict with them when it comes to fiscal redistribution among nation-states in the name of Europe-wide "solidarity". Transfers from North to South mean higher taxes or lower benefits or fewer services to workers in the North, or entail that risk – which is why debt forgiveness, a centralised European investment budget, EMU-wide unemployment insurance and higher European "structural funds" are hard to sell to Northern European voters. Europe-wide social movements find it easy to clamour for "solidarity" at demonstrations in Brussels as they will never have to get their constituents to pay for it; the same holds for European trade unions as long as it is understood that what they say at European social movement occasions is not binding on their national constituents. It remains cheap talk covering up the fact that the very institutional structures in Europe that national governments have used to engineer the move from state-administered to neoliberal capitalism stand in the way of the production of collective-European oppositional interests and their being acted upon in more-than-just symbolic European politics. What we are seeing here is another permutation of an old theme well known from the 1980s and 1990s, when Northern European unions advised their Southern European brothers (and increasingly also sisters) to make stronger efforts to narrow the wage gap between North and South. Of course both sides were aware that this would make employment more secure in the North while likely increasing unemployment in the South. The same was true when in the 1980s the German metalworkers' union, IG Metall, tried to convince trade unions in Italy and elsewhere to fight for a reduction of working time to 35 hours a week, as IG Metall had successfully done, in order to reduce unemployment. Nobody took such advice seriously, not on the giving and not the receiving end, since everybody knew that such "solidarity" would only protect German jobs at the expense of, for example, Italian ones.

Notes

1 One should also remember that social movements are thoroughly local in character in that they much depend for their mobilisation on the physical closeness, the personal contact and the shared experience of the warm bodies of their supporters (as do, to a lesser extent, trade unions, at least those still availing themselves of the strike weapon). This means that they are likely to do better within smaller jurisdictions and vis-à-vis addressees with a more limited territorial reach closer to what may be called the particularism of social life. The Blockupy attack on the ECB, impressive as it was, remained a one-time event that Sr. Draghi has very likely long forgotten.

2 Alternatively the blame is put by national governments on a lack of European institutions and European "integration", as reflected in the survey data that della Porta cites. Such lack, of course, is entirely of the making of Member States and their governments. By complaining about it they activate the "European" illusion, moving address of collective grievances as articulated by social movements and trade unions to a very distant future. This amounts to a "Europeanisation" of hopes and the use of "optimism" as a political tool.

Literature

Schmitter, Philippe C.; Streeck, Wolfgang (1999/1982): *The Organization of Business Interests: Studying the Associative Action of Business in Advanced Industrial Societies*. MPIfG Discussion Paper 99/1.

Streeck, Wolfgang (2005): The Sociology of Labor Markets and Trade Unions. In: Smelser, Neil; Swedberg, Richard (eds.): *Handbook of Economic Sociology*, Second Edition. New York: Russell Sage, 254–283.

Chapter 4

Conceptualising the development of the European political economy from a neo-Gramscian perspective

Andreas Bieler and Hans-Jürgen Bieling

Introduction

Since Robert Cox's seminal articles in 1981 and 1983, neo-Gramscian perspectives have emerged as an inspiring critical approach in the field of International Political Economy (IPE) throughout the 1980s and especially 1990s. One of its prime objectives was the comprehensive analysis of transnational hegemony as a particular mode of capitalist rule, which irrespective of persistent forms of exploitation and marginalisation also includes the consensus of large parts of subaltern social forces. In this sense, transnational hegemony was not simply conceptualised as an order among states, but rather, as stated by Robert W. Cox (1983: 171), as 'an order within a world economy with a dominant mode of production which penetrates into all countries and links into other subordinate modes of production'. Furthermore, Cox (1983: 171–172) continued to emphasise that hegemony represents

> also a complex of international social relationships which connects the
> social classes of the different countries. World hegemony is describable
> as a social structure, an economic structure, and a political structure;
> and it cannot be simply one of these things but must be all three. World
> hegemony, furthermore, is expressed in universal norms, institutions
> and mechanisms which lay down general rules of behaviour for states
> and for those forces of civil society that act across national boundaries –
> rules which support the dominant mode of production.

In correspondence with this general definition, the focus of most neo-Gramscian research was – and perhaps still is – on the emergence and reproduction of neoliberal hegemony, i.e. a market- and competition-centred concept of capitalist modernisation, in manifold contexts: on a global scale, in many developing countries, but also within the European Union (EU). In analysing neo-liberal hegemony, most scholars have taken into consideration the processes of globalisation, financialisation and digitalisation and the changing patterns of production, but also highlighted the more explicitly political manufacturing of a transnational consensus. While some were primarily interested in the activities of most powerful governments (Cox 1987), others analysed the role of transnational business (van der Pijl 1998; Sklair 2001), and others again the impact of collective (organic) intellectuals, research institutes and think tanks (Plehwe et al. 2006).

In view of persistent, in many regards even increasing contradictions of neo-liberal restructuring, quite a few scholars also addressed the role of subaltern forces such as trade unions and social movements in the reproduction of neoliberal hegemony. Analytical core questions in this context had been, to what extent and why these subaltern forces were willing to consent into neoliberal hegemony, and to what extent and why they also proved able to organise resistance and promote initiatives or projects for a more solidaristic mode of social reproduction (Gill 2008: 237–248; Morton 2007: 171–200). In this sense, also the activities of European trade unions were marked by a dialectic of consent and resistance to neoliberal restructuring (Bieler 2006; Clua-Losada/Horn 2015). In some cases and constellations they were partly co-opted by hegemonic forces; in others they showed some willingness to form – sometimes also cross-border – counter-hegemonic alliances.

In this chapter, we aim to explore the partially diverging strategic choices by European trade unions and their impact on the development of industrial relations. We argue that these choices were determined not only by the nature of disposable power resources but also by the broader socio-economic, institutional and cultural context, inclusive of the political self-understanding or identity of unions, also in relation to other social forces. Obviously, this interplay of power resources and the broader political economic context differs in individual Member States as well as in certain periods of European integration and stimulates – irrespective of common problem perceptions – diverging trade union strategies.

To illustrate the overall dynamics and the strategic choices of trade unions as part of European industrial relations, this paper is organised as follows: the next section starts with conceptualising the transformation of industrial relations from a neo-Gramscian perspective, which – beyond all transnational tendencies – is also open to complementary concepts, more sensitive to the particular national economic and institutional arrangements as well as to the discursive struggles within civil societies (2). From there on, we continue to discuss the changing nature of European integration since its re-launch in the late 1980s, i.e. the structurally asymmetrical regulation and the unleashed processes of uneven and combined capitalist development, which also implies more far-reaching consequences for given systems of industrial relations (3). This has become particularly evident during the unfolding European crisis dynamics, which were perceived and strategically encountered, however, fairly different throughout the EU (4). The paper concludes with more general reflections on the chances of trade unions to overcome this strategic divergence, as it limits the capacities to discuss and promote common initiatives for a more solidaristic reform of industrial relations (5).

Dimensions of a critical analysis of industrial relations within the EU

Obviously, the financial crisis and the euro crisis and the political management of both crises constellations impacted differently on the transformation of industrial relations within the EU. To understand and analyse the core mechanisms of theses transformations, a neo-Gramscian approach directs the attention particularly on the complex social relations of (re-)production – and the constellation of social interests and ideas – which evolve differently in different spheres, i.e. within specific national models of capitalism, but also within the European or transnational arena, or within regions and individual firms. Each of these spheres or arenas is characterised by particular institutional settings, power relations and specific social conflicts.

At the core of these conflicts are the relations between capital and labour, and in more organisational terms: between employer associations and trade unions. Both types of organisations – sometimes next to governments – are the core actors in the field of collective bargaining. Inevitably, therefore, any analysis of the transformation of industrial relations has to pay particular attention to the conflicts in this area. At the same time, however, it would be a much too narrow view to focus on this area alone. For, on one hand, the organisation of work and production are not only the result of – multi-level: firm, sector, national – bargaining processes but also influenced by further areas of public policy; and on the other hand, work and production are always related to the organisation of public and private social reproduction, e.g. the provision of the social infrastructure (day care, schools, universities, research institutes, etc.) and the organisation family life. What this implies can be studied with respect to the European crises dynamics since 2008/09 (Bieling/Buhr 2015). It has become evident that in most European countries the overall macroeconomic constellation and the manifold governmental activities – in the first line, the politics of austerity and market-oriented structural reforms – did not broaden, but rather constraint the room for manoeuvre of employees and most trade unions.

In view of the manifold forms of the embeddedness of industrial relations into the broader settings of national and European capitalism, and the endeavour of neo-Gramscian IPE to analyse the hegemonic nature and forms of the social relations of (re-)production, it seems useful to apply the concept of 'labour policy'. This concept was already developed in the 1980s (Jürgens/Naschold 1984) and has been up-dated and specified since then (e.g. Hildebrandt et al. 2007). In the original version, the concept aimed to specify the political impact on the development of work and employment from a regulation theoretical perspective by re-reading some of the core insights with the help of Michael Burawoy's (1979, 1985) analytical differentiation between the 'politics in production' and 'politics of production'. The 'politics in production' concern primarily issues of an effective and, if possible, hegemonic organisation of production, including prevailing power relations and forms of exploitation, along value chains and on the company level. In other words, they are closely related to the productive foundations of capitalist development. In contrast to this, but basically complementary, the 'politics of production' refer to the activities of the state – above all governments, central banks, regulatory agencies, etc. – and civil society actors. These activities mainly address the overall organisation of public life. As they include manifold regulative and redistributive, sometimes even interventionist proposals and measures, they indirectly impact, however, also on work and employment because they aim to change the societal context and the embeddedness of production.

The analytical differentiation between the 'politics in production' and 'politics of production' is absolutely in line with, and supportive of, a neo-Gramscian analysis of industrial relations, as it highlights that work and production should be conceived as complexes of social power relations, the further development of which is severely contested – between employer organisations and trade unions, but also social movements and non-governmental organizations (NGOs) – in more than one arena. The analytical advantage of emphasising the 'politics of production' is at least twofold: first, it helps to overcome the rather firm-centric view of some industrial sociologists ignoring the labour policy dimension of many governmental decisions and programmes launched in the fields of technology, industrial, infrastructure or financial, health or social policy; and second, it builds a bridge to social theoretical reflections regarding capitalist development driven not only by the dynamics of accumulation but also by specific modes of regulation and the social relations of production.

The second aspect makes clear that the social power relations impacting on the development of industrial relations must be analysed in a broader setting. For they are not only determined by the structural (level of (un-)employment), organisational (rate of membership) and institutional power (involvement in political deliberations and decisions) of trade unions and employer associations (Dörre et al. 2009), but also – indirectly – determined by the manifold activities and discourses within civil society. Moreover, the struggles over the content of quite a few areas of the 'politics of production' transcend national borders. If one takes the very important fields of monetary, financial, competition, industrial or even social policy into account, they are defined exclusively or to a large extent in the European context. This makes clear that nowadays any comprehensive analysis of the transformation of industrial relations must include a systematic understanding of the main tendencies and contradictions of the emergent forms of European capitalism.

Asymmetrical integration around neo-liberal restructuring

The revival of European integration since the mid-1980s has been driven by neo-liberal restructuring. The Single European Act (SEA) of 1987, which institutionalised the Internal Market programme, spelled out the goals of the four freedoms, i.e. the freedom of goods, services, capital and people. A bigger market was supposed to lead to tougher competition resulting in higher efficiency, greater profits and eventually through a trickle-down effect in more general wealth and more jobs. National markets should be deregulated and liberalised; national companies were to be privatised. The Economic and Monetary Union (EMU), part of the Treaty of Maastricht in 1991, followed similar neo-liberal directions. The underlying rationale of EMU, its social purpose, is best embodied in the statutory role of the European Central Bank (ECB) and the convergence criteria. As for the former, a common monetary policy is dealt with by the ECB. The primary target of the ECB and its interest rate policy, as spelled out in the Treaty of Maastricht, are the maintenance of price stability and low inflation. Economic growth and employment are only secondary objectives, subordinated to price stability. In relation to the institutional set-up of the ECB, we experience what Stephen Gill calls a 'new constitutionalism', which 'seeks to separate economic policies from broad political accountability in order to make governments more responsive to the discipline of market forces' (Gill 2001: 47). The ECB has to report to the European Council and the European Parliament, but neither states nor supranational institutions are in a position to force any kind of policy upon the ECB. As for the convergence criteria, most importantly, they obliged Member States to have a government budget deficit of no more than 3% of GDP and government debt of no more than 60% of GDP. The EMU member countries, in order to meet the criteria, had to implement tough austerity budgets in the run-up to EMU.

Neo-liberal restructuring, however, has not only been inward facing. It was also projected outwards and here in particular as part of the EU enlargement process from the mid-1990s onwards and the EU's free trade strategy. Neo-liberal restructuring had already been the underlying social purpose of Austria's, Finland's and Sweden's accession to the EU in 1995 (Bieler 2000). The end of the Cold War in the early 1990s provided then the opportunity to extend this towards Central and Eastern Europe (CEE). Potential new members had to achieve a stable democracy, a functioning market economy and the ability to withstand competition within the EU, and to take on the full *acquis communautaire* including the aims of political, and economic and monetary union. Thus, the elements of the enlargement strategy of the

EU clearly demanded adaptation to EU rules and thus measures of liberalisation and deregulation of a more radical, market-oriented variant of
neo-liberalism (Bohle 2006: 69–74). The free trade strategy *Global Europe*,
moreover, was devised as a strategy for the EU's common commercial policy in 2006 (Bieler 2013). Its main focus has been on competitiveness of the
European economy, which is understood to be the best way of achieving
growth and creating new jobs (European Commission 2006: 2). The strategy
emphasises the elimination of non-tariff barriers: access to resources, intellectual property protection, services, investment, public procurement and
competition. The main objective is to obtain far-reaching commitments by
the EU's trading partners in the opening up of their markets (Bieling 2010:
122–144). In short, the EU has been a key driver in furthering neo-liberal
restructuring at the global level.

When European integration was revived from the mid-1980s onwards,
some trade unions had supported it, because economic integration was
expected to be followed by political integration including better social policies across the EU (Bieling 2001: 96–105). And there were some positive
signs. The Treaty of Maastricht, in addition to EMU, added also the Social Chapter to the EU. This has made it possible that, on the initiation
by the Commission, the European-level social partners, i.e. the European
Trade Union Confederation (ETUC) on behalf of trade unions and
BUSINESSEUROPE for the employers' associations as the most important
organisations, can directly negotiate work-related issues. Agreements are
transferred into binding EU law via directives passed by the Council of Ministers without further discussions. In the 1990s, some directives, e.g. on pa-
rental leave, part-time employment and fixed-term employment, have been
passed along this road (Falkner 1998: 99–155). Furthermore, due to pressure
by the new French government of Lionel Jospin at the Amsterdam summit in 1997, an employment chapter was added to the EU and a special job
summit convened in Luxembourg later in the same year. Overall, however,
hopes for a strong social policy have been disappointed. Multi-sector and
sectoral social dialogue has been hardly developed from the 2000s onwards
and more employment is mainly to be created via restructuring through
the deregulation and liberalisation of goods and services as well as capital
and labour markets. EU employment policy is, therefore, in full accordance
with neo-liberal restructuring and has not changed the overall dominant
focus on competitiveness (Hager 2009). In short, the EU Social Dimension
policies can be regarded as part of the market-building process (Leibfried
2005: 257, 262) and European integration is clearly asymmetrical with common social policies being less developed than economic integration.

At the structural level, neo-liberal restructuring was underpinned by increasing transnationalisation of production and finance in the European
political economy. While the annual average of inward Foreign Direct
Investment (FDI) flows into the EU between 1989 and 1994 was $76,634

million (UN 2001: 291), inward FDI in 2007 as a pre-crisis peak year was $842,311 million (UN 2009: 247). The corresponding figures for outward FDI are $105,194 million as annual average between 1989 and 1994 (UN 2001: 296), and $1,192,141 million in 2007 (UN 2009: 247), indicating the closer integration of production processes across borders. As most FDIs are mergers and acquisitions, organised by investment banks on the stock markets, they are closely related to financial market dynamics and the processes of financial integration. Given numerous initiatives in this area, 'the European Union has moved decisively in the direction of a more transnationalised, marketised, and desegmented financial system based on a single legislative framework' (Underhill 1997: 118). Materially, integration was underpinned by manifold processes of financialisation, often triggered by the privatisation of social security (pensions) and public services (rail, telecommunication, post, energy, etc.), so that past decades were characterised by the emergence of a European financial capitalism (Bieling 2013). This increase in structural power of not only financial but also non-financial capital has put European labour on the defensive with transnational capital, unsurprisingly, closely involved in key moments of European integration (van Apeldoorn 2002).

Uneven and combined development and the Eurozone crisis

The onset of the Eurozone crisis is closely related to the global financial crisis. When global financial markets froze and banks and financial institutions ceased lending to each other as well as industrial companies due to high levels of uncertainty, especially peripheral Eurozone countries found it increasingly difficult to re-finance their debts. Closer analysis of the crisis indicates, however, that the global financial crisis only triggered the Eurozone crisis. The main causes of the crisis can be found in the uneven and combined development underpinning the European political economy. Observers of the Eurozone crisis have pointed out how Europe has been divided between export-driven versus debt-driven growth models (Stockhammer 2016). EMU has limited countercyclical state intervention in times of crisis and has relied from the beginning on downward pressure on wages for adjustment alongside the development of financialisation and the creation of national and personal debt for economic growth.

From a post-Keynesian perspective, the main problems of EMU are understood to be the result of insufficient demand and in particular the asymmetries in the formation of such overall demand across the European political economy as a whole (Patomäki 2012: 79). The export-driven growth model of Germany and the debt-driven models of countries such as Greece and Portugal are, thus, mutually dependent on each other. Firms in core countries would not have been able to pursue export-led growth strategies if global aggregate demand had not been supported by the real estate and stock market bubbles that occurred in the periphery. Peripheral countries, unable to compete with German productivity levels and strong export performance, ended up as countries with large account deficits. In the long run, such development strategies based on capital inflows – also FDI, but mainly credits – were unsustainable.

Nevertheless, unevenness across the European political economy is not only due to EMU, but has characterised the European political economy for much longer. Free trade policies, as initially embedded within the EU Customs Union since 1968 and then especially the Internal Market from the mid-1980s onwards – when free trade was extended from trade in goods to trade in services and finance – generally tend to deepen the inequality between countries, as advanced countries with higher levels of productivity benefit disproportionately from trade. 'Unevenness is not…a result of market imperfections, but is in fact a product of the way competitive markets work in the real world' (Kiely 2007: 18). Unevenness has been reflected in different productivity levels with peripheral European countries such as Portugal historically linked to labour-intensive sectors and states such as Germany mainly involved in capital-intensive sectors of global value chains (GVCs). For example, the Portuguese economy is characterised by low-technology, labour-intensive production structures, often poorly organised and based on human resources with low levels of qualification (Rodrigues/Reis 2012: 198). The modernising strategies in the area of industrial production by several successive Portuguese governments have not worked, as Jamie Jordan (2017: 124–128, 154–156, and 159–161) demonstrates in a detailed analysis of the Portuguese Textile and Clothing (TC) and footwear industries as well as motor vehicles. While the former sectors actually expanded during the 1980s and 1990s, this was mainly based on small- and medium-sized companies, which functioned as subcontractors to larger, transnational companies (TNCs) and focussed on labour-intensive assembling of prefabricated parts. As for the latter, in 1995 a motor vehicle assembly plant was opened in Palmela near Lisbon as a joint venture with Ford and Volkswagen. Similar to the TC and footwear industries, although 50% of components were produced nationally, the remaining 50%, mainly capital-intensive production components, were imported from other countries such as Germany, France and the UK. Considering that capital-intensive parts were generally imported from abroad, while Portuguese components and assembling depended on labour-intensive aspects of production, it is clear that Portuguese development was subordinated to requirements of the European political economy.

In the end, Eurozone members were provided with bailout packages by the EU. In May 2010, in March 2012 and again in July 2015 Greece received financial help; Ireland was bailed out in November 2010; in May 2011 it was Portugal's turn, followed by Cyprus in March 2013. Italy and Spain, although they did not have to be bailed out, had to present austerity packages, developed nationally, before EU institutions agreed on the extension of loans to recapitalise their banks. The bailout packages came at a high price. Financial support was made conditional on the implementation of austerity policies including cuts in public services, cuts in public sector employment, the privatisation of national companies and further liberalisation of labour markets (Bieling 2012).

> Hence, the real purpose of the bailout programmes is to restructure political economies and to open up the public sector as new investment opportunities for private finance. The balance of power is, thereby, shifted further from labour to capital in this process.
>
> (Bieler/Jordan 2015)

In addition to disciplining peripheral EU Member States, the economic governance system of the EU as a whole has been restructured. At the EU level itself, the bailout packages were, thus, backed up with a new set of regulations around the so-called 'six pack' on economic governance applicable to all Member States.

> According to these six new EU laws that came into force after their publication in the EU's *Official Journal* on 23 November 2011, Eurozone countries that do not comply with the revised EU Stability and Growth Pact or find themselves in a so-called macroeconomic excessive imbalance position, can be sanctioned by a yearly fine equalling 0.2 per cent or 0.1 per cent of GDP respectively.
>
> (Erne 2012: 228)

These mechanisms have been further enhanced by the 'Fiscal Compact', which came into force on 1 January 2013 requiring that national budgets are in balance or surplus. The whole new economic governance of the EU form of state continues to depoliticise economic-political decision-making enshrining further neo-liberal austerity policies across the EU (Bieler/Morton 2018: Chapter 9).

Industrial relations in the context of the ongoing crisis

In addition to structural imbalance between capital and labour as a result of the transnationalisation of production and finance across the European political economy, the EU's institutional set-up has disadvantaged trade unions. The strategic selectivity of the EU form of state is heavily skewed towards the interests of transnational capital and the way they enjoy privileged access to the key Commission Directorates responsible for Competition, Internal Market and Economics and Finances, while trade unions, social movements and NGOs are generally side-lined (Bieler 2006: 179–182). This is compounded by the way the new economic governance structure has nationalised social conflict, while the main drivers for austerity are implemented at the European level (Erne 2015). Nevertheless, it was also trade unions' agency, which had contributed to labour's inability to stop and re-direct neo-liberal restructuring. As Asbjørn Wahl points out, many of the large, established European trade unions have succumbed to a social partnership ideology. They assume that 'the social progress of the welfare state was not the result of the preceding struggles but of class cooperation and tripartite negotiations in themselves' (Wahl 2011: 35). They overlook that it had actually been labour's ability to balance the power of capital in society, with labour's power having been built up in successful moments of class struggle, which underpinned the gains of the welfare state in Europe after 1945. Tripartite negotiations, i.e. the willingness of employers and state managers to take demands by the working class seriously, were themselves the result of trade unions' structural power in society. By continuing to rely on participating in European and national institutions, while the underlying power structure had changed as a result of the transnationalisation of production and finance, trade unions quite often have forgotten to mobilise members and wider society in concrete struggles against neo-liberalism. In short, it is a combination of a change in structural power in society, particularly skewed institutional arrangements and misguided strategies, which have resulted in a situation, in which organised labour has become largely side-lined in the European political economy.

   The role of German trade unions in the initiative of co-ordinating national collective bargaining at the European level, aiming at ensuring that national unions pursue a common strategy of asking for wage increases along the formula of productivity increase plus inflation rate, is indicative of this double problematic of loss in structural power and strategies overlooking solidarity with other labour movements. While German unions had been the driving force behind the development of this strategy, they were actually the ones that missed targets by the largest amount (Erne 2008: 97). Indeed, for the whole period from the adoption of the Euro in 2000 right up to 2012, the average negotiated salary increase in Germany was 5.5% below productivity increase, and even more drastic the effective average salary increase was a further 9.3% below the negotiated average salary (Lehndorff 2013: 56). On one hand, this had been the result of the 'politics of production', i.e. the weakening of the German trade unions due to domestic restructuring of the welfare state, the so-called Hartz IV reforms, and the related restructuring of the labour market. Partly, however, this has also been the result of the weakness of unions in the 'politics in production', i.e. the general transnationalisation of German production, the lost strike by the IG Metall in Eastern Germany in 2003 and a strategy by German unions to prioritise the situation of German workers above the interests of labour movements elsewhere instead of pursuing common objectives. For example, Berthold Huber, then General Secretary of IG Metall, in 2012 blamed Spanish unions for the fate of the Spanish economy by obtaining 'too high wage increases' at the expense of competitiveness. He, thus, placed himself within a standard neo-liberal analysis of the causes of the crisis (Bieler/Erne 2014: 161–168).

In the European context, the general stance of German unions seems to be representative of 'Nordic' countries, which aimed to address the negative implications of the financial and euro crisis for social and labour relations by resorting to 'crisis corporatism' (Urban 2015). In principle, the crisis corporatist arrangements are based on the competitive corporatist orientations of the pre-crisis era and include irrespective of some social achievements – e.g. a prolonged short-time compensation, car scrappage premiums or involvement in intra-firm working-time flexibilisation – many concessions in terms of wages, working hours as well as labour market and social policy reforms. In many countries of the European periphery, above all in Southern Europe but also in the Balkans, trade unions were confronted with very far-reaching adjustment pressures and public demands for even more concessions so that they – at least temporarily – refrained from upholding corporatist arrangements and resorted to more confrontational strategies (Bieling/Lux 2014; Bieling/Buhr 2015). These more confrontational strategies mainly included public protests such as demonstrations, but also waves of general strikes, both triggered by efforts to ward off the social implications of harsh austerity programmes (Novak/Gallas 2014; Hyman 2015; Hayes 2017).

The indicated divergence of trade union strategies and the rejection of corporatist involvement in the latter group of countries are in some regards illuminating: first, the divergence of union strategies certainly reflects different political traditions and cultures of social struggles. Moreover, however, it also shows that the uneven development within European financial capitalism, particularly under conditions of financial crisis and neo-liberal crisis management, spreads towards the spheres of industrial relations and social and labour market policies, as it generates nationally different, sometimes very specific socio-economic situations and power constellations (Bieling/ Buhr 2015). Second, the resurgence of conflict disposition of trade unions in the peripheral countries occurs under conditions of structural weakness. This weakness partly results from the severity of the crisis in most of these countries. It is, however, further aggravated by the intrusive and disciplinary nature of some European economic governance instruments – more modest within the European semester process, but more far-reaching in the context of structural adjustment in the case of public borrowing from the European Stability Mechanism (ESM) controlled by the troika of the European Commission, ECB and International Monetary Fund (IMF) (Schulten/Müller 2015). The leverage of the disciplinary mechanisms seems particularly strong in Southern Europe, as these countries dispose of instruments of income policy and therefore have only restricted tariff autonomy and as the overall direction in collective bargaining is primarily determined by the results in the public sector. In order to avert and mitigate the pressures of austerity and neo-liberal reforms, resistance aimed at changing the overall economic debate within the EU. For this purpose, the formation of a counter-hegemonic alliance of transnational solidarity was required. However, such efforts failed, as on one hand Nordic unions only reluctantly participated in European days of action and showed generally unwillingness to put the modes of European and national economic regulation into question; and they also failed, as unions showed serious difficulties in gaining public support in civil society – in fact, in Southern Europe they even lost support during the crises years (Hyman 2015: 104–106) – and in cooperating with social protest movements such as M15 in Spain.

In a way, the inability of trade unions to generate new forms of transnational solidarity with strong ties in domestic civil societies under conditions of severe European crises came as no surprise. It was already presaged with the failure of the – principally promising – European Social Forum (ESF) process. In the early 2000s this process seemed to provide an alternative to mainstream trade unions' participation in formal bipartite and tripartite social institutions. It provided regular meeting points of established European trade unions but also of more radical, rank-and-file trade unions as well as social movements and NGOs to exchange their critical positions on neo-liberal globalisation as well as organise various events of contestation at the meetings but importantly even more so between the meetings (Bieler/ Morton 2004). Nevertheless, while enthusiastically welcomed initially especially at the first ESF in Florence/Italy in November 2002, over time this process lost traction as participants became disenchanted, arguing that the forum process had not resulted in joint actions challenging neoliberalism. The forums had failed, it was argued, to develop a significant impact on policy-making in general and on the 'politics of production' in particular. The sixth and final ESF took place in Istanbul/Turkey in 2010. In sum, the European left had already been fragmented and weak even before the financial crisis and subsequent Eurozone crisis struck in 2007/2008, partly due to a change in the balance of power in society in favour of capital, partly due to misguided strategies by trade unions.

Importantly, resistance to neo-liberal globalisation is not automatically progressive. The vacuum on the left provided space, which the extreme right has been successful at exploiting. 'When people are marginalised and underprivileged, if respect and dignity is refused to them, if their social status is threatened, nationalism is one way to compensate for that, in particular, in the absence of an emancipatory alternative' (Wahl 2017: 159). Across Europe, nationalist, xenophobic parties have been on the rise since 2007 with the near victory by the populist right-wing candidate in the Austrian presidential elections in 2016, the strong performance of the Front National candidate Marine LePen in the French presidential elections in May 2017 or the Brexit referendum in the UK in June 2016 as some of the key moments, not to speak about the election of Donald Trump as President of the USA in November 2016. Does this mean that trade unions, the left, have been defeated in Europe? In the final section, we will reflect on ongoing contestation of neo-liberal restructuring and austerity across Europe.

Contradictions, conflicts and prospects

Labour's inability to halt neo-liberal restructuring in Europe in the wake of the global financial crisis does not mean that there have been no successful moments of resistance at the European level. First, between May 2012 and September 2013 the European Citizens' Initiative (ECI) 'Water and Sanitation Are a Human Right' successfully collected close to 1.9 million signatures across the EU, forcing the Commission into an official position on the management of water access. Based on a broad alliance of trade unions, social movements and environmental groups at the European level as well as a whole range of Member States and co-ordinated by the European Federation of Public Service Unions (EPSU), this campaign not only succeeded at demanding safe access to drinking water in Europe and the wider world, but it also mobilised against the liberalisation and privatisation of water (Bieler 2017). Second, there has been a broad alliance against the new free trade agreement between the EU and the USA, the Transatlantic Trade and Investment Partnership (TTIP) (see https://stop-ttip.org/, accessed 03/08/2017). The *Stop TTIP* campaign is based on more than 500 trade unions and civil society organisations across Europe. It has managed to collect more than three million signatures against this Treaty from 7 October 2014 to 6 October 2015. Arguably, it is also due to this campaign that TTIP negotiations are currently on hold and the European public in general is much more aware of the negative implications of these new era free trade agreements. In short, it would be wrong to argue that the European labour movement has been completely ineffective in contesting neo-liberalism.

Moreover, the weak position of trade unions in some Member States should not make us overlook the ongoing resistance in different areas in different countries. As Huke, Clua-Losada and Bailey point out, 'social struggle has not ceased to exist but...has instead shifted in form towards mass mobilisations and collective, autonomous, self-organisation' (Huke, Clua-Losada and Bailey 2015: 745). Focussing on resistance beyond elections and attempts to gain state power reveals that neo-liberalisation is anything but stable and assured in and beyond Europe. It 'should instead be viewed as a fragile, troubled and hard-fought development' (Bailey et al. 2017: 214). As part of the Eurozone crisis, public education came under enormous pressure in Spain, for example. In response, trade unions organising in the sector – together with pupils and their parents – mobilised widely to contribute to a situation in which support for public education remains high. These social movements

> drew on the repertoire of action and political climate created by 15-M. The movements were also often subsumed under the label, *marea verde*, a name derived from green shirts, with the demand for public schools for everyone, which became a symbol of the protest.
>
> (Bailey et al. 2017: 169)

In Greece too, contestation of austerity is ongoing despite the climb-down of the Syriza government in the summer of 2015. As a result of cuts, the health sector in Greece has been decimated with many unemployed Greeks no longer being covered by health insurance and, thus, unable to access healthcare. In response, across the country 'healthcare clinics' have emerged which cater for these people's healthcare needs for free. The clinics are run by volunteers and depend on donations of money, equipment and facilities. While successful in covering people's needs, they also have a political objective. 'Emphasising solidarity as the dominant principle of action repoliticises austerity and restructuring, and how it is having a gen-eralised impact on the socio-economic functioning of Greece and its peo-ple' (Jordan 2017: 253).

Of course, these moments of contestation at the European level and within various Member States have not (yet) succeeded in stopping neo-liberal restructuring and shifting the EU onto a different, more socially just trajectory. Nevertheless, they show that next to the double – domestic and transnational – erosion of solidaristic structures, there are also new im-pulses and practices of solidaristic cooperation; and underneath the appar-ent weakness of European labour, of the European left, there is ongoing conflict, which may well erupt as a more homogenous moment of resistance against neo-liberalism in the future.

The crucial question, however, is how trade unions can mobilise and organise this potential in order to broaden and stabilise solidaristic atti-tudes and practices. It seems clear that efforts in such a direction require some innovative strategies and the formation of new, potentially counter-hegemonic social alliances, which have the potential to transcend national borders. In this sense, the meanwhile rather old slogan 'Another Europe is possible' needs to be revitalised, filled with life and transposed into con-crete political action. To go along this road, both trade unions and social movement must not only cooperate more closely, but also mutually learn from each other, combining new ideas and everyday resistance practices with elements of strategic organisation (Hyman 2015: 115–121). The first and most general aim of such an alliance would be to open the public debate by launching more substantial discourses on the necessity, appropriateness and feasibility of solidaristic political alternatives.

In more concrete terms, this implies moving beyond the defence of social standards and fights against austerity. Required is a more far-reaching prospect of socio-economic transformation following the guiding principle of a new mixed economy, which is based on a combination of private, public and cooperative forms of (re-)production, and in which the solidaristic alternatives inscribed into the outlined practices of resistance can more easily unfold. To facilitate such counter-hegemonic prospects, more specific political projects or initiatives need to be developed, which are mutually sensitive to the implications of labour policy changes in both areas, in the 'politics in production' and the 'politics of production'. In this context, trade unions have to recognise that the latter area – in the domestic and European arena – defines the conditions for the strategic opportunities within the 'politics in production'. To broaden the room for manoeuvre in their main sphere of competence, they have therefore – together with social movements and political parties, also within the European arena – to engage in political projects, which aim to overcome the austerity agenda, confine or even reverse the liberalisation, privatisation and financialisation of the past; restrict corporate tax competition and tax evasion; initiate an effective industrial policy; and promote ecologically sustainable economic branches, an improved public infrastructure and the foundation of new cooperatives. Of course, given the specific constellation of social forces, these aims may generate different political dynamics. In the end, however, they all refer to moving beyond European financial capitalism and the generation of an alternative, transnationally solidaristic 'historical bloc'.

Literature

van Apeldoorn, Bastiaan (2002): *Transnational Capitalism and the Struggle over European Integration*. London: Routledge.

Bailey, David J.; Clua-Losada, Mònica; Huke, Nikolai; Ribera-Almandoz, Olatz (2017): *Beyond Defeat and Austerity: Disrupting (the Critical Political Economy of) Neoliberal Europe*. London: Routledge.

Bieler, Andreas (2000): *Globalisation and EU Enlargement: Austrian and Swedish Social Forces in the Struggle over Membership. London: Routledge.*

Bieler, Andreas (2006): *The Struggle for a Social Europe: Trade Unions and EMU in Times of Global Restructuring.* Manchester: Manchester University Press.

Bieler, Andreas (2013): The EU, Global Europe and Processes of Uneven and Combined Development: The Problem of Transnational Labour Solidarity. *Review of International Studies* 39 (1): 161–183.

Bieler, Andreas (2017): Fighting for Public Water: The First Successful European Citizens' Initiative "Water and Sanitation are a Human Right". *Interface: A Journal for and about Social Movements* 9 (1): 300–326.

Bieler, Andreas; Erne, Roland (2014): Transnational Solidarity? The European Working Class in the Eurozone Crisis. In: Panitch, Leo; Albo, Greg (eds.): *The Socialist Register: Transforming Classes*. London: Merlin Press, 157–177.

Bieler, Andreas; Jordan, Jamie (2015): Austerity and Resistance: The Politics of Labour in the Eurozone Crisis. In: Satgar, Vishwas (ed.): *Capitalism's Crises: Class Struggles in South Africa and the World*. Johannesburg: Wits University Press, 97–122.

Bieler, Andreas; Morton, Adam David (2004): "Another Europe Is Possible"? Labour and Social Movements at the European Social Forum. *Globalizations* 1 (2): 303–325.

Bieler, Andreas; Morton, Adam David (2018): *Global Capitalism, Global War, Global Crisis*. Cambridge: Cambridge University Press.

Bieling, Hans-Jürgen (2001): European Constitutionalism and Industrial Relations. In: Bieler, Andreas; Morton, Adam David (eds.): *Social Forces in the Making of the New Europe: The Restructuring of European Social Relations in the Global Political Economy*. Houndmills: Palgrave, 93–114.

Bieling, Hans-Jürgen (2010): *Die Globalisierungs- und Weltordnungspolitik der Europäischen Union*. Wiesbaden: VS Verlag.

Bieling, Hans-Jürgen (2012): EU Facing the Crisis: Social and Employment Policies in Times of Tight Budgets. *Transfer* 18 (3): 255–271.

Bieling, Hans-Jürgen (2013): European Financial Capitalism and the Politics of (De-)financialization. *Competition & Change*. 17 (3): 283–298.

Bieling, Hans-Jürgen; Buhr, Daniel (eds.) (2015): *Europäische Welten in der Krise. Arbeitsbeziehungen und Wohlfahrtsstaaten im Vergleich*. Frankfurt a.M.; New York: Campus.

Bieling, Hans-Jürgen; Lux, Julia (2014): Crisis-Induced Social Conflicts in the European Union – Trade Union Perspectives: The Emergence of 'Crisis Corporatism' or the Failure of Corporatist Arrangements? *Global Labour Journal* 5 (2): 153–175.

Bohle, Dorothee (2006): Neoliberal Hegemony, Transnational Capital and the Terms of the EU's Eastward Expansion. *Capital & Class* 88: 57–86.

Burawoy, Michael (1979): *Manufacturing Consent. Changes in the Labor Process under Monopoly Capitalism*. Chicago; London: The University of Chicago Press.

Burawoy, Michael (1985): *The Politics of Production. Factory Regimes under Capitalism and Socialism*. London: Verso.

Clua-Losada, Mònica; Horn, Laura (2015): Labour and the Crisis in Europe. In: Jäger, Johannes; Springler, Elisabeth (eds.): *Asymmetric Crisis in Europe and Possible Futures*. London; New York: Routledge, 208–223.

Cox, Robert W. (1981): Social Forces, States and World Orders: Beyond International Relations Theory. *Millennium* 10 (2): 126–155.

Cox, Robert W. (1983): Gramsci, Hegemony and International Relations: An Essay in Method. *Millennium* 12 (2): 162–175.

Cox, Robert W. (1987): *Production, Power, and World Order. Social Forces in the Making of History*. New York: Columbia University Press.

Dörre, Klaus; Holst, Hajo; Nachtwey, Oliver (2009): Organising – A Strategic Option for Trade Union Renewal? *International Journal of Action Research* 5 (1): 33–67.

Erne, Roland (2008): *European Unions: Labor's Quest for a Transnational Democracy*. Ithaca and London: Cornell University Press.

Erne, Roland (2012): European Industrial Relations after the Crisis: A Postscript. In: Smismans, Stijn (ed.): *The European Union and Industrial Relations—New Procedures, New Context*. Manchester: Manchester University Press, 225–235.

Erne, Roland (2015): A Supranational Regime that Nationalises Social Conflict: Explaining European Trade Unions' Difficulties in Politicizing European Economic Governance. *Labor History* 56 (3): 345–368.

Falkner, Gerda (1998): *EU Social Policy in the 1990s: Towards a Corporatist Policy Community.* London: Routledge.

Gill, Stephen (2001): Constitutionalising Capital: EMU and Disciplinary Neoliberalism'. In: Bieler, Andreas; Morton, Adam David (eds.): *Social Forces in the Making of the New Europe: The Restructuring of European Social Relations in the Global Political Economy.* London: Palgrave, 47–69.

Gill, Stephen (2008): *Power and Resistance in the New World Order.* 2nd ed. Houndmills: Palgrave Macmillan.

Hager, Brian Sandy (2009): "New Europeans" for the "New European Economy": Citizenship and the Lisbon Agenda. In: van Apeldoorn, Bastiaan; Drahokoupil, Jan; Horn, Laura (eds.): *Neoliberal European Governance and Beyond: The Contradictions of a Political Project*, Basingstoke: Palgrave, 106–124.

Hayes, Graeme (2017): Regimes of Austerity. *Social Movement Studies Social Movement Studies* 16 (1): 21–35.

Hildebrandt, Eckart; Jürgens, Ulrich; Oppen, Maria; Teipen, Christina (eds.) (2007): *Arbeitspolitik im Wandel. Entwicklung und Perspektiven der Arbeitspolitik.* Berlin: edition sigma.

Huke, Nikolai; Clua-Losada, Mònica; Bailey, David J. (2015): Disrupting the European Crisis: A Critical Political Economy of Contestation, Subversion and Escape. *New Political Economy* 20 (5): 725–751.

Hyman, Richard (2015): Austeritarianism in Europe: What Options for Resistance? In: Natali, David; Vanhercke, Bart (eds.): *Social policy in the European Union: State of Play.* Brussels: ETUI, 97–126.

Jordan, Jamie (2017): *Global restructuring and resistance in an age of austerity: A critical political economy approach to the Eurozone crisis in Greece and Portugal.* Ph.D. thesis. School of Politics and International Relations, University of Nottingham.

Jürgens, Ulrich; Naschold, Frieder (eds.) (1984): *Arbeitspolitik. Materialien zum Zusammenhang von politischer Macht, Kontrolle und betrieblicher Organisation der Arbeit.* Leviathan Special Issue 5. Opladen: Westdeutscher Verlag.

Kiely, Ray (2007): *The New Political Economy of Development: Globalization, Imperialism, Hegemony.* London: Palgrave.

Leibfried, Stephan (2005): Social Policy. In: Wallace, Hellen; Wallace, William (eds.): *Policy-Making in the European Union.* 5th ed. Oxford: Oxford University Press, 243–278.

Lehndorff, Steffen (2013): Un géant endormi? Le rôle des syndicats avant et pendant la crise européenne. *Chronique Internationale de l'IRES* 143–144: 53–64.

Morton, Adam David (2007): *Unravelling Gramsci: Hegemony and Passive Revolution in the Global Political Economy.* London: Pluto Press.

Nowak, Jörg; Gallas, Alexander (2014): Mass Strikes against Austerity in Western Europe – A Strategic Assessment. *Global Labour Journal* 5 (3): 306–321.

Patomäki, Heikki (2012): *The Great Eurozone Disaster: From Crisis to Global New Deal.* London: Zed Books.

van der Pijl, Kees (1998): *Transnational Classes and International Relations.* London; New York: Routledge.

Plehwe, Dieter; Walpen, Bernhard; Neunhöffer, Gisela (eds.) (2006): *Neoliberal Hegemony: A Global Critique*. London; New York: Routledge.

Rodrigues, João; Reis, José (2012): The Asymmetries of European Integration and the Crisis of Capitalism in Portugal. *Competition & Change* 16 (3): 188–205.

Schulten, Thorsten; Müller, Torsten (2015): European Economic Governance and Its Intervention in National Wage Development and Collective Bargaining. In: Lehndorff, Steffen (ed.): *Divisive Integration. The Triumph of Failed Ideas Revisited*. Brussels: ETUI, 331–365.

Sklair, Leslie (2001): *The Transnational Capitalist Class*. Oxford: Blackwell Publishers.

Stockhammer, Engelbert (2016): Neoliberal Growth Models, Monetary Union and the Euro Crisis. A Post-Keynesian Perspective. *New Political Economy* 21 (4): 365–379.

UN (2001): *World Investment Report 2001: Promoting Linkages*. New York: United Nations.

UN (2009): *World Investment Report 2009: Transnational Corporations, Agricultural Production and Development*. New York: United Nations.

Underhill, Geoffrey R. D. (1997): The Making of the European Financial Area: Global Market Integration and the EU Single Market for Financial Services. In: Underhill, Geoffry R. D. (ed.): *The New World Order in International Finance*. London: Palgrave, 101–123.

Urban, Hans-Jürgen (2015): Between Crisis Corporatism and Revitalisation: Trade Union Policy in the Era of European Financial Market Capitalism. In: Lehndorff, Steffen (ed.): *Divisive Integration. The Triumph of Failed Ideas Revisited*. Brussels: ETUI, 269–294.

Wahl, Asbjørn (2011): *The Rise and Fall of the Welfare State*. London: Pluto Press.

Wahl, Peter (2017): Between Eurotopia and Nationalism: A Third Way for the Future of the EU. *Globalizations* 14 (1): 157–163.

Chapter 5

Self-intimidation

Comment on Bieler/Bieling

Georg Vobruba

I.

How can the development and chances of European industrial relations be conceptualised? Bieler and Bieling start by making two crucial theoretical decisions. First they postulate a worldwide "neoliberal hegemony", and second they claim that at the core of all relevant conflicts in the course of European integration and the Euro-crisis "are the relations between capital and labour". If both preconditions are taken seriously, organised labour already has lost. The chapter causes an unintended but important effect: it demonstrates the lack of orientation, hence hopelessness of the "left" (whatever that might be) facing transnationalisation and European integration. There can be no doubt that the paper was written as an attempt to solve serious problems of organised labour, but it must be read as a part of it.

The authors start with introducing "hegemony" as something comprising and dominating almost everything: "World hegemony is describable as a social structure, an economic structure, and a political structure; and it cannot be simply one of these things but must be all three". Immediately the question comes up: how *not* to be a part of it. Generally speaking, approaches aiming critically at society as a hostile totality suffer from two problems. First such approaches face a performative contradiction. Either the observation of the present state of society is correct, then there is no place in it for an independent observer. He/she is part or victim of the hegemony. Or the observer's position is beyond the hegemony, then her/his observation of an all-embracing "neo-liberal" hegemony is false. For hegemony encompasses the whole society and our authors undoubtedly are members of this society, they have accepted that they are part of the hegemony. But our authors apparently have no appetite for complicated epistemological reflections. Instead they seem to look for a middle course. On the one hand, they speak of "world hegemony" and "neoliberal restructuring" of almost everything; on the other hand they hint at "a dialectic of consent and resistance to neoliberal restructuring" and even at the possibility of "counter-hegemonic alliances". But is this in accordance with their theoretical approach? This leads to the second problem. Given a neoliberal hegemony it is hard to say where "resistance" (2) against it could come from. In other words: even before its beginning, the (class-)struggle is already lost. The hegemony-approach fails to provide a criterion appropriate to make a clear distinction between what is included into the hegemony and what is beyond it. Hence the theoretical approach does not guide to any clear point of contact for politics challenging the political and economic mainstream. It seems like the authors are recognising this calamity. As the chapter proceeds the authors discreetly drop their theoretical approach. While, for the reasons just given, this is a good idea, it is costly nevertheless: without a theoretical guideline, most of the text consists of describing the "subordination" of (organised) labour in general and under the condition of the (neoliberal) rule of the EU in particular. Self-intimidation is the result.

II.

Seen through the lens of "neoliberal hegemony theory", European integration and the common European currency are processes that cannot be described different but as "neoliberal restructuring". Under this headline the authors offer an instructive short sketch of "asymmetrical integration". They rightly emphasise that transnationalisation of the economy, European integration and the Euro-crisis put organised labour under pressure. Or the other way around: until the 1980s, the nation-state was a more convenient arena for trade unions' politics. But what is the reason for this? In those better times it was in particular one factor working in favour of the trade unions: governments and associations (trade unions and employers' associations) were mutually connected in complex political exchanges. Associations took over some of the governments' responsibilities; governments in return provided associations with limited co-determination. This arrangement, normally subsumed under the term "neo-corporatism", has had an ambivalent effect. On the one hand it led to high economic performance and enabled trade unions to meet employers' associations at eye level. On the other hand it resulted in unlearning the switching from positive-sum to zero-sum interpretations of the economy and to organised conflict. Surely, countries with competing trade unions were much less able (and willing) to enter neo-corporatist arrangements than countries with monopolistic trade unions. But it can be taken for granted that until the late 1980s neo-corporatist industrial relations performed better than any alternative. The Euro-crisis revealed that surplus Euro-members gradually dispose of cooperative industrial relations, whilst conflictuous relations characterise debt countries. Thus one should at least notice that industrial relations are not invariably a zero-sum game; hence conflict is not at all times and under all conditions the best choice for trade unions' membership. Anyway, it is unlikely for trade unions to manage a switch from cooperation to conflict or the other way around.

Notwithstanding this historic background and the different ways of how trade unions engaged and were able to engage in industrial relations back in the day, as transnational economic entanglements intensified, these neo-corporatist arrangements experienced a process of shrinkage: positive-sum-oriented employer-employee-arrangements were more and more concentrated on export industries, with two distinctive effects. First, these arrangements turned into coalitions against competing sectors of foreign economies. And second, they contributed to a double cleavage within the workforce: between export-oriented and other workers within highly competitive countries and between the workforces of highly and of less competitive countries. All in all this resulted in a complex conflict constellation, which became apparent in the Euro-crisis.

III.

Against this backdrop, the mere description of "the main problems of the EMU…as the result of insufficient demand" is problematic. The authors correctly highlight the fact that export-driven economies were and are dependent on imports of debt economies (although there are also export destinations outside the Euro-area). But until the beginning of the Euro-crisis this was an arrangement that mutually benefitted both sides. From the very beginning of the common currency, huge amounts of cheap money poured into the net-import countries. These loans were a sort of transfer (though lined by creditors' back payment illusion) from the North to the South, causing an excess of demand. Yes, the management of the Euro-crisis imposed, as the authors reaffirm, austerity measures to the debt countries, resulting in "inner devaluation" and massive social-political problems. But there is much more to observe than a pure "neoliberal restructuring": have you ever heard of the hair cut in the year 2013 in Cyprus? Of cheap loans at terms of up to 50 years? Of the ECB desperately trying to pump tons of money into the economy in order to lift the inflation rate? And is there any explanation for the – indeed – stunning patience of the people, apart from dazzlement by "ideology" and "neoliberal hegemony"? Or the other way around: what would be the alternative?

IV.

All in all: the authors point to "a dialectic of consent and resistance" (2). This is definitely a promising point of departure, but it needs further elaboration concerning the structural preconditions for conflicts, an analysis of the complex conflict constellation and the dynamics it triggers. It also needs an understanding of the merits, pitfalls and unintended consequences of the management of the Euro-crisis and an appraisal of trade unions' political room of manoeuvre in it. Our authors miss most of that, mainly because their theoretical approach makes them blind for the ambivalences of the present constellation of the EU trade unions have to cope with.

Chapter 6

The Europeanisation of wage bargaining coordination

Susanne Pernicka and Vera Glassner

Introduction

The focus of this chapter lies on the Europeanisation of wage bargaining coordination, that is, on non-market institutions of wage formation in Europe that have emerged across and beyond national borders. Following Sisson and Marginson (2002: 199) wage bargaining coordination refers to the attempt of collective actors to achieve the same or related outcomes in separate wage negotiations (e.g., similar wage increases within or across sectors and within or beyond national borders). In Western European welfare states historically different forms of wage bargaining coordination have been created, reproduced and transformed. A basic distinction can be made between single-employer bargaining and multi-employer bargaining systems (Sisson/Marginson 2002). Single-employer bargaining refers to wage bargaining coordination within a national or multinational company and its distinct subunits, whereas the bargaining activities of distinct employers or employers' associations and their trade union counterparts are addressed in the case of multi-employer arrangements (Traxler 2003a). This chapter focusses on multi-employer and cross-country coordination within the European Monetary Union (EMU). The rationale behind this specification is that different national wage bargaining institutions within the EMU created severe tensions and contradictions that have been even exacerbated against the background of the most recent financial and Euro crises.

Since the 1990s trade unions from north-western and some southern-European countries (Italy, in particular) were at the forefront of transnational wage bargaining coordination activities in Europe. Within the context of the financial and sovereign debt crises the trade unions found themselves in the positions of "winners" and "losers" of European integration processes that culminated in a widely dysfunctional EMU. The Eastern Enlargement of the European Union (EU), the crisis and crisis politics in particular largely undermined the preconditions for transnational wage bargaining coordination. At the same time, European and international actors, such as the European Commission, the European Central Bank and the International Monetary Fund (also referred to as the "Troika"), have been strengthened to the detriment of national political and industrial relations actors. The establishment of a supranational wage policy regime has reconfigured industrial relations in Europe in a way that makes transnational coordination based on solidarity between trade unions even harder to achieve, let alone ensure its effectiveness.

This chapter explores Europeanisation processes in wage bargaining coordination including (1) trade union initiatives to create and sustain norms and practices of transnational wage coordination; an endeavour that was intensified in the 1990s to prevent ruinous wage competition in view of the forthcoming EMU, and (2) the introduction of a European supranational economic governance regime that includes authoritative forms of wage coordination across different national fields. While the latter seeks to transform national institutions of wage bargaining coordination towards market liberalism, the former follows the principles of social protection and distributional fairness between capital and labour and within the European labour force.

The guiding assumption of this chapter refers to the role of power relations and conflicts within European social and symbolic space. The way particular societies organise their labour markets and wage setting institutions is seen as a result of historical and contemporary conflicts over sets of rules, norms and ideas and their distributional effects rather than as mere outcomes of functional requirements or institutionally determined trajectories. Dominant beliefs and world views often obscure the contested and power-distributional character of institutions (Mahoney/Thelen 2010). The current neoliberal hegemony shapes the perceptions and practices of wage policy actors in a way that leaves almost no room for alternative cognitive framings and normative orientations other than market efficiency. Solidarity-enhancing institutions of wage coordination that aim at reducing wage differentials within and across economic sectors, a function that was firmly established in coordinated market economies until the early 1980s, have widely lost its normative and cultural strength (Crouch 1999) and have never attained high levels of legitimacy on transnational and supranational scales.

While most analyses of wage bargaining institutions are concerned with their differences in economic performance from an internationally comparative perspective (Traxler et al. 2001; Hancké 2013; Hall 2014; Höpner/Lutter 2014), this chapter aims instead at a deeper understanding of the creation, maintenance and transformation of cross-national wage coordinating institutions in Europe. It addresses the following questions: when and why have institutions of European and transnational wage coordination evolved? What forms and functions do these institutions exhibit and why? And what role do trade unions play in the creation and change of transnational and supranational wage coordination institutions?

This analysis is based on a space and power sensitive perspective employed to re-evaluate existing literature and data on wage bargaining coordination in Europe, including policy documents of national and supranational actors. The chapter is structured as follows: "Theoretical perspective" outlines our theoretical perspective; the next section provides a short account on concepts of wage coordination that includes considerations relating to national, transnational and supranational forms of wage coordination. The two ensuing sections present empirical evidence derived from literature and theoretical reflection on the two cases, that is, unilateral transnational wage coordination of trade unions within and across sectors ("The case of unilateral transnational wage coordination of trade unions") and supranational authoritative wage coordination ("The case of European authoritative wage coordination"). "Discussion and conclusions" contains the discussion and conclusions.

Theoretical perspective

Socio-economic conflicts and tensions are viewed as primary drivers of the Europeanisation of national societies and, more specifically, of the institutionalisation processes of European wage coordination. This assumption is derived from two different theoretical concepts, cleavage theory and sociological field theory. The cleavage concept was used by Lipset and Rokkan to describe the main conflict lines (such as between capital owners and workers; between the centre and periphery or between the church and the state) in the historical development of European societies that have been culturally and politically structured primarily within nation-states (Lipset/Rokkan 1967; Kriesi et al. 2012; della Porta 2015). As the European world region has become increasingly economically and politically integrated and the EU has assumed various competencies from national Member States, it can be expected that economic and social divides entail politically and culturally shaped cleavages that reach also across and beyond national borders. Sociological field theory offers a conception of societies as social orders that do not necessarily coincide with the borders of nation-states. A social field is conceived of as a social order in which something is at stake, that has certain rules governing the order, and in which field actors have positions and resources, which correspond to their perceptions and interpretations of the social world (Bourdieu/Wacquant 1996; Fligstein/McAdam 2012). Bourdieu's field theory in particular emphasises the role of power in field construction and focusses on how the structuring of a field gives more powerful actors the tools by which to consistently enforce their interests (Kluttz/Fligstein 2016). Thus, field theory allows analysing conflicts over the forms, functions and the very legitimacy of (emerging) wage coordinating institutions that reach across national borders.

This chapter identifies two lines of conflict over the issue of European wage coordination: class conflicts and centre-periphery conflicts. These two conflict lines differ in terms of the degree of their transnational and supranational institutionalisation. While class conflicts in European wage setting have largely remained hidden despite numerous attempts of trade unions to institutionalise transnational wage bargaining coordination and to prevent national bargainers from both classes (capital and labour) to undercut wages in other countries, centre-periphery cleavages in wage policies have been more openly politicised and socially contested. Centre-periphery conflicts in relation to wage issues were already anticipated as early as in pre-Maastricht political negotiations about the introduction of EMU. As the countries of the Eurozone would be deprived of the exchange rate instrument to adapt to any losses in international competitiveness, it became clear that labour markets, the institutions of wage bargaining coordination and wages would come under severe pressure, particularly in those countries that have not institutionalised wage restraint as a main function of wage coordination (Traxler 2003b). North-western European countries and Germany, in particular, demanded to include a "no bail-out clause" into the Maastricht treaty (now Art 125 TFEU) to prevent any financial transfers to other EMU member countries. Hence, at least formally, financial transfers were ruled out as possible instruments to tackle macroeconomic imbalances that might arise from excessive inflation due to wage increases and rising public debt. However, two decades later, funding problems in Greece, Ireland, Portugal, Spain, Italy and Cyprus that have been exacerbated by the most recent financial crises led supranational, international and intergovernmental actors to ignore primary EU law and to pursue huge international rescue operations. In addition, the EU introduced a supranational regime of economic policy that includes instruments for the coordination of wages that primarily aim to prevent nominal wages to increase beyond certain limits. In this respect it is noteworthy that EU policy actors have no formal competencies in wage-related issues (Art. 153 TFEU). In comparison to centre-periphery conflicts, class conflicts were an issue before the completion of the single market and EMU when the Delors Commission supported transnational wage bargaining coordination, but has been widely neglected later on, and even more so, since the financial and euro crisis.

However, given the tight economic and financial interrelationships of Euro members within the single currency area institutional differences have led to macroeconomic problems that could neither be tackled by assurances and guarantees of the European Central Bank nor by the European fiscal rescue packages provided by north-western to southern European countries (Sinn 2016). Instead, massive austerity politics and legally questionable measures taken by the Troika to disrupt wage coordinating institutions have induced massive political and social upheavals and protests in southern Europe (della Porta 2015; Hofmann 2015) pointing to the social and political dimension of centre-periphery and class conflicts.

This chapter has argued that institutionalisation processes in European wage coordination can only be understood by taking into account societal dynamics, conflicts and power relations in transnational European (and global) space. Rather than looking at international markets and European economic policies as "external" factors to which national institutions and collective actors are expected to respond and/or adapt, we view supranational and transnational institutions of wage coordination as outcomes of complex and contested configurations of actors and institutions, the scales and scope of collective wage coordination being an empirically open question (see Table 6.1).

Table 6.1 Two forms of cross-border wage coordinating institutions in Europe

Forms and functions of European wage coordinating institutions

Forms	Supranational, authoritative wage coordination	Unilateral wage coordination of trade unions within/ across sectors and across countries
Main functions and objectives	Economic competitiveness of national institutions across Eurozone member countries	Transnational solidarity between and within the socio-economic classes of capital and labour
(Intended) economic effects	Convergence of unit labour costs aligned towards developments in north-western European countries	Prevent competitive wage restraint across countries and secure purchasing power of workers

Main drivers of the institutionalisation of European wage coordination

Dominant conflicts and tensions (hidden conflicts)	*Centre-periphery conflicts* Economic, social and cultural divide between north and south within the Eurozone (class conflicts between and within groups of capital owners and workers)	*Class conflicts* Inter- and intra-class conflicts over income and productivity gains across countries (centre-periphery conflicts between more and less competitive countries)

Actors and institutions in emerging fields

Sets of actors	European Commission, European Council, international economic policy actors (European Central Bank, International Monetary Fund)	European and national trade unions; employers are reluctant to embark on transnational wage coordination; no state/ EU-sponsorship
Institutions	(Global), European transnational and national rules, norms and cultural beliefs – orthodox economic model (efficiency enhancing institutions)	(Global), European transnational and national rules, norms and cultural beliefs – heterodox model of solidarity and distributional fairness

Wage coordination within and beyond national borders

We conceive of collective bargaining coordination as a public good for employers, employees and the state. Multi-employer bargaining can fulfil a number of functions for each of these actors (Traxler 1998). For employers it takes wages out of competition, helps to neutralise the workplace from trade union militancy and reduces transaction costs deriving from the regulation of the employment relationship. For trade unions it has a protective (guarantee of minimum standards), voice (participation in wage bargaining) and distributive function (reducing wage inequalities between industrial sectors and occupations). With market internationalisation, the competitive function of wages has partly lost in relevance as employers can make use of differentials in labour costs by cross-border relocation and outsourcing of production and services. In societal and macroeconomic terms collective wage coordination can potentially fulfil the following two functions: (1) it might serve as a means of macroeconomic and political governance, that is, of aligning wage developments with macroeconomic imperatives such as employment and price stability (Hall/Franzese 1998); (2) it might reduce wage differentials within and across economic sectors or countries, and secure a fair income distribution between labour and capital and within the labour force. Wage bargaining coordination has received special attention for its ability to internalise externalities, such as, for instance, excessive wage increases in some particular bargaining units, often sheltered from international competition, and not in others (Traxler et al. 2001; Johnston/Hancké 2009). The capacity to align wage developments with macroeconomic stability and international competitiveness requirements has become even more important and pronounced within EMU. Two ways of internalising externalities are of particular importance: the first aims at achieving outcomes as similar as possible in separate negotiations, a capacity to which Traxler (2003a: 195) referred as *substantive* coordination. The second option, *procedural* coordination (ibid.), is designed to commit the distinct bargaining units to joint rules for formulating demands and conducting negotiations (e.g., productivity and inflation as focal reference for wage policy). While classical studies (see in particular Calmfors/Driffill 1988 and their "hump-shaped hypothesis") claim that extreme degrees of centralisation and decentralisation of bargaining systems perform best in terms of internalising externalities, later accounts have demonstrated that – under certain conditions – intermediate coordination at industry level has a superior capacity to internalise bargaining externalities, particularly in dynamic and internationalised economic contexts (Traxler et al. 2001; Höpner/Lutter 2014). A central precondition for effective wage coordination rooted in the procedural dimension of collective bargaining is the ability of associations to control the behaviour of their constituency, that is, to solve the problem of "free riding" (e.g., by individual employers setting lower wages in order to enhance their cost competitiveness). Problems to govern and control the process of wage bargaining increase with the level of centralisation of collective bargaining as higher-level bargaining units have to make harder efforts to ensure compliance of the rank-and-file. Only under certain legal conditions (e.g., legally binding collective agreements, peace clause in collective agreements) lower bargaining units are ready to follow wage agreements settled at higher (e.g., the national, sectoral or transnational) levels. With respect to this governance function, national collective bargaining arrangements vary widely; while northern and (most) western European wage bargaining institutions ensure high levels of governability, the opposite is the case in southern and eastern European countries.

However, coordination within countries is distinct from coordination across countries (Brandl et al. 2011). Effective transnational free collective bargaining coordination (i.e., unions and employers voluntarily join coordination) presupposes that wage bargaining is substantially and procedurally coordinated at the national and sector level. Authoritative coordination (i.e., wage control) is a means of *ultima ratio* in a situation of extremely poor performance of free collective bargaining (Traxler 2002: 20). With regard to authoritative wage coordination Belgium provides a national example for state-imposed wage coordination. In the wake of forthcoming EMU the country enacted a wage competitiveness law in 1996, stipulating that wage increases should remain below those in the neighbouring countries (Germany, the Netherlands and France). The EU's supranational wage coordination provides evidence for authoritative wage coordination beyond national borders. In comparison to national forms of authoritative wage coordination, the main actors addressed by the supranational monitoring and coordination of wages and wage setting institutions are EU member countries rather than trade unions and employers. Via country-specific recommendations, but also through measures taken by the Troika Institutions, southern European countries in particular have faced growing pressures to dismantle their collective bargaining systems and thus to weaken trade unions at national and sector level (see the following).

The case of unilateral transnational wage coordination of trade unions

In view of the forthcoming EMU that ruled out currency devaluations as a means to improve countries' international competitiveness, trade unions began to coordinate wage bargaining policies across borders in order to mitigate competitive downward pressures on wages and maintain the purchasing power of workers (Table 6.2 provides an overview of the most important transnational coordination initiatives started by trade unions in the 1990s). Transnational businesses as well as their European interest organisations

Table 6.2 Transnational unilateral wage coordination by trade unions

Initiative	EMF	Interregional bargaining coordination networks	Doorn	ETUC
Level	Supranational, sector	Transnational, sector	Transnational, intersectoral	Supranational, intersectoral
Form	Intra-associational norm-setting by European peak organisation	Transnational "pattern bargaining", intra-sectoral	Intra-associational norm-setting by national peak organisations	Intra-associational norm-setting by European peak organisation
Function	Avoidance of competitive wage restraint, safeguarding of workers' purchasing power by guaranteeing a "fair" share in income and productivity gains (transnational solidarity)			
Normative and cultural orientations	Productivity-oriented wage policy Promoted by (metal/industrial sector) unions from DE, AT and Scandinavia No tradition of stability-/productivity-oriented wage policy in southern and eastern Europe, UK, IE, MT, CY	Promoted by (metal/industrial sector) unions from DE, AT and Scandinavia, NL (BE)	Promoted by (metal/industrial sector) unions from DE, AT, NL (BE, FR)	Promoted by (metal/industrial sector) unions from DE, AT, NL, BE and Scandinavia No tradition of stability-/productivity-oriented wage policy in southern and eastern Europe, UK, IE, MT, CY
Geographical scope	Europe	Austria, Germany, Scandinavia, Benelux	Austria, Germany, Benelux, France	Europe

were reluctant to embark on transnational wage coordination in order to make use of national and regional differentials in labour costs by transnational relocation of business sites, outsourcing and off-shoring of production and services. Furthermore, supranational political actors did not support the emergence of strong and encompassing industrial relations that would support transnational wage bargaining coordination. As the issue of wage setting is explicitly excluded from European social dialogues and European Works Councils have proven too weak to ensure coordination at the level of transnational companies (Traxler/Brandl 2009: 181), national and European trade unions unilaterally engaged in cross-border wage coordination. In the metal sector conditions are assumed to be most favourable for transnational bargaining coordination. Companies in the metal sector are tightly integrated in international production and value chains. This provides trade unions with considerable bargaining power deriving from threats to call for industrial action. Trade union density rates are high compared to other sectors and union presence at the workplace is strong. The strong presence of unions in MNCs can be considered as conducive for the transnational mobilisation of workers (Anner et al. 2006; Gajewska 2008). The European Metalworkers' Federation (EMF) had a strong and pioneering role in the cross-border coordination of collective bargaining policies. In a "statement of principle on collective bargaining policy" the EMF and its member organisations agreed on a "regular annual compensation for price increases[1] in order to protect real wages, and to guarantee workers a share in productivity gains" (EMF 1993). The "European coordination rule", adopted in 1998, specifies quantitative normative criteria for wage bargaining but leaves the wage autonomy entirely to the national social partners (EMF 1998). The EMF's coordination rule was adopted not only in view of the forthcoming EMU but also driven by developments at national level. The aforementioned enactment of the Belgian law on "the safeguarding of competitiveness" in 1996 stipulating that wage growth should remain below wage increases in the neighbouring countries is regarded as a crucial driving factor for enhanced coordination initiatives of central western European trade unions (Marginson/Sisson 2006). In the ensuing years, national and European unions started initiatives to coordinate wage bargaining *across sectors* and countries. For instance, the Doorn-group, consisting of the Benelux countries; Germany; and, later on, France, began to hold annual meetings to assess the results of national wage bargaining via the formula agreed, i.e., inflation plus productivity (Pochet 1999; Dufresne/Mermet 2002). The European Trade Union Confederation (ETUC) adopted a resolution on macro-level wage coordination in Europe in December 2000 (ETUC 2000).

Although inter-sectoral, cross-border wage coordination initiatives did not persist due to severe coordination problems among highly heterogeneous national bargaining units and lacking capacities of the European umbrella organisations to ensure compliance of their national member organisations to European wage policy guidelines, wage coordination institutions in the European metal sector proved to be more durable and, from a historical perspective, seem to exhibit a higher degree of institutionalisation (Pernicka/Glassner 2014). Unilateral trade union cooperation in the metal sector dates back to the late 1960s. For instance, the so-called "DACH" initiative, a rather informal network including manufacturing and metal sector unions from Germany, Austria and Switzerland, provided a framework for the regular exchange of information on bargaining policies and other topics and aimed at the coordination of union policies across borders. DACH was formally included in the organisational structure of the International Metalworkers' Federation (IMF) and, later on, the EMF. Another example is the cooperation initiative "Nordiska Metall" founded in 1970 by manufacturing sector unions from Denmark, Sweden, Norway, Finland and Iceland aiming at the coordination of wage bargaining, industrial and health and safety policies. Since the 1990s the Nordic unions intensified their cooperation with the EMF, in particular in collective bargaining, transnational restructuring and other issues. With the accession of Sweden and Finland to the EU in the 1990s, Nordiska Metal became a regional body for the coordination of European policies within the EMF. In the late 1990s interregional bargaining networks, aiming to support the implementation of the EMF coordination rule, were created. These coordination initiatives were driven by the German IG Metall as well as the Dutch, Belgian and Scandinavian unions. Their aim was to promote wage setting strategies that ensure that nominal wages grow in line with national overall productivity increases. For instance, the IG Metall, Belgian and Dutch metalworkers' organisations established a cross-border network for exchange of collective bargaining information and trade union officials in 1997 (Gollbach/Schulten 2000; Schulten 2003). Likewise, a coordination partnership between Austria, Bavaria, Czech Republic, Slovakia, Slovenia and Hungary was established in 1999 by trade unions from these countries that make up the so-called "Vienna Memorandum Group".

With effective support of state actors to ensure bargaining governability lacking in transnational social space, decentral modes of coordination that entail mechanisms such as signalling, pattern setting, imitation and peer pressure are considered to be most feasible to ensure that lower-level bargaining units follow transnational norms and procedures in national negotiations (Traxler/Mermet 2003). However, transnational wage coordination presupposes certain structural, organisational and institutional conditions, including normative orientations, cultural understandings and world views. For the emergence of transnational coordinating institutions this implies first that bargaining actors are embedded in comparable institutional systems of collective bargaining (Pernicka/Glassner 2014). In the northern and central-western European multi-employer bargaining systems both employers and trade unions share understandings of productivity- and stability-orientated wage policies. Relations between business and labour are cooperative and trade unions are regularly involved in public policy-making. Second, bargaining actors within and across countries share common normative orientations in wage policy; that is, the avoidance of competitive wage restraint by the systematic undercutting of wages in trading partners' countries. In the high-wage/high-quality production regimes of northern and western Europe, wage policy norms imply, at least among bargaining actors in the (shrinking) core of industrial/metal sectors, bargaining strategies that ensure wage increases in line with overall productivity growth in order to ensure macroeconomic stability.[2] Third, the creation of informal structures to coordinate bargaining across borders is contested and requires constant efforts of actors to strengthen trust-relations, common norms and understandings about transnational solidarity and cooperation (Pernicka et al. 2015).

At least until the years of the global economic crisis 2008/2009 transnational wage coordination in the northern and western European metal sector was supported by – although weak and informal – transnational institutions, i.e., shared normative and cultural orientations on wage policy, which shaped the strategies of trade unions in neighbouring countries. For instance, the EMF's bargaining coordination rule largely mirrors the notion of stability- and productivity-based wage setting common in Germany and Austria (and to a lesser extent also in the Nordic region) that became incorporated – via learning processes and common practice – into the belief systems of unions from other European regions. Trade union actors themselves were able to actively create structures and promote practices of transnational wage bargaining coordination. As empirical evidence indicates, transnational norms and practices supporting the transnational coordination of wage setting are instable and contested, and inter-class conflicts did not institutionalise in transnational social space, mostly because employers never entered into wage coordination set up by trade unions. Although there are some instances that unions' wage coordination attempts spurred some reaction by employers, such as for instance information exchange on collectively settled wages in member organisation of the Employers' Organisation of Metal Trades in Europe (Marginson/Sisson 2006: 204), these are too weak to constitute a transnational field of voluntary wage policy coordination. In addition, the uneven distribution of economic, social and cultural power resources among business, policy and labour actors across countries hampered the emergence of transnational fields of wage coordination. Although formal arrangements for multi-employer bargaining were in place in most southern Europe countries before the crisis, traditions and understandings about a stability- and productivity-based wage policy never became widely established. In most eastern European countries (with the exception of Slovenia and, partly, Slovakia), the UK and (since more recently) Ireland multi-employer bargaining is non-existent. However, in the recent economic crisis even in countries where national fields of collective bargaining exhibit a higher degree of autonomy and remain more insulated from influences deriving from the supranational economic and wage policy (such as northern and central-western European countries) wage coordination activities (with the exception of the Nordic region) came to a halt. In the initial years of the crisis, social partners' strategies were aimed at the resolution of immediate economic and social problems at national level. For trade unions the safeguarding of employment became a prior goal and the allocation of trade unions' resources to the transnational level became more scrutinised.

When the fiscal and financial crises hit the EU, European policy actors reinforced macroeconomic policy coordination with the aim to enhance international competitiveness of national market economies. Multi-employer bargaining institutions in southern Europe became under severe pressure and were subject to reforms that resulted in their further decentralisation and disorganisation. This contrasts with the earlier support of parts of the European Commission for encompassing and coordinated bargaining structures in Europe. In view of the forthcoming enlargement of the EU considerable financial means were provided to central and eastern European countries in order to build up and strengthen multi-employer bargaining institutions (European Commission 2004, 2006). In the current situation it is unlikely that trade unions, even those in central-western Europe, will revive their transnational wage bargaining coordination activities. The prospect of expanding transnational wage coordination beyond northern and central Europe becomes even more distant.

The case of European authoritative wage coordination

In responding to the euro crisis, in 2011 the EU introduced supranational wage coordination as part of its new economic governance regime. Besides the Stability and Growth Pact (SGP) and the European Semester (ES), that is an annual cycle of economic policy guidance and surveillance, the EU's economic governance also contains a Macroeconomic Imbalance Procedure (MIP), which is a mechanism that aims to "identify potential risks early on, prevent the emergence of harmful macroeconomic imbalances and correct the imbalances that are already in place" (European Commission 2016a). With its primary aim to intensify economic and wage policy coordination, the EU's economic governance facilitates interventions in national wage coordinating institutions (Marginson/Keune 2013; Schulten/Müller 2015). While formally respecting the Member States' autonomy in wage coordination, the MIP entails commitments to ensure that wages do not exceed certain limits set – among other indicators – in the so-called Scoreboard (Keune 2013; Marginson/Welz 2014). However, these nominal wage-related targets evaluate different institutional contributions to macroeconomic imbalances in an asymmetric way (Koll 2013). While "excessive" inflation is seen negative, the Scoreboard leaves deflation unmentioned: the threshold that must not be exceeded is defined as a three years percentage change in nominal unit labour cost which lies at +9% for Eurozone, and +12% for non-Eurozone countries (European Commission 2016a). Besides MIP the so-called Memoranda of Understanding between Troika institutions and national governments have had a much more direct impact by linking financial support to the demand to decentralise wage bargaining institutions (Marginson/Welz 2014: 28). As a consequence, EU southern European countries have faced severe interventions into their national wage coordinating institutions for contributing to *inflationary* tendencies in wage developments. In contrast, national wage bargaining institutions in coordinated market economies in the north-west of the Eurozone enjoy comparatively high levels of social recognition and legitimacy although they created *deflationary* pressures by keeping wages below the levels of productivity and inflation (e.g., German and Austrian competitive corporatism).

It has been argued that the form and functions of cross-border wage coordination are an outcome of the complex dynamics between structural forces, power relations and world views over time. The set-up of power relations is shaped by different speeds and asymmetries of European integration processes across countries and policy fields. Thus, supranational wage coordination cannot be explained by the crisis event alone, but has to be seen as the result of historical power configurations and structural processes that have reinforced and facilitated certain institutions and world views while delegitimising others. The explicit objectives of the EU's supranational wage coordinating institutions correspond more closely to ideas of economic liberalism than to distributive solidarity, and it obviously supports national governments that advocate fiscal discipline and competitive wage restraint within the (current) European centre while weakening national (left-leaning) governments, parliaments and trade unions in the European periphery (Erne 2015). The European Commission and the Directorate-General for Economic and Financial Affairs (DG ECFIN), in particular, are at the forefront of enforcing competitive market logics in southern European countries. Their demand that unit labour costs within the Eurozone should converge in alignment with "best practice" wage coordinating models in north-western European countries is reflected, for instance, in the yearly issued country-specific recommendations of the European Commission. Table 6.3 displays the wage setting and wage policy-related country-specific recommendations for Germany, the Netherlands and Austria as well as for Italy, Portugal and Spain that serve as important examples for north-western and southern Eurozone countries from 2011 until 2016. For the year 2011 the Euro-Plus-Pact commitments are presented (cf. Marginson/Welz 2014: 29f.; European Commission 2016b).

Table 6.3 Country-specific commitments and recommendations on wage setting and wage policy (2011–2016)

Country	Euro-Plus-Pact Commitments 2011	European Semester Recommendations 2011/2012	European Semester Recommendations 2012/2013	European Semester Recommendations 2013/2014	European Semester Recommendations 2014/2015	European Semester Recommendations 2015/2016
DE	–	–	Wages in line with productivity	Wage growth to support domestic demand	–	–
NL	–	–			–	–
AT	–	–			–	–
IT	Wage setting mechanisms	Ensure wage growth better reflects productivity developments	Monitor and if needed reinforce implementation of new wage setting framework	Ensure effective implementation of wage setting reforms to align wages to productivity	Effective implementation of wage setting reforms is still pending	Social partners have not yet reached agreement on the reform of collective bargaining.
PT	Wage setting mechanisms	Implement commitments under Memorandum of Understanding of 2011 ("organised de-centralisation" of collective bargaining)	Implement commitments under Memorandum of Understanding of 2011 ("organised de-centralisation" of collective bargaining)	Implement commitments under Memorandum of Understanding of 2011 ("organised de-centralisation" of collective bargaining)	Ensure effective implementation of "organised decentralisation" in all economic areas	Ensure effective implementation of "organised decentralisation" in all economic areas
ES	Wage setting mechanisms	Comprehensive reform of the collective bargaining process and the wage indexation system	–	–	Promote the alignment of wages and productivity	–

The financial and sovereign debt crises have strengthened DG ECFIN while weakening the DG for Employment, Social Affairs and Inclusion (EMPL) within the European Commission. These new power relations correspond with the changing political positions of the European Commission. Until the crises the EU played a strong role as a promoter of European social partnership and autonomous collective bargaining of employers' and employees associations at national level, with DG EMPL having a more powerful position within the Commission (Keune 2013). It comes as no surprise that DG ECFIN commissioners are more often recruited from liberal and conservative parties, while more "progressive" DGs, such as EMPL, have often been led by social-democrats (Hartlapp et al. 2014: 51).

The creation of a supranational economic governance regime has opened up and partly reconfigured national fields of wage bargaining. Rather than entailing a level playing-field these policies strengthened powerful actors such as highly competitive countries (such as Germany) as well as collective actors (such as urban well-to-do middle classes in Mediterranean countries as well as private and public creditors) that have already benefited from relatively stable monetary conditions and low inflation rates since the inception of EMU (Streeck 2017: 185). As a result, southern European countries and their institutions of bargaining coordination have been consistently challenged and delegitimised in relation to their northern European counterparts, indicating a spatial dualisation in terms of both economic and symbolic power. There is clear evidence that relative economic and financial powers of north-western European countries closely correspond with their symbolic and political power. The functions of collective bargaining coordination in these countries already reflect hegemonic economic models (wage restraint to ensure international competitiveness), while institutions in southern European countries have widely lost their legitimacy. Hence, the most extensive changes induced by the EU and Troika institutions have been targeted at wage coordinating institutions in southern EMU members (Greece, Portugal and Spain) that received financial assistance, while wage-coordinating institutions in national fields in north-western Europe (Austria, Germany, the Netherlands) have remained largely intact.

It is important to note that the EU's new economic governance has the potential to deepen social integration by strengthening supranational political fields. In fact, however, the strong emphasis on neoliberal policies of austerity and international competitiveness has not only contributed to social disintegration and social upheaval particularly in the European periphery. The European model of market liberalism with its common currency area that leaves no room for national sovereignty in monetary policy has also contributed to an economic and symbolic division of two groups of countries: the more and the less competitive ones, neglecting local, regional and national ways of living within capitalism (Streeck 2017: 180).

Discussion and conclusions

This chapter has sought to better understand and explain the Europeanisation of wage coordination. Economic and financial European integration and the introduction of a dysfunctional single currency architecture have not only increased the economic interrelations and interdependencies of wage-setting institutions and actors on different spatial scales (local, regional, national, European) but also contributed to the development of new socio-economic, cultural and symbolic cleavages in European social space. The scope and scale of Europeanisation processes in wage coordination, however, differ in terms of their underlying conflict lines and extent of institutionalisation. While centre-periphery conflicts have been politically and culturally structured at supranational level inducing the creation of a supranational wage policy field with its own logics of action, mechanisms of legitimation and recognition, transnational class conflicts are, though carried out in transnational social space, barely institutionally embedded beyond the level of nation-states. The most recent financial and sovereign debt crises have reinforced material and symbolic power asymmetries between north-western and southern EMU members that supported the creation of supranational authoritative wage coordination. This in turn has reproduced rather than challenged orthodox models of wage coordination with their emphasis on competitive wage restraint while delegitimising and – with the support of international and intergovernmental crisis politics – destroying wage coordinating institutions in southern Europe. In comparison to transnational centre-periphery conflicts over wage issues, there is no such institutionalisation process in relation to class conflicts. International business depends less on associational action and state support than on labour to advance its interests, and it has primarily deployed its economic power to prevent rather than to facilitate transnational wage bargaining coordination. The completion of the internal market and EMU have reinforced prevailing competitive logics in European transnational markets while wage bargaining institutions have been intentionally restricted to the national level. Trade unions' unilateral attempts to coordinate their collective bargaining transnationally focussed on certain sectors and countries, in which transnational cultural power resources as well as national structural and institutional preconditions coincided in a way as to support cross-border cooperation. A field of transnational wage policy coordination based on voluntary negotiations between business and labour has never emerged. Although formal and informal institutions that reconcile both the distributional (i.e., solidarity) function and the macroeconomic function of wage bargaining coordination in the EMU were created, they proved as too weak, fragmented and instable to produce spill-over and learning effects and to reach beyond industrial sectors in northern and central-western Europe. Since wage coordination is a public good that requires compliance of all actors involved in collective bargaining, the transnational forms of wage coordination remained a limited and transitional phenomenon and unions' initiatives largely proved to be marginal in light of lacking support of transnational business and (EU) policy actors. Even transnational inter-class alliances between labour and the organised interests of small and middle-sized enterprises (SMEs) in Europe have not emerged despite their common interest in taking wages out of competition.

Given the transnational economic, political and symbolic power asymmetries, two decisive questions remain: (1) under what conditions would collective actors be willing and able to contribute to a change of the dominant forms and functions of wage coordination in Europe? (2) And how could alternative economic and wage policies look like?

Power configurations and interests change over time and counterforces to market liberalism that predominates in the European field of wage policy might evolve both in the European centre and on the fringes of the Eurozone. In May 2016 economists of the IMF claimed that "austerity do more harm than good" and in a later chapter published in the quarterly magazine of the IMF they pointed out that in practice "episodes of fiscal consolidation have been followed, on average, by drops rather than by expansions in output. On average, a consolidation of 1% of GDP increases the long-term unemployment rate by 0.6 percentage points" (Ostry et al. 2016). Public protests against austerity measures, EU and Troika crisis politics and the destruction of national employment institutions, such as wage coordinating practices, have been most intense in southern Europe. Furthermore, the introduction of a statutory minimum wage in Germany in 2015 provides another strong sign that there are economic and societal limits to the market determination of wages and incomes. On-going disintegration pressures deriving, for instance, from Brexit and the rising popularity of anti-EU political forces might also lead to a reorientation towards less neoliberal policies even within the power centre of the EU. But how might a less neoliberal economic and wage policy look like?

Wolfgang Streeck (2017) and his colleagues at Max Planck Institute for the Study of Societies (Höpner/Lutter 2014) regard the dissolving of the European currency area as the most reasonable way to tackle the competitiveness problem of southern European countries and to counteract the anti-democratic neoliberal EMU project. Streeck, in particular, sees the historically developed institutional differences among European nations as too great to be integrated into a common democracy (Streeck 2017: 189). His pessimistic stance derives from his very eloquently presented historical analysis of the common gold standard, a de facto hard currency regime on world scale, that prevented governments to tackle competitiveness problems by means other than "internal" devaluation (i.e., to push down wages). However, what Polanyi (1944), on which Streeck's historical analysis heavily draws, also pointed out that economically weak countries going off a hard currency regime like the gold standard (or the Euro) involved no less than dropping out of the world (European) economy (ibid., 238). Allowing, for instance, Greece to abandon the Euro and to devalue its currency does not necessarily mean that their economic situation will improve. The empirically relevant question here goes beyond the comparison of macro indicators such as unit labour costs. The largely deindustrialised Greek economy is heavily dependent on the import of basic goods and raw materials such as fuels and chemicals. Currency devaluation would make these imports less affordable and might even decrease its attractiveness as a destination of investments in production, a situation that would hit Greek workers and unemployed people even harder than lowering their (potential) wages. Although a devaluation of the currency would involve a real reduction of state sovereign debt, it cannot be ruled out that the Greek currency comes under severe attack of finance speculations.

The Europeanisation of wage policies and Troika interventions into national wage-setting institutions of indebted countries have to be seen as firmly linked responses to both macroeconomic imbalances that have exacerbated existing centre-periphery conflicts and the expectations of a globally operating financial market that clearly reflects a class-biased policy. Financial markets have been strengthened in favour of large capital owners to the detriment of ordinary citizens. The politicisation of class conflicts still takes place at national and subnational level, while increasingly technocratic European and supranational policy regimes are barely confronted with effective democratic counterforces such as trade unions. However, class conflicts will find their way to the surface in one form or another, as the increase in right-wing populism indicates. Also, admittedly less likely, there is a reorientation of supranational policy actors towards a wage policy that names and shames strategies of wage undercutting and forming policy coalitions against the dismantling of collective wage-setting institutions with the majority of small- and medium-sized companies that are largely in favour of taking wages out of competition.

Notes

1 The EMF has left it open whether national bargaining actors are referring to sectoral or national overall productivity growth. In an internal document adopted in 2011 the EMF was more specific on the issue and mentioned the "national productivity increase" as a reference criterion in wage bargaining.
2 Processes of economic liberalisation have led to the dualisation of the workforce. Hassel (2014) convincingly pointed out that in Germany tighter cooperation within the group of core workers and their interest associations coincided with a growing share of workers at the fringes who receive lower wages and have less stable working conditions. These insider-outsider divisions have undermined the redistributive function of wage bargaining coordination, leading to a concentration of productivity gains in the hands of a few (shareholders, core workers).

Literature

Anner, Mark; Greer, Ian; Hauptmeier, Marco; Lillie, Nathan; Winchester, Nik (2006): The Industrial Determinants of Transnational Solidarity: Global Interunion Politics in Three Sectors. *European Journal of Industrial Relations* 12 (1): 7–27.

Baccaro, Lucio; Howell, Chris (2011): A Common Neoliberal Trajectory: The Transformation of Industrial Relations in Advanced Capitalism. *Politics and Society* 39 (4): 521–563.

Bourdieu, Pierre; Wacquant, Loic (1996): *Reflexive Anthropologie*. Berlin: Suhrkamp.

Brandl, Bernd; Glassner, Vera; Traxler, Franz (2011): Cross-Border Coordination as a Means of Defending National Labour Standards? In: Struck, Olaf (ed.): *Industrial Relations and Social Standards as a Means of Defending National Labour Standards*. München: Rainer Hampp, 89–102.

Calmfors, Lars; Driffill, John (1988): Bargaining Structure, Corporatism and Macroeconomic Performance. *Economic Policy* 6: 13–61.

Crouch, Colin (1999): Adapting the European Model: The Role of Employers' Associations and Trade Unions. In: Huemer, Gerhard; Mesch, Michael; Traxler, Franz (ed.): *The Role of Employer Associations and Labour Unions in the EMU. Institutional Requirements for European Economic Policies*. Aldershot: Ashgate, 27–52.

della Porta, Donatella (2015): *Social Movements in Times of Austerity*. Cambridge: Polity Press.

Dufresne, Anne; Mermet, Emmanuel (2002): *Trends in the Coordination of Collective Bargaining in Europe*. ETUI Discussion and Working Papers 2002.01.02.

Erne, Roland (2015): A Supranational Regime That Nationalizes Social Conflict: Explaining European Trade Unions' Difficulties in Politicizing European Economic Governance. *Labor History* 56 (3): 345–368.

European Commission (2004): *Industrial Relations in Europe*. Luxembourg: Publications Office of the European Union.

European Commission (2006): *Industrial Relations in Europe*. Luxembourg: Publications Office of the European Union.

European Commission (2016a): Macroeconomic Imbalance Procedure (MIP) Scoreboard.http://ec.europa.eu/economy_finance/economic_governance/ macroeconomic_imbalance_procedure/mip_scoreboard/index_en.htm (retrieved on July 3rd, 2016).

European Commission (2016b): European Semester and Country-Specific Recommendations. http://ec.europa.eu/europe2020/making-it-happen/country-specific-recommendations/index_en.htm (retrieved on July 4th, 2016). European Metalworkers' Federation (EMF) (1993): Collective Bargaining Policy in a Changing Europe. Statement of principle on Collective Bargaining, adopted at the 1st EMF Collective Bargaining Conference, Luxembourg, March.

European Metalworkers' Federation (EMF) (1998): Collective Bargaining with the Euro. Resolution Adopted at the 3rd EMF Collective Bargaining Conference, Frankfurt, December 1998.

European Trade Union Confederation (ETUC) (2000): The Coordination of Collective Bargaining, Resolution Adopted at the Executive Committee Meeting, Brussels, December.

Fligstein, Neil; McAdam, Doug (2012): *A Theory of Fields*. Oxford: Oxford University Press.

Gajewska, Katarzyna (2008): The Emergence of a European Labour Protest Movement? *European Journal of Industrial Relations* 14 (1): 104–121.

Gollbach, Jochen; Thorsten Schulten (2000): Cross-Border Collective Bargaining Networks in Europe. *European Journal of Industrial Relations* 6 (2): 161–179.

Hall, Peter A. (2014): Varieties of Capitalism and the Euro Crisis. *West European Politics* 37 (6): 1223–1243.

Hall, Peter A.; Franzese, Robert (1998): Mixed Signals: Central Bank Independence, Coordinated Wage Bargaining, and European Monetary Union. *International Organization* 52 (3): 505–535.

Hall, Peter A.; Soskice, David (2001): *Varieties of Capitalism: The Institutional Foundations of Comparative Advantage*. Oxford: Oxford University Press.

Hancké, Bob (2013): 'The Missing Link. Labour Unions, Central Banks and Monetary Integration in Europe'. *Transfer: European Review of Labour and Research* 19 (1): 89–101.

Hartlapp, Miriam; Metz, Julia; Rauh, Christian (2014): *Which Policy for Europe? Power and Conflict Inside the European Commission*. Oxford: Oxford University Press.

Heidenreich, Martin; Delhey, Jan; Lahusen, Christian; Gerhards, Jürgen; Mau, Steffen; Münch, Richard; Pernicka, Susanne (2012): *Europäische Vergesellschaftungsprozesse. Horizontale Europäisierung zwischen nationalstaatlicher und globaler Vergesellschaftung*. Working Paper No. 1 of the DFG Research Unit "Horizontal Europeanisation".

Hassel, Anke (2014): The Paradox of Liberalization — Understanding Dualism and the Recovery of the German Political Economy. *British Journal of Industrial Relations* 52 (1): 57–81.

Hofmann, Julia (2015): Grenzüberschreitende gewerkschaftliche Antworten auf die Krise. In: Pernnicka, Susanne (ed.): *Horizontale Europäisierung im Feld der Arbeitsbeziehungen*. Wiesbaden: VS Verlag für Sozialwissenschaften, 201–228.

Höpner, Martin; Lutter, Mark (2014): One Currency and Many Modes of Wage Formation. Why the Eurozone Is Too Heterogeneous for the Euro. MPIfG Discussion Paper 14/14.

Johnston, Alison; Hancké, Bob (2009): Wage Inflation and Labour Unions in EMU. *Journal of European Public Policy* 16 (4): 601–622.

Keune, Maarten (2013): Less Governance Capacity and More Inequality: The Effects of the Assault on Collective Bargaining in the EU. In Van Gyes, Guy; Schulten, Thorsten (ed.): *Wage Bargaining Under the New European Economic Governance. Alternative Strategies for Inclusive Growth*. Brussels: ETUI, 283–296.

Kluttz, Daniel; Fligstein, Neil (2016): Varieties of Sociological Field Theory. In: Abrutyn, Seth (ed.): *Handbook of Contemporary Sociological Theory*. New York: Springer, 185–204.

Koll, Willy (2013): *Neue Wirtschaftsregierung und Tarifautonomie in der Europäischen Union. Makroökonomische Koordinierung im Dialog*. Düsseldorf: Institut für Makroökonomie und Konjunkturforschung.

Korpi, Walter (1989): Power, Politics, and State Autonomy in the Development of Social Citizenship. *Sociological Review* 54 (3): 309–328.

Kriesi, Hanspeter; Grande, Edgar; Dolezal, Martin; Helbling, Marc; Höglinger, Dominic; Wüest, Bruno (2012): *Political Conflict in Western Europe*. Cambridge: Cambridge University Press.

Lipset, Seymour; Rokkan, Stein (ed.) (1967): *Party Systems and Voter Alignments: Cross-National Perspectives.* New York and London: The Free Press.

Mahoney, James; Thelen, Kathleen (2010): *Explaining Institutional Change: Ambiguity, Agency, and Power.* Cambridge: Cambridge University Press, 1–37.

Marginson, Paul; Sisson, Keith (2006): *European Integration and Industrial Relations. Multi-Level Governance in the Making.* Basingstoke: Palgrave.

Marginson, Paul; Keune, Maarten (2013): Transnational Industrial Relations as Multi-Level Governance: Interdependencies in European Social Dialogue. *British Journal of Industrial Relations* 51 (3): 473–497.

Marginson, Paul; Weltz, Christian (2014): *Changes to Wage-Setting Mechanisms in the Context of the Crisis and the EU's New Economic Governance Regime.* European Industrial Relations Observatory Online: www.eurofound.eurpa.eu/eiro/studies/tn1402049s/tn1402049s.htm (retrieved on February 20th, 2015).

Martin, Jo Cathie; Swank, Duane (2012): *The Political Construction of Business Interests.* Cambridge: Cambridge University Press.

Ostry, Jonathan D.; Loungani, Prakash; Furceri, Davide (2016): *Neoliberalism: Oversold?* Finance & Development, June 2016. Washington, DC: International Monetary Fund.

Pernicka, Susanne; Glassner, Vera (2014): Transnational Strategies of Trade Unions towards Wage Policy. A Neo-Institutional Framework. *European Journal of Industrial Relations* 20 (4): 317–334.

Pernicka, Susanne; Glassner, Vera; Dittmar, Nele; Mrozowicki, Adam; Maciejewska, Malgorzata (2015): When Does Solidarity End? Transnational Labour Cooperation during and after the Crisis – The GM/Opel Case Revisited. *Economic and Industrial Democracy* 38 (3): 375–399.

Pochet, Philippe (1999): Monetary Union and Collective Bargaining in Europe. Brussels: P.I.E. Lang.

Polanyi, Karl (1944): *The Great Transformation.* New York: Farrar & Rinehart.

Schulten, Thorsten (2003): Europeanisation of Collective Bargaining. Trade Union Initiatives for the Transnational Coordination of Collective Bargaining. In: Keller, Bernd; Platzer, Hans-Wolfgang (ed.): *Industrial Relations and European Integration. Trans-und Supranational Developments and Prospects.* Aldershot: Ashgate, 112–136.

Schulten, Thorsten; Müller, Torsten (2015): European Economic Governance and Its Intervention into National Wage Developments and Collective Bargaining. In: Lehndorff, Steffen (ed.): *Divisive Integration. The Triumph of Failed Ideas in Europe – Revisited.* Brussels: ETUI, 331–363.

Sinn, Hans-Werner (2016): *The Euro Trap. On Bursting Bubbles, Budgets, and Beliefs.* Oxford: Oxford University Press.

Sisson, Keith; Marginson, Paul (2002): Co-Ordinated Bargaining: A Process for Our Times? *British Journal of Industrial Relations* 40 (2): 197–220.

Streeck, Wolfgang (2017): *Buying Time. The Delayed Crisis of Democratic Capitalism.* Second edition. London and New York: Verso.Traxler, Franz (1998): Collective Bargaining in the OECD: Developments, Preconditions and Effects. *European Journal of Industrial Relations* 4 (2): 207–226.

Traxler, Franz (2002): *European Monetary Union and Collective Bargaining.* Working Paper 207, Institut de Institut de Ciències Polítiques i Socials Barcelona.

Traxler, Franz (2003a) Coordinated Bargaining: A Stocktaking of Its Preconditions, Practices and Performance. *Industrial Relations Journal* 43 (3): 194–209.

Traxler, Franz (2003b): The Metamorphosis of Corporatism: From Classical to Lean Patterns. *European Journal of Political Research* 43 (4): 571–598.

Traxler, Franz; Brandl, Bernd (2009): Towards Europeanization of Wage Policy: Germany and the Nordic Countries. *European Union Politics* 10 (2): 177–201.

Traxler, Franz; Mermet, Emmanuel (2003): Coordination of Collective Bargaining: The Case of Europe. *Transfer: European Review of Labour and Research* 2 (3), 229–246.

Traxler, Franz; Blaschke, Sabine; Kittel, Bernhard (2001): *National Labour Relations in Internationalized Markets*. Oxford: Oxford University Press.

Chapter 7

The coordination paradox

A comparative political economy perspective on transnational wage coordination

Martin Höpner

Chapter 6 traces the attempts to coordinate wage policies transnationally from their beginning to the Eurozone crisis. These attempts have clearly not succeeded. "A field of transnational wage policy coordination based on voluntary negotiations between business and labour," Pernicka and Glassner say, "has never emerged."

Is this failure to emerge a problem? At least since the introduction of the euro, it has been a problem indeed. The rules of the game are different once the exchange rate is fixed. In adjustable exchange rate regimes, de- and revaluations can correct heterogeneous unit labour cost and price developments. In monetary unions, by contrast, differential wage dynamics necessarily distort the real exchange rate. This is precisely what has been happening in the Eurozone since 1999 (Flassbeck/Lapavitsas 2015; Sinn 2015: Ch. 4). The lack of transnational wage coordination is therefore not a side aspect of the euro crisis but among its decisive causes.

The prospects for the near future are not good, either. "In the current situation," say Pernicka and Glassner, "it is unlikely that trade unions, even those in central-western Europe, will revive their transnational wage bargaining coordination activities." The European institutions are trying, as the authors show, to fill this gap by establishing a technocratic-authoritative form of wage coordination. The prospect that this second wave of steering attempts will succeed, however, is at least as questionable as its legitimacy.

In the following, I will overcome the impulse to focus my comment on Pernicka and Glassner's concluding remarks, in which they argue against devaluations of overvalued currencies. I will rather complement the authors' pessimistic view on the likelihood that transnational wage coordination will emerge by adopting a comparative political economy perspective. More specifically, I will argue that European wage policy faces a coordination paradox: while in structural terms, internal coordination is the precondition for external coordination, in functional terms, countries with coordinated wage regimes are precisely those that "beggar their neighbours." This paradoxical state of affairs leaves even less room for optimism. European policymakers, I will argue, may therefore face a hard choice between breaking with wage bargaining autonomy and breaking with the fixed inner-European exchange rate.

Coordinated wage bargaining: still superior?

A large comparative political economy literature has dealt with the international variation of wage regimes. It distinguished between two forms: coordinated (or corporatist) and uncoordinated (or non-corporatist) wage bargaining. With regard to economic performance, all the relevant studies have found that coordinated regimes worked at least as well (the hump-shape hypothesis) or, in most cases, significantly better (the linear hypothesis) than their liberal counterparts (see, as just one example, Soskice 1990; see also Streeck/Kenworthy 2005 for an excellent overview).

In retrospect, however, we must doubt whether these insights are as universally true as the corporatists sometimes thought. The superiority of coordinated wage bargaining was dependent on an international economic context that has now changed. In the 1970s and 1980s, when the corporatist literature emerged, the problem to be solved was to prevent nominal wages from overshooting. In this regard, coordinated wage bargaining indeed brought about better outcomes and therefore enabled fiscal and monetary policy to engage in expansive measures without fuelling inflation even more (Scharpf 1991). This problem constellation has gone. Today, we live in a world that was unimaginable some 30–40 years ago, one in which the Bundesbank (!) and the European Central Bank beg the German wage partners to negotiate higher wage increases. This implies that the economic superiority of coordinated wage bargaining has gone, too. Under conditions of undershooting inflation, the undisputed capacity of coordinated wage bargaining to deliver wage moderation is no longer of any help; it is not the solution, but part of the problem.

During the first ten Euro years until the emergence of the crisis, no euro member engaged in more competitive wage restraint than Germany, one of the paradigmatic cases of coordinated wage bargaining. We find a similar pattern in Austria, another paradigmatic case. Some may argue that the German violation of the European Central Bank's (ECB) price inflation target (equivalent to an implicit wage inflation target) happened not due to Germany's coordination features but precisely due to their erosion: weakened trade unions, shrinking coverage of central collective agreements, and the rise of new sectors. This objection, however, does not help. Even if we look at manufacturing alone (where the main features of wage coordination have survived), Germany has undershot. Germany is the only one of the 12 founding members of the Eurozone in which nominal unit labour costs fell, until the crisis struck, both economy-wide and in manufacturing. As Mark Lutter and I have shown elsewhere (Höpner/Lutter 2018), wage coordination generally depressed nominal unit labour cost increases until the crisis, a finding that holds even if one controls statistically for growth, unemployment, left-wing parties in government, the size of the service sector, and other factors.

And things do not look any better once we take stock of post-crisis developments. The countries with overshooting nominal wages until 2008 were mainly cases of uncoordinated, non-corporatist wage bargaining. Since 2009, however, Portugal, Spain, and Greece have deflated their nominal unit labour costs enough to correct their previous overshooting (for details see Höpner/Seeliger 2017: 8–11). Today, the problem cases are not the so-called crisis countries anymore, but those with coordinated wage bargaining. These countries – first and foremost Germany and Austria – refuse to help by correcting their previous undershooting. This has had disastrous consequences for Southern Europe – which therefore has to engage in even more painful real devaluation than previously – as well as for the Eurozone as a whole, which, under such conditions, persistently operates on the brink of deflation.

Coordinated wage bargaining, in other words, contributed substantially to the emergence of euro crisis, as well as to its persistence. With regard to transnational coordination, we therefore face a paradox. Of course, internal coordination remains the crucial structural precondition of transnational coordination; what cannot be steered internally can by no means be coordinated across borders. In functional terms, however, coordinated wage bargaining turned out to be transnational wage coordination's greatest enemy.

Sectoral conflicts shape the prospects of transnational coordination

Let us elaborate on this paradox a bit further. Pernicka and Glassner rightly distinguish between two types of conflict that have to be taken into account in our context, one between classes and the other between countries. A closer look at the conflict between countries makes yet another conflict dimension visible, the conflict between economic sectors.

What is good for the export sector is not necessarily good for the domestic sector, too. If the nominal exchange rate is fixed, competitive disinflation necessarily increases international cost competitiveness. The export sector therefore favours not only modest wage policies but also strict fiscal rules that prohibit potentially inflationary fiscal expansion. From the perspective of domestic sector firms, however, the problem constellation differs. With regard to wage increases, domestically oriented firms face a collective action dilemma. They favour low cost pressure individually but depend on internal demand increases collectively. With regard to budget policy, they have no interest in the "black zero" whatsoever, neither in the private part of the public sector nor, especially, in its public part.

This conflict dimension sheds light on the nature of the conflict between Eurozone countries. As the emerging literature on growth regimes demonstrates, countries differ in terms of their export orientation (Baccaro/ Pontusson 2016). All Southern European countries have smaller export sectors than we would expect from their size. Their economies depend on the growth of domestic demand and have little to gain from competitive disinflation. Germany, Austria, and other export-oriented countries, by contrast, have large export sectors. They have a growth option that domestically oriented countries lack: holding down internal demand, thereby disinflating and absorbing the demand that other countries have created.

The struggle that Pernicka and Glassner label the "centre-periphery conflict" is therefore not only a conflict between countries with different wage regimes but, more fundamentally, a conflict between different inner-European varieties of capitalism (see Hall 2014; Streeck 2015; Scharpf 2016; Nölke 2016 provides an excellent overview that locates the growth regime literature within the broader varieties of capitalism literature). This insight makes it even clearer why the emergence of European wage coordination is highly unlikely. Internal demand-driven economies suffer from the beggar-your-neighbour-policies of their export-oriented counterparts and would therefore clearly gain from transnational wage coordination and inflation convergence, but they lack the structural preconditions. And those who tend to possess the respective structural preconditions are, paradoxically, precisely those who would suffer from better wage coordination because the structure of their economies makes beggaring their neighbours – in other words, "competitive mercantilism" – an attractive option indeed.

Wage bargaining autonomy or fixed exchange rates

We have seen that the euro has increased the functional need to harmonise wage inflation and, therefore, to coordinate wage bargaining transnationally. This functional requirement does not imply, however, that the institutional, organisational, and motivational preconditions of transnational wage coordination are present. The comparative political economy perspective which I propose here confirms Pernicka and Glassner's pessimism: the preconditions for transnational wage coordination have not emerged in the Eurozone and nor are they likely to in the foreseeable future. The emergence of voluntary, horizontal wage coordination in order to correct the inner-European distorted real exchange rates is not within our range of options. It would be irresponsible to arouse false hopes in this respect because they would necessarily lead to wrong policy recommendations (see also Höpner/ Seeliger 2017).

Is there no solution to the problem? Pernicka and Glassner rightly point our attention towards the macroeconomic monitoring and correction procedures that have been created since 2010. Given that they also cover wages, they are part of the quest for functional equivalents to the failed horizontal coordination attempts. But it is hard to imagine that these instruments will work, either. "Wrong" policy decisions on the part of governments can be sanctioned, but the Commission cannot punish trade unions for their demands or employers for the wages they pay their workers. Under conditions of free collective bargaining, the new procedures, as long as they concern wages, remain in the field of signalling and of "soft" steering. They might help if the problem to be solved was based purely on information gaps. But as we have seen, such an interpretation would be naïve: in reality, the problems are based on structural heterogeneity, on a lack of steering capacity, and on different power relations between sectors within the Eurozone countries.

The story, however, does not end here. The Troika's impact on the so-called "programme countries" has demonstrated that the autonomy of wage bargaining, which we have taken for granted so far, can be broken (Rödl/Callsen 2015). In principle, "hard" measures such as cuts on minimum wages minimum wages, union busting, the destruction of declarations of general applicability of collective agreements, and even the entire destruction of such agreements are possible. The Eurozone members may therefore, in the medium to long-term, face a hard choice, namely between fixed exchange rates and the autonomy of collective wage formation. Under conditions of structural heterogeneity, they do not harmonise. Anyone wishing to save the euro, at whatever cost, may have to sacrifice wage bargaining autonomy, whereas whoever thinks that this price is too high will have to engage in discussions about alternatives to the euro.

Literature

Baccaro, Lucio; Pontusson, Jonas (2016): Rethinking Comparative Political Economy: The Growth Model Perspective. *Politics & Society* 44 (2): 175–207.

Flassbeck, Heiner; Lapavitsas, Costas (2015): *Nur Deutschland kann den Euro retten. Der letzte Akt beginnt.* Frankfurt a.M.: Westend.

Hall, Peter A. (2014): Varieties of Capitalism and the Euro Crisis. *West European Politics* 37 (6): 1223–1243.

Höpner, Martin; Lutter, Mark (2018): The Diversity of Wage Regimes: Why the Eurozone Is Too Heterogeneous for the Euro. *European Political Science Review* 10 (1): 71–96.

Höpner, Martin; Seeliger, Martin (2017): *Transnationale Lohnkoordination zur Stabilisierung des Euro? Gab es nicht, gibt es nicht, wird es nicht geben.* MPIfG Discussion Paper 17/13.

Nölke, Andreas (2016): Economic Causes of the Eurozone Crisis: The Analytical Contribution of Comparative Capitalism. *Socio-Economic Review* 14 (1): 141–161.

Rödl, Florian; Callsen, Raphaël (2015): *Kollektive soziale Rechte unter dem Druck der Währungsunion: Schutz durch Art. 28 EU-Grundrechtecharta?* Frankfurt a.M.: Bund-Verlag.

Scharpf, Fritz W. (1991): *Crisis and Choice in European Social Democracy.* Ithaca/London: Cornell University Press.

Scharpf, Fritz W. (2016): *Forced Structural Convergence in the Eurozone – Or a Differentiated European Monetary Community.* MPIfG Discussion Paper 16/15.

Sinn, Hans-Werner (2015): *Der Euro. Von der Friedensidee zum Zankapfel.* München: Hanser.

Soskice, David (1990): Wage Determination: The Changing Role of Institutions in Advanced Industrialized Countries. *Oxford Review of Economic Policy* 6 (4): 36–61.

Streeck, Wolfgang (2015): Why the Euro Divides Europe. *New Left Review* 95 (Sept./Oct.): 5–26.

Streeck, Wolfgang; Kenworthy, Lane (2005): Theories and Practices of Neocorporatism. In: Janoski, Thomas; Alford, Robert R.; Hicks, Alexander M.; Schwartz, Mildred A. (eds.): *The Handbook of Political Sociology.* Cambridge: Cambridge University Press, 441–460.

Chapter 8

Ambiguities of social Europe

Political agenda setting among trade unionists from Central and Eastern Europe and Western Europe

Martin Seeliger

Introduction

In the course of European integration, trade unions face two challenges. While in qualitative terms, negative integration (Scharpf 2012) has increased the pressure on unions to organize resistance within a cross-border context, the recent enlargement rounds have also increased the heterogeneity among the Member States (Höpner/Schäfer 2010). As a result, the development of common policy positions among European trade unions is becoming more and more difficult.[1]

Against that backdrop, this text analyses the development of common policy positions between European trade unions. With reference to the discussions on the Freedom of Services and a European minimum wage, we shall investigate the extent to which trade unions from the Central and Easter European (CEE) countries are participating in the development of policy positions among European-level trade union organizations.

In this context, an important framework condition lies in vast power asymmetries between organizations from West and East. Larger membership gives the former both economic resources and a stronger voting position within European trade union structures. Moreover, their established position within the field of European-level trade unionism attributes more experience to them and bestows on them a higher status in agenda setting. Analysis of the two fields shows how the frame of Social Europe is mobilized in one case to maintain Western European standards (Freedom of Services) and is blocked at the same time in the other case by the established organizations from the Northwest, given that it mainly serves the interests of CEE trade unions (European minimum wage). On this basis, the article makes a threefold contribution to the social inquiry of European trade unionism: (1) the instrumental meaning of "Social Europe," (2) the necessity of a position midway between optimistic and pessimistic viewpoints on East-West trade union cooperation, and (3) the importance of social skills among European-level trade union actors.

International trade unionism in the EU

Research on labour relations has mainly focussed on conflict between capital and labour. While trade unions have traditionally served as cartels of wage earners, European integration has had a fundamental impact on the relations between capital, labour, and the state as the classical triangle of industrial relations. Recent developments such as European Monetary Union or the single market have increased pressure on the working class through downward competition between different countries. In order to maintain their bargaining capacity, trade unions from the different European Union (EU) countries need to formulate common political positions on wage and employment standards. Yet, against the background of the widening spectrum of national institutional settings and a growing gap in terms of national wealth, common political positions become more and more difficult to establish.

Within the EU, cross-border cooperation of trade unions is the political key to establishing such common positions. Because it is the most comprehensive instance of workers' representation within the EU, this study focusses on the European Trade Union Confederation (ETUC). Consisting of the ten European industry federations as well as 90 national trade union organizations from 39 European countries, the ETUC provides today more than ever before a "'superstructure' for European cross-national collaboration" (Turner 2005: 75). As a forum for the exchange of information and consultation, Hyman (2005: 171) assigns to the ETUC an important "coordination role" in its efforts "to transform the diverse and at times conflicting aims of its affiliates into a coherent policy agenda." In addition to its character as a forum for internal negotiations among the member organizations, the ETUC holds another important capacity for the European labour movement: it formulates "the general interpretive frames for collective action" (Gajewska 2009: 82).

Looking back at the past two decades of trade union politics on the Continent, the most comprehensive and well known of these frames can be found in the concept of Social Europe (see the introduction of this volume). Over the last years, the use of the concept has largely been transformed to address consequences for labour linked to the Eastern enlargement of the EU. As the liberalization of the common market proceeds and, likewise, the diversity of national settings increases, so does the need to maintain these standards – at least for those affected negatively. By looking at the implicit conception of "Social Europe" held by trade union organizations from the old and the new Member States, this article shows how it is understood in very different ways according to the particular contexts.

In the evaluation of the literature on European trade unionism, the positions in the discussion of this concept and its meaning for labour in the course of EU integration can be connected to "the broad – albeit somewhat oversimplified camps of 'Euro-optimists' and 'Euro-pessimists'" (Platzer 1997: 68). While the definition of the central problems seems generally similar, these two camps differ greatly with regard to the potential of European trade unionism (see the introduction to this volume).

While the pessimists address the problems of institutional heterogeneity within the EU, optimists highlight the potential benefits of a diverse leadership (Gumbrell-McCormick/Hyman 2013: 193) that represents all the backgrounds involved. Facing the limited success of the regulatory initiatives that have emerged from the camp of European-level labour representatives – not only in recent years (Turner 1996) – most optimistic arguments for the potential benefits of international trade union cooperation currently are limited (not the least due to a lack of good empirical news) to a mainly conceptual character.

Does this mean that there is no concrete hope for European labour? Do the structural weaknesses of European-level trade union federations undermine all capacities to develop common policy positions beyond national egoisms? Is European labour facing the bleak perspective of a "race to the bottom," in terms of not only political capacity but also standards of work; employment; and, ultimately, quality of life? As a point of departure for empirical research, this study takes up the argument about the heterogeneity of the EU as an economic space.

By looking at the constellation in the field of European trade unionism, it becomes apparent that cooperation within the EU's international arena is shaped by significant power asymmetries between trade unions from the East and those from the West. To learn about the integration of CEE representatives in European-level rule setting, the research focussed on the involvement of Hungarian, Polish, and Swedish national trade union federations in European-level debates. The selection of the debates on the Services Directive and the European minimum wage reflects the challenges trade unions are facing in the process of European integration because of the institutional heterogeneity among the EU-28 (Höpner/Schäfer 2012).

Regarding the first issue, the negotiations on the Services Directive in the internal market (short: Services Directive) will be analysed to show how a common political position could emerge around this topic. For the unions, the territorial validity of collective bargaining agreements was at stake, which some companies hoped to undermine by applying foreign standards through cross-border services. The fact that a joint international campaign finally led to a significant change in the Directive that preliminarily dismantled its destructive potential leads Bernaciak (2011: 33) to suggest that "there exists consensus among European labor over the desired shape of social Europe."

In the second issue, the discussion about a European minimum wage has recently brought about a compromise, with a demand for a common bottom-limit to wages at 50 per cent (and later 60 per cent) of the national median wage. While the CEE representatives have been among the protagonists of this idea, the resistance of the Nordic trade unions has made implementation of this compromise rather difficult.

While the issue at stake in both policy fields seems at first glance to be the wage level, a closer look reveals that conflicts arise in both cases over the more fundamental dynamics of the national collective bargaining systems, namely the mode according to which wages are set between the reference frames at the national and the EU levels. In the following section we introduce the theoretical framework of the study.

Theoretical framework

The attempt to understand international trade union cooperation as a reaction to (and thus a part of) European integration is best interpreted as a process of political mobilization. Since agency – understood as (individual or collective) actors' capacity to act purposefully (although with possible unintended consequences) – is at the core of processes, this study takes an action-theoretical starting point. The following paragraphs introduce the theoretical framework established to understand the multi-level dynamics among the different organizations.

Goal setting within ETFs between institutional nationalism and international socialization

ETFs are constituted by national member organizations, each representing workers from the different EU Member States. For this reason, the formulation of common organizational goals stands out because of its genuinely contested character and because it involves continual negotiation among the members. As international delegates represent the interests of their national reference group, these negotiations bear the risk that representatives will only take these interests into account. Such "institutional nationalism" (Streeck 1995: 120) can impede or even prevent the pursuit of common goals.

Since membership is voluntary, European federations cannot bindingly impose or enforce rules onto the national organizations. Therefore, internal goal setting often functions according to a mode termed "persuasion" by Ahrne and Brunsson (2008: 121). According to them (ibid.), "[p]ersuasion does not threaten the autonomy of the persuaded party because it has not been forced to comply, but has decided for itself to embrace new values and norms." While the voting mechanism depends on a fixed set of rules, the federations comprise a broad range of committees, working groups, and informal settings. It is in these micro-contexts that the exchange and negotiations between single members are usually translated into processes of concrete agenda setting.

At the same time, meta-organizations (Ahrne/Brunsson 2008) such as the ETUC or the ETFs often follow a logic of collective identity formation. For Risse (2010: 88), this very formation of collective identities serves in the long run as a necessary precondition for the stable formulation of common political interests. For the multi-level system of the EU, such socialization dynamics are of central significance. Accordingly, Haas (1958: 16) understands political integration as

> the process whereby political actors in several distinct national settings are persuaded to shift their loyalties, expectations and political activities toward a new centre, whose institutions possess or demand jurisdiction over the pre-existing national states.

According to Checkel (2005: 804), such a shift in loyalties towards a common reference frame beyond national particularities stems from a routine in everyday cooperation, in the course of which these positions are continuously being negotiated and revised. However, it has to be noted that, despite their influence on the national delegates, the ETFs lack the formal capacity to influence the strategies of their national member organizations (Meardi 2012).

Framing interest representation through the use of "social skill"

From the perspective taken in this study, interaction is not limited to the microcosm of a certain group but takes place within a broader symbolic framework. Drawing on the example of the general strike as a tool of trade union action in late 19th-century France, Ansell (1997: 360) points out how, beyond micro-level interactions, such processes of joint position making require "a shared interpretative framework that facilitates coordination, exchange, and ultimately commitment." The concept of "social skill" developed by Fligstein (2001) aims to understand how appropriately "skilled actors … empathetically relate to the situations of other people and, in doing so, are able to provide those people with reasons to cooperate" (Fligstein 2001: 112). A particular advantage in strategic negotiations derives from their ability to draw up an interpretative framework:

> The basic problem for skilled social actors is to frame "stories" that help induce cooperation from people by appealing to their identity, belief, and interests, while at the same time using those same stories to frame actions against various opponents.
>
> (Fligstein/McAdam 2011: 50f)

A particularly effective moment to apply such frames is the initial agenda setting of a debate: "If a skilled actor can get others to accept what the terms of discussion are, the negotiation is half won" (Fligstein 2001: 114).

As Hyman (2013: 175) states, trade union democracy requires an "internal social dialogue" at eye level. In his work on "deliberative democracy" Habermas (1992) shows how democratic decision-making requires equal access to information, absence of external and internal constraints (material and non-material), and the inclusion of the highest possible number of concerned actors (also see Erne 2008). At the same time, discussions within the ETFs are by no means guaranteed to take place on such an equal footing. Here, different representatives of the member organizations try to influence the outcome of the goal-setting processes not only through immediate bargaining but also through the setting of particular agendas. In doing so, they can draw on different statuses, as well as different sets of material (money) and ideal (knowledge) resources.

Summary of the theoretical framework

Since ETFs have little power to oblige their members, the establishment of common policy positions needs to be achieved and maintained mainly through consensus. Such consensus can be achieved in the interplay of daily cooperative routines and explicit bargaining. Because of the consensual tendency in decision-making, goals are often achieved through the implementation of particular interpretative frames that indicate why certain policy goals are desirable. The most common frame in relation to questions about European-level rule setting is the concept of Social Europe. Connected to this frame is also a common identity, which stems first from the fact that all the national working classes participate in the European labour market.

The concept of "social skill" enables us to understand how the terms of discussion are set by members who can convincingly establish certain symbolic frames. As long as the capacity to implement such frames differs among individuals and groups within the federations, the deliberative character of internal debates is genuinely called into question by the risk that actors will impose their interpretation (and perhaps their will) on others – in other words, not by discussion but by persuasion or force. After introducing the methodology of the study in the following section, we describe how this works in practice.

Methodology

The findings presented here stem from a research project on international trade union cooperation in the EU. Although the selected countries' institutional settings differ greatly with regard to how they shape the two policy fields under study, their selection does not intentionally reflect any particular typology from the field of comparative political economy. Instead, they were chosen to represent different parties in conflicts within these policy fields found in the literature (Gajewska 2009; Furaker/Selden

2011) and in the course of the fieldwork. A total of 88 interviews were con-
ducted with representatives from nine European countries as well as from
the ETUC and the European Industry Federations. A four-month stay at
the European Trade Union Institute, moreover, enabled the author to join
several meetings of ETUC committees and conduct participatory observations. The selection of interview partners covers the most important
federations from three countries – Sweden: LO, TCO, and SACO; Poland:
OPZZ, Solidarnosc, and Forum; and Hungary: LIGA and MSZOSZ. The
empirical part of this article will therefore focus on the 22 interviews with
representatives from the respective countries and with 16 representatives
from the EIFs and the ETUC. The interview partners representing the national trade unions were from the international secretariats and collective
bargaining departments.

Empirical findings

National backgrounds with regard to policy fields

On the basis of its close cooperation with the national Social Democratic
Party, of Sweden's large export surpluses, and of a welfare system that has
favoured union density, the Swedish labour union movement is "uniquely
powerful compared [to] its counterparts elsewhere in the world" (Peterson
et al. 2011: 624). Despite recent trends in the decentralization of collective
bargaining and attacks on the right to engage in industrial action (Svensson
2013), the Swedish model can be considered perhaps the most robust in the
EU. Against this background, Götz and Haggrén (2009: 15) recognize a
Eurosceptic tendency among Scandinavian labour, which manifests itself in
"a belief in the superiority of the Nordic industrial relations regime." From
this point of view, the transfer of competencies to the European level appears to be a threat to the national sovereignty necessary to maintain work
and employment standards.

   At the same time, in Poland, Gardawski et al. (2012: 11) identify its
"chronic fragmentation combined with 'competitive pluralism' and interunion rivalry" as a central historical feature of the Polish trade union
movement. While nowadays the Polish economy is among the fastest
growing in the EU, its persistent weakness in the post-communist era has
prevented the national labour force from successfully claiming its share
of the new wealth (Polakowski 2013). Due to disputes over assets, it was
only in 2006 that national federations managed to join forces in the field
of European politics.

   A similarly fragmented system can also be found in Hungary (Neumann
2012). However, despite a number of attempts (Németh 2014), no recon-
ciliation has yet been achieved. Even more strikingly than in Poland, in-
formalization in the labour market and in trade union structures weaken

the foundations of national labour union power. This is also reflected organizationally: only 10–20 per cent of membership fees reach the federations. These limited national capacities among the Eastern European trade unions make the European level look like a promising regulatory arena. Summing up socio-economic developments in the CEE countries over the first decade in the post-enlargement era, Kohl (2015) recognizes persisting inequalities between the regions. At the same time, from the viewpoint of the Eastern European labour representatives, "the enlarged Union is not only a marketplace but is based on a promise to be a Social Europe with specific prospects of improved living and working opportunities for all" (ibid.: 306). As the agenda of a Social Europe programmatically implies the gradual improvement of wage and employment standards in the process of European integration, CEE unions have come to identify over the years with the concept in a way that shapes their perspective on the European policy arena. Hence, Greskovitz (2015: 281) notes that these organizations tend to "frame their demands in European labor rights terms and use such regulations to externalise domestic conflicts." In the following, this adaptation process will be introduced in more detail.

With regard to the Freedom of Services, key differences hinder the development of a shared policy position among the selected countries (Meardi 2002). In the early 2000s (the time frame during which the discussions took place), the East-West divide was illustrated by CEE per capita GDP, which was only 45 per cent of the EU average (Bernaciak 2010: 21). Moreover, vast differences in terms of national labour and employment regulations and wage levels caused significant potential for conflict over the issue on the European level. Similarly, with regard to the European minimum wage, differences between national bargaining systems impede the development of a common policy position. Table 8.1 summarizes the features of the countries under examination.

In the following two sections we illustrate how the common positions of the national trade unions in these two areas have emerged in the course of European representative work.

Table 8.1 Bargaining systems in the countries under examination in 2010[a]

	Bargaining coverage (%)	Organized workers (%)	Statutory minimum wage (euros)
Sweden	88	70	–
Poland	25	12	2.21
Hungary	33	12	1.95

a http://de.worker-participation.eu/Nationale-Arbeitsbeziehungen/Quer-durch-Europa/Gewerkschaften

Discussion on the European Services Directive

The first proposal for the European Services Directive was made by the Internal Market and Services Directorate General and submitted to the European Commission in January 2004 as part of the Lisbon Strategy. The study prognosticated the creation of 2.3 million new jobs and a 30 per cent increase in turnover in cross-border services. Article 16 of the Directive, however, gave rise to major resistance from European trade unionists. This is the clause on the country-of-origin principle (Menz 2010: 977) with which the authors of the Directive hoped to establish the employment conditions of the sending country as the standard employment framework for cross-border allocation of services within the EU. Under such conditions, businesses would be able to hire foreign employees to work on the receiving country's territory under contractual conditions of the sending country. Against the backdrop of growing wage differentials in the course of Eastern enlargement, the structural advantage for workers from CEE countries would therefore endanger Western European wage and employment standards.

Highlighting how the negotiations on the Directive were "clearly an issue dividing along national lines," Gajewska (2009: 55) points to a cleavage between Eastern and Western European countries on the issue. As a former ETUC representative claims, the formation of policy positions was accompanied from the beginning by a constant "fear of the hordes from Eastern Europe."[2] Fuelled by the shorthand announcement of the Directive, the discussion of the country-of-origin principle threatened to divide European trade unions.

Adherence to the European Social Model among CEE unions has not only been motivated by a general cross-border solidarity. With a particular focus on Polish trade unions, Bernaciak (2007: 35) points out three factors that brought their representatives to underline "the necessity of preserving the European Social Model in the West," not only from an internationalist viewpoint, but also from a perspective focussed on domestic aspects. According to her, these are "the prospects for upward convergence of working conditions across the enlarged EU," the protection of national wage- and working-norms for the case that countries with lower standards joined the EU, and a "legal chaos, that would emerge after the adoption of the country of origin principle." Her conclusion, according to which "positions of Polish and Western European unionists were congruent from the very outset during the anti-Directive campaign" (ibid.: 39), is not fully supported by the findings of this research.

A former representative of the European Federation of Building and Wood Workers (EFBWW) describes the liberal position of the Eastern European representatives:

> It was difficult because of the Polish colleagues. They were the biggest group among the Eastern Europeans and were thus representing the

strongest interest. And they said it is important that our people find work. And if they can find work in Holland, Germany, Belgium, we are satisfied. Of course, they will not get the same wages as the workers from the Western European countries.

As another EFBWW representative recalls, a high-ranking ETUC official from Eastern Europe repeatedly expressed the position that the Freedom of Services should not be limited by national regulations and that this would this allow for a "level playing field" of international competition. The same statement was made by several (Western European) representatives of ETFs engaged in the discussion at the time. According to them, Eastern European trade unions were pursuing a low-wage strategy in order to create a comparative advantage. A debate was therefore needed.

The starting point of finding a common position between East and West is highlighted by a trade unionist from the Swedish confederation TCO. The starting point was:

> very early in the process, when the directive came. I think it came in January or something. And I read it before Christmas. And then we had a lot of work during the winter and spring. Because we saw that if some Eastern unions would say that this is a very good idea, we would be very weak. It was extremely important that ETUC could say we have all our 60 members and even the members from the Eastern Europe standing together.

A representative from the Swedish LO confirms that at this stage "there were some tensions between East and West," related mainly to the objection of protectionism. On one side, the Eastern Europeans ascribed to their Western European colleagues the tendency to block national labour markets for foreigners. Among the latter, in turn, the threat of cheap labour led to a perception that "the Eastern unions ... are ready to sign agreements, as long as their members get a job," as a representative from the European Transport Federation put it.

In the course of the next few months, several meetings at both the European and the bilateral levels were held to establish a position on a joint lobbying strategy for the ETUC and its national members. As the interviewees from both CEE countries state, the turn towards the Western European position only followed a long debate among the domestic trade union confederations, at the end of which CEE unions agreed to oppose the country-of-origin principle in the directive. A key role in these negotiations is generally assigned to the international representatives, who contributed to the implementation of the idea of equal standards for everyone.

A representative from Hungary's MSZOSZ explains how this discussion resonated in the headquarters of his national federation:

> We were having conflicts among ourselves in this very room, where I was attacked by some of our trade unionists. "It is better if our people make less, because they get a job. It's better than if they stay home!"

Finally, a common position was reached to demand the exclusion of the country-of-origin principle from the Directive. Central to this was that the Eastern European representatives accepted an argument according to which Western standards in terms of pay and employment could eventually be established only if these standards were not undermined by intra-European competition.

> We told them that it's important to be solidarity on the issue with the Directive. But not in a moral tone, but to prevent our drifting apart. And so we sat down to talk it over. And when it's about important stuff, about collective bargaining, there is unity. The closer we get to the core business, the more it is possible to get everyone into one boat.
>
> (ETUC representative)

The first sentence here already hints at who called the shots in this discussion. As another trade unionist from Solidarnosc confirms, the Polish representatives could not take a very active role in this discussion: "Maybe we were not asked, but we were aware of all that." This impression is also underlined by a representative from OPZZ, who highlights a protectionist tendency in these discussions. The political line of the Western trade unionists, according to him, thus implies the maintenance of social standards at the cost of excluding foreign workers: "Of course the Germans want to protect their markets from our workers. That's natural, but initially, it was not the idea. So we had to come up with something."

Explicitly referring to the concept of Social Europe as it was applied by the representatives from the West to justify the modification of the Directive, a trade unionist from Hungary's MSZOSZ problematizes a lack of involvement by his national colleagues:

> I think that the so-called Social Europe was a model of the Western European countries and the Eastern Europeans were not participating. And they saw this model endangered through Eastern enlargement.

Similarly, a Polish representative of the ETUC claims that the concept of Social Europe is "pretty much a Western idea." "In fact," he goes on, "the whole integration process was like that. You have never had this kind of negotiation on an equal footing. It was a matter of joining the block with some rules." According to the CEE unionists, the entire agenda setting in the question about the Services Directive was established by the Western representatives from the European level and the respective countries. This lack of representation is also confirmed by the Hungarian colleague, who explains that they "joined in later. It's normal. It's like a family and you're coming from outside. And the question is, if the family can still function as a family." For the CEE representatives, developing a joint position on the Freedom of Services was – at least from this perspective – a matter of adhering to the Western idea of a Social Europe. Compliance with the consequences was, according to the interviewees, not reached through deliberate discussion at eye level but in a rather persuasive way.

Debate on the European minimum wage

The original idea of a European minimum wage was brought into the political discussion by a handful of trade unionists in 2004 (Schulten 2014). From the very beginning, the Swedish representatives spearheaded the opposing coalition, which, in addition to the Scandinavian countries, consisted of the organizations from Austria and Italy. While Dufresne (2015) points out that German, British, and French trade unions have been a driving force behind the project of a European minimum wage, findings from this research point to a leading role of CEE trade unions as well as representatives from the ETFs (mainly the ETUC, EPSU, ETF, and EFFAT). Subsequent to the ETUC congress of 2007, the first ambitions in this direction were carefully taken up in the Seville Manifesto. This declaration, published by the ETUC executive committee, announces the aspiration to

> explore continually the scope for united campaigns at European level, led by the ETUC, for common standards on minimum pay and income and for collective bargaining strategies.

After four years of discussion within the framework of the ETUC, especially against the backdrop of the Troika's intervention in national bargaining systems, the Athens Congress of 2011 specified the strategy on the topic, although without explicitly committing to particular measures. In general it would work

> in pursuit of fair wages for all European workers, including supporting union campaigns for effective minimum wages in those countries where the unions consider them necessary.[3]

In a preparatory statement for the ETUC Winter School[4] of 2012, this idea was further specified. According to the proposal, the new aim was that

> wherever it exists, the effective national minimum wage should be at least equal to 50% of the average wage or 60% of the median wage.[5]

The current nominal position wage was finally adopted at the ETUC Winter School held in Copenhagen in February 2012. Here, the following wording describes the ETUC's aim in this regard:

> The ETUC recommends that where it exists the effective national minimum wage should be at least equal to 50% of the average wage or 60% of the median wage. ETUC actively supports its affiliates in their actions to gradually reach this goal, in accordance with their national circumstances. Countries which have already achieved this goal should aim for a more ambitious target.
>
> (ETUC 2012: 8)

Compared to the older version, one significant change can be found in the text. While the former proposal referred to the demand for a European minimum wage as a fixed and compulsory goal, the new version reduces this goal to a recommendation. Here, the wording "in accordance with national circumstances" maintains the leeway necessary to establish particular national solutions (Furaker/Selden 2013: 517). It is only against the backdrop of this mitigation that the participants agreed to make this position a demand for a public campaign directed at national governments to be launched by the ETUC with the support of national and European federations. While we find a statement advocating that "statutory minimum wages, where trade unions want them, should be set with the involvement of social partners" (ETUC 2015) in the publication documenting the ETUC's 2015 congress in Paris, after several years of discussion, no such campaign has yet been launched.

The failure to materialize such a campaign, despite the compromise achieved in the Winter School, seems remarkable. The fact that, despite the fierce opposition of the Nordic countries, the participants could formulate a common position on the European minimum wage is ascribed by a colleague from the ETUC to its proponents' argumentative strategy:

> I think in the dynamics of the meeting, yes, it amounted to a technique, because there was first a more radical proposal that was discussed in the official text. And then representatives were resisting this. And then it was thrown into the discussion, okay, let's have a compromise. Let's have the standard of the Council of Europe. Of course, no one in the audience was exactly aware what these standards were. So they subscribed to the compromise and let it pass. But it is still the language, where those affiliates agree to it.

As the Scandinavian representatives were not aware of the implications, they unconsciously agreed to a decision that in reality they could not support.

Viewed in this light, it does not seem surprising that no campaign has yet been launched. In fact, as one Polish colleague explains, the incident was followed by heated discussions:

> We had a kind of informal meeting in London, and the president of all the Nordics, of the FTF white-collar workers, she was really defending this. And our president and her, there was a clash. The language was hostile. Both stepped forward on both sides.

Swedish representatives express a twofold concern about the European minimum wage: a loss of influence in the field of collective bargaining and a relocation of political capacity from the national to the European level as a threat to national autonomy. Particular political salience perceived by the Swedish trade unions can be derived from the following statement by the LO representative:

> The moment someone in [their] capacity as an ETUC official has [to] say that the ETUC supports the European minimum wage, we will do our best to sack that person. Because that person will work directly against our interest. We do not want intervention in our wage issues.

Besides this preference for the national arena, the fear of a gradual development has led to a refusal to engage in a campaign on the European minimum wage. Interviewees ascribe the reason for this to the Swedish industrial relations system and the country's strong social policy. Doubts about the idea of introducing a statutory minimum wage stem from the fear of employer-employee bargaining becoming superfluous through a mandatory bottom-limit. In order to maintain their influence as collective-bargaining actors, Swedish confederations therefore oppose the introduction of such a bottom-limit. Moreover, in the current tendency to strive for European-level regulations, the representative perceived an exaggerated, overhasty integrationism, which might endanger this mode of national regulation: "I think the problem with the European project is the impatience. And I cannot say that the patience is there" (LO Sweden).

Among the Eastern European organizations, a different perspective prevails. In view of the low degree of organization and the correspondingly low bargaining coverage in these countries, the decision to raise their lower wage floors would not only protect the low-paid segments, but, within the framework of the recent austerity measures, it could be an argument in favour of EU intervention.

Discussions on this matter within the ETUC usually take place in either the executive committee or the collective bargaining committee, where attempts to adhere to a common position have been blocked repeatedly by

Swedish and Italian representatives. Yet from the viewpoint of the Swedes, the current position describes a suitable compromise:

> The compromise right now is that ETUC supports the introduction of minimum wages or *erga omnes* clauses at national level. And ETUC will help any affiliate to achieve that. But ETUC cannot advocate European competence as to minimum wages.

Since it should be apparent that the other national affiliates are *not satisfied* with the current state of affairs, this quote points to a possible strategy of intentionally deferring the project. When we consider the few references found in the public-relations material of the ETFs, it does seem to be the case that a more substantial campaign could theoretically be aspired to, but it is not being put into practice.

On the topic of their role in the conception and practice of Social Europe, the interviews show that CEE representatives do not see their political aims reflected in the ETUC's agenda. While Polish members (possibly due to their relative strength in members and resources in relation to the other CEE countries) are apparently not so pessimistic about international co-operation, the representative of Hungary's MSZOSZ again highlights the persisting marginality of the Eastern Europeans:

> It's not well balanced, we're newbies. Although you shouldn't be a newbie if you've been in for 20 years. But we're weak and do not have the resources to offensively engage in all discussions. ... The powerful trade unions can work on the topics and set the priorities. And we're totally lacking that. We can just react.

As in the discussion about the Freedom of Services, the debate on the European minimum wage thus indicates the strong power imbalance between East and West at the European level. The concluding section summarizes the empirical results and relates them to the theoretical framework.

Summary

While a common policy position could be established in both cases, the two policy fields under inquiry differ in two regards. First, in the debate on the Services Directive, a joint position was arrived at in a process of successful lobbying, while the compromise in the discussion on the European minimum wage has so far remained strictly rhetorical. Second, the way in which the common policy position was formulated varies. In the first case representatives from the CEE countries were persuaded to adhere to the proposal of Western representatives, but in the second case, trade unionists from Poland and Hungary have taken a much more active role in the debate on the European minimum wage.

Whereas the implementation and maintenance of minimum standards constitute the object of regulations in both issues, attempts have been made by various actors to frame each issue differently, thus resulting in an increasingly evident emergence of a particular perspective on each issue. The superior political position of the Western federations derives from a combination of their greater numbers and resources, combined with their longer experience in mutual cooperation. In light of this, it is especially Western representatives who attempt to plausibly represent an idea of Social Europe that reflects their particular interests.

In the debate on the Services Directive this strategy works very well, but the case of the European minimum wage is less clear-cut. Here, the active commitment of the federations from the CEE countries to a campaign on the issue led to fierce resistance from Scandinavian representatives. They reject the idea of EU influence on wage setting, not only because they perceive it as a threat to their established role in the national collective-bargaining arena, but also because the idea of any EU interference in their national system is viewed as endangering national autonomy. At the same time, unions from the CEE countries are highly motivated to take their claim to the European level because of their comparatively weak national bargaining systems.

A comparative perspective on the two policy fields now reveals how the idea of Social Europe is put into practice in the process of European-level policy-making. While the European level does seem to be the appropriate locus of regulation when it serves the interests of Western trade unions, the same logic does not apply when it is to their disadvantage. As a consequence, the question arises about how well European trade unionism can achieve an egalitarian mode of decision-making that transcends mere lip service or blockades between diverging positions.

Conclusion

Against the backdrop of the institutional heterogeneity of the EU-28, we examined in this article the extent to which trade unions from the CEE countries participate in the development of policy positions among ETFs as meta-organizations. By taking into account the multi-level character of their organizations, it was shown how trade unionists set goals in their daily cooperative routine by negotiating interpretative frames. As the political agenda of such organizations is often set by a smaller subset of countries located in regional proximity to each other, particular attention was directed at the integration of CEE representatives into the European arena. While the consideration of Swedish, Polish, Hungarian, and ETF representatives does not cover the entire constellation among European trade unionists, the focus serves to illustrate the difficulty of joint goal setting.

While the matter at stake in both policy fields seems at first to be wage levels, a closer look reveals that in both cases conflicts arise about the more fundamental dynamics of the national collective bargaining systems, namely the mode in which wages are set between the reference frames at the national and the EU levels. Here it becomes apparent that different perceptions of the European arena motivate the national representatives to take different and partly incompatible political approaches. Especially in the case of the European minimum wage, the defensive position taken by the Nordic affiliates can be captured with Streeck's (1995: 120) concept of "institutional nationalism": the allocation of competences at a European level is accepted to the degree that does not derogate the pursuit of primary national interests. While the CEE representatives view the European arena as an appropriate locus for rule setting and policy-making, the Nordic representatives seem to be strongly dissatisfied with such a prospect. The programmatic character of this discussion makes the European minimum wage a touchstone of trade union positions towards European integration. Moreover, it may not be surprising that there is a clear tendency among the ETUC representatives to support the idea of a European minimum wage, because it gradually helps strengthen the European arena of collective bargaining. This tendency is reflected in the effort of ETUC representatives to convince the Swedes to agree with the proposal for a bottom-limit at the meeting in Copenhagen. The fact that they did not manage to persuade the Nordics illustrates the predominant impact of national institutionalism over transnational deliberation.

In relation to currently established research, the findings therefore reflect an ambiguous picture. While there were joint policy positions, they are either not effective (policy field 2) or were established in a nondeliberative manner (policy field 1). Thus some doubt must be expressed with regard to the idea put forth by Gumbrell-McCormick and Hyman (2013: 193) that a diverse leadership among European trade unions could lead to a broader repertoire of political action. If, on the one hand, we regard the participation of the CEE delegates as leadership, then no new political opportunities are opening up. If, on the other hand, we take their marginal status as an indicator of a power disequilibrium among national representatives, the idea of democratic leadership as such is called into question. By drawing on the concept of European-level socialization, the findings presented here support the counter-thesis of a persistent "importance of domestic politics" (Zürn/Checkel 2005: 1068). The strong impact of the Western affiliates within the ETUC enables them to influence the discussion in both policy fields in a way that sets their particular interests as the legitimate goal.

At the same time, an integrative moment among national trade unions is created by referring to the idealist framework of Social Europe. Despite disagreements, especially on the matter of the European minimum wage, the concept's meaning remains quite clear: in a nutshell, it is about maintaining the economic standards achieved by the Western European working class, not just as a goal in itself but as a reference point for class struggle in Central and Eastern Europe.

Studies on this topic have highlighted the fruitful cooperation between trade unions from the Western European and the CEE countries (for example, Gajewska 2009). Compliance with the traditional (i.e., Western European) concept of Social Europe by the representatives from new Member States is derived from their anticipation of the influence that market integration will have on their national labour markets (such as the evolution of equal labour and employment standards). The motives for compliance have therefore been framed as the interplay of self-interest and solidaristic orientation (Bernaciak 2012: 14).

Without contradicting these conclusions, the findings of this article can help us understand the cooperation process between CEE and Western trade union representatives. By describing the origins of the concept of Social Europe as "pretty much a Western idea," the Polish ETUC representative points to the ambiguities among the different interpretations. Thus, we can conclude that the concept was neither externally imposed in an explicit way nor deliberately embraced by the representatives from the CEE countries. Unlike the account proposed by Bernaciak and Gajewska, our findings show how the integration of the CEE representatives into the campaign against the Services Directive and also on the European minimum wage was based on influence exercised by the trade unionists from the ETFs and national organizations (in this text exemplified by the Swedes).

With reference to Fligstein's (2001) concept of social skill, this reluctance to integrate other viewpoints can, in the case of the European minimum wage, possibly be traced back to a misunderstanding over the proposal discussed at the ETUC Winter School. Here, their superior knowledge enabled the ETUC representatives to include the Nordics in the compromise. It could, moreover, be shown how representatives from Western European as well as European-level trade union organizations managed to establish the frame of Social Europe as an appropriate pattern for interpreting the situation in the case of the Freedom of Services. The presentation of a future scenario in which all European countries adapt to Western employment standards convinced Eastern European representatives to accept the idea of refraining from a strategy of offensive wage-competition.

It seems remarkable that it is first and foremost the Swedish representatives who can mobilize the frame in accordance with their pre-interpretation of an issue. If, to put it bluntly, a political measure serves their interests, it is included in the conception of Social Europe. If, however, they perceive the measure as a threat, they will frame it as a loss of national autonomy. In the case of the Services Directive, this frame setting is accompanied by the compliance of the Eastern European representatives. While there were objections to the alleged "protectionism" of Western representatives, especially among the domestic representatives, discourse inside the ETUC excluded such viewpoints as illegitimate. At the same time, the case of the debate on the European minimum wage shows how the role of the CEE representatives has changed over time. While they were unable to voice a firm position on the issue of the Services Directive, their strong demand for a campaign on a European wage floor shapes the debate in a way that makes Social Europe a contested framework. As actors mobilize the frame in order to pursue their own political goals, we can clearly detect an instrumental dimension within the concept of Social Europe.

Despite this development, the empirical material shows how the criteria necessary for a deliberative discussion (Habermas 1992) serving as a foundation of "internal social dialogue" (Hyman 2013: 175) were neglected in practice. While the European-level federations principally seem to represent their national members, their internal dynamics follow a logic of internal power imbalances and persuasion. Since these preconditions were not given, the deliberative character of the discussion does not seem to be confirmed, after all. As the interviews show, the participants themselves also perceive this deficit in the debate. At the same time, the way in which the Nordic representatives were led to compromise on the proposal about a European minimum wage shows how such ethical standards are being neglected in the practice of policy discussion. A more integrative model of policy-making will require the empowerment of CEE representatives, even at the cost of Western privileges in agenda setting.

In order to enable a more egalitarian mode of goal setting and decision-making, IG-Metall board member Hans-Jürgen Urban (2009: 313) states that the European trade unions require a democratic discursive space. As long as major discrepancies in terms of resources and degree of numerical representation exist between the countries, no such development seems very probable. One possible solution, as suggested by Evans (2010: 365), would be to increase financial support for European-level organizations through strong organizations from the core countries. However, this would require the willingness of the Western representatives to engage in real debates on an equal footing with their colleagues from the East.

Notes

1 I would like to thank David Schick, Martin Höpner, Guglielmo Meardi, Lea Elsässer, and Neil Fligstein for their helpful comments.
2 Similarly, Meardi (2002) refers to the integration of Polish workers into the EU labour market as a "Trojan Horse" for Western European labour.
3 www.etuc.org/IMG/pdf/Rapport_Congres_2011_DE_DEF.pdf (25.10.2015).
4 The Winter School is an organ that serves as forum for debates, on the basis of which the General Secretary is obliged to draft recommendations to the ETUC's Executive Committee.
5 www.etuc.org/sites/www.etuc.org/files/07-EN-Preparation-of-the-Winter-School.pdf (25.10.2015).

Literature

Ahrne, Göran; Brunsson, Nils (2008): *Meta-Organizations*. Cheltenham: Edward Elgar.

Ansell, Chris (1997): Symbolic Networks: The Realignment of the French Working Class, 1887–1894. *American Journal of Sociology* 103 (2): 359–390.

Bernaciak, Magdalena (2007): *Stop Bolkestein! An Analysis of East-West Trade. Union Mobilization. Against the Draft Services Directive*. Paper presented at Central European University.

Bernaciak, Magdalena. (2012). Social Dumping: Political Catchphrase or Threat to Labour Standards?. *Working Paper* 2012/06, European Trade Union Institute, Brüssel.

Bernaciak, Magdalena (2010): Cross-Border Competition and Trade Union Responses in the Enlarged EU. European Journal of Industrial Relations 16 (2): 119–135.

Bernaciak, Magdalena (2011): East-West European Labour Transnationalism(s). In: Bieler, Andreas; Lindberg, Ingemar (eds.): *Global Restructuring, Labour and the Challenges for Transnational Solidarity*. London: Routledge, 33–47.

Checkel, Jeffrey T. (2005): International Institutions and Socialization in Europe. *International Organization* 59 (4): 801–826.

Dufresne, Anne (2015): Euro-Unionism and Wage Policy. In: Menz, Georg et al. (ed.): *Social Policy and the Euro Crisis*. New York: Palgrave, 86–113.

Erne, Roland (2008): *European Unions. Labor's Quest for a Transnational Democracy*. Ithaca/London: Cornell University Press.

ETUC (2012). Solidarity in the Crisis and beyond: Towards a Coordinated European Trade Union Approach to Tackling Social Dumping. Discussion Note for the ETUC Winter School in Copenhagen, 7–8. February.

ETUC 2015: *Paris Manifesto*. Brussels: ETUC.

Evans, Peter, 2010: Is It Labor's Turn to Globalize? *Global Labour Journal* 1 (3): 352–379.

Fligstein, Neil, 2001: Social Skill and the Theory of Fields. *Sociological Theory* 19 (2): 105–125.

Fligstein, Neil; Doug McAdam, 2011: *A Theory of Fields*. Oxford: Oxford University Press.

Furaker, Bengt; Selden, Kristina Loven (2013): Trade Union Cooperation on Statutory Minimum Wages? *Transfer* 19 (4): 507–520.

Gajewska, Katarzyna (2009): *Transnational Labour Solidarity: Mechanisms of Commitment to Cooperation within the European Trade Union Movement*. London: Routledge.

Gardawski, Juliusz et al., 2012: *Trade Unions in Poland*. Brussels: ETUI. Report 123.

Götz, Norbert; Heidi Haggrén (eds.) (2009): *Regional Cooperation and International Organizations*. London: Routledge.

Greskovitz, Béla (2015): Ten Years of Enlargement and the Forces of Labour in Central and Eastern Europe. *Transfer* 21 (3): 269–284.

Gumbrell-McCormick, Rebecca; Hyman, Richard (2013): *Trade Unions in Western Europe*. Oxford: Oxford University Press.

Haas, Ernst B. (1958): *The Uniting of Europe*. Stanford: Stanford University Press.

Habermas, Jürgen (1992): Faktizität und Geltung. Frankfurt a.M.: Suhrkamp.

Höpner, Martin; Schäfer, Armin (2010): A New Phase of European Integration. *West European Politics* 33 (2): 344–368.

Höpner, Martin; Schäfer, Armin (2012): Embeddedness and Regional Integration. *International Organization* 66 (3): 429–455.

Hyman, Richard (2005): Trade Unions and the Politics of the European Social Model. *Economic and Industrial Democracy* 26 (1): 9–40.

Hyman, Richard (2013): European Trade Unions and the Long March through the Institutions. In: Fairbrother, Peter; Lévesque, Christian; Hennebert, Marc-Antonin (eds.): *Transnational Trade Unionism. Building Union Power*. London: Routledge, 161–179.

Johnston, Alastair Iain (2005): Conclusions and Extensions Toward Mid-Range Theorizing and Beyond Europe. *International Organization* 59 (4): 1013–1044.

Kohl, Heribert (2015): Convergence and Divergence – 10 Years Since EU Enlargement. *Transfer* 21 (3): 285–311.

Meardi, Guglielmo (2002): Trojan Horse for the Americanization of Europe? Polish Industrial Relations toward the EU. *European Journal of Industrial Relations* 8 (1): 77–99.

Meardi, Guglielmo (2012): *Social Failures of EU Enlargement. A Case of Workers Voting with their Feet*. London: Routledge.

Menz, Georg (2010): Are You Being Served? *Journal of European Public Policy* 17 (7): 971–987.

Németh, Edith. (2014). *Aufgeschoben, nicht aufgehoben: Der schwierige Weg zu einer neuen Dachgewerkschaft in Ungarn*. Bonn: Friedrich-Ebert-Stiftung.

Neumann, László (2012): Hungarian Unions. Responses to Political Challenges. *Management Revue* 23 (4): 369–385.

Peterson, Abby et al. (2011): Swedish Trade Unionism. A Renewed Social Movement? *Economic and Industrial Democracy* 33 (4): 621–647.

Platzer, Hans-Wolfgang (1997): *The Europeanisation of Industrial Relations*. In: Forschungsgruppe Europäische Gemeinschaften (FEG), Studie Nr. 10. Marburg.

Polakowski, Michal (2013): *Poland – Labor Relations and Social Dialogue 2013*. Warschau: Friedrich-Ebert-Stiftung.

Risse, Thomas (2010): *A Community of Europeans?* Cornell: Cornell University Press.

Scharpf, Fritz (2012): *Legitimacy Intermediation in the Multilevel European Polity and Its Collapse in the Euro Crisis*. MPIfG Discussion Paper 12/6.

Schulten, Thorsten (2014): *Mindestlohnregime in Europa*. Bonn: Friedrich-Ebert-Stiftung.

Streeck, Wolfgang, 1995: Politikverflechtung und Entscheidungslücke. In: Schettkat, Ronald et al. (ed.): *Reformfähigkeit*. Frankfurt a.M./New York: Campus, 101–130.

Svensson, Torsten (2013): Sweden. In: Frege, Carola; Kelly, Paul (ed.): *Comparative Employment Relations in the Global Economy*. London: Routledge, 227–244.

Turner, Lowell (1996): The Europeanization of Labour. European Journal of Industrial Relations 2 (3): 325–344.

Turner, Lowell (2005): From Transformation to Revitalization. *Journal of Industrial Relations* 32 (4): 383–399.

Urban, Hans Jürgen (2009): Gewerkschaftliche Revitalisierung in einem neoliberalen und postdemokratischen Europa? In: Scholz, Dieter et al. (Hg.): *Europa sind wir*. Münster, Westfälisches Dampfboot, 304–317.

Vaughan-Whitehead, Daniel (2003): *EU Enlargement versus Social Europe?* Cheltenham: Edward Elgar.

Zürn, Michael; Checkel, Jeffrey T. (2005): Getting Socialized to Build Bridges. *International Organization* 59 (4): 1045–1079.

Chapter 9

Comment on Seeliger

Guglielmo Meardi

The contribution by Martin Seeliger makes three important contributions to the understanding of the contested process of trade union Europeanisation. First, it reveals the instrumental meaning of 'Social Europe', dependent on relative power positions of the actors that use it to justify their negotiation standpoints and to mobilise for them. Second, it provides an empirically grounded and conceptually sophisticated mid-way position between 'optimists' and 'pessimists' on the sensitive issue of East-West union relations, which are arguably the hardest test yet of trade union capacity to elaborate positions that cover areas with different institutional, social and economic situations. Finally, it provides an understanding of the role of European-level actors (European Trade Union Federations, ETF, European Trade Union Congress, ETUC) as brokers of compromise who, despite very limited resources and formal powers, have developed the right 'social skills'. If we put these contributions together, we could draw from them the prediction that Europeanisation of trade unions – against the most Eurosceptical views – has a chance to advance, but that it will do so – against the most Euro-enthusiastic views – only in a slow and uneven way.

Power, international integration and skills are not simple concepts, of course, and the aforementioned three contributions deserve further attention and research.

Power relations on social Europe

The frustration of trade unionists from Central and Eastern Europe (CEE) towards the western-dominated European union structures is becoming increasingly apparent. It contrasts with the Euro-enthusiasm of 20 years ago, when those unionists were being invited to join the ETUC and the European Works Councils. With insight, just as the length of the European Union (EU) accession process and the unbalance of the so-called 'negotiations' on the *acquis communautaire* frustrated leaders and public opinions in the accession countries, the process of enlarging the ETUC in the early 1990s may have been too slow and somehow patronising, creating the germs for later bad feelings. Yet 20 years afterwards, it is likely that it is the current power and interest differences to be most relevant for East-West relations. And these differences are not disappearing in the current EU: in fact, centrifugal pressures are visible, and East-West diffidence is being match, since the beginning of the Euro-crisis, by similar North-South incomprehension.

Yet the power relations may be more complex than they appear. Seeliger describes the two important campaigns on minimum wages and Bolkestein as substantially western unionists' victories. The ETUC joint position on freedom of services in 2005 was not a simple imposition from the western constituencies, though. More complex exchanges were at play. The eastern unions accepted to oppose the service directive, in exchange of the western unions' acceptance of free movement and opposition (in principle) of transitional periods, which was reflected in the ETUC Declaration of 5–6 December 2005. Freedom of movement is something trade unionists from Central Europe had become very sensitive about, after feeling short-changed at the time of the enlargement. In 2000, the German Trade Union Congress (DGB) and Solidarity leaders, Dieter Schulte and Marian Krzaklewski, had signed a joint declaration on free movement that the Polish side took as support in the opposition to transitional limits – however, the DGB subsequently asked for 'temporary measures' and tacitly supported the imposition of a seven-year transitional period. I remember the overall feeling of betrayal among Central Eastern European trade unionists. On the 1st of May 2004, the date of EU enlargement, I was at the Liga trade union stand at the traditional Mayday party in the City Park of Budapest. A trade unionist received a text from some Belgian union colleague, wishing all the best with Mayday and the EU, but when he read it out, his comrades replied drily 'ask him when they are going to open up to free movement'. Positions have evolved since, and some CEE trade unionists now privately admit, especially now that Central Europe starts being affected by immigration too, that transitional periods did make sense. But it is still an issue of great symbolism, and the 2005 ETUC declaration was important: it was followed by the end of transitional periods in most old Member States in 2006–2008 (including Spain, Italy, the Netherlands and France). The ETUC position on the service directive is therefore not a simple western victory, as it was partially compensated in other parallel fields. Moreover, power relations evolve, and Seeliger already notices a substantial improvement of the new Member States' union position between his two cases: from 2005 and 2011 their influence has clearly increased.

And CEE trade unions are not alone. European social issues are not a simple East-West confrontation, as debates on the working time directive have proved. CEE labour does find some support in specific western unions in several circumstances, if for coincidental reasons rather than as an effect of coordination. This happens in particular with British and Southern

European unions. On posted workers, an issue very similar to that of the Bolkestein directive, Swiss unions have since the mid-2000s led the calls for an ETUC campaign for a 'same pay for same work in the same place' policy. This has been effectively resisted not only by eastern but also by some western (Italian, French, and especially British) unions: 'institutional nationalism' is not, it appears, exclusive of Scandinavian unions. On the minimum wage, Spanish and Greek unions are quite close to the standpoint of CEE unions. And they also use the 'social Europe' idea to their own end. If 'social Europe' has so far been used predominantly by (North)-western unions, this does not exclude elaborations and usages from the East (and South) as well.

The nature and future of the East-West divide

This brings to the nature of the East-West trade union relations in general. A strength of Seeliger's analysis is that it avoids simplistic, stereotypical explanations in terms of culture or basic legacy of the past. We are now over a generation after 1989 and current differences in interests and power are more relevant that inherited attitudes.

If we take a broader perspective and compare the rather unique configuration of trade unions in the enlarged EU with the most direct available comparator, i.e. trade unions in North-American Free Trade Agreement (NAFTA), it is possible to reach a much more positive view of the achievements of European unions. The economic gap between Mexico and the USA/Canada, and their respective weight in terms of population in 1995 were quite similar to those between old and new Member States in 2004. Collaboration between Mexican and US trade unions is overall much weaker, and confrontations between the two sides much more open than the rather disguised tensions that Seeliger describes: Mexican unions still subscribe to anti-Yankee rhetoric, and some US unions have expressed support for Trump's policies on NAFTA and on immigration from Mexico. Of course, NAFTA is a much different construct than the more politically integrated EU. But this is exactly the key point: despite all its flaws, that are today more evident than ever, the EU has had some remarkable traction in creating elements of a European polity where actors meet, discuss, often disagree but attempt to reach compromises.

The economic gap between East and West means that while both sides talk of solidarity – which may be seen as an achievement compared to other possible rhetorical repertoires – the meanings are rather different. In the West, solidarity is meant as 'obeying to the same rules' and 'fair competition': whether on concession bargaining in multinational companies, on posted workers or more broadly on tax incentives for investors and sharing the burden of refugee waves. In the poorer East, solidarity is meant in a much simpler redistribution sense: the richer West should transfer resources to the poorer East, in particular through investment, as it would happen in any large economy with economic regional differences. This redistribution argument does have a historical component: CEE – the eastern narrative goes – did not benefit from the Marshall plan, being by contrast dilapidated by the Soviet Union, and to compete in the same market needs to quickly catch up in terms of technology and infrastructure.

The definition of such divide in concomitance with tensions in the Eurozone might eventually redefine the East-West differences as centre-periphery ones. Yet, it is still too early for this. New Member States' actors, notably in Eurozone Slovakia, resist transfers to Greece with the argument that they are still (with the exceptions of Slovenia and the Czech Republic) significantly poorer than Greece in terms of GDP per capita. To explain their opposition to enter the EMU at any time soon, Solidarnosc officers start with 'why should we rush to have to pay for the Greeks?' The specific historic-structural gap between East and West seems therefore to be continuously reproduced in today's politics, and not to disappear. In an EU governance structure that incentivises national political actors to always blame the EU and other Member States, in a pattern of 'renationalisation of conflict' (Erne 2015), the fact that trade unions are still committed to social Europe and collaboration (although certainly not anymore to the EMU!), even when they differ on specific meanings of such terms, testifies that Europeanisation has set some strong, probably inextirpable roots. But it will probably take a very long season before those roots can produce appreciable fruits.

Where do unions' international 'social skills' come from?

The application of the concept of 'social skills' is one of the most original points in Seeliger's analysis. It appears that such skills allow European trade union organisations to overcome, in some cases, the well-known deficiency of their association power. In general, it is 'soft' factors like this (e.g. ideas about networks, socialisation) that help the 'Euro-optimist' side of the debate, while the 'hard' institutional and economic factors tend to support the 'Euro-pessimist' one. But do social skills also help the old Member States' union keep their control of European union organisations, at the cost of those from the new Member States?

There is here much scope for dissecting and explaining what these skills are and where they come from. Seeliger points at the utility of actors' familiarity with procedures, agenda and policy formulation in international organisations, and provides evidence on how western actors possess more of such skills than their eastern counterparts. The issues are how such evidence can be generalised, and how can we analytically distinguish between 'skills' and 'resources'. It is probably not true, in general, that eastern trade unionists are less qualified than their western ones: given the unions' stronger concentration, in the new Member States, in the public sector and among skilled workers, their levels of education are generally higher than in western Europe, where unions are (still) more strongly rooted in blue-collar professions. So it is probably job-specific skills, rather than general ones, that are lacking. Seeliger does not mention a specific skill that is of great importance in international contacts, especially if of a political nature: language competence. Some, but not yet enough, research attention has been paid to the role of language in international union collaborations, e.g. in the European Works Councils (Miller et al. 2000). It is commonly observed that British, Dutch and Scandinavian unionists possess a much better English fluency than their colleagues from other countries, and that this allows them a clear advantage in deliberative discussions. However it would be interesting to test whether the new Member States are really where the unionists with the worst English come from: my non-systematic observations point rather at the Southern Europeans (Italians, Spanish and to a lesser extent French) as worst placed. With regard to other languages that may be used in Brussels corridors or in European Works Councils (EWC) meetings, participants from the new Member States tend to have a weaker-than-average knowledge of French, but not necessarily of German. It may be expected that language provision and competences may be addressed, to some extent and over time, by adequate training and translation measures – but that in itself remains a political issue.

Seeliger rightly points to the funding structure of CEE trade unions, which, for instance in Poland and Hungary, allocate a smaller proportion of members' contributions to the national level. This translates into a 'top-light' structure that affects organisation capacities in centralised functions such as international relations. Moreover, such weakness is exacerbated by lower membership levels, much lower membership fees especially if counted in Euros, and in some cases (e.g. in Solidarnosc) weak industrial, sector-level structures, which are required for participating in European Trade Union Federations and in European Sectoral Social Dialogue. If this is considered, the problem may well not be one of 'skills', but of resources: CEE unionists may well start their functions with higher skills than the western ones, but if they lack the organisational, training, expert and financial support of their western counterparts, they will still arrive to European meetings less prepared. Which reminds us of the importance of the complex power unbalanced outlined earlier.

Specific skills are indeed important for European-level trade union activity. And they are needed for effective *research* on European trade union activity, and Seeliger's research is among the most convincing application of such skills, and possibly representative of a new generation of researchers with transnational capacities allowing them to go beyond the state of the arts and 'old' ways of thinking about Europe.

Literature

Erne, Roland (2015): A Supranational Regime that Nationalizes Social Conflict. Explaining European Trade Unions' Difficulties in Politicizing European Economic Governance. *Labor History* 56 (3): 345–368.

Miller, Doug; Tully, Barbara; Fitzgerald, Ian (2000): The Politics of Language and European Works Councils: Towards a Research Agenda. *European Journal of Industrial Relations* 6 (3): 307–323.

Chapter 10

EWC – ineffective bureaucratic body or institutionalising labour regulation at European company level?

Ludger Pries

Are European Works Councils (EWC) successful in exercising significant information and consultation functions within processes through which management and employees regulate their interests? Or are they merely a clearing-house for contacts between employee representatives from different countries and operations? From the perspective of management, do EWCs represent a burdensome bureaucratic, and possibly costly, additional institution that has to be dealt with? Or are they an important means for communication and possibly even a serious negotiating partner? Do trade unions see EWCs as helpful forums within the Europeanisation of interest representation, or are they viewed sceptically, possibly mistrustfully, as bodies that might act as competing ("syndicalist") institutions or, at most, a place at which divergent local interests encounter each other? Are EWCs little more than bodies that exist in name only, and whose work and activities pass unnoticed by the employees they aim to represent?

For many years, especially after the EWC Directive had been adopted in 1994, political debates and scientific research were concentrated in crosscut analysis of the number of EWCs established, their working conditions, and outcome. After almost a quarter of a century with the EWC Directive in force, there are opportunities for a longitudinal perspective and balance of the trajectory of EWCs. The crucial question is not just: "how many EWCs do exist and how are they working?", but the query must be: "what is the balance of the learning curve and institution building trajectory of EWCs?" In this chapter the emergence of EWCs is approached from a historical perspective of *institutionalising a European body of interest mediation and regulation* on the basis of highly differing local and national traditions and conditions of labour and its regulation.

Many arguments could be given for having such a longitudinal look at EWCs as an *institution in the making*. Therefore, first a brief overview will be given on the development of scientific research on EWCs ("Trajectories of conceptual framings and empirical research on EWCs"). Then the regulative trajectory of legal framing at European and national levels will be sketched out ("The regulative trajectory of EWC"). In "The trajectory of EWC numbers and characteristics" the on-going process of increasing numbers and differentiating characteristics of EWCs will be demonstrated, and finally some conclusions will be drawn characterising the EWC as an emerging European institution ("The EWC as an emerging European institution").[1]

Trajectories of conceptual framings and empirical research on EWCs

Interest in researching EWCs as the first cross-border institution for company-level employee representation pre-dates the 1994 adoption of the EWC Directive, but was given a substantial boost from then and following its transposition into national law until 1996. EWC research has drawn on a number of disciplinary approaches and perspectives. Roughly spoken, three phases of scientific studies on EWCs could be distinguished: the period until the adoption of the Directive in 1994, the transition period until the first decade of the new century, and since the new century. Although no clear cut could be drawn, during these three stages the main research questions and focus, and the conceptual framing varied a lot. In the following studies will be mentioned not necessarily according to their publication date, but to their main topics and framing of research.

Before enacting the EWC Directive in 1994, studies were mainly case oriented and analysed the specific functioning of – mainly company based – positive experiences of workers' participation across borders.[2] In an analysis of economic and political factors explaining the existence or non-existence of any kind of European workers' representation body, political factors were identified as having greater explanatory power than socio-economic variables; the study concluded that "voluntary supranational works councils are rooted in diverse national political and institutional conditions, especially the power and access to political and legal resources of national unions and employers" (Streeck/Vitols 1995: 268).

During the second period beginning with 1994 research was basically concerned with the implementation of the EWC Directive, with the successful establishment of EWCs and the actual activities of EWCs. From a legal perspective the specific modalities of national transposition of the Directive, either in a single country (Bercusson/Dickens 1996 for the UK; Blanke 1999 for Germany) or as a comparison of several countries (Bueggel 2002), were studied. An extensive number of studies concentrated on the content of EWC agreements. These studies demonstrate that the actual form and mode of operation of EWCs is not primarily determined by the EU Directive itself or its respective equivalent in national law, but primarily by national labour regulation traditions and by the EWC agreements negotiated by employers and employees' representatives at company level (Carley/Hall 1996; Marginson et al. 1998; Carley/Marginson 2000; Gilman/Marginson 2002).

As influencing factors mainly the *line of business* and the *headquarters* of an international company, the significance of the model EWC, as conceptualised in the supplement to the directive ("statutory model effect"), and the model character, namely "learning effect" of former EWC agreements, were identified.

Formal-legal research considered especially the effectiveness with which the Directive had been transposed (e.g. with country studies on France, Germany, Belgium, and the Netherlands in Rigaux/Dorssemont 1999; Gohde 2005). A smaller number of economic studies adopted a quantitative perspective, examining, for example, the relationship between the establishment of EWCs and salient company characteristics, such as branch or company size. An econometric analysis of voluntary EWC agreements by Addison/Belfield (2002) did not establish any significant correlation between productivity/company performance and the existence of an EWC. A more recent study by Vitols (2009: 7) looked at the social welfare impact of EWCs for shareholders, creditors, managers, and employees. It concludes that EWCs have no negative impacts on creditors and shareholders, and "clear positive benefits" (ibid.) for managers and employees.

Political science research concentrated on factors such as power, interests, institutions, and dynamic processes within a European multi-level system (Jachtenfuchs/Kohler-Koch 1996). Research from the perspective of industrial relations theory mainly focussed on the nexus constituted by the triangle of labour (workplace employee representatives and trade unions), capital (company managements and employer associations), and the state looking at EWCs' functions and operational characteristics. Ramsay (1997) looked at the extent to which EWCs promote the democratisation of work. Many studies asked whether the establishment of EWCs might add impetus to a European system of employment regulation. The EWC Directive was seen as a major step in this direction (Martin/Ross 1999; Hoffmann et al. 2002; Lecher/Platzer 2003). For Müller/Platzer (2003) the new quality of EWCs as an institution was related to three aspects: regulation, subsidiarity, and the priority of negotiation.

A number of studies concentrated on the *real function and operating mode* of EWCs differentiating four dimensions: relations between EWCs and management, EWCs and labour unions, EWCs and national interest representations, and EWC internal relations (Lecher et al. 1999; Waddington/Kerckhofs 2003; for management's view e.g. Waddington et al. 2016). Most focussed on "the 'different types' of EWC, the 'variables' influencing their operation and the 'phases' through which they develop" (Waddington/Kerckhofs 2003: 302). Lecher et al. develop a typology of European Works Councils distinguishing symbolic, service-providing, project-orientated, and participation-orientated EWCs and concluded that "(...) only a part has so far developed the traits of a real player" (Lecher et al. 2001: 200). Significant differences in participation quality were found in another broad study concluding that in many EWCs important issues are either not brought up or the quality of intra- and inter-organisational cooperation is low (Waddington/Kerckhofs 2003).[3] In this period, actor-centred views at the company level prevailed; structural factors – as national regimes of employee representation, sector- and company-specific factors, and management attitudes – were handled as context variables of EWCs (Marginson et al. 2004: 212; Telljohann 2005; Kotthoff 2006). Marginson et al. (1998) found three context factors as crucial: (1) the existence of a European management, (2) the degree of production integration at EU level, and (3) type of company ownership.

Summarising, this second period of EWC research was characterised by understanding how EWCs emerged, established, and began to work. A classical industrial relations perspective dominated with a capital-labour axis as the frame of reference. A minority of studies analysed in a broader view EWCs' impact on democracy and political regimes in general. But neither the political science-orientated European integration research (Jachtenfuchs/Kohler-Koch 1996), nor the debate on the convergence or divergence of national institutional systems in the process of globalisation (Coates 2000; Hall/Soskice 2001), nor organisation-sociological and transnationalisation research were systematically considered in EWC studies.

A third period of EWC research began during the first decade of the new century. It could be characterised by (1) shifting from a small number of case studies towards either representative or systematically contrasting research designs; (2) shifting from dealing EWCs, their structure, and outcome as the *explanandum* towards analysing EWCs also as an independent social force of democracy and economic performance; (3) approaching EWCs in their overall role and impact on European institution building; and (4) integrating increasingly conceptual frames of other disciplines than industrial relations research (Platzer 2009; Da Costa et al. 2012; Gold/Rees 2013; Marginson et al. 2013; Platzer/Rüb 2014).

The European automobile end-manufacturers (OEMs) were pioneers in establishing EWCs. By 1996, that is before expiry of the Art. 13 phase, *all* European OEMs had such committees (Hancké 2000: 55). EWCs also were established in almost all important supplier companies. Transnationalism and organisational research were introduced in broader studies of the car industry (Hertwig et al. 2011; Hauser-Dietz et al. 2016). EWCs were conceptualised as internationally operating non-profit organisations embedded in internationally operating for-profit organisations; EWCs were seen as platforms for intra-organisational information, consultation, and bargaining on workers' side as well as for inter-organisational information, consultation, and sometimes negotiation with management. Cross-border structure of companies *as well as* their EWCs were analysed in their *spatial distribution* of resources (material and personnel, power, culture, and knowledge) and their *coordination* of organisational activities.

A further line of studies in this period looks at EWCs not as *explanandum* but as *explanans* of changes in national employment relations or company structures. Hofmann et al. identified significant differences in the influence of EWCs upon national labour relations and concern-wide interest regulation structures and found an "increase in the amount and quality of information made available throughout the companies, resulting in increased transparency of business decisions and their IR consequences" (Hoffmann et al. 2002: 21). However, this only holds in companies where management has a positive stance with regard to EWC and, moreover, provides contact persons specifically for EWC representatives.

Summarising, during the three periods of EWC research sketched out so far, different theses on the possible meaning, effectiveness, and overall societal impact of EWCs can be distinguished. Roughly spoken, a more sceptical standpoint can be distinguished from a more optimistic view. For the first, Streeck (1997) criticised the missing regulatory power of EWCs, which lags far behind, that made possible by the German model of workers' participation. He also criticises the deficient link between the EWC as institution and the European socio-political regime. In this spirit EWCs are (dis)qualified as "neither European nor works councils" (Streeck 1997: 328). In a similar vein, Keller (2001) stressed the danger of "social dumping" because the EWC is not an appropriate instrument to cope with neither intra-company, nor between-company competition. For Hancké (2000) competition between different locations of the same company had even intensified since 1996 and "EWCs have failed to become a pan-European vehicle for trade union coordination" (ibid.: 55). Schulten (1997: 97) argued that there exists a "danger of a European neo-syndicalism" (with EWCs as potential partners for collective bargaining and therefore possible competitors of trade unions).

By contrast, the optimistic position argued that despite their initially limited power EWCs could develop into effective cross-border interest representation bodies. Lecher et al. (1999) argued that EWCs could develop into supportive pillars of a system of European industrial relations (ibid.: 256f). Müller/Hoffmann (2002) stated that "the actual practice usually exceeds the formal content of EWC agreement" (ibid.: 108). Telljohann (2005) found in a study of 50 EWCs that these could assume roles that went beyond their formal legal provisions (also Müller/Platzer 2003: 79).

In sum, there are little socially relevant transnational objects that have generated so much empirical studies and efforts of theoretical reflections than did the EWCs. Interestingly, during the 1990s this research mainly began by national teams or individuals based on their specific country-related tradition and training. But then scholars increasingly related their scientific efforts to the increasing amount of transnational literature on EWCs. In this respect, EWCs actually triggered the emergence of a transnational, mainly European scholarship of conceptual and empirical inquiries. It is of great interest to see how the regulative framing of EWCs developed over this period.

The regulative trajectory of EWC

The main purpose of this chapter is not analysing the development of the legal framework and regulative infrastructure of EWCs as put down in national legislation and especially in the agreements at company level. Such a systematic longitudinal cut would be of high interest but is not the main focus of this chapter; neither is there the space for dealing with other important Regulations and Directives.[4] Just some brief stages of this regulative trajectory will be sketched out. The general directive on the introduction of EWCs was passed by the European Council of Secretaries on the 22nd of September 1994 as "Council Directive 94/45/EC of 22 September 1994 on the establishment of a European Works Council or a procedure in Community-scale undertakings and Community-scale groups of undertakings for the purposes of informing and consulting employees".[5] It was the outcome of more than ten years of on-going discussions and prior attempts. The first projects of extending workers' representation across the boundaries of one nation-state were the decision of the French building company Saint Gobain Comité de Group in 1983 to include representatives of workers from outside France. In October 1985 the French electronic company Thompson signed an agreement with the European Metalworkers Federation EMF to introduce an EWC. One year later the European Commission (EC) made a "proposal to create a financial mechanism that would support 'pan-European meetings between workers' representatives in European transnational companies" (ETUC 2004: 8). In 1990 a first proposal of the EWC Directive was launched but could not be adopted because for "economic policy" there still reigned the principle of unanimity.[6]

As the social partners could not reach an agreement the EC launched and adopted the EWC Directive finally in 1994. It stipulated that in all companies with locations in at least two EU Member States (MS), each with at least 150 employees and an overall minimum of 1,000 employees in the EU, an EWC could be built.[7] In order to respect the plurality of nationally grown customs and practices of labour regulation, there was not fixed definition of how such an EWC should be built, how it should be composed and structured, and how it should work. The Directive obliged all MS that had backed it[8] to specify in national law until September 1996 several aspects like national delegating procedures for EWC. In Germany, e.g., the respective law was passed on the 28th of October 1996 by the parliament. Concerning the constitution process of EWC the Directive defined two mechanisms. During the period from September 1994 to September 1996 so-called *voluntary agreements* could be signed between workers' and employer's representatives at company level according to Article 13.

As these *voluntary agreements* did not necessarily have to accord with the alternative procedure laid down by the Directive and could deviate from the envisaged design of EWC, many companies were interested in grabbing the opportunity of reaching a voluntary agreement on the procedure of information and consultation before the alternative mechanism for constituting an EWC would take effect (Hoffmann 1997: 120; Lecher et al. 2001: 194). This second mechanism was defined in Articles 5 and 6 of the Directive and specified the building of a *special negotiating body* as the workers' representation at EU level that should negotiate with the *central management*. Election or delegating mechanisms for the *special negotiating body* should be defined in the national transposition laws of the EWC Directive. As Articles 5 and 6 required a lot of formal bargaining and included national provisions that still were to be defined, between September 1994 and September 1996 there developed much "bargaining under the shadow of the law", and some 400 so-called Article 13 agreements were finalised (Platzer et al. 2001; Kerckhofs 2003).

In Article 15 the Directive of 1994 previewed that

> not later than 22 September 1999, the Commission shall, in consultation with the Member States and with management and labour at European level, review its operation and, in particular examine whether the workforce size thresholds are appropriate with a view to proposing suitable amendments to the Council, where necessary.[9]

The actual revision process took much longer; in 2000 (long after the deadlines defined in Council Directive 94/45/EC) the EC published a report but still did not initiate the formal revision process. The first stage of the formal consultation process of the European social partners on the possible revision of the Directive started until April 2004 (ETUC 2004: 9f). Whereas unions pushed for a rapid revision, there was resistance especially from employers' side.[10] After a long period of discussions the EC finally launched a proposal for the revision, and in May 2009 the "Directive 2009/38/EC of the European Parliament and of the Council" was adopted.[11]

In a summary of the revision process, its outcomes are characterised by an Austrian union officer as a

> classic compromise. On the one hand, in comparison with the existing *acquis* the new text of the Directive contains substantial clarifications and improvements on a number of important points, which in practice will yield positive benefits, not only in new establishments, but also in the everyday operations of EWCs. The intensive lobbying of the European employers' federations, which continued right up to the wire, contributed to watering down what were originally more far-reaching plans. As a result, there was little scope for a number of central trade union demands.
>
> (Greif 2009)

In a general statement the European Trade Union Confederation (ETUC) underlined as positive points of the "New European Works Council Directive": more precise and encompassing definitions of basic terms like information and consultation rights, possible strengthening of the transnational competence of EWCs by when defining *possible* effects of company decisions at EU level, better possibilities of coordination between European and national levels of interest representation, improved (financial) means for EWC work, stronger integration of trade unions in EWC work, and extended possibilities for establishing an EWC (ETUC 2010).

A recent extensive research on the transposition of the 2009 EU Directive into national law of the 28 EU MS draws the quite sceptical conclusion that

> the quality of national transpositions differs significantly across the EU. The diversity of solutions comes as no surprise due to the inherent characteristics of any directive and EU Member States' different traditions and systems of industrial relations. What does come as a surprise, however, is the very peculiar mix consisting of, on one hand, at times very formalistic copy/paste transposition laws in some respects, combined with, on the other hand, very general, imprecise and vague with regard to aspects where the Directive needs sharp, concrete and well-defined implementation.[12]

The 2009 EWC Directive had programmed in Article 15 that "No later than 5 June 2016, the Commission shall report to the European Parliament, the Council and the European Economic and Social Committee on the implementation of this Directive, making appropriate proposals where necessary".[13] In light of this next revision round the coordinator of the transposition study concludes to

> have documented obvious and flagrant shortcomings in national laws transposing the Recast Directive. With this evidence in hand any evaluation by the European Commission that is similar in terms of perfunctoriness and laxness to that of the previous Implementation Report of 2000 (...) seems unthinkable.
>
> (Jagodzinski 2015: 190; De Spiegelaere 2016)

A generally more optimistic conclusion of the regulative trajectory of the EWC Directive is drawn in a research that focussed not on the national transposing laws, but on the effects of the 2009 Directive on the company agreements that regulate the work of EWCs. Based on the analysis of almost 1,100 EWC agreements the authors find

> a combination of direct effects from the recast and a general learning effect in the negotiation and renegotiation of EWC agreements. Which is dominant, depends on the issue under examination. The impact of the law tends to accelerate the development of EWCs as an institution in process.
>
> (De Spiegelaere/Waddington 2017: 1)

In light of the recast of the Directive in 2009 and corresponding management policies and practices, in a recent analysis of EWCs the authors (Waddington et al. 2016: 75) conclude:

> The notion of EWCs being on a learning curve is substantiated by responses to interviewees to questions on the Recast Directive. The dominant response from interviewees was that the Recast Directive generated no need for change as EWC practices and agreements were already compliant with the new requirements prior to the adoption of the Recast Directive.

In sum, this short review of the regulative trajectory reveals a surprising European and national dynamic of developing the formal-normative framework of EWC. After long debates the Directive of 1994 set substantially new standards and initiated a process of defining a European legal framework for workers' participation in companies active in several EU MS. The 1994 Directive was transposed into national laws, and a substantial revision process led to a recast of the Directive in 2009. Less than ten years later there began the next round of revision of the 2009 Directive. Meanwhile employer associations tended to slow down the revision processes and further legal development of the Directive; unions generally criticised it as too slow. Social partners and scientists agree that the 2009 Directive represents a substantial deepening and differentiation of the 1994 Directive, although national transposition in many MS seems to have been more a mechanic copy-paste process. The latter could be interpreted in at least two ways. First, it could be a signal of a certain resistance or lack of interest of MS and/or their social partners to fully integrate and adapt the European EWC framework into national legislation. Second, it could reflect the fact that EWCs, meanwhile, are accepted as part of European institution building and that transposing the 2009 Directive is perceived just as "business as usual". The following sections allow for a better grasp of the actual development of EWC practice.

The trajectory of EWC numbers and characteristics

According to the phases of the regulatory trajectory of EWC, it is to expect that the total number of EWCs, their distribution according to countries of companies' headquarters, their type according to the character of corresponding agreements, etc. also reveal specific routes of development since the 1990s. A first phase runs from the mid-1980s to 1994, and it was a time when voluntarily agreed-upon employee bodies of information and consultation were created. In this period 49 EWCs were created in 46 companies.[14] The second phase reaches from the period of the passing of the

EU directive in September 1994 to its transformation into national law in September 1996. During this phase a high number of so-called voluntary agreements were reached on the basis of Article 13 of the EWC directive. As these did not necessarily have to accord with the procedure laid down by the directive and it was possible to deviate from the envisaged design, many companies were interested in grabbing the opportunity of reaching a voluntary agreement on the procedure of information and consultation before the directive took effect (Hoffmann 1997:120; Lecher et al. 2001: 194). During this period of "bargaining under the shadow of the law" the number of agreements grew rapidly. Almost 400 so-called Article 13 agreements were finalised (Kerckhofs 2003). A third, so-called Article 6 phase runs from the period after September 1996, that is after the deadline for implementing the 1994 Directive into national law, until the turn of the century. During this period EWCs were founded and stabilised according to standard legal procedures, and the growth of the overall number of EWCs still was significant. A fourth period begins with the new century and could be characterised by a still but smoothly growing number of EWCs.

Figure 10.1 reveals the four phases mentioned before. Substantial expansion of the number of EWCs concentrates in 1996 as indicated in the total number of active EWCs and in the number of newly created EWCs in that year. The number of dissolved EWCs in general is very low at about 2%, it oscillated between 2% and 4.6% between 1998 and 2007, and it was lower

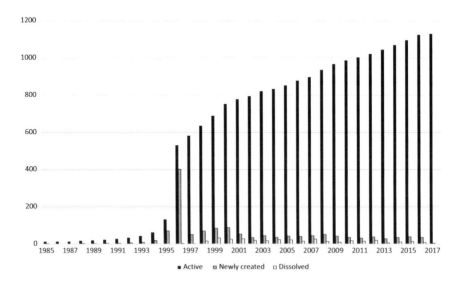

Figure 10.1 EWCs and SE works councils 1985–2017.

Source: own elaboration based on ETUI (www.ewcdb.eu/stats-and-graphs); numbers for 2017 provisional.

than 2% since 2008. According to European Trade Union Institute (ETUI) there are 1,083 multinationals having an (or sometimes more than one) EWC; in total there existed 1,126 EWCs in 2017.[15] Dissolutions of EWCs often are due to mergers or other changes of companies (De Spiegelaere/ Jagodzinski (2015: 15). When interpreting Graph 1 one has to take into account the significant increase of the numbers of EU MS, especially with the EU-8 extension in 2004. It is worth to note that the dynamics of EWC growth was not significantly broken by the financial and economic crisis of 2007. The general observation to be made is that in terms of their volume EWCs extended very dynamically until 1996, then at a slower but still substantial pace and since the 21st century in a moderate manner. The number of workers represented by EWCs grew constantly to some 19–20 million.[16] De Spiegelaere/Jagodzinski (2015: 13) summarise:

> The effect of voluntary establishment of EWCs has never been reproduced since 1996. It did not happen in 2004 with the EU enlargement after the accession of ten new Member States; nor did the 2007 EU enlargement have a significant effect on the number of EWCs created. With the entry into force of the EWC Recast Directive (2009/38/EC) in 2011, a similar window of opportunity as in 1994–96 was opened for agreements signed between 2009 and 2011. Yet this time, contrary to expectations of the European law-makers, no radical change in the number of EWCs created was observed.

A closer look to how the total number of EWCs is composed and developed by important characteristics reveals some interesting results. As mentioned in "The regulative trajectory of EWC", there are two different types of agreements that could be the basis for an EWC, Article 6 and Article 13. Until 1996, the latter gave more freedom to the negotiating partners, whereas the former only permits agreements in the direct regulation framework of the 1994 and 2009 Directives and the corresponding national transpositions. As already mentioned, during the second phase of the regulatory trajectory and of the practical expansion of EWCs there prevailed agreements according to Article 13. This situation changed substantially until 2015: "Most of the EWCs (49%) are the so-called Article 6 EWCs. These EWCs are fully regulated by the EWC Directive of 1994 and the 2009 Recast Directive. On the other hand, 39% of the existing EWCs are 'pre-directive' EWCs" (De Spiegelaere/Jagodzinski 2015: 13). Almost half of the pre-directive EWCs renegotiated their original agreement (ibid.: 14). There is also a trend that the share of EWCs founded in the new and in certain aspects extended legal figure of the European Company SE[17] is increasing: "9% of current EWCs are established in SEs and the share is rising" (ibid.: 13). The distribution of EWCs in the different economic sectors is not completely equilibrated.

More than 850 EWCs (three quarters) concentrate in three sectors: metal industry, service sector, and chemical industry:

> In sectors such as textiles, transport and public services, the numbers of EWCs are significantly smaller and the number of newly created EWCs tends to increase slightly over time. Generally speaking, the reason for the variation in numbers of EWCs between sectors is their differing characteristics. Specifically, one of the main reasons for these significant sectoral differences in terms of EWCs is the presence of multinationals covered by the directive.
>
> (ibid.: 16)

Concerning the countries of headquarters of companies with an EWC, from the very beginning there was a high concentration of EWCs in companies headquartered in Germany (21%), the USA (15%), France (12%), United Kingdom (10%), and Sweden and the Netherlands (6% each).[18] This country structure and its relative stability over time are not as surprising. It reflects mainly the strength of the corresponding countries' multinationals in the main sectors of EWC concentration:

> More than half of all EWCs are established in firms headquartered in Germany, France, the UK, Sweden or the Netherlands. Given the size of these economies this should come as no surprise. What is striking, however, is the low number of EWCs set up in companies headquartered in the new Member States that joined the EU after 2004. There are only five Hungarian companies with an EWC and one company from each of Czechia, Poland and Cyprus.
>
> (ibid.: 18)

Interestingly, almost a quarter (23%) of all EWC companies have their headquarters in the USA, Switzerland, Japan, and Canada, that is, outside the EU. In qualitative case studies it could be shown that many companies not headquartered in the EU were quite sceptical at the beginning of EWC work, but found the positive functions it could have for the company as well (e.g. Hauser-Ditz et al. 2016). It is also worth to mention that almost 42% of the companies with an EWC employ less or up to 5,000 employees in the European Economic Area (EEA).[19] Thirty-four per cent of EWC companies have more than 10,000 workers, and only 17% are medium sized (between 5,000 and 10,000). This polarised structure between companies with smaller or very high numbers of employment in the EEA.

A final structural element of EWCs to mention is their composition by representatives of management *and* workers or only of workers (Figure 10.2). Since the beginning there was a predominance (of about two thirds) of EWCs as mixed bodies, often called the French model because it assimilates

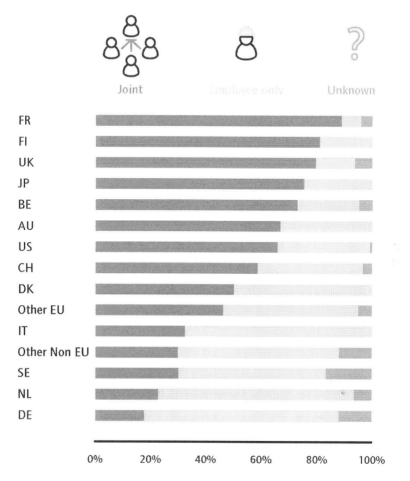

Figure 10.2 EWC composition according to headquarter of company.
Source: De Spiegelaere and Jagodzinski (2015: 20).

to the French national way of workers' participation in the comités d'entreprise. In contrast, the other EWCs are purely employee representations – the so-called "German model". There is no general trend to increase or marginalise one of these two options, but mainly a stable distribution of the relative weight of both models according to country traditions of labour regulation. One identifiable tendency is that those newly established EWCs in SEs are mainly structured according to the German model; 69% of all SE works councils are composed only by employees (but EWCs in Ses represent only a tenth of all EWCs): "This is not surprising given the fact that most SE works councils operate in companies headquartered in Germany" (De Spiegelaere/Jagodzinski 2015: 20; see also ibid.: 44f). It has to be seen in the future if SEs will extend significantly in number and how their composition will develop.

Summarising, the development of EWCs since the 1990s reflects not only a considerable regulative trajectory, but also an expansion of the number of EWCs active in Europe. Therein, the number of Article 6-based EWCs is increasing substantially since the Article 13 option ended in 1998. Article 6-based EWCs have a higher probability to make full use of the provisiones of the EWC Directives. Although still in a clear minority position, the number of EWCs in SEs is growing, and their competences go even further:

> They do stand out as being more extensive than the average in terms of competences (both procedural and substantive), numbers of meetings and facilities for employee representatives such as training and guaranteed access to premises. In their essential characteristics, however, SE works councils may be said to resemble EWCs in virtually every respect.
> (De Spiegelaere/Jagodzinski 2015: 45)

All in all, the actual volume and structure of EWCs does not indicate any crisis or decrease of this relatively new European institution. The opposite could be stated: in little more than two decades EWCs established and are of increasing significance as innovative institutions of labour regulation at European company level.

The EWC as an emerging European institution

Looking at EWCs in a longitudinal perspective finally invites us to draw some conclusions on this emerging European institution of labour regulation. We take the concept of institution and institution building not just in a legal way but understand institution in a sociological way as (1) inherited action programmes (laws/rules, norms, cognitive maps) that (2) structure certain areas of social life and action of extended social groups; (3) could extend at local, national, supranational, global, or transnational level; (4) emerge and stabilise by habitualising, making explicit, typifying, and formalising; and (5) provide for social identity, stability, integration, and predictability (Pries/Seeliger 2013). In such a perspective during the last quarter of a century the EWC emerged and institutionalised in an unpredicted speed and intensity. In this historically quite short period the EWC demonstrated a strong and dynamic trajectory concerning his regulative trajectory, as presented in section "The regulative trajectory of EWC". Since the 1994 Directive the number of EWCs increased considerably, and most of them stabilised as transnational bodies intra-organisational and inter-organisational networking, information, consultation and sometimes negotiation, as demonstrated in "The trajectory of EWC numbers and characteristics".

Finally, in "Trajectories of conceptual framings and empirical research on EWCs" it could be shown that EWCs also led to an institutionalised branch of scientific research with a vivid theoretical and empirical trajectory.

Approaching EWCs in a dynamic perspective of trajectory and a process of institutionalisation invites us to ask for their development potential in the future. At least three tendencies could be identified that are not necessarily established in a huge number of EWCs already but classify as emerging capabilities. First, EWCs could have an impact on the *Europeanisation of labour regulation* that goes far beyond its initial objectives and the companies directly involved. As demonstrated in many studies EWCs in general fuel a culture of social dialogue, of taking workers' interest as a necessary part of economic and social life, and of looking for win-win solutions in situations of conflict – in place of a logic of class conflict and lose-lose outcomes. Whereas management, especially of those countries not used to deal with plant or company level workers' representative bodies, during the first years after the 1994 Directive was sceptical or negative of EWCs, it then learned that EWCs could be useful for intra-company communication (Hauser-Ditz et al. 2016) and even for company restructuring.

Waddington et al. (2016: 77) conclude,

> that the breadth of the value added by EWCs has been extended since initial studies of the topic [...] as managers have 'tailored' EWCs to serve the interests of companies. In particular, interviewees report the benefits of bottom-up communication via the EWC that were not mentioned in earlier studies and the introduction of more sophisticated means to use EWCs to facilitate and expedite corporate restructuring.

From the viewpoint of trade unions (ETUC 2010: 4) EWCs could be crucial for a multi-level Europeanisation of union cooperation and labour regulation, as they offer "an important opportunity for employee representatives and their trade unions at the local and national levels to further develop and deepen their own communication and cooperation processes on a day to day basis at the company level and beyond".

The possible Europeanisation effects of EWCs are especially important for the new EU accession states. In a study Voss (2006) found that due to historical experiences of state socialism and the role of official unions in the Czech Republic, Hungary, Poland, and Slovakia there is little tradition of balanced bargaining between the social partners, and management is quite sceptical with respect to workers' participation. The author underlines the "importance of the European Works Councils as the key institution of employee cross-country information, consultation and, to an increasing extent, negotiation processes with management" (ibid.: 46). Ziltener/ Gabathuler (2016) found that EWCs are of great importance for Switzerland as a non-EU country as Swiss employees are integrated in some 150 EWCs and play a significant role there.

A second potential refers to the *actual negotiation capacity of EWCs*. From the very beginning the more sceptical voices on the role of EWCs, mainly from unions and some scientists, stressed the fact that EWCs only were given legal competencies of information and consultation but not of negotiation. Thus, compared e.g. to the German Works Councils they seemed to be week or, in a quite defeatist way, "neither European nor works councils" (Streeck 1997: 328). But such critiques often were unsophisticated, first because not analysing EWCs in a dynamic perspective as potentialities, and second because taking legal norms as realities. The last aspect is misleading in two ways. First, legal norms must not be lived in practice; even in a country like Germany the majority of Works Councils actually is not fully exploiting its co-determination rights (Hauser-Ditz et al. 2008). Second, social practice could go far beyond legal norms. In the case of EWCs, Mark Carley (2001: 16) in 2001 found some cases, where company agreements on the work of EWCs explicitly included right to negotiate joint texts: "the agreements on which the EWCs at Air France, Danone and Sara Lee Personal Products are based provide explicitly for joint texts to be negotiated".

In a joint research project on eight UK- and USA-headquartered companies with an EWC Marginson et al. (2004: 221) found quite strong co-determination:

> In four cases [...] the implementation of one or more management decisions was reported to have been modified as a result of the EWC process. And in one of these cases [...] EWC intervention has also changed the substance of a management decision. In the other four cases the EWC has had an impact on neither the substance nor the implementation of management decisions.

For implementing transnational agreements in European companies the active involvement of actor groups is more important than the legal-formal competencies given by such contracts (Sobczak 2012).

A third crucial potentiality of EWCs that goes far beyond their regulative framing and primary role refers to their possible *leverage effects* for specific countries and actor groups. Some already mentioned sceptical views hold that EWCs often are just extensions of the powerful centres of labour regulation in the home country of European companies. In a recent study Cavallini et al. 2016 started from this position:

> Much of the literature suggests that employee representatives from the home country of a multinational company are likely to mould EWC

structures in accordance with their own national backgrounds and have greater confidence in dealing with central management in EWC meetings.

(ibid.: 115)

Taking the case of the EWC at UniCredit and analysing the role of Italian, German, and Austrian employee representatives they found

that minority delegations, when they have the benefit of strong national institutional arrangements and less fragmented union patterns, are more likely to be cohesive and experienced and therefore are able to challenge management and sometimes win significant arguments over strategy.

(ibid.)

Obviously it depends on actor constellations and strategies to exploit the potentials of EWCs for local or national interests. There is also empirical evidence that EWCs could be used to extend the positions of workers' representative bodies especially in countries with weak legal resources (e.g. Costa 2013). EWCs also could extend their legally given role and function by dealing with International Framework Agreements (IFAs; Dehnen 2013; Dehnen/Pries 2014). In an extensive analysis of IFAs and based on additional case studies in three companies Dehnen (2013: 577) also includes the role of Global Union Federations (GUFs) and concludes that EWCs "can become main actors in negotiating and implementing international framework agreements (IFAs) about core labour standards in multinational companies. [...] internal bargaining between EWCs and GUFs influences negotiations with management". In a recent study several scholars discussed the opportunities of a "transnational collective bargaining at company level" and the role of EWCs in this (Schömann et al. 2012). EWCs finally have a potential not only for European actor groups and extended topics of negotiation, but could induce or fuel the global level of interest representation and labour regulation. There is not only intensive interaction between existing World Works Councils and their corresponding EWC partners (Rüb 2002), but EWCs could also be the platform for extending their activities and induce the building of worldwide labour regulation in companies (De Spiegelaere/Jagodzinski 2015: 13).

All in all, in a longitudinal perspective of the three decades EWCs more and more became an increasingly important European institution of transnational labour regulation. EWCs still have a lot of potentialities. They could be considered a crucial instrument of societal Europeanisation and as an institution in process (Waddington 2011). As demonstrated by the complex processes of European rule setting and national adaption or, vice versa, national or company initiatives that influence European regulative framing, EWCs are far away from leading to a homogenisation and convergence of labour regulation in the EU; however, there is not only heterogeneity and divergence. As demonstrated for the process of identity building and belongings (Pries 2013) and for business strategies in general (Pries/ Erol 2017) there seems to work a complex dialectic of convergent divergence and of divergent convergence of local, national, and European labour regulation. Future research could demonstrate that is at the very centre of Europeanisation in general and also in the field of EWC's institutionalisation.

Notes

1 I appreciate research assistance of Katrina Böse.
2 See e.g. Blanpain (1998: 30ff) and the literature cited there.
3 Four hundred seventy-two EWC-members from five countries and 222 companies were interviewed (ibid.; 332).
4 See e.g. Council Regulation (EC) No. 2157/2001 of 8 October 2001 on the Statute for a European company (SE) and Council Directive 2001/86/EC of 8 October 2001 supplementing the Statute for a European company with regard to the involvement of employees: http://eur-lex.europa.eu/legal-content/EN/TXT/?uri=uriserv:l26016; EU general rules on employee information and consultation: http://eur-lex.europa.eu/legal-content/EN/TXT/?uri=URISERV%3Ac10817; for general overview see www.worker-participation.eu/.
5 See http://eur-lex.europa.eu/legal-content/EN/TXT/?uri=URISERV%3Ac10805 and http://eur-lex.europa.eu/legal-content/EN/TXT/?uri=celex:31994L0045.
6 For the development and continuous topic extension of the Qualified Majority Voting, see e.g. www.euro-know.org/europages/dictionary/q.html.
7 As an alternative to an EWC as a special body the directive offered the option of defining procedures of information and consultation at the European level of a company – this option was of minor importance in the implementation of the EWC-Directive; the basic idea of information and consultation rights in all companies in the EU was strengthened with the Directive 2002/14/EC (general framework for informing and consulting employees in the EU); see http://eur-lex.europa.eu/legal-content/EN/TXT/?uri=URISERV%3Ac10817.
8 Great Britain made use of its opting-our option and withdrew from the entire process, but only to join the EWC plan after Labour's electoral victory in 1997.
9 http://eur-lex.europa.eu/legal-content/EN/TXT/?uri=celex:31994L0045.
10 See http://eur-lex.europa.eu/legal-content/EN/TXT/?uri=COM:2008:0419:FIN, point 10. For employers' resistance and the revision debate e.g. Altmeyer (2004).
11 See http://eur-lex.europa.eu/procedure/EN/2008_141 and http://eur-lex.europa.eu/legal-content/EN/TXT/?uri=CELEX:32009L0038.
12 Jagodzinski (2015: 180); see also http://blogs.lse.ac.uk/netuf/2016/05/24/european-works-councils-at-a-turning-point/; http://blogs.lse.ac.uk/netuf/2015/12/18/european-works-councils-progress-and-a-long-road-ahead/; for the transposition report in the UK e.g. see www.gov.uk/government/uploads/system/uploads/attachment_data/file/210140/a10-895-implementation-european-works-council-directive-response.pdf.
13 http://eur-lex.europa.eu/LexUriServ/LexUriServ.do?uri=OJ:L:2009:122:0028:0044:EN:PDF.

14 See Kerckhofs (2003: 15); the term "EWC" is used here as a catch all for quite different forms of collective bodies of workers' participation that often had quite different denominations.
15 See www.ewcdb.eu/stats-and-graphs.
16 De Spiegelaere and Jagodzinski estimate some 19 million for 2015; as the total number of EWCs increased, the number probably is a little bit higher in 2017; see http://blogs.lse.ac.uk/netuf/2015/12/18/european-works-councils-progress-and-a-long-road-ahead/.
17 For details of the Societas Europaea SE see www.etui.org/Topics/Worker-Participation/European-Company-SE; Stollt and Wolters (2011); Rosenbohm (2014).
18 See www.ewcdb.eu/stats-and-graphs; De Spiegelaere and Jagodzinski (2015: 16).
19 For the EEA see e.g. www.efta.int/eea.

Literature

Addison, John T.; Belfield, Clive R. (2002). 'What Do We Know about the New European Works Councils? Some Preliminary Evidence from Britain'. *Scottish Journal of Political Economy* 49 (4): 418–444.

Altmeyer, Werner (2004): Arbeitnehmer hoffen auf eine Halbierung. *Personalführung* 9, 66–70.

Bercusson, Brian; Dickens, Linda (1996): *Equal Opportunities and Collective Bargaining in Europe.* Dublin: European Commission.

Blanke, Thomas (1999): Recht und Praxis der Europäischen Betriebsräte. *Kritische Justiz* 32 (4): 497–526.

Blanpain, Roger (1998): *European Works Councils in Multinational Enterprises. Background Working Experience.* Multinational Enterprises Programme, Working Paper No. 83. Geneva: ILO.

Bueggel, Anneliese (2002): *Comparative Tables on EWC Legal Proceedings (Court and Out-of-Court/Extrajudicial) in the EU Member States.* www.emf-fem.org/content/download /17654/184737/ version/2/file/English.pdf (accessed 30 April 2010).

Carley, Mark (2001): *Bargaining at European Level? Joint Texts Negotiated by European Works Councils.* European Foundation for the Improvement of Living and Working Conditions. Dublin: Eurofound.

Carley, Mark; Hall, Mark (1996): Comparative Analysis of Agreements. In: *Social Europe, Agreements on Information and Consultation in European Multinationals* Supplement 5/95, 13–40. Luxembourg: Office for Official Publications of the European Communities.

Carley, Mark; Marginson, Paul (2000): *Negotiating European Works Councils. A Comparative Study of Article 6 and Article 13 Agreements.* European Foundation for the Improvement of Living and Working Conditions. Dublin: Eurofound.

Cavallini, Michaela; Gold, Michael; Royle, Tony; Senatori, Iacopo (2016): Home Country Advantage? The Influence of Italian, German and Austrian Employee Representatives in the UniCredit European Works Council. *European Journal of Industrial Relations* 22 (2): 115–130.

Coates, David (2000): *Models of Capitalism. Growth and Stagnation in the Modern Era.* Cambridge: Polity Press.

Costa, Hermes Augusto (2013): European Works Councils between Formal Requirements and Good Practices: The Potential for Further Development Based on Evidence from Portugal. *Transfer: European Review of Labour and Research* 19 (4): 553–567.

Da Costa, Isabell; Pulignano, Valeria; Rehfeldt, Udo; Telljohann, Volker (2012): Transnational Negotiations and the Europeanization of Industrial Relations: Potential and Obstacles. *European Journal of Industrial Relations* 18 (2): 123–137.

De Spiegelaere, Stan (2016): *Too Little, Too Late? Evaluating the European Works Councils Recast Directive.* Brussels: ETUI.

De Spiegelaere, Stan; Jagodzinski, Romuald (2015): *European Works Councils and SE Works Councils in 2015. Facts & Figures.* Brussels: ETUI.

De Spiegelaere, Stan; Waddington, Jeremy (2017): Has the Recast Made a Difference? An Examination of the Content of European Works Council Agreements. *European Journal of Industrial Relations*, Online First.

Dehnen, Veronika (2013): Transnational Alliances for Negotiating International Framework Agreements: Power Relations and Bargaining Processes between Global Union Federations and European Works Councils. *British Journal of Industrial Relations* 51 (3): 577–600.

Dehnen, Veronika; Pries, Ludger (2014): International Framework Agreements: A Thread in the Web of Transnational Labour Regulation. *European Journal of Industrial Relations* 20 (4): 335–350.

ETUC (European Trade Union Council) (2004): *Revising the EWC Directive.* Brussels: ETUC.

ETUC (European Trade Union Council) (2010): *On the Offensive for More and Stronger European Works Councils. The New European Works Council Directive ('Recast').* Brussels: ETUC.

Gilman, Mark; Marginson, Paul (2002): 'Negotiating European Works Councils: Contours of Constrained Choice'. *Industrial Relations Journal* 33 (1): 36–51.

Gohde, Hellmut (2005): *Company Agreements – A Practical Guide. European Works Councils. Analysis and Recommendations.* Frankfurt a.M.: Bund-Verlag.

Gold, Michael; Rees, Chris (2013): What Makes an Effective European Works Council? Considerations Based on Three Case Studies. *Transfer, European Review of Labour and Research* 19 (4): 539–551.

Greif, Wolfgang (2009): The Revised Directive on European Works Councils. Download: www.worker-participation.eu/content/download/2368/21387/file/FAQ-revision-EN-final.pdf.

Hall, Peter A.; Soskice, David (eds.) (2001): *Varieties of Capitalism: The Institutional Foundations of Comparative Advantage.* Oxford: Oxford University Press.

Hancké, Bob (2000): European Works Councils and Industrial Restructuring in the European Motor Industry. *European Journal of Industrial Relations* 6 (1): 35–59.

Hauser-Ditz, Axel; Hertwig, Markus; Pries, Ludger (2008): *Betriebliche Interessenregulierung in Deutschland. Arbeitnehmervertretung zwischen demokratischer Teilhabe und ökonomischer Effizienz.* Frankfurt a.M./New York: Campus.

Hauser-Ditz, Axel; Hertwig, Markus; Pries, Ludger; Rampeltshammer, Luitpold (2016): *A Solution for Transnational Labour Regulation? Company Internationalization and European Works Councils in the Automotive Sector.* New York: Peter Lang.

Hertwig, Markus; Pries, Ludger; Rampeltshammer, Luitpold (2011): Stabilizing Effects of European Works Councils: Examples from the Automotive Industry. *European Journal of Industrial Relations* 17 (3): 209–226.

Hoffmann, Aline; Hall, Mark; Marginson, Paul; Müller, Torsten (2002). *If the Shoe Fits: The Effects of European Works Councils on Industrial Relations at National Level in Eight US- and UK-based Multinationals.* Unpublished paper. Coventry: University of Warwick.

Hoffmann, Reiner (1997). Europäische Betriebsräte – ein Baustein zur Europäisierung industrieller Beziehungen. In: Deppe, Joachim; Hoffmann, Reiner; Stützel, Wieland (eds.): *Europäische Betriebsräte. Wege in ein soziales Europa.* Frankfurt a.M./New York, 115–131.

Jachtenfuchs, Markus; Kohler-Koch, Beate (1996): Regieren im dynamischen Mehrebenensystem. In: Jachtenfuchs, Markus; Kohler-Koch, Beate (ed.): *Europäische Integration.* Opladen: Westdeutscher Verlag, 15–44.

Jagodzinski, Romuald (ed.) (2015): *Variations on a Theme? The Implementation of the EWC Recast Directive.* Brussels: ETUI.

Keller, Berndt (2001): *Europäische Arbeits- und Sozialpolitik.* München: Oldenbourg.

Kerckhofs, Peter (2003): Europäische *Betriebsräte. Fakten und Zahlen,* Brüssel: ETUI.

Kotthoff, Hermann (2006): Lehrjahre des Europäischen Betriebsrats. Zehn Jahre transnationale Arbeitnehmervertretung. Berlin: edition sigma.

Lecher, Wolfgang; Nagel, Bernhard; Platzer, Hans-Werner (1999): *The Establishment of European Works Councils. From Information Committee to Social Actor.* Aldershot: Ashgate.

Lecher, Wolfgang; Platzer, Hans-Werner (2003): Europäische Betriebsräte. In: Schroeder, Wolfgang; Weßels, Berhard (ed.): Die *Gewerkschaften in Politik und Gesellschaft der Bundesrepublik Deutschland.* Wiesbaden: VS Verlag, 588–613.

Lecher, Wolfgang, Platzer, Hans-Werner; Rüb, Stefan; Weiner, Klaus Peter (2001): *European Works Councils: Developments, Types and Networking.* Aldershot: Ashgate.

Marginson, Paul; Gilman, Mark; Jacobi, Otto; Krieger, Hubert (1998): *Negotiating European Works Councils. An Analysis of Agreements under Article 13.* European Foundation for the Improvement of Living and Working Conditions. Dublin: Eurofound.

Marginson, Paul; Hall, Mark; Hoffmann, Aline; Müller, Torsten (2004): The Impact of European Works Councils on Management Decision-Making in UK and US-Based Multinationals: A Case Study Comparison. *British Journal of Industrial Relations* 42 (2): 209–233.

Marginson, Paul; Lavelle, Jonathan; Quintanilla, Javier; Adam, Duncan; Sánchez-Mangas, Rocío (2013): Variation in Approaches to European Works Councils in Multinational Companies. *ILR Review* 66 (3): 618–644.

Martin, Andrew; Ross, George (1999): In the Line of Fire. The Europeanization of Labor Representation. In: Martin, Andrew; Ross, George (ed.): *The Brave New World of European Labour. European Trade Unions at the Millennium.* New York/Oxford: Bergahn, 312–367.

Müller, Torsten; Hoffmann, Aline (2002): Euro-Betriebsräte unter der Lupe. Zusammenfassender Bericht über die Forschungsliteratur. *Industrielle Beziehungen* 9 (1): 103–111.

Müller, Torsten; Platzer, Hans-Werner (2003): European Works Councils: A New Mode of EU Regulation and the Emergence of a European Multi-Level Structure of Workplace Industrial Relations. In: Keller, Berndt and Platzer, Hans-Werner (ed.): *Industrial Relations and European Integration*. Ashgate: Aldershot, 58–84.

Platzer, Hans-Werner (2009): Approaching and Theorizing European Works Councils: Comments on the Emergence of a European Multi- Level – Structure of Employee Involvement and Participation. In: Hertwig, Markus; Pries, Ludger; Rampeltshammer, Luitpold (eds.): *European Works Councils in Complementary Perspectives*. Brussels: ETUI, 47–69.

Platzer, Hans-Wolfgang; Rüb, Stefan (2014): It Takes Two to Tango: Management and European Company Agreements. *Transfer, European review of labour and research* 20 (2): 255–270.

Platzer, Hans-Wolfgang; Rüb, Stefan; Weiner, Klaus-Peter (2001): European Works Councils – Article 6 Agreements: Quantitative and Qualitative Developments. *Transfer: European Review of Labour and Research* 7 (1): 90–113.

Pries, Ludger (2013): Ambiguities of Global and Transnational Collective Identities. *Global Networks* 13 (1): 22–40.

Pries, Ludger; Erol, Serife (2017): Social Change and Business Development through Transnational Companies in Turkey. In: Eurasian Studies in Business and Economic, Vol. 7. In: Bilgin, Mehmet H.; Danis, Hakan, Demir, Ender; Can, Ugur (eds.): *Regional Studies on Economic Growth, Financial Economics and Management. Proceedings of the 19th Eurasia Business and Economics Society Conference*. Berlin: Springer, 11–32.

Pries, Ludger; Seeliger, Martin (2013): Work and Employment Relations in a Globalized World: The Emerging Texture of Transnational Labour Regulation. *Global Labour Journal* 4 (1): 26–47.

Ramsay, Harvie (1997): 'Fool's Gold? European Works Councils and Workplace Democracy. *Industrial Relations Journal*, 28 (4): 314–323.

Rigaux, Marie-Francoise; Dorssemont, Filip (1999): European Works Councils. A Legal Analysis of the European Works Council: Towards a Revision of the Directive (EC) No. 94/45? Antwerp.

Rosenbohm, Sophie (2014): *Verhandelte Mitbestimmung: Die Arbeitnehmerbeteiligung in der Europäischen Aktiengesellschaft*. Frankfurt am Main: Campus.

Rüb, Stefan (2002): *World Works Councils and Other Forms of Global Employee Representation in Transnational Undertakings. A Survey*. Arbeitspapier 55. Düsseldorf: Hans-Böckler-Stiftung.

Schömann, Isabelle; Jagodzinski, Romuald; Boni, Guido; Clauwaert, Stefan; Glassner, Vera; Jaspers, Teun (2012): *Transnational Collective Bargaining at Company Level. A New Component of European Industrial Relations?* Brussels: ETUI.

Schulten, Thorsten (1997): Europäische Modernisierungskoalitionen? Der Beitrag Europäischer Betriebsräte zur Neuordnung der Arbeitsbeziehungen in Europa. In: Flecker, Jörg (ed.): *Jenseits der Sachzwanglogik. Arbeitspolitik zwischen Anpassungsdruck und Gestaltungschancen*. Berlin: Edition Sigma, 71–102.

Sobczak, André (2012): Ensuring the Effective Implementation of Transnational Company Agreements. *European Journal of Industrial Relations* 18 (2): 139–151.

Stollt, Michael; Wolters, Elwin (2011): Worker Involvement in the European Company (SE). A Handbook for Practitioners. Brussels: ETUI.

Streeck, Wolfgang (1997): Neither European nor Works Councils: A Reply to Paul Knutsen. *Economic and Industrial Democracy* 18 (2): 325–337.

Streeck, Wolfgang; Vitols, Sigurt (1995): The European Community: Between Mandatory Consultation and Voluntary Information. In: Streeck, Wolfgang; Rogers, Joel (eds.): *Works Councils: Consultation, Representation and Cooperation in Industrial Relations.* Chicago: University of Chicago, 243–281.

Telljohann, Volker (2005): The European Works Councils – A Role beyond the EC Directive? *Transfer. European Review of Labour and Research* 11 (1): 81–96.

Vitols, Sigurt (2009): European Works Councils: *An Assessment of their Social Welfare Impact.* Working Paper 2009.04 of the European Trade Union Institute, Brussels.

Voss, Eckhard (2006): *The Experience of European Works Councils in New EU Member States.* Dublin/Luxembourg: European Foundation for the Improvement of Living and Working Conditions/Office for Official Publications of the European Communities.

Waddington, Jeremy (2011): European Works Councils: The Challenge for Labour. *Industrial Relations Journal* 42 (6): 508–529.

Waddington, Jeremy; Kerckhofs, Peter (2003): European Works Councils: What Is the Current State of Play? *Transfer. European Review of Labour and Research* 9 (2): 322–339.

Waddington, Jeremy; Pulignano, Valeria; Turk, Jeffrey; Swerts, Thomas (2016): *Managers, Business Europe and the Development of European Works Councils.* Working Paper 2016.06. Brussels: ETUI.

Ziltener, Patrick; Gabathuler, Heinz (2016): Swiss Multinational Companies and Their European Works Councils: European Voluntarism Meets Swiss Voluntarism. *European Journal of Industrial Relations* 22 (4): 353–369.

Chapter 11

The European Works Council – not an effective means against site-competition and multiscalar social fragmentation

Stefanie Hürtgen

In his contribution, Ludger Pries in this volume analyses European Works Councils (EWCs) as European institutions in the making, growing in numbers and institutionalized formation and accumulating historical experiences and "learning curves". In arguing so, Pries is a prominent part of a strong and wide tradition in EWCs research, whose concern is the theoretical and empirical manifestation of the transnational institutional and social establishment of EWCs. From this perspective, EWCs are not loosely coupled conglomerates of workers from different locations and countries or even part of a systemic trade union "institutional nationalism" (Streeck 1997), but – despite existing setbacks, for example during the crisis 2008ff. – are inherently European, transnational organizations with sometimes impressive solidaristic practices of mutual exchange and support (see for example Kotthoff/Whittall 2014).

My argument is not to deny the transnational character of EWCs. Both from the "objective" institutional and from the "subjective" social side it is appropriate to consider EWCs as transnational regulating bodies – and, indeed, their exchange and networking activities are sometimes remarkable, helpful in particular for employees with weak local union structures or with local unions under management's attack (Hürtgen 2008; Lüthje et al. 2013: 200ff.). What I criticize, however, is that Pries (and this important scientific stream in general) does not ask about the potency of EWCs regarding social protection. Instead, Pries implicitly gives the impression that processes of institution building and learning would as such strengthen European social embeddedness. EWCs have been promoted by trade union activists precisely for becoming a central part of what is still known as "Social Europe". Their role was thought to stop or at least to diminish social competition and "whipsawing" among workers along production sites and nation-states. This is, hence, the main question and reference to ask today: whether or not EWCs achieve, via democratic voice, the protection or even the strengthening of European companies' workers' social integration. This question goes beyond a consideration of EWCs as emerging and learning institutions, and it is necessarily linked to a more socio-economic perspective on Europeanization, with EWCs being part of the process. In this perspective, however, a much more critical view of EWCs is required. As I will explore, they can hardly be conceptualized as socially corrective on the European scale. Today, EWCs are neither able to stop or regulate cross-border site-competition, nor are they in other ways an effective means to represent the social and democratic dimension in the on-going process of economic Europeanization. This, of course, is not their "fault" but the result of the specific institutional and socio-economic setting of Europe itself. When discussing EWCs, it is therefore necessary to take an interdisciplinary approach, including the sociology of work and industry, debates from the Global Production Network (GPN) literature and Critical European Political Economy.

I develop my argument, accordingly, in two steps: first I have a look at the literature on global and European production networks and the qualitative new form of social competition. In the next step I will develop a more detailed view of labour in contemporary Europeanization, taking Critical European Political Economy and, again, the sociology of work and industry to demonstrate the structurally – although not the subjectively – limited character of EWCs' role for a necessary social Europeanization.

European production networks and social competition

Since the early 1970s, with the development and rising size of multinational companies in Europe and beyond, ideas to create transnational workers' committees evolved (Levinson 1972; Tudyka et al. 1978; Schulten 1996). Hereby and from the very beginning the building up of autonomous information channels among different European productions sites was crucial to prevent the "playing off" against each other via the management's non-targeted or targeted disinformation. Indeed, very early on workers in different regions have been confronted with cost-cutting demands (working-time flexibilization, pay cuts, etc.) with reference to (seemingly) more responsiveness from the workers' side in other European production sites. Even today, the existence or not of autonomous information channels is one of the most important topics for EWC-members and their practices; in their view it often marks the line between the EWC as a "real" workers' representation and the EWC as only the management's tool for communication. However, contemporary cross-border site-competition goes far beyond (dis-)information politics.

Rather, contemporary site-competition must be seen in the light of quasi-generalized competitive social fragmentation via multidimensional divisionalization of work and production. Ideologically manifested as enterprises' "modernization" and "innovation", this organizational divisionalization directly targets the enhancement of workers' efforts, flexibility and efficiency (Marchington et al. 2005; Lüthje et al. 2013; Sisson 2015: 19). Global and European production today is systematically divided, decentralized production: it is divided in separated, budgetary more or less "autonomous" units such as cost-centres, business-units, customer lines, working groups, departments and also production sites (often run as cost-centres). However, the turning away from "Fordist" vertically integrated production towards decentralization is only one side of the whole process. It goes hand in hand with new forms of centralized control, i.e. quasi-permanent translocal as well as transnational evaluation of quality and cost via modern digital tools and equipment. Accounting, that is the translation of all kinds of single social activities and working results into numeral codes and entities, is part of this centralized (digital) control, allowing more and more detailed surveillances and comparisons. The systematic comparison in output, flexibility, quality and costs includes the individual units of an organization, but it goes beyond organizational borders as "European sourcing" also involves external providers and suppliers, putting both "in-house-production" and "external offers" into competitive relation to each other. The result is post-Fordist "lean" and highly flexible European production via multiple socio-spatial fragmentation on the one hand and centralized control and evaluation on the other. It goes along with complex socio-spatial competitive divisionalization on all organizational and socio-spatial scales of the network, within as well as beyond nation-states, in the light of what the management interprets as constrains of the market.

In fact, post-Fordist markets are highly insecure and competitive, due to the relative saturation, overcapacities of production in many branches, high insecurity and pressure through financialization and shareholder-logics and the strong acceleration of product-cycles. The "organizational revolution" of European production (Sauer 2013), e.g., gives management a tool to mitigate their profit-squeeze-risks in a new dimension of flexibilization. In this sense, Ian Greer and Marco Hauptmeier (2015) speak about site-competition and whipsawing in general as "marketization". All the individual, socio-spatially divided units compete for positive evaluation and (prolonged) adequate resources and benefits, i.e. mainly remuneration and contract-awards, a new dimension of social fragmentation and competition on the workers' side: "Discipline [and self-discipline of workers, SH] is secured [...] through the 'whip' of the market, in the form of the potential loss of contracts that connect networked organizations, and often the provision of (temporary) workers within them" (Grimshaw et al. 2005: 12). Patterns of social and economic competition are changing rapidly in their forms and in space and time, following what in the sociology of work and industry is known as the "permanent restructuring" of the production network (Sauer 2013). Local outsourcing and the use of different (precarious) workforce-categories as well as permanent "best of" competition (benchmarking) among cost-centres and production sites in different regions and countries are part of this process, but also featured is the (permanent) redefinition of a firm's profitable "core-competences" under permanently changing market conditions; the latter include consequences in production awards, investment decisions but also closure, selling and relocation (Ahlers et al. 2009; Coe/Hess 2013; Trappmann 2015).

In short: economic and social competition among the workforces of different European production sites goes far beyond the "old" question of competitive pressure via disinformation even when this sometimes still exists. But on a larger perspective, European site-competition is part of a multidimensional and multiscalar competitive fragmentation throughout the whole of Europe (and beyond), and it is a structural feature of contemporary economic Europeanization.

Europeanization and social dumping

In relation to this socio-economic development, EWCs' (juridical) instruments, mainly the right to gather and to get information, are by no means adequate. I share the idea that EWCs are European institutions with sometimes a lot of very interesting activism from the members' side, trying to enlarge their framework of action and establishing sometimes far-reaching solidarity and supportive activities. Nevertheless, when the reference is to stop or at least to mitigate social fragmentation and competition, i.e. what Magdalena Bernaciak (2015) calls European social dumping, we have to admit that EWCs have only dramatically weak institutional power (for the power resources approach see Schmalz/Dörre 2014). This argument is more important as EWCs are not (yet?) part of the wider structure of European trade unionism and collective action. Indeed, there has been a lot of hope that EWCs will be part of what we can call a European trade union movement (Hürtgen 2008), for example the famous "first European strike" in 1997, at the car-maker Renault against closure in Belgium, kindled this hope (Imig/Tarrow 2000). However, European collective action remains rare, and there is neither a strong normative logic nor a "thick" institutionalization of European trade unionism *against social competition*, in which EWCs could be a part. Instead, European trade unions themselves are often involved in logics of national and local competition (Bieling/Schulten 2001), sometimes even weakening European activism by EWC-members (Hürtgen 2008), or they are worn out by multiple procedures of nonbinding "social dialogues". In other words: to identify EWCs as a learning, developing institution does not say that much when we do not – at the same time – consider its potency in relation to social protection (which, in the end, is the condition for a real democratic voice). But here, optimism is misplaced: "Worker representatives, however sophisticated their countervailing strategies may be and however many years they have had to develop them [...] cannot really stop social dumping under the current institutional set-up of capitalism in Europe" (Greer/Hauptmeier 2015: 126).

Even under conditions of strongly developed autonomous exchange networks, as was the case for a while at GM Europe or at Fiat, for example, EWCs are not able to hinder closures or to prevent concessions. Instead, strong EWCs typically follow "share the pain" strategies, i.e. the acceptance of concessions and their more or less equal share among all production sites. This coordinated European concession bargaining is in favour of strengthening competitiveness again, now in relation to other players in the European market (Leutert 2012/2013[1]; Pernicka et al. 2015). The widely documented development of profound European norms and supporting practices, hence, is not enough to counter systematic and structural European and multiscalar competition.

Multiscalar regime competition and Europeanization

I started this response by saying that in EWCs literature generally and in Pries's consideration in particular, EWCs institution building is often implicitly treated as an inherent part of a developing social Europe and rising social embeddedness. This impression occurs because research and theory-building concentrate on institutional procedures and social activities and identities while the crucial question of workers' effective social protection, a genuine starting point for those efforts of transnational coordination, is widely absent. Implicitly, instead, there is a deduction from "effective" EWCs (conceptualized as having a high degree of activities and agreement-conclusion on the European scale, see for example Mählmeyer et al. 2017) to effective social development, at least in the future. The aforementioned "share the pain" strategies, for example, are mostly interpreted, when problematized at all, as situation- and firm-specific challenges and not as what they are: highly developed transnational, but socially restrictive, workers' representations on the European scale. One could speak about a regulated social competition instead of an unregulated one. But in both forms of competition social restrictiveness and even social regress are systematically inscribed in the system. And this is not due to the limits of subjective EWCs members' willingness, as the empirical research shows, but due to the character of the EWC-institution itself. In fact, both forms of competition often even deepen *local* social fragmentation and accelerate the circumventing of national labour standards, for example in the form of flexibilization and destandardization of employment-conditions via opening clauses or acceptance of local outsourcing or precarious work as part of the concession bargaining process (Hürtgen 2008).

Put differently: a significant part of EWCs literature does not link its research to debates on contemporary Europeanization and its inherent feature of accelerated social competition (or even: social dumping, Bernaciak 2015). In fact, not only in political science but also in industrial relations actual Europeanization has been widely analysed as a system of social "regime competition" (Streeck 1997; Bieling/Schulten 2001; Apeldoorn 2009; Bohle 2009; Erne 2015). Sharpening social competition, in these analyses, is a structural feature of contemporary Europeanization, namely via political recommodification and the widely and on-going acceptance of firms' demands for flexibilization and cost-cutting.

However, regime competition today is not limited to the national scale. This is the misleading approach by for example Wolfang Streeck (1997), who considers EWCs conglomerates of *national* representatives, in competition with each other and therefore structurally unable to develop something like a "European interest". But as I have discussed with regard to GPN and work-sociology literature, social competition today subverts, includes and exceeds the national scale – it is a multiscalar social fragmentation and competition, by no means limited to only one of the multiple socio-spatial scales (Hürtgen 2015). This includes, indeed, the building up of EWCs as a European institution, often marked by transnational identities and activities. Nevertheless, elaborated EWCs activities are also bound to "their" firm on a European scale and its competitive advantage in relation to others, for example other European car-makers. Whereas social protection and social embeddedness in Polanyi's sense is the limitation of this rush for competitive advantages with regard to labour and via a generalized, societal binding norm-setting, EWCs perfectly demonstrate that regulation as such does not limit social pressure and social competition (Greer/Hauptmeier 2015: 127). What is needed is *social* regulation, i.e. the obligatory social norm-setting on all socio-spatial scales, namely the European one. Without that social regulation, i.e. the institutionalized decommodification of labour, EWCs at their best and despite a lot of impressive and far-reaching activities can only *regulate* social restriction, but they cannot stop it or even turn it into a socially progressive perspective. The same as the workforces they represent, they are bound to the priority of being exploited and, hence, to the private firm's interest in a strong position in European and worldwide economic competition. Only strongly institutionalized and binding social norms – not only beyond nation-states, but also beyond European firms and production networks and on the local as well as regional scale – can effectively mitigate an economic firm's pressure on labour. Without that, EWCs are genuinely European, but socially nearly insignificant – despite a lot of impressive engagement by their activists. "Just as national bargaining and co-determination rules proved to be inadequate for coping with an internationalised economy, so the EWCs at the scale of the firm were never going to be very useful for coping with the consequences of fierce competition" (Greer/Hauptmeier 2015: 135).

Note

1   The title of this interview with the former Ford's EWC secretary Georg Leutert is misleading. He speaks less about "mutual learning" than about the structural limits of EWCs strategies.

Literature

Ahlers, Elke; Kraemer, Birgit; Ziegler, Aatrid (2009): *Beschäftigte in der Globalisierungsfalle?* Baden-Baden: Nomos.
Apeldoorn, Bastiaan (2009). The Contradictions of 'Embedded Neoliberalism' and Europe's Multi-Level Legitimacy Crisis: The European Project and Its Limits. In: Apeldoorn, Bastiaan; Drahokoupil, Jan; Horn, Laura (eds.): *Contradictions and Limits of Neoliberal European Governance. From Lisbon to Lisbon.* Basingstoke: Palgrave, 21–43.
Coe, Neil M.; Hess, Martin (2013): Global Production Networks, Labour and Development. *Geoforum* 44 (1), 4–9.
Bernaciak, Magdalena (ed.) (2015): *Market Expansion and Social Dumping in Europe.* London/New York: Routledge.
Bieling, Hans-Jürgen; Schulten, Thorsten (2001): Competitive Restructuring and Industrial Relations within the European Union: Corporatist Involvement and Beyond? WSI Discussion Paper No. 99, Düsseldorf.
Bohle, Dorothee (2009): Race to the Bottom? Transnational Companies and Reinforced Competition in Enlarged European Union. In: Drahokoupil, Jan; Horn, Laura (eds.): *Contradictions and Limits of Neoliberal European Governance. From Lisbon to Lisbon.* Basingstoke: Palgrave, 163–186.
Erne, Roland (2015): A Supranational Regime that Nationalizes Social Conflict: Explaining European's Trade Union's Difficulties in Politicizing European Economic Governance. Labor *History* 56 (3), 345–368.
Greer, Ian; Hauptmeier, Marco (2015): Marketization and Social Dumping: Management Whipsawing in Europe's Automotive Industry. In: Bernaciak, Magdalena (ed.): *Market Expansion and Social Dumping in Europe.* London/New York: Routledge, 124–139.
Grimshaw, Damian; Marchington, Mick; Rubery, Jill; Willmott, Hugh (2005): Fragmenting Work across Organizational Boundaries. In: Marchington, Mick; Grimshaw, Damian; Rubery, Jill; Willmott, Hugh (eds.): *Fragmenting Work. Blurring Organizational Boundaries and Disordering Hierarchies.* New York: Oxford University Press, 1–38.
Hürtgen, Stefanie (2008). *Transnationales Co-Management. Betriebliche Politik in der globalen Konkurrenz.* Münster: Westfälisches Dampfboot.
Hürtgen, Stefanie (2015). Transnationalisierung und Fragmentierung. Euro-Betriebsratshandeln als multiscalare Praxis. In: Pernicka, Susanne (ed.): *Horizontale Europäisierung im Feld der Arbeitsbeziehungen.* Wiesbaden: Springer, 17–54.
Imig, Doug; Tarrow, Sidney (2000): Political Contention in an Europeanising polity. *West European Politics* 23 (4): 73–93.
Kotthoff, Hermann; Whittall, Michael (2014): *Paths to Transnational Solidarity. Identity-Building Processes in the European Works Councils.* Pieterlen: Peter Lang.
Levinson, Charles (1972): *International Trade Unionism.* London: Allen and Unwin.
Leutert, Georg (2012/2013): Das Voneinander-Lernen spielt eine große Rolle. Nikola Tietze und Ulrich Bielefeld im Gespräch mit Georg Leutert, Sekretär des EBR von Ford. *Mittelweg 36* 21 (6): 53–79.
Lüthje, Boy; Hürtgen, Stefanie; Pawlicki, Peter; Sproll, Martina (2013): *From Silicon Valley to Shenzhen. Global Production and Work in the IT Industry.* Lanham: Roman & Littlefield.

Mählmeyer, Valentina; Rampeltshammer, Luitpold; Hertwig, Markus (2017): European Works Councils during the Financial and Economic Crisis: Activation, Stagnation or Disintegration? *European Journal of Industrial Relations* 23 (3), 225–242.

Marchington, Mick; Grimshaw, Damian; Rubery, Jill; Willmott, Hugh (2005): *Fragmenting Work. Blurring Organizational Boundaries and Disordering Hierarchies.* New York: Oxford University Press.

Pernicka, Susanne; Glassner, Vera; Dittmar, Nele; Mrozowicki, Adam; Maciejewska, Malgorzata (2015): When Does Solidarity End? Transnational Labour Cooperation during and after the Crisis – The GM/Opel Case Revisited. *Economic and Industrial Democracy*, 38 (3): 375–399.

Sauer, D. (2013): *Die organisatorische Revolution. Umbrüche in der Arbeitswelt – Ursachen, Auswirkungen und arbeitspolitische Antworten.* Hamburg: VSA.

Schulten, Thorsten (1996): European Works Councils. Prospects for a New System of European Industrial Relations. *European Journal of Industrial Relations*, 2 (3): 303–324.

Schmalz, Stefan; Dörre, Klaus (2014): Der Machtressourcenansatz: Ein Instrument zur Analyse gewerkschaftlichen Handlungsvermögens. *Industrielle Beziehungen* 21 (3): 217–234.

Sisson, Keith (2015): Private Sector Employment Relations in Western Europe. Collective Bargaining under Pressure? In: Arrowsmith, Jim; Pulignano, Valeria (ed.): *The Transformation of Employment Relations in Europe. Institutions and Outcomes in the Age of Globalization.* London/New York: Routledge, 13–32.

Streeck, Wolfgang (1997): Industrial Citizenship under Regime Competition: The Case of European Works Councils. *Journal of European Public Policy* 4 (4): 643–664.

Trappmann, Vera (2015): Social Dumping with No Divide: Evidence from Multinational Companies in Europe. In: Bernaciak, Magdalena (ed.): *Market Expansion and Social Dumping in Europe.* London/New York: Routledge, 140–156.

Tudyka, Kurt P.; Etty, Tom; Sucha, Marian (ed.) (1978): *Macht ohne Grenzen und grenzenlose Ohnmacht. Arbeitnehmerbewusstsein und die Bedingungen gewerkschaftlicher Gegenstrategien in multinationalen Konzernen.* Frankfurt a. M.: Campus.

Chapter 12

The road to pan-European codetermination rights

A course that never did run smooth

Sara Lafuente Hernández[*]

Introduction

The relevance of European integration for codetermination has gone largely unnoticed in European industrial relations, except for a few studies on the European company (Societas Europaea) and its legal statute. The literature is overwhelmingly focussed on workers' information and consultation rights, given the pioneering directives on European works councils (EWCs) and their wide uptake in the European Union (EU). Conversely, codetermination is largely anchored in national policies, industrial relations' traditions and national corporate law.

However, the Treaty on the Functioning of the European Union (TFEU) includes codetermination in the social policy section, calling on the EU to support and complement the activities of Member States (Article 153.1 (f) TFEU version 2012). The EU has already made use of this competence, adopting three directives of relevance to codetermination rights.[1] A focus on the limited objectives, scope and impact of these explicit regulations overshadows the fact that codetermination is primarily affected (and weakened) by the operation of the internal market, freedom of establishment and the free movement of capital.

Evolving over time, the term "codetermination" is ambiguous (Jackson 2012: 491). It refers to a form of workers' involvement in corporate governance, in which workers have a right to be represented with a distinct voice on company boards, influencing decisions with a right to vote[2] (Conchon 2015). Unlike other workers' rights, codetermination rights are embedded in corporate governance structures, thus not only governed by labour law but also strongly dependent on company law. Such a form of workers' involvement exists in at least 14 European Economic Area (EEA) countries (ETUI/ETUC 2017: 34).[3] Most regulations date from the 1970s or 1990s and relied on the German model of industrial democracy as a proxy for their development. Despite divergent institutional design, functions and practice

* European Trade Union Institute (financially supported by the European Union for this study)

(Waddington/Conchon 2016), codetermination is generally a well-rooted and highly valued institution in most of these countries.

In Member States with limited or no practice of this form of participation, codetermination is gradually permeating the agenda. Political parties, mostly socio-democratic, have included proposals for economic democracy in their programmes, reintroducing or extending codetermination rights (i.e. Czech Republic in 2017; France in 2013/2015), or furthering public debate in the matter (i.e. Italy, the United Kingdom). A number of national trade unions have also developed positions in support of codetermination, even in countries with traditionally conflictual industrial relations (Conchon 2013; ETUI/ETUC 2017). At EU level, the European Parliament's Committee on Employment and Social Affairs also put board-level workers' representation on its agenda and proposed drafting a resolution[4] in line with the European Trade Union Confederation's (ETUC) demand for a directive on minimum standards of board-level employee representation applicable to EU corporate forms (ETUC 2016). Such developments highlight the important role of agency and policy transfer across regulatory levels and societal contexts in shaping institutions, revealing a dynamic relationship between European integration and codetermination as an element of social policy (Jacquot/Woll 2010).

This chapter takes stock of the relationship between Europeanisation and protection of codetermination rights. Drawing on a literature review, a regulatory analysis and a secondary data analysis, it dissects the current institutional anchorage of codetermination in EU law and analyses underlying political processes and implications for the effective protection of codetermination rights. From a labour perspective, the chapter investigates to what extent codetermination rights and their practice are affected explicitly by EU regulation and implicitly by the functioning of the EU internal market. My argument is that if codetermination is deemed to fulfil its dual orientation,[5] then it urgently needs to be balanced with the current scope of market operations via an overarching and protective EU legislative approach. The Case Konrad Erzberger v. TUI AG resolved by the Court of Justice of the European Union (CJEU)[6] had the merit of highlighting certain relevant implications for codetermination rights and national protective systems in an integrated European order, but more largely for workers' rights in transnational corporate groups.

The chapter is structured as follows. The first section describes the ground-breaking SE Directive framework governing codetermination rights. The second section reflects on its footprint for subsequent EU corporate law instruments. The main features, protection objectives, achievements and limitations of the SE framework and related pieces of European company law are discussed in their comprehension of codetermination rights. The third section addresses, from a broader perspective, the exposure of codetermination rights to transnational corporate strategies secured by EU internal market rules, pinpointing some relevant regulatory loopholes and negative consequences for the enforcement and effectiveness of

codetermination rights, resulting from conceptual distinctions and prior-
itisations between ownership and management, and financial, corporate
and labour law. Finally, the fourth section presents the aforementioned
Erzberger Case, depicting its antecedents, the parties' main positions and
a critical review of certain aspects of the judgement. Focussing on the political implications rather than on a strict legal analysis, I argue that the CJEU
withdrew from a catalyst role in furthering EU protection of codetermination rights. The decision uncovered the pressing need for an overarching EU
legal framework to protect codetermination as a workers' right in corporate
groups.

The SE Directive: a ground-breaking
scoop with dubious results

The European legislator has already used its mandate to legislate on codetermination, albeit limited to specific EU corporate forms. The most
important institutional novelty came in 2001 with the adoption of the SE
Statute[7] and its complementary Directive. The SE Directive defines employees' involvement as "any mechanism, including information, consultation
and participation, through which employees' representatives may exercise
an influence" on company decisions (Article 2(h). Participation involves exercising such influence

> by way of: (1) The right to elect or appoint some of the members of the
> company's supervisory or administrative organ, or (2) The right to rec-
> ommend and/or oppose the appointment of some or all of the members
> of the company's supervisory or administrative organ.
>
> (Article 2(k)

The SE Directive thus reconciles the main approaches found in national
Member States' institutional frameworks (i.e. Germanic and Dutch).

This final version of the Directive was far less ambitious than the original
Commission proposals for an EU-law-based public limited liability company form with overall and far-reaching codetermination rights (Davies
2003: 96; Conchon 2015: 31). The SE Directive failed such harmonisation
expectations, following an arduous political process where workers' involvement was the most contentious issue. Hybrid and complex (Lenoir 2008),
the resulting SE regime is dependent on EU law, 30 different national transpositions, national laws in other domains (i.e. tax, insolvency, administrative or intellectual property law), an SE's articles of association and, if any,
case-by-case negotiated agreements on workers' involvement including very
laconic rules. The Directive retained a flexible and path-dependent solution
as a way out of the political impasse, combining (i) a negotiation procedure
between management and a special negotiating body (SNB) representing

employees for establishing workers' involvement in corporate governance, (ii) a "before-after" rule, affecting workers' participation in company boards where workers had board representation in pre-SE times and (iii) a set of standard rules on workers' board participation (among others) whose transposition into national law applies by default when the parties so agree, or when no agreement has been reached within the deadline but management still wants to register the SE and the SNB has not terminated negotiations.

On the negotiated procedure, the SE Directive framework is said to be inspired by the EWC Directive, though with certain peculiarities. Negotiations (required to register the SE) start at management's initiative, are relatively quicker (six months, extendable to one year if so agreed) and are not dependent on workforce thresholds. Workers in small SEs are also entitled to negotiate workers' involvement[8] (Stollt/Wolters 2011: 24; Rehfeldt 2011: 100), which includes a broader range of rights – information and consultation, but also possible board-level participation. Unless otherwise specified, I refer from now on to board-level participation rules. Though in theory negotiations can always cover participation, solely the "before-after" rule activates the "shadow of the law" effect of the standard rules concerning participation. Even then, the SNB can agree to reduce the "level" of participation rights when the SE is established by merger, as a holding or a subsidiary.[9] In such cases, if a high share of employees of the participating companies were previously covered by the participation rules in question (at least 25% employees in the case of a merger, or 50% in the case of a holding or subsidiary), then the level can only be reduced by qualified majority (two-thirds of the SNB members, representing at least two Member States and two-thirds of employees). Otherwise, the parties are free to set the terms of an agreement on participation. They only need to specify the number of members, their rights and appointment procedures. They can also directly refer to the transposed standard rules in the Member State registering the SE.

The "before-after" principle represents a compromise between Member States: on the one hand safeguarding pre-existing codetermination rights and reducing the risk of "escape" from national codetermination rules; on the other hand, preventing an "export" effect in situations where no previous codetermination rights existed. It means that, under certain conditions, pre-existing codetermination rights are maintained upon a company's conversion to an SE. It would seem that the safeguarding rationale was intended to rule out competition between company forms in countries with codetermination rights, rather than expanding EU workers' rights via protective social legislation. As some scholars rightly put it, defensive objectives took precedence over proactive ones (Davies 2003: 84–87; Keller/Werner 2008: 170).

As for the (transposed) standard rules on workers' participation, they apply in any transformation case. Conversely, when the SE is established by merger,[10] as a holding or subsidiary, thresholds of at least 25%/50% employees with previous participation rights again apply, although they can be lowered by an SNB decision.[11] If several forms of participation existed previously, the SNB can decide which one takes precedence; otherwise, a rule fixed by the Member State will prevail. The standard rules define the main features of codetermination in an SE. When they apply, the new SE must abide to "all aspects" of the retained employee participation, and extend them cross-borders to all subsidiaries and establishments. Interestingly, participation is conceptualised here as a specific right of employees. Appointed employee members are full members of the board with the "same rights and obligations as the members representing the shareholders, including the right to vote", though they never have the casting vote in the event of a tie.

Three mechanisms favour the internationalisation of SE board participation: the SNB opens mandates to different countries; in the standard rules, participation rights extend to the whole SE workforce including all entities within the EEA; finally, board-level seats are allocated according to the size of national workforces. A trend towards internationalising workers' board participation can be generally observed. Most SE agreements with negotiated codetermination allow delegates mandated by different countries to sit on the board, and some even require such diversity. Recent data on worker directors supports this finding: 20% of the 219 SE workers' directors were mandated in a country different from the SE registering country, and at least one-third of SE boards with employee representation had two or more countries represented on the workers' side (ETUI 2017a). While the regulation and practice of internationalised codetermined SE boards diverge from national characteristics under transnational influences (Waddington/Conchon 2017: 49; Rosenbohm 2014), worker directors' rights and duties are still largely dependent on national laws and company organs' decisions, leading to divergency in protection and mandate conditions, and sometimes provoking uncertainty in the implementation of mandating procedures. Other Europeanisation dimensions in codetermined boards, such as the interactions and possible conflicts between worker directors from different industrial relations' cultures, use of board representation or adaptation to the boards' multinational composition, need further investigation in qualitative research.

All in all, the statistical evidence does not support an optimistic view in terms of SEs' potential to spread codetermination in Europe. In 2017, there were 2,827 SEs established in the EEA (ETUI 2017b),[12] but according to Eurostat, at least 174,513 enterprises were foreign-controlled (by other Member States) in 2014 in the EU28 (Eurostat 2017).[13] Either for lack of information or due to insufficient economic, tax or organisational advantages (Davies 2003: 77–78; Lenoir 2008), companies did not fundamentally use the SE regime to operate transnationally, apparently resorting to other alternatives. The SE Directive's flexible and path-dependent approach has been unable to spread codetermination practices, or even to foster negotiations on participation rights. SEs are split into three categories in the European Company database according to their relevance for workers' involvement rights: (1) "UFO" is a temporary category for registered SEs with no data available on employees or real business (i.e. 1959 of the 2,827 existing SEs); (2) "empty/ micro" refer to SEs up to five employees (i.e. 396)[14]; and (3) "normal" SEs are those having more than five employees (i.e. 472 SEs); of these, just 72 had negotiated workers' board participation (ETUI 2017a). The geographical distribution is very uneven across Europe. Apart from Germany which hosts more than half of "normal" SEs (243), and the Czech Republic, which is specialised in letterbox SEs, most countries have very few (if any) SEs (Figure 12.1). This national bias is mirrored in the figures on codetermined SEs and worker directors' mandates, both led by Germany (ETUI 2017a). Mirroring this imbalance, the study of SEs and their codetermination practices is very much in the hands of the German research community (e.g. Eidenmüller et al. 2012; Rosenbohm 2014; Rose/Köstler 2014), attracting less attention in other national contexts (González Begega/Köhler 2016: 84).

Yet, employers have found ways to use SEs in their global corporate strategies to facilitate financial restructuring or institutional shopping. The current SE regulatory framework allows for cuts in previous codetermination rights, even when negotiations take place on establishing the SE. Though a complete circumvention of pre-existing codetermination systems was generally prevented, the SE Directive's precautions still permitted a ruling-out of national provisions for increasing or adapting codetermination rights (provoking a so-called "freezing" effect in German companies transformed into SEs).[15] Also, the negotiation process was sometimes the opportunity for cuts in board size, or for trade-offs detracting from existing codetermination rights (Rehfeldt 2011: 107).

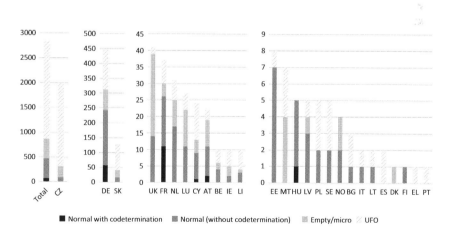

Figure 12.1 European Companies (SEs) per country and type in EEA.
Source: Own elaboration from the ECDB (ETUI 2017b), last checked 9 Aug. 2017.
Note: Croatia, Iceland, Romania and Slovenia have no registered SEs.

In conclusion, the SE Statute and Directive contributed to the emergence of real European codetermination as an employee right in at least 72 SEs, but without substantially promoting the expansion of codetermination rights in the EU. Despite careful safeguarding rules, the effect of this EU legislation was often not even neutral for pre-existing rights.

The SE "no export–no escape" footprint in EU corporate law

The SE Directive's compromise had greater impact than it might seem. The safeguard without export of pre-existing codetermination rights set the benchmark and inspired discussions, concerns and solutions in subsequent EU company law.

First, the European Cooperative Society (SCE) Statute in 2003[16] introduced a legal form of cooperative based on EU law, to help cooperatives operate transnationally in the EU. In contrast to other transnational investor-based company forms, an SCE aims to satisfy its members' needs and support their economic and social activities. It can be created by merger, by conversion or from scratch by at least five people, with a minimum capital of €30,000. A complementary directive on employee involvement[17] lays down rules similar to the SE Directive, with four main differences: the rules do not apply to SCEs set up by natural persons employing less than 50 employees; workers may be members of the SCE board but also participate in its general meeting; structural changes explicitly trigger renegotiations on workers' involvement and gender balance affects SNB composition. Workers' involvement rules are slightly better than SE standards, although, given the nature of a cooperative, their adequacy might be questioned (Snaith 2006).

More objectionable is the SCE Statute's social impact, which is marginal due to regulatory complexity and lack of awareness (Cooperatives Europe et al. 2010) and has not improved over time. Conflicting goals and structural differences between investor-controlled and cooperative societies surely play a role. Rising from 17 SCEs in 2010, 58 had been established by 2017, though only one (German) had negotiated codetermination rights (ETUI 2017b). This low number explains the limited research interest in the topic, although SCEs have comparatively attracted more Southern European research than SEs (e.g. Chomel 2004; Fernández Guadaño 2006; Pastor Sempere 2009).

Over the last decade, the European Commission put forward four other legislative proposals with possible implications for codetermination rights. While the European Private Company Statute (2008), the European Foundation Statute (2012) and the Single-Member Private Limited Liability Companies (2014) all failed to see the light of day due to irreconcilable disagreement on how employee involvement should be treated (Conchon 2015: 35), the Cross-Border Mergers (CBM) Directive[18] succeeded.

Entering into force in 2007, it introduced an EU instrument to facilitate cross-EEA mergers, streamlining procedures and reducing costs for companies. In contrast to the SE Directive, the CBM Directive did not complement a specific EU corporate form, but only clarified the merger procedure itself. Prior to its adoption, workers with advantageous national codetermination rights systems in one merging company could lose rights if the resulting company registered in a country with no, or less advantageous, participation rules. The CBM Directive included provisions to protect such pre-existing rights. As regards information and consultation, national provisions referred to the general framework of information and consultation (Directive 2002/14/EC) and the specific one for mergers under the Acquired Rights' Directive 2001/23/EC (ARD)[19] but also those referred to in Directive 98/59/EC in the case of collective redundancies. Once the merger is completed, the EWC Directive could apply if the resulting company meets the conditions to create a transnational information and consultation body. Clearly, the split rules and moments for negotiating codetermination and information and consultation rights are not conducive to a congruent articulation of workers' involvement in the new company, a mismatch addressed by the European Trade Union Confederation (ETUC) in its proposed integrated architecture for workers' involvement rights (ETUC 2016).

Turning now to workers' involvement provisions in the CBM Directive, they were unanimously considered to cut back codetermination rights' protection in comparison to the SE Directive (Cremers/Wolters 2011: 8; Eidenmüller et al. 2012: 222; Conchon 2013: 304). While the cutbacks intended to accelerate the merger process, they also hampered the effective application of more advantageous codetermination rights, de facto contradicting and undermining the negotiation and protection purposes. First, the CBM Directive set a threshold of at least 500 employees with previous codetermination rights, below which management was exempted from the Directive's participation rules and those of the registering country directly applied, without blocking the merger. Moreover, the general assembly of shareholders could decide to apply the standard rules directly, skipping negotiations. In the same vein, when the resulting company adopted a monistic corporate governance structure, codetermination rights could be limited to one-third of the board seats without negotiating the matter. Management was little encouraged to enter negotiations under the CBM Directive. When negotiations did take place but failed, the standard rules only applied if one-third of workers previously benefitted from participation rights (again, a higher threshold than the one-fourth required in the SE Directive). Finally, when the resulting company maintained codetermination rights, these were only protected in subsequent mergers for the next three years, after which the safeguards declined. These rules are still in force, as Directive (EU) 2017/1132/EC on company law literally replicated them in its Article 133 on employee participation.

In a context of financial crisis, the CBM Directive was very much used between 2008 and 2012, with CBMs increasing from 132 in 2008 to 361 in 2012 (Bech-Bruun/Lexidale 2013: 975). The steady incremental trend continued: at least 1,936 CBMs were registered between 2013 and 2017 (Biermeyer/Meyer 2018: 5).[20] An ETUI study identified at least 75 CBM cases reflecting employee participation issues in their merger plans (Biermeyer/Meyer 2015), suggesting that CBMs might be of greater impact for codetermination rights than it was originally foreseen.

Even so, the CBM Directive has limited scope. With some explicit corporate exceptions,[21] it covers full mergers of limited liability companies formed under the law of an EEA country, registered and with main place of business are different/alternative possibilities in the EEA and governed by the law of at least two Member States. Partial mergers (i.e. where not all assets and liabilities are transferred to the resulting company) or share exchanges[22] would be excluded, although commonly used to achieve equivalent results. What happens then to workers' codetermination rights in the uncovered cases?

The EU blind spot: protecting codetermination rights in the face of transnationalisation and company mobility

Despite impacting national codetermination rights, most corporate cross-border strategies are not covered by the protective measures described so far. Capital transnationalisation and cross-border company mobility largely operate under EU secondary rules with no safeguards for codetermination rights, or under the direct rule of national regulatory competition sheltered by EU internal market principles. Thus, business has still many routes at hand to circumvent and weaken national codetermination rights (Conchon 2013: 305).

Directive 77/187/EC on Acquired Rights, along with its modified (Directive 1998/50/EC) and revised (Directive 2001/23/EC) versions (ARD), was specifically adopted to harmonise legislations and safeguard workers' acquired rights in transfers of business (meaning a change in employer). Despite ARD and SE Directive legislative processes unfolding simultaneously, the protection of codetermination rights, either in an individual or a collective guise, did not feature in the ARD debates and there is no mention of this issue in the ARD. This may come as a surprise considering that the ARD framework covers not only domestic but also cross-border transfers, the focus of protection being on the transferred unit. Nevertheless, codetermination rights could arguably fall under the scope of the ARD's protective measures in at least two ways.

On the one hand, Member States must ensure that "employee representatives" preserve their status, functions and protection until new representative bodies are formed under the laws of the new employer (transferee).

At first, board-level employee representatives were explicitly excluded from the notion of "workers' representatives", discussed at length in the debates leading to the adoption of ARD 77/187/EC. However, against the backdrop of the internal market's impact and the revision of the Collective Redundancies Directive 98/59/EC, it was decided to bring this Directive 98/59/EC's and ARD's definitions of employee representatives into line with each other. The exclusion of board-level representatives was thus withdrawn in the ARD 1998 modified version, a decision supported by social partners, Member States and the Economic and Social Committee. Such a reversal suggests that there was no political will to fundamentally disconnect codetermination rights from the scope of the acquired rights' protection.

On the other hand, the terms and conditions of collective agreements signed with the employer transferring business (transferor) must be maintained for the duration of the agreement, at least until a new one enters into force or one year after the business transfer. The new employer could be bound by codetermination rights as with other collectively bargained transferred conditions, if such rights were established by collective agreement (e.g. in SEs, in companies emerging from a CBM or in companies governed by certain national jurisdictions, particularly in Nordic countries). In such cases, a collective agreement could provide more immediate and effective protection for codetermination rights than rules based on the transferor's mandatory national law. Admittedly, considering recent CJEU case law in this context (e.g. Alemon-Herron C-426/11), such safeguards on codetermination rights would likely be deemed an excessive burden on the transferee's freedom to conduct its business.

Finally, employee representation at the board level could be understood as belonging to the realm of working conditions, in an interpretation favourable to workers' rights. Such an interpretation would significantly broaden the ARD's protective scope. For now, however, the fact that codetermination rights are not even considered in the Directive suggests that the prevailing notion of codetermination at the EU level remains primarily connected to corporate law rather than to protective labour law and working conditions.

Second, companies can easily circumvent national codetermination systems through using freedom of establishment (Article 49 TFEU), which CJEU case law has interpreted as allowing companies to register in a country while conducting their real business elsewhere.[23] In the absence of protective measures in EU secondary law on cross-border transfers of seat,[24] countries connecting codetermination to the structure of legal entities can suffer circumventions when they host companies registered in foreign jurisdictions lacking similar rules on codetermined corporate governance. This practice led to workers from at least 94 foreign-registered companies operating in Germany being deprived of board codetermination rights in 2015 (Sick 2015: 6). The circumvention stems here from a problem of jurisdiction and conflict of laws, favouring company law regulatory competition. Therefore, in the context of the "company law package" proposed by the European Commission,[25] the ETUC called inter alia for the "real seat" principle to be strengthened and codetermination rights safeguarded.

Third, codetermination is rendered ineffective by the operation of national corporate and financial rules under the free movement of capital rule (Article 63 TFEU). The ARD, SE or CBM Directives do not cover transfers of assets or ownership via stock acquisition or other share deals (e.g. Case C-234/98 Allen v. Amalgamated Constructions), although capital concentrations were also addressed by the Commission's initial ARD proposal in 1974, and the ETUC asked in 2007 for the ARD's scope to be revised to include transfers by change of ownership. The only existing EU secondary law on trading shares includes neither safeguards nor negotiating procedures for workers' involvement, despite the legislative process having unfolded since the 1970s, as for the ARD and SE Directives. The Takeover Bid Directive[26] aims to provide legal certainty for takeovers and acquisitions of control through share-trading on regulated markets, granting shareholders, employees and stakeholders minimum information rights and protecting holders of securities in companies governed by Member State laws. The Directive establishes guidelines on procedures, form and content of information and consultation to the offeror and offeree's employees, but simply refers to national legislation for codetermination matters (Cremers/Vitols 2016).

Beyond changes in employer, transactions resulting in changes in ownership or control of company groups can significantly affect codetermination rights in a context of globalised shareholder capitalism. In the absence of overarching EU regulation or established CJEU case law on transnational company groups for the purpose of protecting employee rights, transnational corporate structures can take shelter under free movement of capital rules, as provide for in national corporate and financial laws. From a labour perspective, three main implications arise for codetermination rights in this context.

First, rules governing the parent company board and workers' rights in subsidiaries may depend on different jurisdictions, leading to conflict-of-law situations and legal uncertainty, with major repercussions on codetermination. The very political compromise between national codetermined systems and a power balance institutionally embedded in labour and corporate laws is jeopardised when the logic of international law and conflicts of laws comes into play and considers corporate and labour law as distinct and competing fields (Deakin 2007: 1168).

Second, transnational corporate realities may act against achieving the thresholds required for codetermination or increased representation rights. A German court,[27] deviating from established national doctrine, argued that employees of foreign subsidiaries should be taken into account in the calculation of codetermination thresholds in parent boards of German transnational groups, on grounds that the German Codetermination Act made no distinction between employees of national or foreign subsidiaries. Such an interpretation could have enhanced labour rights in very internationalised companies. The judgement was appealed against and reached the highest court, who finally ruled in line with CJEU Erzberger, in the understanding that counting methods and issues discussed in the latter Case were intrinsically linked.[28]

Third, transnational corporate realities lead to situations in which workers with a similar organisational relationship towards a parent company have, in terms of their dependency on global corporate decisions, different positions in their access to codetermination rights, depending on the jurisdiction of their employment. The mismatch is particularly striking when a holding centralises strategic decisions and controls country-based performance and/or human resources policies (i.e. operating as "one-company").

Some national codetermination legislations have adapted to transnational realities. In Norway and Denmark, employees and management jointly decide on the scope and implementation of codetermination rights in groups, so that subsidiaries, regardless of their location, can (at least theoretically) be included in election procedures. In France, the global workforce is counted to determine thresholds giving access to representation rights, and when an EWC exists, it may have a role in appointing one worker director employed in any location of the group (ETUI/ETUC 2017: 63). However, the challenges of corporate transnationalisation and mobility mentioned earlier largely surpass national regulatory capacities and institutional solutions.

Erzberger v. TUI AG Case: another bump on the road to pan-European codetermination rights?

The CJEU has recently taken sides in the application of national codetermination rights to transnational corporations in Case C-566/15 Konrad Erzberger v. TUI AG. In these preliminary proceedings, a German court requested the CJEU to rule on whether national regulations complied with EU principles of equal treatment and workers' freedom of movement (Articles 18 and 45 TFEU) when foreign subsidiary workers were prevented from taking part in parent-company board elections.

The Case should be comprehended within the German context and debate. The German codetermination system in public limited companies is characterised by a two-tier corporate governance structure, where a company's executive and supervisory boards are entrusted with management and control functions respectively. Theoretically, the executive board decides on day-to-day business while the supervisory board oversees the former, appointing and dismissing directors, setting their remuneration and inspecting annual accounts. The supervisory board is granted an authorising role over relevant transactions by the German Stock Corporation Act of 1965, meaning that in practice it fulfils a "co-deciding control" function (Hopt 2016) often interfering in the executive board's worldwide decisions.[29] A core aspect of the German codetermination system is that workers are entitled to elect half of supervisory board members according to strict procedural rules and a regime of rights and obligations relating to unions, employees and companies, following the highly legalistic and regulated nature of German industrial relations (Jacobi et al. 1992).[30] The dominant German legal doctrine considers that workers can only elect representatives and stand as candidates for election when their employment contract falls under German law, i.e. workers of foreign subsidiaries of the same group are excluded from election rights in application of the so-called territoriality principle.

The German Codetermination Act (1976) has been under employer fire ever since it was adopted, and even subjected to constitutional challenges. More recently, a legal academic debate questioned whether German codetermination complied with equal treatment and free movement principles, as it excluded workers outside Germany from voting rights and mandates (Hellwig/Behme 2009; Habersack et al. 2016). Some minority shareholders (of which the claimant in the Case at hand proved particularly active) adopted litigation strategies before German courts, challenging the supervisory board composition on grounds that they were in breach of these EU principles (Pütz and Sick 2015; Hofmann 2017). The vested interest of shareholders in defending workers' rights is questionable, their underlying political motivation seemingly being to disrupt the German codetermination system.

The Case attracted much attention, being characterised as a dispute confined to the national context between "business-attackers" threatening the German – and potentially other – social market economies (Hofmann 2017) and "labour-defenders" of German codetermination, while the broader implications for labour in a context of European integration and financialisation of the economy tended to be overlooked. Were the CJEU to find any discrimination or obstacle to free movement, it could oblige Germany to amend, or even completely remove, the controversial rule for all economic players.

Erzberger claimed that Articles 18 and 45 TFEU had been violated in composing the workers' delegation to the supervisory board, as workers from foreign subsidiaries had not taken part in the elections. German law should have been applied, granting equal voting rights to all TUI workers in the EU, irrespective of the law governing their contract and upholding the rights of German workers moving to a foreign subsidiary. Using slightly different reasonings, the European Commission and the EFTA Surveillance Authority supported this view, arguing that the German territorial restriction was not proportional, as other countries had found more inclusive solutions in their codetermination systems.

By contrast, TUI AG rejected any breach of EU law, arguing that workers in Germany had equal access to board elections irrespective of their nationality, and that there was thus no discrimination. The problem concerned jurisdiction: in the absence of EU regulation, election-related codetermination rights could not fall under the scope of EU freedom of movement rules, but under the principle of territoriality, i.e. preventing Germany from enforcing its laws outside its jurisdiction (Mulder 2017). Workers' representatives, German authorities and other intervening Member States (i.e. Austria, France, the Netherlands and Luxembourg) shared this view. If any restriction on free movement was to be observed, it was in any case justified on grounds of public interest, and was proportional and appropriate considering the relevance for the German social order to ensure the enforcement of election procedures and transparency. It should be pointed out here that supervisory board elections in Germany are entirely organised by employees and unions under strict procedural rules, in contrast to Denmark or Norway, where company case-by-case negotiations with management constitute the key legal procedure.

The German Codetermination Act was declared fully compliant with EU law. Given "the absence of harmonisation or coordination measures at Union level" in the field of workers' collective representation rights in transnational company boards, Member States have the right to "set the criteria for defining the scope of application of their legislation" provided that these criteria are "objective and non-discriminatory".

As we have argued elsewhere (Lafuente Hernández and Rasnača 2019), it would be misleading to interpret the verdict as a case in support of trade unions' demands and collective labour rights in Europe. The restrained and pragmatic judgement instead served Member States' sovereign causes through shielding their own national social systems, without clear positive offsets for labour rights in transnational corporate scenarios.

The CJEU highlighted a blind spot in EU law: neither codetermination rights nor the relationship between foreign subsidiary workers and their parent company are expressly regulated in EU law. But its reasoning fell short in that it categorically closed any avenue to enforce workers' representation rights in transnational companies via a broader interpretation of workers' free movement rules.

The CJEU did not engage with notions such as "legal personality",[31] control, dependency or unity of direction, usually evaluated by national labour courts when enforcing workers' rights in groups of undertakings. Corporate decisions often equally affect workers across a whole group, irrespective of the location of their employment contracts or their formal direct employer. In this context, a situation where workers within the same group are excluded from collective rights vis-à-vis the parent company enjoyed by their peers, solely based on their contract's location, hardly qualifies as perfectly "objective and non-discriminatory". The CJEU did not clarify why and under which circumstances such exclusions could be deemed objective and non-discriminatory.

The Court missed the opportunity to set EU precedent for a more protective understanding of codetermination rights in transnational groups,[32] even when EU legislation appears the most appropriate remedy to secure equal access to employees' rights across groups of undertakings in the EU.

Conclusion

This chapter takes stock of ways in which European integration affects codetermination rights. The combined assessment of fragmented, poor and underused EU provisions on participation rights in corporate governance (i.e. SE, SCE and CBM Directives) and of EU business and capital freedoms directly impacting national codetermination rights highlights serious regulatory shortcomings in countering risks associated with transnationalisation and company mobility for effective codetermination at all levels.

The Erzberger Case confronted the CJEU with several contradictions between national-based interpretations of codetermination rights and transnational corporate reality. The CJEU judgement could have interpreted codetermination in a light of employee rights, helping to secure national codetermination legitimacy and stability in the long-term. It preferred not to choose that path.

There is still a long way to walk in the realm of political action. From an EU law perspective, codetermination lacks an unambiguous connection to labour law. By subordinating the EU's principle of workers' freedom of movement to Member States' internal rule, the CJEU implicitly gives precedence to a concept of codetermination primarily based on corporate law and national jurisdiction applicable to parent company boards. This deviates from the SE Directive's approach, and from national codetermination systems based on complementarities between corporate and protective labour law rules, in turn automatically excluding codetermination from the scope of other protective EU labour law norms (i.e. ARD). As pointed out by Simon Deakin, in a context of globalisation where shareholder value prevails, courts ultimately solve the tensions between corporate and labour law realms by resorting to conflict-of-law rules. But the choice of jurisdiction implies a political choice, inexorably subordinating the goals and values of one realm to the other (Deakin 2007: 1168).

From a labour perspective, defending the national status quo without addressing the break in national power balances caused by the way the internal market operates could nurture a significant twist in the use of codetermination. Cooperation and legitimisation of managerial decisions would prevail, without workers being able to influence strategic corporate decisions. A consistent strategy to hinder the erosion of national codetermination systems in the long run calls for European political action and legislation, assigning codetermination rights to the transnational level of corporate decision-making. This might be inseparable from including other countries and other industrial relations' traditions in board representation. Admittedly, while such diversity could destabilise labour power in certain contexts, it would eventually foster new transnational political compromises and strategy-building.

In a context of globalisation, EU legislation can obviously not solve all possible risks of hollowing out codetermination rules. Yet the regulatory field seems the most appropriate available to tackle problems arising from the EU internal market and transnational company structures and mobility. If codetermination rights are taken seriously at national level, then overarching legislative action protecting them at EU level seems a sine qua non for their survival.

Notes

1 Directives 2001/86/EC of 8 October (SE Directive) and 2003/72/EC of 22 July (SCE Directive) respectively supplementing the Statutes for a European Company and a European Cooperative Society with regard to the involvement of employees, and Directive 2005/56/EC of 26 October on cross-border mergers of limited liability companies (CBM Directive).
2 Unless otherwise specified, the chapter will use this restricted notion of codetermination, distinct from other forms of workers involvement in corporate governance (e.g. management, general assembly of shareholders, consultative or observing roles, or extended information and consultation rights at the level of establishment).
3 Some regulations on codetermination rights exist in Spain, Portugal, Ireland, Greece and Poland, but they were either marginally implemented or dramatically impacted by recent political and economic developments.
4 European Parliament (2016) Draft Report on workers representation on board level in Europe (2015/2222(INI), of 26 Feb. 2016.
5 The institution of codetermination embodies a political compromise in promoting social development, between democratic participation/control of economic power and shareholder value, union power and cooperation to reduce labour conflict (Jackson 2012: 492; Page 2011:10). An evaluation of the substantial political, ideological, cultural or institutional differences between national codetermination systems would exceed the scope of this chapter.
6 Judgement of the Court (Grand Chamber) of 18 July 2017 C-566/15 *Konrad Erzberger vs TUI AG* [2017] ECLI:EU:C:2017:562 (*Erzberger* Case).
7 Regulation 2001/2157/EC of 8 October on the Statute of a European Company (SE).
8 Negotiations on workers' involvement can only be triggered at the moment of establishment, i.e. they are hampered when (as is often the case) the SE is empty at establishment (a "shelf SE") and recruits workers at a later stage. However, a line of German case law interprets that negotiations must still take place after later recruitment (e.g. OLG Düsseldorf, 30 March 2009, 3 Wx 248/08).
9 The highest "level" of participation boils down to the highest share of board members appointed/elected/opposed or recommended by workers, and determines which codetermination system prevails when several collide. Other

elements impacting workers' influence in the board (e.g. internal composition of the workers' side, size, rights, role of the board) are ignored by the SE Directive (Davies 2003: 86). SEs are founded as a holding, as a subsidiary or by merger or transformation of existing companies. A negotiated reduction of the level of participation is prohibited solely in the latter case.

10 Member States can opt out of standard rules in merger cases.

11 The implementation of both negotiation procedures and standard rules greatly depends on the corporate path to SE establishment.

12 The European Company database (ECDB) is probably the most reliable collection of SE data. Even so, some data may be outdated or incomplete, due to the lack of mandatory registration at EU level (the TED registry is less accurate), the diversity in national registries and data access rules, and the difficulty in tracing empty SEs after foundation.

13 Eurostat uses shares ownership as the main proxy for assessing business control, although in combination with other indicators when available, such as statutory decisions over company policy or directors' appointments.

14 Austria sets the lowest threshold: five employees. This is the threshold needed to set up a works council entitled to appoint board members on behalf of employees. However, in some national registries employee figures are not broken down to that number; therefore the "empty/micro" category includes SEs up to five employees, while the "normal" category starts at six. For the ECDB, SEs having employees are assumed to have a real activity.

15 No normative provision obliges to reopen negotiations when structural changes or workforce increases occur. However, the Directive's aim is to secure acquired codetermination rights not only at the time of the SE's establishment but also in the case of *"structural changes in an existing SE and to the companies affected by structural change processes"* (recital 18).

16 Regulation 1435/2003 on the Statute for a European Cooperative Society.

17 Directive 2003/72/EC supplementing the Statute for a European Cooperative Society with regard to the involvement of employees.

18 Directive 2005/56/EC on cross-border mergers of limited liability companies was repealed by Directive (EU) 2017/1132/EC of 14 June 2017 relating to certain aspects of company law. This fledging "EU corporate law code" brought together six existing corporate law Directives for the sake of clarity and legal certainty, but it did not alter their substance, so new transpositions were not even required. Therefore, unless otherwise specified, I will refer as "CBM Directive" to Chapter II (Articles 118–134 and 161) of Directive (EU) 2017/1132 in force, which fully captures the content of the repealed CBM Directive 2005/56/EC.

19 Directive 2001/23/EC of 12 March 2001 on the approximation of the laws of the Member States relating to the safeguarding of employees' rights in the event of transfers of undertakings, business or parts of undertakings or businesses.

20 An ongoing project ("Cross-border company mobility") partly financed by ETUI is gathering data from 2000 to 2008 and from 2012 onwards. See: www.maastrichtuniversity.nl/research/institutes/item/research/cross-border-corporate-mobility-eu.

21 Exceptions were included in Article 3.3., now Article 120.3 of Directive (EU) 2017/1132.

22 These are transactions by which a company acquires a majority holding in the capital of a company, and, in exchange, transfers its own shares to the shareholders of the latter.

23 Daily Mail C-81/87 and Centros C-212/97 are exemplary cases of the CJEU doctrine supporting "incorporation" *vis-à-vis* "real seat" theories in corporate law.

24   A 14th Directive on transfer of companies' registered office has been in the pipe-
     line of European Commission's proposals since 1997 without ever being formal-
     ised. The protection of codetermination was again highly contentious. The EU
     "company law package" and the CJEU judgement on case C-106/16 *Polbud –
     Wykonawstwo sp. z o.o.* [ECLI:EU:C:2017:804] reinvigorated discussions around
     the regulation of cross-border transfers of seat.
25   The package consists in two Directives proposed to amend Directive (EU)
     2017/1132 and expected to be adopted by the end of the European Parliament's
     legislature in 2019. One deals with cross-border conversions, mergers and di-
     visions, the other with the use of digital tools and processes in company law.
     Although initially included, the conflict-of-laws issue was finally withdrawn
     from the proposal and put off for an eventual later specific legislation.
26   Directive 2004/25/EC of 21 April on takeover bids.
27   Frankfurt Regional Court in judgement of 16 Feb. 2015, 3–16 O 1/14.
28   Oberlandesgericht Frankfurt am Main, 25.05.2018 – 21 W 32/18 (*Deutsche
     Börse*).
29   According to its report of activities of 2015–2016, the TUI AG supervisory
     board participated in decisions dealing with the business model, growth strat-
     egies and cross-national transactions (i.e. sales, divestments, companies' ac-
     quisition, investment allocation) and matters concerning global organization,
     human resources policies (i.e. gender quota, employee shares) or health and
     safety structures. www.tuigroup.com/en-en/investors/corporate-governance/
     report-of-the-supervisory-board [checked 1 Jul. 2017].
30   Three laws provide for codetermination rights in Germany: the Codetermina-
     tion Act in the Coal, Iron and Steel Industry (1951) and its Supplementary Act
     (1956); the Third Codetermination Act (2004, former Works Constitution Act
     of 1952) and the Codetermination Act (1976), establishing a mandatory quasi-
     parity rule in companies with more than 2,000 employees, which is the one ap-
     plicable to TUI AG.
31   The Advocate General (AG)'s Opinion suggested that the legal status of foreign
     entities was the ultimate yardstick to constitute a cross-border element, render-
     ing free movement rules applicable to the case. But is the legal status decisive
     (i) because it determines the jurisdiction applicable to the entity – still left up to
     national rules? (ii) because it affects the nature of the relationship between the
     worker and his/her parent company? It was not explicit whether the connection
     with EU law is rooted in the entity's law, or in the law applicable to the employ-
     ment relationship.
32   The AG's Opinion addressed the issue as problematic and encouraged Euro-
     pean legislation on minimum labour standards across company groups.

Literature

Bech-Bruun; Lexidale (2013): *Study on the Application of the Cross-Border Mergers
    Directive*. Directorate General for the Internal Market and Services, European
    Commission.
Biermeyer, T.; Meyer, M. (2015): *Identification of Cross-Border Mergers Where the
    Issue Employee Participation Has Arisen (2008–2012)*. Internal Research Paper,
    ETUI, Brussels.
Biermeyer, T.; Meyer, M. (2018): *Cross-Border Corporate Mobility in the EU. Empir-
    ical Findings 2018*. Report, ETUI and Maastricht University.

Chomel, C. (2004): The Long March of the European Cooperative Society. *Revue internationale de l'économie sociale* 02/2004 (291): 1–5.

Cremers, J.; Vitols, S. (eds.) (2016): *Takeovers with or without Worker Voice: Workers' Rights under the EU Takeover Bids Directive*. Brussels: ETUI.

Cremers, J.; Wolters, E. (2011): *EU and National Company Law – Fixation on Attractiveness*. ETUI Report 120. Brussels: ETUI.

Conchon, A. (2013): National Participation Rights in an EU Perspective: The SE Rules as a Key Safeguard. In: Cremers, J.; Stollt, M.; Vitols, S. (eds.): *A Decade of Experience with the European Company*. Brussels: ETUI, 291–310.

Conchon, A. (2015): *Workers' Voice in Corporate Governance: A European Perspective*. ETUI and TUC.

Cooperatives Europe, Euricse and Ekai (2010): *Study on the Implementation of the Regulation 1435/2003 on the Statute for European Cooperative Society (SCE)*. Final Report for the European Commission.

Davies, P. (2003): Workers on the Board of the European Company? *Industrial Law Journal* 32 (2): 75–96.

Deakin, S. (2007): A New Paradigm for Labour Law? *Melbourne University Law Review* 31: 1161–1173.

Eidenmüller, H.; Hornuf, L.; Reps, M. (2012): Contracting Employee Involvement: An Analysis of Bargaining Over Employee Involvement Rules for a Societas Europaea. *Journal of Corporate Law Studies* 12 (2): 201–235.

ETUI (2017a): European Worker Participation Competence Centre (EWPCC) database (accessed 20.2.2017).

ETUI (2017b): European Company Database. http://ecdb.worker-participation.eu (accessed 9.8.2017).

ETUI; ETUC (2017): *Benchmarking Working Europe 2017*. Brussels: ETUI.

ETUC (2016): *Orientation for a New EU Framework on Information, Consultation and Board-Level Representation Rights*. Position paper. https://www.etuc.org/sites/default/files/document/files/en-position-wblr.pdf [checked 29 Oct 2018]

Eurostat (2017): *Data on Foreign Control of Enterprises by Controlling Countries Intra EU28 [fats_g1b_08]*. http://appsso.eurostat.ec.europa.eu/nui/submitView TableAction.do [checked 17 Jul 2017].

Fernández Guadaño, J. (2006): Structural Changes in the Development of European Co-operative Societies. *Annals of Public and Cooperative Economics* 77 (1): 107–127.

González Begega, S.; Köhler, H.D. (2016): La Sociedad Europea (SE). ¿Una Oportunidad Perdida para la Democracia Industrial en Europa? *Cuadernos de Relaciones Laborales* 33 (1): 65–91.

Habersack, M.; Behme, C.; Eidenmüller, H.; Klöhn, L. (eds.) (2016): Deutsche Mitbestimmung unter europäischen Reformzwang. *Fachmedien Recht und Wirtschaft*, Frankfurt-am-Main.

Hellwig, H.-J.; Behme, C. (2009): Gemeinschaftsrechtliche Probleme der deutschen Unternehmensmitbestimmung. *Die Aktiengesellschaft* 54 (8): 261–278.

Hofmann, A. (2017): *Who Goes to Court? Social Partners and the Asymmetry of EU Law*. Paper for the Council for European Studies 2017 Conference, University of Glasgow.

Hopt, K.J. (2016): *The German Law of and Experience with the Supervisory Board*. Law Working Paper No 305/2016, European Corporate Governance Institute.

Jackson, G.; Müllenborn, T. (2012): Understanding the Role of Institutions in Industrial Relations: Perspectives from Classical Sociological Theory. *Industrial Relations* 51 (S1): 472–500.

Jacquot, S.; Woll, C. (2010): Using Europe: Strategic Action in Multi-Level Politics. *Comparative European Politics* 8 (1): 110–126.

Jacobi, O.; Keller, B.; Müller-Jentsch, W. (1992): Germany: Codetermining the Future. In: Ferner, A.; Hyman, R. (eds.): *Industrial Relations in the New Europe.* Oxford: Basil Blackwell, 218–269.

Keller, B.; Werner, F. (2008): Negotiated Forms of Worker Involvement in the European Company (SE). First Empirical Evidence and Conclusions. *The International Review of Management Studies* 19 (4): 291–306.

Lafuente Hernández, S.; Rasnača, Z. (2019): Can Workers' Rights Ever Catch Up? The Erzberger Case and EU Cross-Border Reality. *Industrial Law Journal* 48 (1): 98–116. First published 14 November 2018.

Lenoir, N. (2008): The Societas Europaea (SE) in Europe. A Promising Start and an Option with Good Prospects. *Utrecht Law Review* 4 (1): 13–21.

Mulder, B.J. (2017): The Law Concerning the Election of Employees' Representatives in Company Bodies. Note in the Light of the CJEU Case Konrad Erzberger v TUI AG, C 566/15. *European Labour Law Journal* 8 (1): 96–104.

Rehfeldt, U. (2011): L'Européanisation de la participation des salariés dans les sociétés européennes par la négociation: potentialités et limites. *La Revue de l'IRES* 2011/4 (n°71): 89–114.

Rose, E.; Köstler, R. (2014): Mitbestimmung in der Europäischen Aktiengesellschaft (SE). Frankfurt am Main: Bund Verlag.

Rosenbohm, S. (2014): *Verhandelte Mitbestimmung. Die Arbeitnehmerbeteiligung in der Europäischen Aktiengesellschaft.* Frankfurt: Campus Verlag.

Page, R. (2011): *Co-determination in Germany – A Beginner's Guide*, Arbeitspapier 33, Hans Böckler Stiftung. www.boeckler.de/pdf/p_arbp_033.pdf.

Pastor Sempere, C. (2009): La Sociedad Cooperativa Europea domiciliada en España. *Revista de Estudios Cooperativos, 01/2009* 97 (5): 117–144.

Pütz, L.; Sick, S. (2015): *Acid Test ECJ – Undermine or Strengthen Co-Determination? The ECJ Examines Conformity of German Co-Determination under European Law.* Report 17/2015. Hans Böckler Stiftung, Düsseldorf.

Sick, S. (2015): *Der deutschen Mitbestimmung entzogen: Unternehmen mit ausländischer Rechtsform nehmen zu.* Hans Böckler Stiftung Report. www.boeckler.de/pdf/p_mbf_report_2015_8.pdf.

Snaith, I. (2006): Employee Involvement in the European Cooperative Society: A Range of Stakeholders? *International Journal of Comparative Labour Law and Industrial Relations* 22: 213–230.

Stollt, M.; Wolters, E. (2011): *Worker Involvement in the European Company (SE). A Handbook for Practitioners.* Brussels: ETUI.

Waddington, J.; Conchon, A. (2016): *Board-Level Employee Representation in Europe. Priorities, Power and Articulation.* New York and London: Routledge.

Waddington, J.; Conchon, A. (2017): *Is Europeanised Board-Level Employee Representation Specific? The Case of European Companies (SEs).* Working Paper 2017-02. ETUI, Brussels.

Chapter 13

Europe is not the answer

Some remarks on the future of worker co-determination in Europe

Benjamin Werner

The involvement of workers in the governance of corporations – the central organisation of the capitalist economy – has always been a contentious issue, since it limits the power of owners and management. Also, occurrence and form of co-determination vary significantly in Europe, from non-existence in the UK to Germany's far-reaching "Mitbestimmung" (Aguilera/Jackson 2003; Conchon 2011). Given this political salience as well as the great diversity in national co-determination practices, a European-wide harmonisation of this central aspect of corporate governance has always failed so far (Wouters 2000; Werner 2013: 30–43). Agreement could only be reached if crucial points were made non-binding. The SE Directive reflects this perfectly: which co-determination rights apply in an SE depends on several conditions that vary from case to case in order to avoid both strengthening of worker-involvement in Member States with weak co-determination and weakening of stronger co-determination systems. Thus, until today there is no European minimum standard for co-determination and the few existing European regulations that affect this issue are intended to be neutral towards the national models.

This observation is also the starting point of Sara Lafuente Hernández's critical assessment of the relevance of European integration for co-determination. However, she takes this further in two important regards: first, she demonstrates convincingly that even the thin achievements in EU secondary law like the SE and especially the provisions of the Cross-Border Mergers Directive are far from neutral. Instead, these provisions can be – and actually are – often used to weaken worker-involvement rights (obviously against the regulations' intention). And second, she argues rightly that European internal market law, especially in form of extensive European Court of Justice (ECJ) jurisprudence, is helping businesses significantly to escape and undermine existing co-determination rights on the national level. Taken together these arguments make it very clear that European integration in its current form is not a boon but a bane for worker co-determination in Europe. Rather than protecting or promoting this form of "industrial democracy", European law is currently undermining it. Sara

Lafuente Hernández, therefore, calls for new political action and legislation on the European level to stop and maybe even reverse this corrosive effect of European law for co-determination rights.

As already indicated, I share her general assessment of the impact of European integration on co-determination. European law is currently indeed neither defender nor promoter of this form of "industrial democracy" but one of its worst enemies. However, I think that one aspect of Sara Lafuente Hernández' argumentation must be emphasised much more, and that is the role of the ECJ and its case law. The threat of this aspect for co-determination rights is not only bigger and more severe than her article suggests, but it is also highly relevant for the question of what can be done to protect co-determination rights from the "European danger" – an implication Sara Lafuente Hernández is not reflecting at all.

Regarding the severity of the ECJ case law, it has to be pointed out, first, that the Court's decisions regarding the freedom of establishment have recently been radicalised. As Sara Lafuente Hernández rightly describes, the ECJ has ruled that this Internal Market freedom allows entrepreneurs to choose the most attractive legal order when *establishing* a company. This opened indeed the possibility to circumvent more demanding company law standards, among them mandatory co-determination requirements (Armour/Ringe 2011). But recently, in its *Polbud*[1] decision the ECJ has drastically expanded this possibility and, therefore, dramatically intensified corporate "regime-shopping" in Europe. Now even already *existing* companies are allowed to change their legal form any time and without any obligation to have an economic link to the member state which provides the new corporate legal form. Thus, by now companies always have the right to enjoy the legislation that best suits them. This has potentially dramatic consequences for co-determination since it weakens the power of workers vis-à-vis management and owners drastically. The capital side can now always threaten to change the company's legal form to one without co-determination in order to force the workers to support company decisions against their interests.

Yet, the co-determination undermining capacity of ECJ case law stems not only from these decisions on the freedom of establishment. There is, second, also danger lurking from the case law on the free movement of capital (Werner 2013, 2016), an aspect Sara Lafuente Hernández does not mention. In its decisions on so-called "Golden Shares", the ECJ ruled that any national regulation restricting the power of shareholders in a company constitutes a restriction of the free movement of capital. Such restrictions are only allowed, if they can be justified by reasons of general interest and fulfil certain criteria of proportionality. So far, this case law concerned only a very special case of shareholder power restriction, namely Golden Shares – a legal instrument that allows the state to keep control over ownership and crucial management decisions of privatised companies without being the major shareholder. But law experts have pointed out that these rulings would also affect many other national measures restricting shareholder power (Ringe 2008; Gerner-Beuerle 2012). And it is not hard to understand that co-determination would be one of the most obvious examples in this regard – to limit the power of management and owners is, after all, the basic idea of co-determination. Whether this restriction can then be justified or not is far from certain. Even if the ECJ accepts that co-determination can be justified, the member state concerned would also need to explain why the concrete form of worker-involvement is necessary and appropriate. And why should the ECJ accept a high co-determination standard (like in Germany) as proportionate when other, less far-reaching national co-determination models demonstrate – at least in the eyes of the judges – that the protection of workers' interests in a corporation can also be realised with much less restrictive measures? Thus, in contrast to the case law on freedom of establishment, this jurisprudence threatens co-determination rights directly. It has the potential not only to rule out existing co-determination models (at least the stronger ones) but also to block any attempts to strengthen worker-involvement rights on national as well as European level.

Therefore, these developments alone demonstrate that the ECJ and its case law have to be watched much more closely than many observers realise. But it might be even more important to understand technically how far-reaching these lines of case law are (Schmidt 2018). Besides the co-determination undermining content, it is also crucial to see that the ECJ case law described earlier operates on a different level than European secondary law. This case law interprets fundamental rights of the EU Treaties and is thus part of the EU's primary law. And European legislation (i.e. secondary legislation) cannot overrule this primary law; only Treaty change can do that. In consequence, the only way to get rid of the co-determination undermining ECJ case law is to change the European Treaties – an option which, in light of the fact that a common denominator for a European-wide co-determination standard was never in sight, is realistically not available. And as long as this case law continues to exist, any secondary law has to be in line with it. Thus, I disagree with Sara Lafuente Hernández who calls for further action on the European level in order to stop or even reverse the negative impact of Europe for co-determination. Apart from the fact that also this secondary law would have to surmount high majority thresholds that are practically unsurmountable given the great diversity of interests, such action would, in my view, also be very much futile in light of the subordinate status of secondary law.

To my mind, the only way to protect and to strengthen co-determination is to pursue national measures. Such a strategy would comprise, first of all, of course, national attempts to introduce and to extend existing national models of worker-involvement in corporations. The several national discussions described by Sara Lafuente Hernández in Member States like France or the UK are encouraging and promising signs that currently there might indeed be a window of opportunity for such national developments. Proponents of co-determination on the European level should use their knowledge and influence to nurture these processes as constructive and helpful as possible. Second, such a strategy would then comprise the development of national measures (tailored to the specific domestic context, of course), which are able to protect the national co-determination model as much as possible. One example in this regard could be a national measure (a law, etc.) that extends the domestic co-determination model to all economically active corporations in the given member state irrespective of their legal form.[2] In my view, this is a very promising option to counter the devastating case law on the freedom of establishment, especially the *Polbud* decision. Of course, it might be that both parts of this national strategy to strengthen co-determination rights will be tested before the ECJ. But I am quite sure that there are ways to be successful, either by convincing the Court that the national co-determination rights are not violating the internal market freedoms, or by finding ways to contain the consequences of negative decisions. This is, for sure, a rather conflictive strategy and might be called "protectionist" and "non-European". But to protect co-determination rights such national efforts are, at least in the short or medium term, much more promising than hoping for a break-through on the European level – which will almost certainly never happen.

Notes

1 Case C-106/16 (Polbud), Judgment of the Court (Grand Chamber) of 25 October 2017.
2 German unions are calling for such a measure since years now, but unfortunately to no avail so far.

Literature

Aguilera, Ruth V.; Jackson, Gregory (2003): The Cross-National Diversity of Corporate Governance: Dimensions and Determinants. *Academy of Management Review* 28 (3), 447–465.

Armour, John; Ringe, Wolf-Georg (2011): *European Company Law 1999–2010: Renaissance and Crisis*. Brussels: European Corporate Governance Institute (ECGI).

Conchon, Aline (2011): Board-level employee representation rights in Europe: Facts and Trends. Report 121. Brussels: European Trade Union Institute (ETUI).

Gerner-Beuerle, Carsten (2012): Shareholders between the Market and the State. The VW Law and Other Interventions in the Market Economy. *Common Market Law Review* 49 (1), 97–144.

Ringe, Wolf-Georg (2008): The Volkswagen Case and the European Court of Justice. *Common Market Law Review* 45 (2), 537–544.

Schmidt, Susanne K. (2018): *The European Court of Justice and the Policy Process. The Shadow of Case Law*. Oxford: Oxford University Press.

Werner, Benjamin (2013): *Der Streit um das VW-Gesetz. Wie Europäische Kommission und Europäischer Gerichtshof die Unternehmenskontrolle liberalisieren*. Frankfurt a.M.: Campus.

Werner, Benjamin (2016): Why Is the Court of Justice of the European Union Not More Contested? Three Mechanisms of Opposition Abatement. *Journal of Common Market Studies* 54 (6), 1449–1464.

Wouters, Jan (2000): European Company Law: Quo Vadis? *Common Market Law Review* 37 (2), 257–307.

Chapter 14

European economic governance, autonomy of collective bargaining and democratic capitalism

Daniel Seikel

Introduction

The autonomy of collective bargaining in the euro-countries is under attack. The euro crisis brought the issue of divergent wage developments in the euro area to the fore. In response to the crisis, a new economic governance architecture for the Eurozone was devised. New procedures were set up at European level, which provided European institutions with new regulatory competences regarding national wage policies.

The ambushes on collective bargaining systems launched from the European level are especially noteworthy since the autonomy of collective bargaining is explicitly protected by European Treaty law (cf. Höpner/Rödl 2012; Rödl/Callsen 2015). The so-called 'restrictive clause' of Article 153 (5) Treaty on the Functioning of the European Union (TFEU) explicitly states that the regulative competences of the EU 'do not apply to pay, the right of association, the right to strike or the right to impose lock-outs'. Furthermore, Article 28 of the Charter of Fundamental Rights stipulates that

> [w]orkers and employers, or their respective organisations, have, in accordance with Community law and national laws and practices, the right to negotiate and conclude collective agreements at the appropriate levels and, in cases of conflicts of interest, to take collective action to defend their interests, including strike action.

Nevertheless, European institutions have directly intervened in an unprecedented way in the wage setting of several euro-countries (Müller 2015: 6). Furthermore, a new governance architecture was set up at European Union (EU) level to control national wage developments.

As Schulten and Müller (2015: 352) state, the establishment of the new European governance regime 'marks a paradigm shift from acceptance of free collective bargaining to direct political intervention in national collective bargaining outcomes and processes'. Moreover, the new European interventionism 'must be seen as a political project to weaken European trade unions' (Schulten/Müller 2015: 354). These observations serve as the starting point for the following examination. The present article analyses how the euro crisis management and the new European economic governance regime affect the autonomy of collective bargaining as well as the bargaining power of trade unions in the Member States participating in the Economic and Monetary Union (EMU). In this article, the autonomy of collective bargaining refers to the legally guaranteed prerogative of trade unions and employers to regulate central aspects of the economic and work life through collectively binding agreements (Kocher 2010: 482; Seikel/Absenger 2015: 52).

As will be shown, the new European competences are in fundamental conflict with the autonomy of collective bargaining. Moreover, I outline how different reform measures imposed on programme countries have led to a substantial deterioration of the bargaining power of trade unions. In addition, I argue that the weakening of autonomous collective bargaining undermines one of the cornerstones of post-war democratic governance: by restricting the autonomy of collective autonomy the new European economic governance regime weakens one of two channels by which capitalism has been democratically domesticated since the end of the Second World War.

The remainder is structured as follows: building on the concept of democratic capitalism, Section 2 depicts democracy-related functions of the autonomy of collective bargaining. Section 3 briefly explains why wages have become a focal point of the EU's crisis strategy. In Section 4, the institutional innovations implemented in response to the euro crises are described. The article focusses on new regulatory procedures that target national wage developments. Thereafter, I analyse the way in which new procedures affect the autonomy of collective bargaining and the power resources of trade unions (Section 5). Section 6 summarises and discusses the findings.

Two channels of democratisation: autonomy of collective bargaining and democratic capitalism

Recently, Wolfgang Streeck (2011, 2013) has revived the concept of democratic capitalism and applied it to the development of democratic and capitalist countries from the end of the Second World War until today. Core to this concept is the observation of a fundamental tension between capitalism and democracy which is rooted in the conflict between the quest for economic liberalisation of capitalists on the one hand and aspirations for social regulation of wage-earners on the other. Historically, capitalist societies have been able to reconcile the contradictions between the two positions only temporarily (Streeck 2009: 227, 2011: 24): only during the first decades after the Second World War was it possible to balance this tension over a relatively long period of time (Streeck 2013: 11, 2014: 40). The three decades after the Second World War can be seen as the golden era of democratic capitalism. Yet, beginning at the end of the 1960s, the post-war regime of democratic capitalism slowly started to erode (Streeck 2013: 10). By and by, democratic capitalism entered a state of permanent crisis. In response to repeated economic crises, policy-makers started to shift the balance between the market and the state successively to the detriment of the state and democracy (2014: 116). Streeck (2013: 27–28) described this process as an 'immunisation' of the economy against democracy and as 'de-economisation' of democracy. However, every new arrangement that was able to stabilise capitalism for a time sowed the seeds for the next crisis (Streeck 2011: 24) – from inflation to mass unemployment, from mass unemployment to public debt, from public debt to volatile financial markets, from volatile financial markets to financial and economic crisis, including the euro crisis.

How was capitalism democratised after the Second World War? In modern Western democracies, there are usually two channels through which capitalism has been democratically regulated. The first channel for exerting democratic control over the economy is the electoral channel, i.e. political democracy. Political democracy is based on representative parliamentarianism and/or elements of direct democracy. The prerequisite of political democracy is the general primacy of political decisions over economic decisions. This primacy of the political sphere rests on a chain of five interlinked elements: (1) the state monopoly of the use of force and (2) its use to establish the rule of law (3) constitutionally guaranteed political citizenship rights that (4) empower citizens to vote for parliaments which (5) issue collectively binding laws to which individual economic contracts are subordinated.

The second channel of democratic regulation of capitalism is economic or industrial democracy.[1] Economic democracy rests on collective social rights that balance the power asymmetry between capital and labour, e.g. the freedom of association, the right to strike or the binding nature of collective agreements (cf. Schmid 1951: 118, 120). Institutionalised labour relations form the second arena besides parliaments in which the struggle for economic and political power takes place (Streeck 2006: 5). The corporatist integration of the labour movement after the war was a cornerstone of democratic capitalism. It secured a certain level of democratic co-determination in the economic sphere (Eberl/Salomon 2017: 5). As the corporatism literature of the 1970s onwards shows, alongside party systems and parliaments, interest organisations with quasi-public status made an important contribution to governance (Molina/Rhodes 2002: 305). Legally enforceable collective agreements enabled employers and trade unions to act as second legislator (Schmid 1951: 119).

Institutionalised collective social rights restrict a pure capitalistic logic in two ways. First, the determination of wages and other working conditions is not based on the market mechanism in the first place but on collective bargaining. Hence, the regulation of working conditions – i.e. the price of labour – is not determined by supply and demand of labour alone but also by the balance of power between capital and organised labour. As a principle of economic organisation, bargaining power is fundamentally different from market-driven price setting. Second, given the asymmetric power distribution between employers and individual workers, individual workers are in a weak bargaining position vis-à-vis employers. Collective labour law balances this uneven distribution of power between capitalists (seeking economic liberalisation[2]) and wage-earners (seeking social regulation). Here, trade unions play an especially important role. In order to curb the power of business, trade unions are entrusted with the task of acting as countervailing power. Economic democracy, thus, is a means to domesticate the economy not directly by the state but out of the economic sphere itself in the sense of autonomous self-regulation of the economy.[3]

Both channels of democratic domestication of the economy – the electoral and the corporatist – have been hollowed out throughout the last decades (cf. Streeck 2006: 20–31). This process is the most important element of the trend towards what Crouch (2004) has called 'Post-Democracy' (Eberl/Salomon 2017: 5). During the euro crisis, both political and economic democracy received another severe blow. The remainder of the article focusses on the consequences of the euro crisis for economic democracy.

Wages, collective bargaining and competitiveness in the euro crisis

Why have wages become a focal point of the European crisis response? The answer to this question is connected to the broadly prevailing diagnosis, that the euro crisis is rooted, to a large extent, in diverging wage developments across the Eurozone (cf. Collignon 2009; Flassbeck/Lapavitsas 2013; Höpner/Lutter 2017).

According to Höpner and Lutter (2017), the substantial institutional heterogeneity of collective bargaining systems – especially between the 'coordinated' systems of northern European countries and 'uncoordinated' ones in southern Europe – led to divergent developments of wages and unit labour costs (see Figure 14.1). This resulted in a deterioration of price competitiveness of southern European countries vis-à-vis 'wage moderating' countries in northern Europe, in particular Germany. The result was a massive piling up of current account imbalances between the countries of the Eurozone, leading to private and/or public debt in the deficit countries (Höpner/Rödl 2012: 220). This view is also shared by the European Commission (2012: 15):

> Large and sustained increases in ULCs [unit labour costs] may lead to the erosion of competitiveness, especially if combined with a widening current account deficit and declining market shares for exports. For instance, in the years preceding the present crisis, wage growth outstripped productivity improvements in many Member States, inducing sharp increases in ULC.

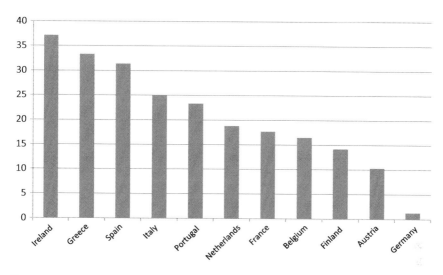

Figure 14.1 Cumulated annual growth rates of nominal unit labour costs in percent (2000–2008).

Source: Eurostat; http://ec.europa.eu/eurostat/tgm/table.do?tab=table&init=1&language=en&pcode=tipslm20&plugin=1 (last accessed: 18.08.2016).

Since membership in the EMU reduced available national macroeconomic instruments for economic adjustment (exchange rate, interest rate, fiscal policy, wage policy) to wage policy, European institutions and most of the national governments saw the moderation of wages as the primary means for the economic recovery of countries in crisis (Höpner/Rödl 2012: 220; Rödl/Callsen 2015: 15; Schulten/Müller 2015: 331). For many influential political actors, flexibilisation of collective bargaining became the key prerequisite for the functioning of the monetary union (Rödl/Callsen 2015: 15). What followed was a general overhaul of the European economic governance architecture with the aim – apart from enforcing fiscal discipline – of bringing national wage developments in line with the necessities of EMU.

The next section reviews the institutional innovations at EU level targeting national wages and collective bargaining systems.

Wages in the new European economic governance framework

In response to the euro crisis, European policymakers introduced two main innovations: a financial assistance procedure, including the European Stability Mechanism (ESM) and the Troika, and a far-reaching reform of the Stability and Growth Pact (SGP) (Müller 2015: 9).

The new financial assistance procedure

Next to reducing public debt, one of the main objectives of the new European economic governance regime is to align wage growth with the development of productivity (Rödl/Callsen 2015: 15). However, the already existing huge trade balance and current account deficits of countries in need of urgent financial assistance, such as Greece, Spain, Portugal and Ireland, had to be addressed first. In order to correct trade balance deficits, European policymakers dictated a strategy of internal devaluation, i.e. lowering wages, social transfers and public expenditures in order to increase price competitiveness and consolidate public finances (Müller 2015: 19).

During the negotiations of the first rescue package for Greece in 2010, a procedure for granting financial assistance for euro-countries in distress was developed (Müller 2015: 10). In this context, the so-called Troika was established (Müller 2015: 5). The Troika is a three-headed structure consisting of European Commission, International Monetary Fund (IMF) and European Central Bank (ECB) (Müller 2015: 5).[4] It negotiates the 'conditionalities' for receiving financial assistance. Countries receiving financial aid have to commit themselves to far-reaching structural reforms that are formalised in a 'Memorandum of Understanding' (MoU) (Müller 2015: 10–11). The Troika monitors the implementation of and compliance with assistance programmes and MoUs (Müller 2015: 11).[5]

So far, reform programmes have pursued two objectives: enforcement of strict austerity and supply-sided structural reforms of labour markets and wage-setting systems. As Schulten and Müller (2015) show, programme countries had to freeze or even cut minimum wages as well as salaries in the public sector.[6] As a consequence, wages in the public sector of these countries fell by five percentage points to 30%, abolition of additional monthly salaries, pension entitlements, food allowances and subsidies not included. Furthermore, a bundle of different measures aimed at decentralising collective bargaining was imposed on countries in crisis. First, 'favourability clauses' had to be eradicated. As a consequence, collective agreements at company-level may contain conditions less favourable than those of sectoral or national collective agreements. In some cases, company-level agreements gained precedence over sectoral agreements. Second, non-trade union workers' representatives had to be authorised to conclude collective agreements. Third, declaring collective agreements generally applicable was made more difficult. Fourth, Troika countries had to reduce the duration and 'after effects' of (expired) collective agreements.

Institutional reform of the European economic governance architecture

In addition to the new financial assistance procedure, the general economic governance architecture of the EMU was thoroughly reformed. The so-called Six-Pack (2011) is the central element of the reform.[7] The legislative

package entails three elements. First, it establishes the 'European Semester' that aims at a systematic ex-ante coordination of national economic
policies and budgets. Second, the reform tightens the economic deficit procedure (EDP).[8] Third, the Six-Pack implements a new procedure for the
prevention and correction of macroeconomic imbalances, the macroeconomic imbalance procedure, including the excessive imbalance procedure
(EIP). Euro Plus Pact (2011), Fiscal Compact (2012) and Two Pack (2013)
complement the Six-Pack. All these procedures and regulations over-
lap and form one integrated macroeconomic governance regime for the
Eurozone (Gloggnitzer/Lindner 2011: 49; Salines et al. 2012: 672; van Aken/
Artige 2013: 148; Bauer/Becker 2014: 220; Seikel 2016: 5–6). In the following, I focus on the procedures that target wages: the European Semester,
the Euro Plus Pact and the EIP.

European Semester

The reforms in the aftermath of the crisis have complemented the previous
European economic governance structure with the European Semester: a
new procedure of ex-ante coordination of economic and fiscal policies and
budgetary surveillance. In order to improve policy coordination and monitoring, the national budgetary scheduling was synchronised with the annual
cycle of the European Semester. The European Semester starts before the national budgetary consultations. Euro-countries have to submit their budget
drafts in October. In November, the Commission publishes the annual
growth survey and alert-mechanism report and issues opinions about the
budget drafts. In April, the non-euro-countries submit their budget drafts.
At the same time, all Member States present 'national reform programmes'
on economic policies and 'stability programmes' (euro-countries) or 'convergence programmes' (non-euro-countries) on fiscal policies. In June or
July, the Council adopts country-specific recommendations proposed by the
Commission (Degryse 2012: 29; Seikel 2016: 6).[9] These recommendations
have to be addressed in the national reform programmes, stability and convergence programmes of the following year. Country-specific recommendations are not binding but can become obligatory through the EDP and the
EIP (Schulten/Müller 2015: 333, 337). So far, experiences with the new European Semester show that country-specific recommendations usually aim at
reducing public debts, raising the retirement age, deregulating labour markets and achieving a moderate wage development (Bieling 2012).[10] Germany,
however, was requested to support a more dynamic wage development.

Euro Plus Pact

As a supplement to the European Semester, the heads of government
adopted the Euro Plus Pact.[11] It aims at additional, legally non-binding policy coordination. Its main objective is the improvement of competitiveness.

It focusses on wage and productivity developments and 'competitive adjustment needs'. Further objectives are the fostering of employment, sustainability of public finances and financial stability. The Euro Plus Pact contains a set of indicators and principles. According to the Euro Plus Pact, wages should evolve in line with productivity. This is assessed by monitoring unit labour costs. The Euro Plus Pact indicates how Member States shall ensure the alignment of wages and productivity:

-   [R]eview the wage setting arrangements, and, where necessary, the degree of centralisation in the bargaining process, and the indexation mechanisms, while maintaining the autonomy of the social partners in the collective bargaining process;
-   ensure that wage settlements in the public sector support the competitiveness efforts in the private sector (bearing in mind the important signalling effect of public sector wages).

Member states have to specify measures for achieving the targets of the Euro Plus Pact in their stability and convergence programmes. Thus, the provisions of the Euro Plus Pact are integrated in the European Semester.

Excessive imbalance procedure

As another innovation, the new European economic governance regime is no longer restricted to the surveillance of fiscal policies (public debt and public deficit) but also takes into consideration macroeconomic imbalances such as current account deficits (Degryse 2012: 39; Schulten/Müller 2015: 333). In contrast to the EDP, the EIP does not contain quasi-automatic trigger indicators.[12] Instead, the Commission assesses a number of indicators that are included in the new so-called Economic Scoreboard (Salines et al. 2012: 673). The Scoreboard serves as an early-alert mechanism. It contains a number of internal and external macroeconomic indicators, including minimum and maximum thresholds for every indicator (European Council 2011b; European Commission 2012; see Table 14.1).

If the Commission detects an excessive imbalance on the basis of a qualitative assessment of these indicators, the country concerned has to submit a corrective action plan within a defined period of time (European Council 2011b). In case a country does not take necessary measures or proposes measures that the Commission deems to be insufficient, the Commission can start an EIP and impose sanctions (see Table 14.2). Only euro-countries can be sanctioned. As mentioned, in context of the EIP, the country-specific recommendations of the European Semester can become obligatory. Recommendations about corrective actions can concern all policy areas, including wage policy, social policy and labour market policy (Höpner/Rödl 2012: 219).

Table 14.1 Indicators and indicative thresholds of the Economic Scoreboard

	Indicator	Euro-countries	Non-euro-countries	Time period
Internal imbalances	General government debt	Upper limit 60% of GDP	Upper limit 60% of GDP	–
	Private sector debt	Upper limit 160% of GDP	Upper limit 160% of GDP	–
	Unemployment rate	Increase of 10%	Increase of 10%	3-year-average
	Private sector credit flow*	Upper limit 15% of GDP	Upper limit 15% of GDP	–
	Deflated house prices	Increase of 9%	Increase of 12%	Annual change
External imbalances	Current account balance	Surplus of 6% of GDP	Surplus of 6% of GDP	3-year-average
		Deficit of 4% of GDP	Deficit of 4% of GDP	
	Nominal unit labour costs	Increase of 9%	Increase of 12%	Over 3 years
	Real effective exchange rate	Increase of 5% Decrease of 5%	Increase of 11% Decrease of 11%	Over 3 years
	Export market share	Decrease of 6%	Decrease of 6%	Over 5 years
	Net international investment position **	Lower limit of −35% of GDP	Lower limit of −35% of GDP	–

* Net amount of debt securities and loans for the private sector.
**Difference between external financial assets and liabilities.

Source: European Commission (2012).

Table 14.2 Overview of the EIP

Stage I	Council decides with qualified majority if excessive deficit exists and recommends corrective measures
	Member state submits corrective action plan
	Council approves corrective action plan or requests member state to submit a new corrective action plan within two months
	Member state regularly submits progress reports
Stage II	Council decides that member state has not taken recommended corrective actions
	Commission imposes an interest-bearing deposit of 0.1% of GDP if Council does not reject sanction within ten days with qualified majority
Stage III	If two successive Council decisions determine that
	a corrective actions are insufficient
	b or corrective actions have not been taken
	The Commission imposes (a) an annual fine of 0.1% of GDP or (b) a conversion of the interest-bearing deposit into an annual fine if Council does not deny sanction within ten days with qualified majority
	Council can change recommendation with qualified majority

Source: European Council (2011a, 2011b).

Consequences for the autonomy of collective bargaining, wages and trade unions

What are the consequences of the institutional innovations introduced in the aftermath of the euro crisis? Schulten and Müller (2015) have provided a comprehensive empirical analysis of the concrete effects of recent European interventions on minimum wages, salaries and collective bargaining systems.[13] Building on their findings, this section (a) discusses the implications for the autonomy of collective bargaining and (b) analyses their effects on the bargaining power of trade unions.

In the case of the new financial assistance procedure, the effects on the autonomy of collective bargaining are straightforward and do not need much elaboration. The authoritarian top-down imposition of downward wage flexibility in Ireland, Greece, Portugal and Spain[14] is an outright violation of the autonomy of collective bargaining (Rödl and Callsen 2015: 15–16). The legality of the Troika and the MoUs is highly doubtful (see Höpner/Rödl 2012; Fischer-Lescano 2014; Rödl/Callsen 2015). In Greece, minimum wages were normally settled by the social partners at national level. Under pressure from the other euro-countries, the Greek government was forced to replace collective bargaining by a *statutory* minimum wage (Schulten/Müller 2015: 344). Collective bargaining in the public sector of the programme countries has de facto been temporarily suspended (Glassner 2010: 23; Schulten/Müller 2015: 341). In all crisis-ridden countries collective bargaining systems have been decentralised. As a result, collective bargaining systems of the programme countries have virtually collapsed. Their collective bargaining systems have become closer to the single-employer bargaining systems in central and Eastern Europe than to the multi-employer bargaining systems in northern European countries. The structural reform programmes have led to unprecedented decentralisation and de-collectivisation of industrial relations (Müller 2015: 22). Between 2008 and 2013, the number of workers covered by collective agreements fell in Portugal from 1.7 million to 200,000 and in Spain from 10 million to 7 million. In Greece, the number of collective agreements at the sectoral level fell from 202 in 2008 to 14 in 2013, in Portugal from 172 to 27 and in Spain from 1,448 to 706 (Schulten/Müller 2015: 349–352). As a consequence real wages have declined dramatically (see Figure 14.2).

What effect did the imposed reform programmes (see Section 4.1) have on the power resources of trade unions? Five conclusions can be drawn: first, by making the criteria for declaring collective agreements generally applicable more restrictive in Greece and Portugal, the influence of trade unions on the state has been pushed back (cf. Hassel 2014: 30–31). From a political economy perspective, this aspect is particularly important in the case of the 'mixed market economies' of southern Europe where the state has a central role for the coordination of the economy. In this setting, access to the state

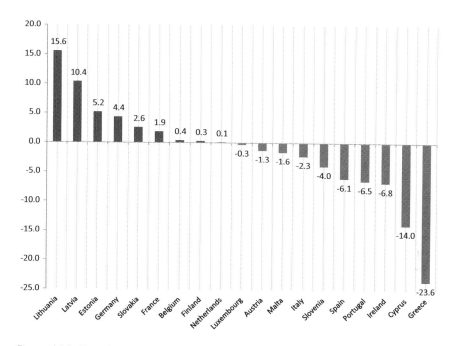

Figure 14.2 Development of real wages 2010–2014 in percent.
Source: Schulten and Müller (2015: 351).

is a key power resource. In the past, trade unions and employers used this influence to veto policy changes or to demand compensation and protection from the state (Hassel 2014: 4, 7, 2015: 235; Molina/Rhodes 2007: 227–228). By making it more difficult to declare collective agreements as universally binding, trade unions lost the possibility to stabilise collective bargaining via the state. For trade unions this is problematic because in the collective bargaining systems of southern European countries this practice was central to achieving a comparatively high degree of collective bargaining coverage. Second, in Ireland, Greece, Portugal and Spain, trade unions have been weakened in their strongholds: the public sectors. Given the wage-leadership of public sector collective bargaining in southern European countries (Hancké 2013; Schulten/Müller 2015: 340–341), wage demands of trade unions for other sectors are also affected. Two further, not mutually exclusive, effects are possible: a direct moderating effect on wages in the private sector (short-term) and a reversal of wage-leadership from 'sheltered' to 'exposed' sectors which could lead to a subordination of wage developments in the rest of the economy to cost competitiveness objectives of export firms (long-term). Third, the abolition of 'favourability clauses' and giving company-level agreements precedence over sectoral agreements in Greece and Spain has several effects. It leads to a deterioration of protection for workers since sectoral agreements no longer provide a guaranteed minimum level of working conditions that may not be undercut. Furthermore, for companies, deviating from sectoral agreements becomes much more attractive since it creates the possibility to obtain more favourable conditions. Finally, since an 'isolated' workforce is more susceptible to blackmail, giving company-level agreements precedence over sectoral agreements, like in Greece and Spain, increases the inclination of workers for concession bargaining. Workers can more easily be forced to accept worse working conditions in exchange for job security. Fourth, the authorisation of non-trade union workers' representatives to conclude collective agreements in Greece, Portugal and Spain weakens trade union representation at the workplace. But more important, trade unions lose their monopoly to conclude collective agreements. Hence, workers have fewer incentives to join a trade union. Fifth, the consequence of the reduction of the 'after effect' of expired collective agreements in Greece and Spain is particularly devastating for trade unions and workers. The effect of this measure is illustrated by Figure 14.3.

The measure shifts the default positions (SQ to SQ') for negotiations between the employer and employees to the detriment of the latter. With 'after effect', a new collective agreement (C) will probably be close to SQ because the expired collective agreement remains in force as long there is no new compromise between the parties. The abolition of the 'after effect' fundamentally changes the bargaining situation. If negotiations with employers fail, working conditions no longer fall back on the provisions of the expired but still valid agreement (SQ). Instead, in case of no agreement between trade unions and employers, single employers are free to autonomously set the working conditions. Since trade unions can be put under pressure to choose between a disadvantageous agreement (C') and an even worse situation without any agreement (SQ'), this change puts trade unions and workers in a much worse bargaining position vis-à-vis the employer. The latter can shape collective agreements much more to his advantage. The cumulated

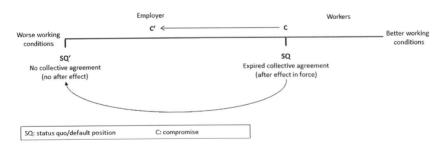

Figure 14.3 Effect of abolition of 'after effect' on bargaining constellation.

effect of all these changes leads to a considerable and systematic weakening of the bargaining power of trade unions.

Beyond the new financial assistance procedure, the reform of the SGP has provided European institutions with additional permanent competences for national wage policies which are not only restricted to the Troika countries but affect *all* euro-countries – despite the 'restrictive clause' of Article 153 (5) TFEU. Whereas the fate of the Troika is uncertain (Müller 2015), the procedures and rules of the new European economic governance architecture are firmly institutionalised. Thereby, the subordination of collective bargaining under the primacy of competitiveness is particularly problematic. The overarching objective is to bring wages in line with productivity. Here, the way the Commission has operationalised this objective deserves special attention. The Economic Scoreboard contains provisions for nominal unit labour costs (see Table 14.1). The upper limit is set to an increase of 9% over three years. There is no lower limit. This means that strong increases of wages and nominal labour costs can be punished. In contrast, weak wage developments that undercut wages in the rest of the Eurozone – having an equally macroeconomically de-stabilising effect – cannot be sanctioned. Hence, this rule significantly limits the leeway for an expansionary or solidaristic wage policy but does not pose any barriers for restrictive wage policies. This asymmetric approach to diverging wage developments puts the load for economic adjustment solely on deficit countries. This reflects the balance of power between deficit/debtor states and surplus/creditor states. The upper limit for nominal labour costs developments clearly restricts the autonomy of collective bargaining insofar as it indirectly establishes a 'ceiling' for wage growth. According to the definition of unit labour costs,[15] wages concluded by the social partners may not be higher than 3% above productivity growth on average per year. This rule implies that social partners may conclude wages only within the margins set by the European Commission, i.e. as long as they do not affect the price competitiveness of companies overly negatively. The theoretical consequences for the wage development can be illustrated by a hypothetical scenario of low productivity growth and high (exogenously driven) inflation. Assuming that productivity grows by 10% over three years, nominal wages would be allowed to rise by roughly 20% in this period. If we assume an inflation rate of 30% in the same time, this would mean a decline of real wages by 10%.

It is important to note that attempts by governments to influence wage developments in the context of an internal devaluation strategy are not new, as the literature on the social pacts of the 1990s in preparation for EMU accession in many European countries shows (Rhodes 2001; Hassel 2003). However, the differences between the governance modes of neo-corporatist concertation and direct hierarchical intervention deserve attention. In contrast to today, in the times of social pacts, governments and employers seemed to prefer austerity policies *with* the involvement of trade unions over austerity policies *without* trade union participation (Streeck 2006: 25). Governments needed the cooperation of trade unions because they could not influence wage levels directly and to keep the political costs of economic adjustment as low as possible, i.e. preventing electoral punishment (cf. Streeck 2006: 25–26). Trade unions often accepted wage moderation in exchange for some form of material compensation like pension increases. The new authoritarian and interventionist governance mode de-politicises and judicialises the politics of economic adjustment and welfare state restructuring. It reduces the dependence on trade union cooperation and removes the link to electoral accountability.[16] Elected governments only execute decisions made elsewhere at European level, in the Commission, the ECB or the euro group. There are no effective procedures to hold these actors accountable. Thus, austerity policy has become insulated against electoral restraints. In contrast to the 'class corporatism' of the post-war era or the neo-corporatism of the 1990s, the state does not have any longer 'to share public power with organised class interests disadvantaged by free-market capitalism' (Streeck 2006: 26).

Conclusions

In this article, I have shown how policy-makers in the EU have responded to the euro crisis. For this purpose, I have described those institutional innovations that directly target national wage developments. In addition, I have illustrated how these changes affect wages, collective bargaining and trade unions.

As became apparent, the EU's response to the crisis has clearly restricted the autonomy of collective bargaining. The violations by the Troika are especially drastic. Collective bargaining systems in the programme countries have been dismantled. In Section 4, I have outlined how the different reform measures have weakened trade unions in the programme countries. The implications of the reformed SGP for collective bargaining are equally important since the new procedures and rules are relevant for all euro-countries, not only for programme countries. The reformed SGP institutionalises a supply-sided view according to which wages are reduced to a cost factor. However, for trade unions, collective bargaining is a means to pursue a variety of objectives, such as the improvement of living conditions, the redistribution of wealth and the stimulation of demand and economic growth. The current path of monetary integration subordinates these objectives under the primacy of macroeconomic stability of the euro as a currency. This is not only a radical redefinition of the purposes of collective bargaining but also a total overburdening of the institutions, practices and actors of collective bargaining. Even the harshest and most sceptic critics of the structural market-liberalism of European integration could not have possibly imagined such a radicalisation of economic integration.

From a more theoretical perspective, I have shown that industrial relations were one of two channels by which capitalism was democratically domesticated after the Second World War (Section 2). By undermining the institutions of economic democracy and shifting the power balance between labour and capital, the new European economic governance regime makes euro-countries not only less social, but also less democratic.

Notes

1 I thank Wolfgang Streeck for pointing me towards this aspect.
2 From this power-based perspective, the interest for economic liberalisation can be understood as an interest for an 'increase of the degree of employers discretion' (cf. Baccaro/Howell 2017).
3 This mode of autonomous self-regulation is interesting for the state because of lower implementation costs and higher implementation effectiveness (Streeck/Schmitter 1985: 20). In addition, corporatism allowed for constituting polities and societies around organised classes and to deal with class conflict in a way compatible with liberal democracy while generating superior governability and economic performance (Streeck 2006: 12).
4 Meanwhile, the ESM joined the Troika which was officially re-named as 'Institutions'.
5 Decisions about granting financial assistance are not taken by the Troika but by the IMF executive board and ESM Board of Governors which consist of finance ministers of the other euro countries (Müller 2015: 11).
6 Wages in the public sector are important for both austerity and structural reform objectives since labour costs in the public sector represent a considerable proportion of national expenditure. In addition, public sector wages often serve as point of reference for collective bargaining in the private sector (Müller 2015: 19; Schulten/Müller 2015: 340–341).
7 The Six-Pack entails five regulations and one directive.
8 For a detailed analysis of the new system of surveillance, co-ordination and correction of national *fiscal* policies, see Seikel (2016).
9 For the schedule of the European Semester, see http://ec.europa.eu/europe2020/images/europeansemestser_big_en.jpg.
10 For an overview of wage-related recommendations, see Schulten and Müller (2015: 338 339)
11 http://www.consilium.europa.eu/uedocs/cms_data/docs/pressdata/en/ec/120296.pdf (last access: 19.08.2016).
12 The SGP sets the limit to public debt to 60% of GDP and to the annual public deficit to 3% of GDP.
13 See already Schulten and Müller (2013).
14 Spain is not subjected to the control of the Troika. However, Spain had to apply for financial assistance in order to stabilise its banking sector and had to commit itself to structural reforms in exchange.
15 Unit labour costs are defined as ratio of compensation per employee to real GDP per person employed (European Commission 2012: 15).
16 I thank Wolfgang Streeck for pointing out this aspect.

Literature

Baccaro, Lucio; Howell, Chris (2017): *European Industrial Relations since the 1970s: Trajectories of Neoliberal Transformation*. Cambridge: Cambridge University Press.

Bauer, Michael W.; Becker, Stefan (2014): The Unexpected Winner of the Crisis: The European Commission's Strengthened Role in Economic Governance. *Journal of European Integration* 36 (3): 213–229.

Bieling, Hans-Jürgen (2012): EU Facing the Crisis: Social and Employment Policies in Times of Tight Budgets. *Transfer* 18 (3): 255–271.

Collignon, Stefan (2009): The Failure of the Macroeconomic Dialogue on Wages (and How to Fix It). In: Letelier, Rute; Menéndez, Agustín José (eds.): *The Sinews of European Peace: Reconstituting the Democratic Legitimacy of the Socio-Economic Constitution of the European Union*. Oslo: ARENA Center for European Studies, 427–467.

Crouch, Colin (2004): *Post-Democracy*. Cambridge: Polity Press.

Degryse, Christophe (2012): *The New European Economic Governance*. ETUI Working Paper 2012.14. Brussels: ETUI.

Eberl, Oliver; Salomon, David (2017): Soziale Demokratie in der Postdemokratie. In: Eberl, Oliver; Salomon, David (eds.): *Perspektiven sozialer Demokratie in der Postdemokratie*, Wiesbaden: Springer VS, 1–15.

European Commission (2012): *Scoreboard for the surveillance of macroeconomic imbalance*. European Economy Occasional Papers 92.

European Council (2011a): Regulation (EU) No 1174/2011 of the European Parliament and of the Council of 16 November 2011 on Enforcement Measures to Correct Excessive Macroeconomic Imbalances in the Euro Area. OJ L 306 of 23.11.2011, 8–11.

European Council (2011b): Regulation (EU) No 1176/2011 of the European Parliament and of the Council of 16 November 2011 on the Prevention and Correction of Macroeconomic Imbalances. OJ L 306 of 32.11.2011, 25–32.

Fischer-Lescano, Andreas (2014): *Human Rights in Times of Austerity Policy. The EU Institutions and the Conclusion of Memoranda of Understanding*. Baden-Baden: Nomos.

Flassbeck, Heiner; Lapavitsas, Costas (2013): *The Systemic Crisis of the Euro – True Causes and Effective Therapies*. Studien der Rosa-Luxemburg-Stiftung. Berlin: Rosa-Luxemburg-Stiftung.

Glassner, Vera (2010): *The Public Sector in the Crisis*. ETUI Working Paper 2010.07. Brussels: ETUI.

Gloggnitzer, Sylvia; Lindner, Isabella (2011): Economic Governance Reform and Financial Stabilization in the EU and in the Eurosystem – Treaty-Based and Intergovernmental Decisions. *Monetary Policy & the Economy* Q4/11: 36–58.

Hancké, Bob (2013): *Unions, Central Banks, and EMU. Labour Market Integration in Europe*. Oxford: Oxford University Press.

Hassel, Anke (2003): Konzertierung als Instrument zur Anpassung und die europäische Währungsunion. In: Jochem, Sven; Siegel, Nico A. (eds.): *Konzertierung, Verhandlungsdemokratie und Reformpolitik im Wohlfahrtsstaat: Das Modell Deutschland im Vergleich*. Opladen: Leske und Budrich, 70–106.

Hassel, Anke (2014): Adjustments in the Eurozone: Varieties of Capitalism and the Crisis in southern Europe. *LSE 'Europe in Question' Discussion Paper Series 76/2014*. London: London School of Economics and Political Science.

Hassel, Anke (2015): Trade Unions and the Future of Democratic Capitalism. In: Beramendi, Pablo; Häuserman, Silja; Kitschelt, Herbert; Kriesi, Hanspeter (eds.): *The Politics of Advanced Capitalism*. Cambridge: Cambridge University Press, 231–256.

Höpner, Martin; Lutter, Mark (2017): The Diversity of Wage Regimes: Why the Eurozone Is Too Heterogeneous for the Euro. *European Political Science Review* 10 (1): 71–96.

Höpner, Martin; Rödl, Florian (2012): Illegitim und rechtswidrig: Das neue makroökonomische Regime im Euroraum. *Wirtschaftsdienst* 2012 (4): 219–222.

Kocher, Eva (2010): Europäische Tarifautonomie – Rechtsrahmen für Autonomie und Korporatismus. *juridikum* 4/2010: 465–483.

Molina, Óscar; Rhodes, Martin (2002): Corporatism: The Past, Present, and Future of a Concept. *Annual Review of Political Science* 5: 305–331.

Molina, Óscar; Rhodes, Martin (2007): The Political Economy of Adjustment in Mixed Market Economies: A Study of Spain and Italy. In: Hancké, Bob; Rhodes, Martin; Thatcher, Mark (eds.): *Beyond Varieties of Capitalism. Conflict, Contradictions, and Complementarities in the European Economy*. Oxford: Oxford University Press, 223–252.

Müller, Torsten (2015): *The King Is Dead – Long Live the King: What Follows after the Troika?* ETUI Working Paper 2015.09. Brussels: ETUI.

Rhodes, Martin (2001): The Political Economy of Social Pacts: "Competitive Corporatism" and European Welfare Reform. In: Pierson, Paul (ed.): *The New Politics of the Welfare State*. Oxford: Oxford University Press, 165–194.

Rödl, Florian; Callsen, Raphael (2015): Kollektive soziale Rechte unter dem Druck der Währungsunion. Schutz durch Art. 28 EU-Grundrechtecharta? Frankfurt a.M.: Bund-Verlag.

Salines, Marion; Glöckler, Gabriel; Truchlewski, Zbigniew (2012): Existential Crisis, Incremental Response: The Eurozone's Dual Institutional Evolution 2007–2011. *Journal of European Public Policy* 19 (5): 665–681.

Schmid, Carlo (1951): Soziale Autonomie und Staat. *Gewerkschaftliche Monatshefte* (3): 116–123.

Schulten, Thorsten; Müller, Torsten (2013): A New European Interventionism? The Impact of the New European Economic Governance on Wages and Collective Bargaining. In: Natali, David; Vanhercke, Bart (eds.): *Social Developments in the European Union 2012. Fourteenth Annual Report*. Brussels: ETUI, 181–213.

Schulten, Thorsten; Müller, Torsten (2015): European Economic Governance and Its Intervention in National Wage Development and Collective Bargaining. In: Lehndorff, Steffen (ed.): *Divisive Integration. The Triumph of Failed Ideas in Europe – Revisited*. Brussels: European Trade Union Institute, 331–363.

Seikel, Daniel (2016): Flexible Austerity and Supranational Autonomy. The Reformed Excessive Deficit Procedure and the Asymmetry between Liberalization and Social Regulation in the EU. *Journal of Common Market Studies* 54 (6): 1398–1416.

Seikel, Daniel; Absenger, Nadine (2015): Die Auswirkungen der EuGH-Rechtsprechung auf das Tarifvertragssystem in Deutschland. *Industrielle Beziehungen* 22 (1): 51–71.

Streeck, Wolfgang (2006): The Study of Organized Interests: Before "The Century' and After. In: Crouch, Colin; Streeck, Wolfgang (eds.): *The Diversity of Democracy. Corporatism, Social Order and Political Conflict*. Cheltenham: Edward Elgar, 3–45.

Streeck, Wolfgang (2009): *Re-Forming Capitalism. Institutional Change in the German Political Economy.* Oxford: Oxford University Press.

Streeck, Wolfgang (2011): The Crises of Democratic Capitalism. *New Left Review* (71): 5–29.

Streeck, Wolfgang (2013): *Gekaufte Zeit: Die vertagte Krise des demokratischen Kapitalismus.* Berlin: Suhrkamp.

Streeck, Wolfgang (2014): How Will Capitalism End? *New Left Review* (87): 35–64.

Streeck, Wolfgang; Schmitter, Phillippe C. (1985): Community, Market, State – and Associations? The Prospective Contribution of Interest Governance to Social Order. In: Streeck, Wolfgang; Schmitter, Phillippe C. (eds.): *Private Interest Government. Beyond Market and State.* London: SAGE, 1–29.

van Aken, Wim; Artige, Lionel (2013): Reverse Majority Voting in Comparative Perspective: Implications for Fiscal Governance in the EU. In: de Witte, Bruno; Héritier, Adrienne; Trechsler, Alexander H. (eds.), *The Euro Crisis and the State of European Democracy.* Florence: European University Institute – EUDO, 129–161.

Chapter 15

Going beyond institutional restrictions

Conflict as a challenge

Johannes Kiess

Assessing the consequences of European integration is a complex endeavour, as is European integration as a whole: the integration process and the EU itself, a "moving target" for the descriptive and analytical attempts of social scientists (Bieling/Lerch 2013), has led to very different theoretical and political approaches to understand its nature; formation; characteristics; and, indeed, consequences (see the introduction to this volume). What I want to emphasise here is that, most of the time, the reasons for disagreement lie in differing distinctions and definitions of the subject of study and differing perspectives. In other words: what part you look at will determine what you learn; and what you learn from case studies obviously determines what you conclude.

Against the perspective taken by Daniel Seikel that focusses on the top-down imposition of restrictions to collective bargaining, I argue that the worsening of trade union bargaining power and collective bargaining autonomy is much more dependent on the overall ability to activate resources for mobilisation than on European integration. While the authoritarian imposition of neoliberal reform agendas on Southern European Member States during the crisis indeed must be criticised, this is only half the story and stopping here may accidentally lead to wrong conclusions. I argue that European integration is not the only channel of deregulation and also not the source of it. The politics of deregulation and liberalisation have too long of a history to be dependent on European economic governance (EEG); other levels of governance are structured similarly and are as likely (or unlikely) to offer opportunities for strategic choice for trade unions.

In the following I will first attempt to broaden the perspective and argue that the pressures on European trade unionism are by no means only produced by European integration. Rather, the structural imbalance between labour and capital (Danielian/Page 1994), neoliberal hegemony (Blyth 2002; Peck 2010; Crouch 2011; Harvey 2011), and political abandoning of the "social dimension" – which indeed goes at the heart of democracy itself, as Seikel argues – go beyond the scope of European integration. Second, I will argue that because of this, the analysis and any consequences drawn from it need to include more than just one instrument (not) available for strategic choice. While collective bargaining especially in Southern Europe is indeed under pressure, trade unions can and must turn to other, new instruments and strategies (see Chapter 18 in this volume), regardless of under the conditions of European integration or in a national framework. While Seikel is careful not to jump to conclusions (i.e., dismantling the common currency), I argue that the authoritarian regime imposed on (not only) collective wage bargaining by the Troika and under the leading role of individual nation-states (i.e., most prominently, Germany) needs to be seen as a case study for the much more general phenomenon of authoritarian capitalism. The European level is an arena of conflict like others; the point being that it exists and that it needs to be dealt with head-on (rather than rejected by turning to the national level *or* celebrated in negligence of European heterogeneity).

European integration within historical and global context

The "ambushes on collective bargaining systems launched from the European level" described in Seikel's chapter indeed should be seen as the latest attacks on labour and labour power resources, however, originating not from the European level *per se* but resulting from broader historical developments and the structural conflict between capital and labour itself. I briefly mention three main points to support my claim for broadening up the perspective. First, there is an elaborate literature describing the triumphal march of neoliberal ideology towards hegemony in Western societies (e.g., Blyth 2002, 2015; Peck 2010; Chomsky 2011; v Centeno/Cohen 2012; Widmaier 2016), including the established political parties left and right, as well as majorities of the electorates. To take one prominent example, Marc Blyth (2002) has dissected carefully the almost religious power of ideas such as "private is better than public", "the market always prevails over the state", and "unions disturb the well functioning of markets". The dominance of these ideas may have gained from the conservative claim of the "end of history" and can be traced in the programmes of "third way" Social Democracy. Neoliberal ideas, in any way, were gaining traction before the 1990s and before European integration was shifting gears with the Treaty of Maastricht. No doubt, neoliberal ideas have influenced the design of European institutions ever since, dominated during the Barroso commission, and shaped the Troika responses to the crisis. But European institutions did not invent this programme, although it is now distributed through its channels of power as well. Likewise, the European integration process is not necessarily subscribed to this programme (although the case law of the European Court of Justice (ECJ) may paints another picture, see Chapter 13 in this volume).

Beyond the ideological power of the neoliberal paradigm, which has left little room for Keynesian or any other policies more prone to support corporatist institutions and collective bargaining in particular, the change of organisation of the labour market (Peck 1996) has interfered with collective bargaining as a system and trade union bargaining power in particular. My second point is therefore that the restructuring of labour markets and global competition had a fundamental impact on trade unions. Consequently, trade union density has declined all over the world and already before the Euro-crisis (Ebbinghaus/Visser 1999; Visser 2006; Waddington 2015), not only in Europe and under the pressures of European integration. With the decline of union power, other institutions have been weakened, too. For example in Germany, the shrinking mobilisation power of trade unions has consequently weakened the organisation of employers (Behrens 2011; for France see Woll 2006) as well as tariff commitment.[1] Other factors, such as the weakness of (centre) left parties and their subordination to neoliberalism combined with the abandoning of traditional alliances with trade unions, have accompanied this development. The Euro-crisis indeed served as a window of opportunity to introduce neoliberal austerity policies (Crouch 2014) to all those countries (because of their fiscal dependence) and collective bargaining systems (because of their structural weakness) that were not able to defend themselves anymore. However, it stands that the decline of union power was not linked to European economic integration in the first place.

Third, global competition makes it necessary that trade unions not only strive for higher living standards, redistribution, etc., as Seikel describes their objectives, but also seek to secure employment through wage moderation. Not only the "current path of monetary integration" subordinates collective bargaining to macroeconomic stability, as Seikel argues. Global competition all along did and does so increasingly with the industrialisation of developing countries. The specific situation today is that monetary integration has produced a short period of prosperity in the European South through the introduction of the Euro that led to the (artificial) convergence of interest rates. This prosperity is now taken away rather instantly which produces hardship but would not have been softer or more democratic if the markets alone would have "solved" it (i.e., most likely by dismantling the Euro with drastic effects on prices through external devaluation). Clearly, with different economic ideas and power balances, much better (i.e., labour-friendly) solutions would have been possible. Those have not been available.

In short, the crisis of democratic capitalism and more particularly corporatism pre-dates European integration or rather that era of European integration actually interfering with people's lives (starting with the Treaty of Maastricht 1992). Moreover, the crisis of collective bargaining is by no means specific to Europe or the Euro-zone, as in the UK and the USA this chapter was already opened in the 1980s by Thatcher and Reagan, respectively. Often, employment crises open the opportunity for labour market "reforms" and austerity (Farnsworth/Irving 2012; Hirsch/Schnabel 2014). Thus, the Euro-crisis and the authoritarian introduction of austerity policies is only one example for what is happening more continuously across the world based not least on the hegemony of a specific set of ideas. Neoliberal reform agendas and attacks on collective bargaining exist with, through, and within but also without, against, and outside European governance institutions.

Strategic choice as the only choice

While we have to take very serious the fact that the most recent attacks on labour are channelled via the European level, one must also consider that strategic decisions in the past (e.g., establishing the common currency area), even if ex-post discovered as "wrong", may not be reversible in a way that would re-establish or strengthen what is now under attack. This needs further explanation and I refer to Georg Vobruba's work for the following argument. European monetary integration has two ambivalent effects (Vobruba 2017: 66): One is indeed that competition between firms but also labour across the Member States increases because the protective mechanism of exchange rate adjustments is lost (see Chapter 7 in this volume). It is a mechanism which the Commission of the European Communities (1990: 24) foresaw and counted on from the beginning: "A credible monetary union will affect the behaviour of wage-bargainers. They will be more careful about risking becoming uncompetitive, given that devaluation will not be an option". However, there is also the effect of a stable currency that, as of now, has proved surprisingly strong – even during the most critical phase of the Euro-crisis. The ambivalence here is that the currency is decommoditised while labour becomes commoditised further. Ignoring this ambivalence leads, first, to ignoring the protective consequences of the common currency also for welfare in the Member States (Vobruba 2017: 66). Second, exchange rate adjustments are not as effective as one may think. And third, the costs of dissolving the Euro are far greater than not introducing it would have been. For these reasons, *ex nunc*, the common currency is part of the institutional framework in which trade unions act, and their situation will certainly not improve if one country just leaves the Euro.

But this does not mean that trade unions and their (potential) allies in social movements and left parties are necessarily defenceless and without choice. Even in "hard times" there are resources and options that can be used for mobilisation within an unfriendly environment.[2] Following power resource approaches (Korpi 1983; Korpi/Palme 2003; Schmalz/Dörre 2013; Paster 2015) such resources are to be found in more than one dimension and include more than just one instrument. Seikel refers in his argument to the institutional power that indeed is weakened by recent developments of the Euro-zone regime. From a conflict theoretical perspective the European level constitutes a conflict constellation in which it is, compared to classic nationally framed industrial relations, less clear who is in conflict with whom, but which is nevertheless not per se a lost battleground. Rather, we may even expect renewed mobilisation on a number of frontiers: Brexit and other political conflicts could pressure the EU eventually to be more receptive towards making concessions in the social dimension; German ordoliberal hegemony may produce further resistance (while it was never dominating, for example, European Central Bank (ECB) monetary policy to the extent some imply in the first place) and new alliances among other Member States; and for trade unions themselves there are new strategies available developed during the years of austerity helping the renewal of the labour movement (see e.g. Chapters 2 and 18 in this volume). The *empirical* question then is whether trade unions are able to mobilise and play a decisive role in this new conflict constellation. Heterogeneity of national trade union organisations is an obstacle; shared grievances may be a uniting factor.

Thus, along the lines of "strategic choice", there is a need to question the inevitability ringing – at least to some extent – in pessimistic political-economic approaches that narrow empirical reality down into strictly path-dependent models. Trade unions do have scope of action beyond the regime of EEG, and while there are of course more favourable environments imaginable, it is at least questionable if they had more scope without the Euro. Having said this, one must still agree with the sceptical assessment of how collective bargaining developed in recent years and how chances stand for a quick revitalisation of labour power. Therefore, I pointed at the (lack of) organisational resources and mobilisation potential as the main reasons for the weakening (or strengthening) of bargaining power, which, however, implies a more empirically open judgement. Those who are able to organise and enforce their interests make the rules – regardless of the level of regulation, be it global, European, or national. The dominance of neoliberalism (Crouch 2011; Schmidt/Thatcher 2013) is rather independent from the level of governance.

Conclusion

To summarise, it is precisely "the way the Commission has operationalized this objective [of EEG]" that deserves attention. This "way", however, cannot be understood without the context of continued restructuring of Western capitalism more generally. The power balance was not so much shifted by EEG; rather EEG is a means or a result of this shift. The difference between both assessments is a matter of defining the object of study, which is moving and changing. This becomes apparent as we include further crises and their consequences with external origin into the conceptional analysis of institutional power balances. Think of the global migration crisis, Brexit, Trump, etc., which all impacted the possibilities of political conflict at the European level. A very much pressing problem is indeed the power imbalance between debtors and creditors, i.e., the economic core and the South, and it did lead to "authoritarian top-down imposition of downward wage flexibility" (Chapter 14). But this is only one aspect of the picture if we broaden the perspective to global competition and its effects on national labour markets. In this light and from a power resources approach that understands capitalism always as an uphill battle for labour, the search for allies and new strategies is the most promising counter-strategy to authoritarian EEG.

Notes

1 www.boeckler.de/wsi-tarifarchiv_2257.htm (last checked July 24, 2017).
2 After all, capitalism is always an "unfriendly environment".

Literature

Behrens, Martin (2011): *Das Paradox der Arbeitgeberverbände: von der Schwierigkeit, durchsetzungsstarke Unternehmensinteressen kollektiv zu vertreten.* Berlin: Ed. Sigma.

Bieling, Hans-Jürgen; Lerch, Marika (2013): Theorien der europäischen Integration: ein Systematisierungsversuch. In: Bieling, Hans-Jürgen; Lerch, Marika (ed.): *Theorien der europäischen Integration.* Wiesbaden: Springer, 9–31.

Blyth, Mark (2002): *Great Transformations. Economic Ideas and Institutional Change in the Twentieth Century.* Cambridge: Cambridge University Press.

Blyth, Mark (2015): *Austerity. The History of a Dangerous Idea.* Cambridge: Cambridge University Press.

Centeno, Miguel A.; Cohen, Joseph N. (2012): The Arc of Neoliberalism. *Annual Review of Sociology* 38 (1): 317–340.

Chomsky, Noam (2011): *Profit Over People: Neoliberalism and Global Order: Neoliberalism and the Global Order.* New York: Seven Stories Press.

Commission of the European Communities (1990): One Market, One Money. An Evaluation of the Potential Benefits and Costs of Forming an Economic and Monetary Union. European Economy 44. Brussels.

Crouch, Colin (2011): *The Strange Non-Death of Neoliberalism.* Cambridge: Polity Press.

Crouch, Colin (2014). Introduction : Labour Markets and Social Policy after the Crisis. *Transfer: European Review of Labour and Research* 20 (1): 7–22.

Danielian, Lucig H.; Page, Benjamin I. (1994): The Heavenly Chorus: Interest Group Voices on TV News. *American Journal of Political Science* 38 (4): 1056.

Ebbinghaus, Bernhard; Visser, Jelle (1999): When Institutions Matter: Union Growth and Decline in Western Europe, 1950–1995. *European Sociological Review* 15 (2): 135–158.

Farnsworth, Kevin; Irving, Zoë (2012): Varieties of Crisis, Varieties of Austerity: Social Policy in Challenging Times. *Journal of Poverty and Social Justice* 20 (2): 133–147.

Harvey, David (2011): *A Brief History of Neoliberalism.* Oxford: Oxford University Press.

Hirsch, Boris; Schnabel, Claus (2014): What Can We Learn from Bargaining Models about Union Power? The Decline in Union Power in Germany, 1992–2009. *The Manchester School* 82 (3): 347–362.

Korpi, Walter (1983): *The Democratic Class Struggle*. New York: Routledge.

Korpi, Walter; Palme, Joakim (2003): New Politics and Class Politics in the Context of Austerity and Globalization: Welfare State Regress in 18 Countries, 1975–95. *American Political Science Review* 97 (3): 425–446.

Paster, Thomas (2015): *Bringing Power Back in: A Review of the Literature on the Role of Business in Welfare State Politics*. MPIfG Discussion Paper 15/3.

Peck, Jamie (1996): *Work-Place: The Social Regulation of Labor Markets*. New York: Guilford Press.

Peck, Jamie (2010): *Constructions of Neoliberal Reason*. Oxford: Oxford University Press.

Schmalz, Stefan; Dörre, Klaus (2013): *Comeback der Gewerkschaften?: Machtressourcen, innovative Praktiken, internationale Perspektiven*. Frankfurt a.M.: Campus.

Schmidt, Vivien A.; Thatcher, Mark (2013): *Resilient Liberalism in Europe's Political Economy*. Cambridge: Cambridge University Press.

Visser, Jelle (2006): Union Membership Statistics in 24 Countries: An Analysis of 'Adjusted' Union Membership Data in 24 Countries. *Monthly Labor Review* 129 (1): 38.

Vobruba, Georg (2017): *Krisendiskurs: die nächste Zukunft Europas*. Weinheim: Beltz Juventa.

Waddington, Jeremy (2015): Trade Union Membership Retention in Europe: The Challenge of Difficult Times. *European Journal of Industrial Relations* 21 (3): 205–221.

Widmaier, Wesley (2016): The Power of Economic Ideas – Through, Over and In – Political Time: The Construction, Conversion and Crisis of the Neoliberal Order in the US and UK. *Journal of European Public Policy* 23 (3): 338–356.

Woll, Cornelia (2006): National Business Associations under Stress: Lessons from the French Case. *West European Politics* 29 (3): 489–512.

Chapter 16

Contention in times of crisis

British and German social actors and the quest of framing capitalism

Johannes Kiess

Introduction

Pressure on European trade unions has increased considerably with the unfolding of the social and political consequences of the Great Recession. Most importantly, the somewhat dormant North-South divide has opened up again as a significant challenge for the European integration project. The Troika policies specifically have established an authoritarian regime on social policies and wage setting mechanisms (see Chapters 6 and 14 in this volume) putting into question the vision of a European Social Model. As a result, the challenges for trade unions across Europe are becoming even more diverse. Beyond that, the immanent conflict between Eastern and Western countries is ever more existing (chapter 8). Moreover, following the "successful" Brexit vote in June 2016, for the first time, a member state is (most likely as of spring 2018) leaving the European Union (EU). These are truly interesting times in which the notion "crisis" is used almost on a daily basis in more respects than can be listed here. But what does it actually mean to speak about crisis?

Following this initial question, this chapter investigates the social construction of crisis, the relative positioning of actors, and their advocating of institutional change by re-framing capitalism. I claim that, despite the centrality of institutional restrictions for their action capacity, there is also the need to look at what actors are actually saying and doing, and what frames they use. This perspective adds to research investigating power resources available for trade unions and rediscovering strategic choice in the renewal of action capacity (Schmalz/Dörre 2014; Lévesque/Murray 2013). Frames, I argue, are an important vehicle to utter such strategic choice: with frames, actors mobilize members and allies, introduce and reinforce narratives in public debate, and, last but not least, challenge or reinforce ideological hegemony. With this focus, the similar battles of trade unions and their counterparts in Germany and the UK about the re-framing of capitalism become visible. While this analysis does not disregard the findings of institutionalist or rational choice approaches, it aims at broadening our understanding of the challenges of European integration for trade unions by adding an ideational dimension.

The following section gives a short summary of previous research findings. By introducing an actor-centred concept of crisis framing in Section 3, I claim that crises are always subject to social construction. Crises thus are conceptualized as societal decision situations, in which the understanding and framing of a given situation prevails over any "objective" notion of crisis. In Section 4, I describe the research design of this case study before I discuss the findings in Section 5. In the conclusion, I draw attention to the importance of framing and ideological hegemony and what lessons should be considered for the debate on the challenges of European integration.

Framing the crisis

Looking for the starting point of the contemporary crisis in Europe, we see a crisis with changing faces – more concretely, narratives are changing quite rapidly over time. Whereas the actor-centred framing perspective proposed here (see Section 3) is mostly ignored, the literature does discuss the social construction of crisis, the interests behind the promotion of specific narratives, and the change of narratives over time. For instance, in early 2009, the dominant frames of the financial and economic crisis were those of "epochal change" and "conjunctural rupture" (Thompson 2009). Both readings imply very different consequences. Epochal change may mean that the dominance of modern financial capitalism and neo-liberalism eventually comes to an end; conjunctural rupture only calls for transitional interventions for a still well-running system. Of course the emergence of frames is not random. Quiring et al.'s (2013) study on media frames in Germany concludes that the relatively narrow number of thematic frames they found is due to the need for status, resources, thematic connection, and a sense for a cultural point of connection to establish them. Furthermore, narratives are connected to the construction of legitimacy for the system but also for those actors or governments in place. Likewise, blame attribution simplifies the complex reality of a crisis and makes it attractive for strategic use within domestic and European policy fields (Sommer et al. 2016).

Soon, at the end of 2009, most public and political attention shifted from global economic and financial to the so-called "state debt crisis" or "Eurocrisis". Bieling even argues that the refocussing of the debate was "organized" by, inter alia, "financial market actors, the European Commission, as well as the creditor and surplus Member States, first and foremost Germany" (Bieling 2013: 320; my translation). A similar argument is made by Colin Hay for the UK: after initial irritation, the preferred economic policies of the British government were pure austerity and aimed at deficit reduction following the now established reading of the crisis as a crisis of debt instead of a crisis of growth (Hay 2013; cf. Temple et al. 2016; English et al. 2016).

This very different course of the crisis discourse, especially compared to the Keynesian 1970s, was only possible because of the "political influence of sectorally based coalitions of firms and unionized workers demanding protection or compensation in the 1970s and the absence or weakness of such coalitions in 2008–2010" (Pontusson/Raess 2012: 15). The difference of then and now, thus, "can be seen, in part, as a result of deindustrialization, globalization, and the decline of organized labor since the early 1980s" (ibid.). In other words, the interests of actors, their beliefs, their strategic aims, and their ability to build coalitions seem to shape crisis reactions, and not so much the "objective" severity of a crisis (Heinrich/Kutter 2014).

Different crises debated in public discourse – e.g. the global financial crisis, the state debt crisis, the industrial productive crisis, or the political legitimacy crisis – have very different meanings, are addressed by different actors, and to varying degrees across countries (Zamponi/Bosi 2016). Based on newspaper analysis, Kutter (2013) reconstructs different stages within the public debate, most importantly the financial market crisis from 2007 to 2009 and, after 2009, the emergence of a state debt crisis. In consequence, the "Greek economic crisis" emerged. As a trope, the Greek crisis "resonates across Europe as synonymous with corruption, poor government, austerity, financial bailouts, civil unrest, and social turmoil" and it "transcends local and national borders" (Knight 2013: 147; cf. Wodak/Angouri 2014; Schmidt 2013). Moreover, for example in Germany (Kiess 2015) and Austria (Ziem 2010) the crisis was externalized successfully, not least *to* Greece.

By using metaphors, actors develop crisis scenarios that appear threatening and dramatic (Ziem 2010: 167). Particularly (public) emotions play an important role as another look at the case of the UK shows; although national debt numbers were relatively moderate until 2010 (lower national debt than the other G7 members, Canada, France, Germany, Italy, Japan, and the USA), government reaction moved towards austerity with comparisons to Greece and with the following story: "Our national debt is higher than it's ever been. Our deficit and debt interest payments are unmanageable. Our debt crisis was caused by the overspending of the previous government's. We are on the brink of bankruptcy" (Kushner/Kushner 2013: 8). The capability of this story "to gain traction with ordinary people, is rooted in fear, anxiety and the almost effortless way in which the personal is woven into the national" (ibid.: 9). Stirring up fears of national financial apocalypse in consequence established a political and public consensus including 75% of the public and all three relevant parties (labour, conservatives, and liberals) (ibid.: 13).

Was this unchallenged and without an alternative? Marc Blyth (2013: 208ff) argues that the passing of time and the lack of an alternative theoretical paradigm hindered institutional change, not least because the people who were in charge before the crisis were still in charge in and after the crisis. He concludes that "it is politics, not economics, and it is authority, not facts, that matter for both paradigm maintenance and change" (ibid.: 10). In agreement with this reading, Matthijs (2016) shows how German dominance in Europe led to the enforcement of ordoliberal monetary and fiscal policy, especially in Greece. Alternative paradigms (de-growth, post growth, heterodox economics, etc.) were not able to challenge the hegemony of neoliberal mainstream economics (Urhammer/Røpke 2013: 69). Still, however, alternative readings were uttered, for example by trade unions, as will be shown later.

There is an ever growing literature on policy reactions and the change of industrial relations during the crisis (Brandl/Traxler 2011; Busch et al. 2013; European Commission 2012, 2015; Gennard 2009; Heyes 2013; Holst 2013; Heinrich 2014; Lehndorff et al. 2017). No emphasis, however, seems to lie on frame articulation by social actors – even though the role of (individual) interest groups in the bargaining on growth programmes and new regulations is, of course, discussed (e.g. Heinrich 2014) and at least discourse analytical studies have pointed at the importance of framing (e.g. Hegelich 2010; De Ville/Orbie 2014). Also the "communicative power of the unions as a form of trade union 'soft power'" (Urban 2012: 222) has been studied in other contexts. This chapter seeks to combine these approaches and add to the existing literature on the crisis with a systematic investigation of social actors' framing of the crisis.

Following the previous literature review, my research questions are: which argumentative strategies do actors implement to frame the crisis? In opposition to whom do they position themselves and with what reasons? Which aims do they pursue, how do they describe and explain the crisis, and what solutions are advocated? Finally, does the variety of crisis framings follow varieties of capitalism? Or is it class conflict, regardless of institutional context, that structures crisis framing?

The social construction of crises

Investigating the Great Recession, its causes, as well as social and political consequences, I argue, needs to build on a comprehensive understanding of "crisis". What does attributing a situation with the word "crisis" mean? What do the Euro-crisis and other crises have in common in terms of the structure of the respective social situation? Is crisis just some "difficult" situation? But for whom, then, is it a "difficult" situation? And, more importantly, who says a situation is "difficult"? These questions are especially pressing for what is referred to as the "Great Recession" and the "Euro-crisis". Most importantly in this cascade of crises with changing names, the attributed causes and consequences changed as well, as did responsibilities and accountabilities. Taking the concept of crisis for granted, thus, falls short of understanding why and also how an actor calls a situation a crisis. A proper analysis must therefore build on a concept of crisis that takes actor's crisis framing into consideration.

From this perspective, the semantics of the crisis, the observations and framing by actors, as well as these actors' relative positioning become the main focus of analysis. The hypothesis of the research project this paper is based on summarizes these assumptions: actors try to strategically frame crises in order to push for decisions (i.e. specific crises policies) favouring their interests. This framing, it is assumed, follows two general logics as the crisis framing is aimed at persuasion in two arenas according to the central organizational interests of social actors (Schmitter/Streeck 1999: 11): On the one hand, regarding the "logic of membership", organizations have to produce a "minimal degree of internal cohesion, a sense of solidarity in spite of existing internal divisions, and legitimate leadership strong enough to impose discipline and individual sacrifice on their members". On the other hand, to cope with the "logic of influence", organizations "have to be able to formulate their goals in terms of commonly accepted values" (ibid.), i.e. they need to frame their interests as public interest (Bohmann/Vobruba 1992). Because of this and because they also seek different goals, crisis framings differ, obviously, between labour and business organizations but also between sectors, as well as between sector and umbrella organizations (Kiess 2015). Furthermore, one may assume that the framing differs between institutional environments and national contexts in which actors are framing the crisis. Liberal market economies (LMEs) like the UK differ from co-ordinated market economies (CMEs) like Germany in a number of ways, including coordination between state and social actors (Hall/Soskice 2001).

How crisis is socially constructed and crisis metaphors work can be examined with different analytical tools adopted and advanced in media studies, cultural studies, and discourse analysis. At the core of varying framing approaches lies the rejection of a thorough norm of objectivity: "[…] objectivity is not possible, since every transmission of information entails selection; selection is itself, however, already an evaluation because it expresses a preference for something particular and ignores everything else in that moment" (Matthes 2007: 22; my translation). The theory of speech act (cf. Austin 1975) lies focus on technical characteristics of crisis framing. Nagel et al. (2008: 307) differentiate in their study on apocalyptic rhetoric the semantics, meaning the images used, the syntax, referring to the dramaturgic construction, and the rhetoric function of the *speech act* and whether this act is "illocutionary" (aimed at a specific goal) or "perlocutionary" (having an impact on alter). All of this happens in or rather in relation to the public sphere and is communicated through the media. This is especially true for crises: a crisis without attention in the public sphere would not be understood as a crisis.

Following Goffman's conceptually fundamental book *Frame Analysis* (1986), Benford and Snow (2000) identify three basic elements of intentional framing: diagnostic framing (description and cause attribution), prognostic framing (prescriptions for action), and motivational framing (why should one care). The literature consistently emphasizes that these elements of frames are by no means plain facts, but discursively formed and as such always a matter of conflict about meaning (Raupp 2013: 184; cf. Entman 2004; Gamson/Modigliani 1989). The initial motivational framing of a crisis is already changing the interpretative frame and thus its diagnostic and prognostic implications. However, in the concept followed here, framing is distinguished from pure agenda-setting: "The primary difference on the psychological level between agenda setting and priming, on the one hand, and framing, on the other hand, is therefore the difference between whether we think about an issue and how we think about it" (Entman 2007; Scheufele/Tewksbury 2007: 14). It is indeed the "how" we are interested in here. The usage of the word crisis calls on interpretational frames (Scharloth et al. 2010: 99) that are shared and communicated and, thus, crises are always socially constructed.

As argued, for social movements and social actors alike framing is an important tool to seek influence but also to ensure allegiance of their members. Frames contain offers for identification for members, followers, and potential partners; provide ideological orientation; connect to normative principles of the group; and may relate to shared historic knowledge. They aim not least at emotions and affective (dis)approval, based on shared values, resentments, prejudices, myths, etc. as well as respective action (Koch-Baumgarten 2010: 35). Rather than creating new ideas or presenting the greatest truth, the strategic framing of social actors is mostly concerned with the "splicing together of old and existing ideas and the strategic punctuating of certain issues, events, or beliefs" (Johnston/Noakes 2005: 8). Its success is dependent, inter alia, on access to and control over resources, the existence of strategic alliances, as well as knowledge and abilities that actors can build on to support their frames (Pan/Kosicki 2001: 44).

Of course, emphasizing the social construction of crisis does not mean that there is no "real" crisis:

> [T]o say that a situation is real is not the same as saying that its reality is self-evident. The ways in which a situation is named, described, explained and historically positioned both shape its context and determine the plausibility of one contextual account over another.
>
> (Coleman 2013: 330)

With each diagnosis and theory comes a narrative, an idea of who is to blame, and a strategy of how to solve the crisis. This means that there are "no innocent descriptive presentations that should be taken just at face value" (Thompson 2009: 520). This is, of course, not only true for crises. Every policy in complex modern societies needs a narrative, i.e. scenarios and arguments "which underwrite and stabilize the assumptions for policymaking in situations that persist with many unknowns, a high degree of interdependence, and little, if any, agreement" (Roe 1994: 34). The discursive turn in policy analysis has appreciated this and the following case study aims at establishing this perspective to trade union studies.

Germany and the UK: two "most different cases"

Within the Varieties of Capitalism (VoC) literature and in accordance with other comparative frameworks the UK is described as LME. LMEs are

> characterized by low levels of business coordination and state intervention, and deregulated markets serve as the primary coordinating mechanism for economic activity. As a consequence, firms are often unable to resolve collective action problems and are rarely in a position jointly to provide basic supply-side goods that sustain vocational training, R&D, and long-term finance.
>
> (Fioretos 2001: 221)

In comparison, Germany is referred to as CME. CMEs are characterized by a much higher degree of coordination among firms but also among the state, business, and labour. CMEs are thus expected to be

> more willing to invest in *specific* and *co-specific assets* (i.e. assets that cannot readily be turned to another purpose and assets whose returns depend heavily on the active cooperation of others), while those in liberal market economies should invest more extensively in *switchable assets* (i.e. assets whose value can be realized if diverted to other purposes).
>
> (Hall/Soskice 2001)

The *VoC*-approach was criticized for, among other things, not acknowledging conflict and for concentrating almost entirely on firms, neglecting the role of labour power (Howell 2003; Hancké et al. 2008). This chapter includes labour as a central actor in the shaping of models of capitalism (Korpi 2006). The central empirical question thus is whether there are differences in the strategic crisis framing between British and German organizations and how these differences relate to the respective institutional framework. Germany and the UK can be regarded as most different cases. However, similarities may point to more fundamental principles that forego the evolvement of institutional differences.

The analysis builds on a collection of all press releases disseminated by German and British actors between 2008 and 2014. For Germany, the German trade union congress (*Deutscher Gewerkschaftsbund*, DGB) and the business organizations' umbrella organization (*Bundesvereinigung der deutschen Arbeitgeberverbände*, BDA) have been selected, for the UK the *Trade Union Congress* (TUC) and the *Confederation of the British Industry*

(CBI). All four are umbrella organizations and not directly involved in wage negotiations, which are usually organized on the sectoral or firm level. In the CBI, firms can become individual members whereas in the BDA, only sectoral and regional associations are direct members. These and other organizational differences are, however, probably not as relevant as differences in the overall institutional framework. Overall, the organizations' roles and structural places in the respective system of industrial relations are comparable.

On the basis of press releases it is not possible to measure the success of framing strategies, i.e. whether certain frames dominate public discourse and whether such hegemony has had an impact on government policies in response to the crisis. The constellation involving organizations, the public, the media, and politics is far too complex to permit such an analysis (Koch-Baumgarten 2010). However, it is possible to show how the crisis was framed and, indeed, socially constructed by actors, while they tried to pursue their own agendas concerning, for example, wage increases, state interventions, tight budget control, and so on. For this purpose, press releases – which are issued specifically to communicate an organization's positions on particular topics – can be considered the most qualified data.

In a first step, all press releases containing the word "crisis" were selected comprising the sample to be analysed. In Germany and for both organizations, the absolute (and relative) number of press releases referring to "crisis" grew from 2008 on, peaked in 2009, and then decreased over the course of the period investigated (see Table 16.1). For the British case there are no press releases of the CBI available anymore for 2008. From the press releases at hand it looks like the numbers of crisis-related press releases are considerably higher compared to the German BDA, but with a similar decrease over time. The numbers for the TUC, however, show a different pattern compared to Germany: there is a first peak in 2009 after which crisis-related press releases decrease slightly, only to go up again in 2012, reaching an all-time high in 2013. In a second step, all documents containing the word "crisis" were analysed following the three main dimensions introduced earlier (significance, diagnosis, and prescription of the crisis). It was also noted whether the press release contained a reference to the European level as this

Table 16.1 Number of press releases containing "crisis/crises" per year (own data)

	2008	2009	2010	2011	2012	2013	2014
DGB	28	100	73	47	46	26	24
BDA	3	30	20	5	7	10	3
TUC	23*	57	40	40	53	62	26
CBI	**	**	**	34	24	13	20

*seven were not related to the financial and economic crisis **not available.

might indicate a shift from the national to the supranational level. As discussed, we can expect externalization strategies in which actors frame the crisis as only being an issue abroad.

Varieties of crisis framing in Germany and the UK

In this section, the crisis framing of four organizations is analysed based on their press releases containing the word "crisis" and following a distinction common in literature between three dimensions of framing (significance, diagnosis, and prognosis). In the most basic dimension of motivational framing, the speaking actor describes the crisis in its scale and severity: emphasizing or negating the severity of a situation increases or decreases pressure to address a problem. In the diagnostic dimension, the causes of the crisis are named, and specific actors are often blamed for having caused or for not having done enough to prevent the crisis. The prognostic dimension refers to the consequences of the crisis and, more importantly, what to do about it. This section gives a comparative overview of differences according to class (labour vs. business) and institutional framework (CME vs. LME). Translations from German to English are mine; press releases are cited by their issuing date.

The DGB's hope for a "Social Europe" and "a change in politics"

In the motivational framing, the DGB spoke of a "system crisis" (DGB 1 May 2009), emphasizing the fundamental questioning of the contemporary mode of capitalism. In early 2009, it expected a loss of at least half a million jobs in Germany alone and cautioned against the social and political consequences of the economic crisis if people lost trust in politics. Second, the DGB included the European level in its analysis as early as 2009: the crisis was so severe, the DGB asserted, that it transcended national borders (DGB 1 June 2009). Third, an important recurrent motif is the direct reference to the crisis of 1929 or indirect references with phrases like "worst in 80 years" and "since the Second World War" (e.g. DGB 13 October 2009, 16 March 2010). This is a common form of "frame amplification" (Snow et al. 1986): by referring to the widely shared knowledge about an earlier, very serious event the DGB amplified the notion of severity. In 2010, the DGB insisted that "[w]e are not in year one after the crisis; this is year three of the crisis" (DGB 1 May 2010). One year later then, the crisis in Germany was declared over (DGB 19 January 2011), but, at the same time, the European crisis threatened the whole Euro-zone (DGB 16 May 2011). In following years, the DGB kept discussing the European crisis, the social dislocations within Europe, and rising unemployment in Europe.

In its diagnostic framing, the DGB criticized long-term developments that helped paving the way into the crisis, starting with the (partial) privatization of the German retirement system (DGB 4 November 2008). As the main causes of the crisis it named misguided strategies of most banks, short-term profit maximization, and growing inequality, which triggered financial speculation (e.g. DGB 10 April 2008). The most crucial problem, however, was the lack of control over market actors, implying the general need of the state controlling markets. The DGB also criticized employers' positions formulated by a famous and very influential bank manager: the DGB

> would dispute vigorously the claim of Mr Ackermann that we are all in the same boat. The working people and their unions did not sit in one boat with the perpetrators of the crisis. We are not among those who caused the crisis. Part of the responsibility for causing the crisis must be assigned to, among others, irresponsible bankers.
>
> (DGB 6 April 2009)

This framing persisted over time but became more defensive as the window of opportunity for "a change in politics" was not used (DGB 1 September 2011).

The DGB did try to use the crisis as a critical juncture by calling for significant changes in policy-making and to depart from austerity policies of previous years. This included calls to make the German "social market economy" "really social" again (DGB 22 January 2009) and to establish a new financial and economic system (DGB 24 March 2009). On the European level, too, the DGB continuously demanded a "new European institutional framework" (DGB 10 February 2009), which was to include a European financial transaction tax, a stronger European Parliament, and a "social dimension" for Europe. Already in mid-2009, however, the tide was slowly turning and the statements became more defensive, emphasizing that it was unfair not to re-regulate the financial system and not to make bankers and wealthy pay for the crisis. From 2010 onwards the prognostic framing consisted mainly of rejecting austerity measures and criticizing the German and European crisis management (e.g. DGB 1 November 2012, 25 March 2013). Instead of competition, wage decreases in the crisis countries, and austerity, the DGB furthermore persistently advocated a European Marshall Plan (DGB 23 January 2013) and thus public spending as the working solution to the crisis.

From this short summary of the DGB's strategic interventions in the public discourse the central themes are very clear: the crisis was caused by systemic flaws of the contemporary mode of capitalism, flaws that persist regardless of the national variety of capitalism. Considering the retreating tone of later press releases, it seems as the crisis was a missed opportunity for strengthening the German CME or, in the DGB's words, to make the "social market economy" "social" again, and establishing similar standards at the European level. Its pro-integrationist rhetoric was accordingly consistent and explicit.

The BDA: from appeasement to externalization

In the narrative of the BDA, too, the crisis hit the German economy hard (BDA and BDI 13 March 2009). Contrary to the DGB's warnings though, the crisis according to the BDA did not have severe impacts on jobs and apprenticeships for young people (BDA 31 March 2009). While not negating the crisis in general, the BDA was attempting to downplay its significance. It focussed at the same time on upholding its narrative of a structural shortage of skilled workers (BDA 29 September 2009), which it linked to one of its most important political projects in recent years: raising the retirement age. In the first quarter of 2010, the worst was over and the economy was growing again, yet now the BDA continued to emphasize risks to the economy. From late 2011 until mid-2013, effectively all crisis-related press releases by the BDA addressed the crisis as a question of state debt (in other European countries) and, by doing so, externalized the crisis.

The BDA's first explicitly diagnostic framing did not appear before summer 2009. It then argued that higher taxes, especially for corporations, would "aggravate the crisis" (BDA 30 June 2009). Throughout, the BDA pointed to its own contributions in helping to overcome the crisis, namely, by making the labour market more flexible and by cooperating with the unions in the crisis (BDA 22 January 2010, 30 June 2010, 08 January 2013). By 2011, the state debt crisis had been identified by the BDA as a risk, caused by state debt crises and the backlash effects those had on the financial economy (BDA 16 March 2012). The causes of the crisis were thus re-framed from a banking and economic crisis – with causes that were not referred to explicitly because this would have contradicted the BDA's own positions on issues like liberalization and de-regulation – to a state debt crisis in which the causes (misguided fiscal policy) could be brought in line with the BDA's agenda (i.e. cutting government expenditures, liberalization, etc.).

Likewise, the BDA tried to use the crisis in its prognostic framing to amplify positions that it had already advocated before. Significant wage increases, European efforts for stricter environmental and climate policies, or more state intervention in consumer and energy policy were all labelled as detrimental in the light of the uncertainties associated with the financial crisis (BDA 12 November 2008, 10 December 2008). One measure that was especially emphasized and acclaimed in the second German growth package announced in early 2009 was the new debt brake. Whereas some initial state intervention at the peak of the financial crisis may have been inevitable, the BDA quickly rushed to argue that the best solution to the crisis was to keep budgets tight and to lower taxes for companies. This approach shifted towards the European state debt crisis as the BDA, like the DGB, advocated more integration – though aiming for an LME setting on the European level in line with its national liberalization agenda.

The TUC's uphill battle in a (neo-)liberal market economy

Compared to the German DGB, the British TUC commented on the crisis surprisingly late, long after the financial crisis had unfolded. However, the crisis was also framed as endangering jobs and pensions of millions, causing strain and poverty throughout the country (TUC 20 and 27 October 2008, 17 December 2008). The TUC also saw the crisis as both a chance (TUC 24 March 2009, 13 September 2009) and a risk (TUC 30 June 2009). The comparison with the 1930s was first made in a press release from 20 May 2009 calling the crisis the "worst recession since the 1930s, with jobs being slashed and homes repossessed on an alarming scale". Another historic reference, this time to the Thatcher years, was brought up by arguing that not acting on youth unemployment would "leave a generation of young people on the scrap heap, as happened in the 1980s" (TUC 12 October 2009). Contrary to Germany, where growth packages limited effects on the labour market, the TUC labelled the crisis in the UK also later as "jobs crisis" and "unemployment crisis" (TUC 13 and 25 March 2010, 25 May 2010, 11 October 2010) affecting predominantly workers of colour, female, and young workers. Important in the TUC's framing were also the description of the UK being "trapped in double dip recession" (TUC 24 September 2012). It is striking that the crisis was not understood as European in the TUC's press releases in any respect; the crisis thus was not externalized.

Early on, the TUC identified high levels of inequality as the main cause of the crisis. It was the "fat-cats" that "were paid these huge amounts to construct a financial system so insecure, the tax-payer has had to find billions to bail it out. It now threatens to bring down the jobs and homes of ordinary people across the country" (TUC 17 October 2008). The British unions further declared that "[r]eckless bonuses for top bankers, tax haven secrecy and business opposition to regulation were all key ingredients in the financial crisis that is now causing people up and down the country to lose their jobs and homes" (TUC 11 March 2009, cf. 12 March 2009). However, not only bankers were blamed but also

> all the policy makers of the last few decades who believed that they should let the market rip, that public services should become profit centres and who were happy to see the gap between the super-rich and the poor get bigger every year.
>
> (TUC 27 March 2009)

The causes of the (social) crisis were not economic but political and "home made" by unjust government reactions to the crisis (TUC 19 July 2010, 10 September 2010, 9 March 2011, 5 September 2011). Another cause of the crisis was seen in the "weakness of shareholder involvement" (TUC 16 November 2010).

The TUC tried hard to use the crisis as an argument for fundamental policy change, e.g. avoiding "a return to 'beggar-thy-neighbour' approach of competitive wage moderation and reductions in social protection" (TUC 27 September 2008), stopping austerity rules (TUC 7 October 2008), and substituting the "greed economy" with a "green economy" (14 June 2009). On the international level the TUC called at the G20 "that the Washington consensus of deregulation, privatisation and unfettered markets must end" (TUC 13 November 2008, 9 March 2009). Together with the DGB they lobbied for a global financial transaction tax (TUC & DGB 12 March 2010), which was seen as a way to use the crisis for real change (TUC 10 February 2010, 27 January 2011). On the domestic level, the TUC was urging the government to "introduce a fund for businesses forced to move to short-time working" (TUC 20 May 2009) and argued for "more collective bargaining, investment to boost workers' skills, stronger corporate governance including action to crack down on top pay, and encouraging the growth of well-paid jobs beyond financial services and the City" (27 January 2012) – all attributes that fit the description of CME. By the end of 2010, most of the prognostic framing targeted the spending cuts, which continued the UK's (neo-)liberal path of subsequent decades (Kiess et al. 2017).

While the tone sometimes was more aggressive, the content of the DGB's and TUC's press releases appears very similar. Even concrete policy ideas were shared across countries; however, only in Germany did some of these similar claims actually become policy (e.g. short time work). The TUC was clearly trying to push for social standards and re-regulation like the DGB, but in a more hostile environment and to no avail. International (and European) initiatives (e.g. the financial transaction tax) did not fail because of disagreements between the unions but because of their all-together continuously weak power position.

The CBI: don't change but improve

Unfortunately, the CBI does not store press releases longer than 24 months. Still, the data collected is interesting compared with its German counterpart and with the TUC. In 2011 the CBI announced that business had returned to (almost) pre-crisis level (CBI 4 April 2011), including the financial sector (CBI 4 July 2011). The crisis then consisted of growth risks imposed upon the UK by the instability of the Euro-zone: the crisis was clearly marked as an external threat (CBI 27 July 2011, 1 and 8 August 2011). This frame was kept up throughout 2012 (e.g. CBI 1 October 2012, 1 November 2012) and also in 2013, whereas it seems to have lost importance (CBI 13 November 2013).

The CBI, again like the BDA, did not often engage in diagnostic framing, i.e. naming causes of the crisis. Still, the *topos* of crisis externalization is reoccurring constantly: economic conditions had deteriorated "[d]ue to external factors bearing down on us" (CBI 10 November 2011). Next to the risks imposed by the Euro-crisis and the risk of another financial crisis, the biggest problem for business was "financial market volatility" (CBI 20 November 2011). Throughout 2012 the Euro-crisis was blamed for having "led to falling orders and stagnant output" (CBI 6 February 2012) and by the end of 2013 these conditions had "tightened the supply of credit to SMEs in particular". The Euro-crisis itself was consequently described as a state-debt problem (CBI 13 November 2013) with no mentioning of the preceding financial crisis.

The CBI's priority was to halt re-regulation of the banking industry since wrong regulations would hurt overall business and thus diminish growth (CBI 4 February 2011, 4 July 2011): "[w]e need less regulation, more public service reform and a faster pace on infrastructure development and renewal" (CBI 1 September 2011). At the European level, the CBI was supporting the financial stability measures (27 October 2011) but also called for diversifying economic engagement to non-European countries (21 November 2011). The Euro-zone crisis was also taken to argue for reducing the size of the UK pension system as pensions are seen as a risk factor for budgets in hard times (CBI 12 December 2011). Up to that point and including the claim for reduced pension schemes, the CBI's prognostic framing is very similar to the BDA's. In 2013, however, the CBI called for stronger regulation of banks and more supervision "to avoid another financial crisis and create a more stable system" (CBI 2 April 2013). Another rather unexpected claim was the (cautious) call for a more coherent approach to industrial policy in the UK (CBI 13 November 2013). Regarding the European level, the CBI demanded early enough and quite aggressively to assess the benefits of EU membership since the crisis might trigger far-reaching changes of the EU (CBI 17 December 2012, 21 June 2013). This is very different to the liberal-integrationist framing of the BDA. Similarities existed, however, in the strategy of externalizing the crisis as a risk for growth imposed by the Euro-zone or rather individual weak members and the demand for LME-shaped institutions on both the national and European level.

Conclusion: two varieties of capitalism, four versions of the crisis?

This explorative study of press releases issued by the German and the British trade union congresses and their employer counterparts aimed at identifying similarities and differences in their attempts to frame the crisis. The way an actor frames a crisis, or any situation for that matter, is a strategic choice and an important part of the struggle over policies, institutional change, and ideological hegemony. In the crisis it seemed possible, even if only for a short time, to challenge the hegemonic paradigm of financial capitalism. Interestingly, the analysis revealed that despite the institutional differences between the UK and Germany, the basic conflicts and the main narratives were very similar.

At the organizational level and following Schmitter and Streeck's (1999) conceptual framework, I assumed that the logics of influence and membership would matter for the crisis framing. Trade unions and business associations react to both the needs and sensitivities of its members and the conditions of goal formation and asserting influence in a given institutional setup. Not surprisingly, the crisis framing of course did follow the "domestic" situation and day-to-day developments of public debates to a large extent. The actor's framing attempts react to, enforce, and form this discourse. Comparing Germany and the UK, many differences in the framing are thus due to institutional and political contexts and the effects these have on the positions of the actors. Many differences also result simply from situational effects like the fast economic recovery of Germany already by the end of 2009.

Looking closer at some of the similarities in the strategic crisis framing though challenges readings that exaggerate structural-institutional differences. Following *VoC*, I expected that institutional differences between countries also mattered for the strategic framing of the crisis as, e.g., business in Germany should aim to strengthen CME institutions. Against this backdrop, general similarities between DGB and TUC as well as BDA and CBI are striking. The German model of CME could have implied that the BDA was interested in concerted action and re-regulation. While there was indeed considerable cooperation during the crisis in Germany which sparked debates about the character of this crisis corporation (Lehndorff 2011; Urban 2012) and whether it was to lead to more permanent coordination, the crisis framing tells a different story. The BDA consistently framed the crisis along the main themes: deregulation, liberalization of the labour market, and austerity. In their crisis framing they were brothers in mind with the CBI and by no means with the DGB. The DGB and the TUC also framed the crisis similarly albeit following the national crisis experiences: whereas the DGB took on the European crisis, the TUC stuck to the domestic employment and living standards crisis. In their claims for re-regulation, democratization of the economy, and international regulation (e.g. with a financial transaction tax), however, they followed the model of CME like the DGB.

Against the *VoC*, I argued based on power resource perspectives that because either form of market economy is a result of conflicting interests, the framing might not differ too much, as the institutional framework is a result of varying power balances and not of different interests. In other words, while trade unions and their counterparts find themselves in different institutional settings in Germany and the UK, they still have the very same goals when they embark to strategically intervene in public discourse. This argument would explain how actors framed the crisis in order to attack or reinforce ideological hegemony. In their framing of the crisis, actors do not defend "their" model of capitalism but try to use the opportunity for institutional change in their interests. This supports the critique from power resource approaches targeting the negligence of (class) conflict by the VoC-approach. Thus, I argue, it seems worth to put more emphasis on the common goals, ideologies, and indeed narrative resources of trade unions across national VoC. This could lead to new consciousness of shared interests and ideological positions across European trade unions that would help in the common quest against neoliberal hegemony within nation-states and on the European level. This may not produce results quickly but the emergence of neoliberalism, too, was a "great transformation" (Blyth 2002). The reassurance of common ideological starting points and compatible framings of the crisis thus may strengthen at least the dimension of ideational resources of European trade unions. In a world of increasingly divided public spheres, even within nation-states, this may prove to be more vital than in previous decades.

Literature

Austin, John Langshaw (1975): *How to Do Things with Words*. Harvard University Press.

Benford, Robert D.; Snow, David A. (2000): Framing Processes and Social Movements: An Overview and Assessment. *Annual Review of Sociology* 26: 611–639.

Bieling, Hans-Jürgen (2013): Die Krise Der Europäischen Union Aus Der Perspektive Einer Neogramscianisch Erweiterten Regulationstheorie". In: Atzmüller, Roland; Becker, Joachim; Brand, Ulrich; Oberndorfer, Lukas; Redak, Vanessa; Sablowski, Thomas (eds.): *Fit Für Die Krise? Perspektiven Der Regulationstheorie*. Münster: Westfälisches Dampfboot, 309–328.

Blyth, Mark (2002): *Great Transformations. Economic Ideas and Institutional Change in the Twentieth Century*. Cambridge: Cambridge University Press.

Blyth, Mark (2013): Paradigms and Paradox: The Politics of Economic Ideas in Two Moments of Crisis. *Governance* 26 (2): 197–215.

Bohmann, Gerda; Vobruba, Georg (1992): Crisis and their Interpretations. The World Economic Crises of 1929 ff. and 1974 ff. in Austria. *Crime, Law and Social Change* 17: 145–163.

Brandl, Bernd; Traxler, Franz (2011): Labour Relations, Economic Governance and the Crisis: Turning the Tide Again? *Labor History* 52 (1): 1–22.

Busch, Klaus; Hermann, Christoph; Hinrichs, Karl; Schulten, Thorsten (2013): *Euro Crisis, Austerity Policy and the European Social Model. How Crisis Policies in Southern Europe Threaten the EU's Social Dimension*. Berlin: Friedrich-Ebert-Stiftung.

Coleman, Stephen (2013): How to Make a Drama Out of a Crisis. *Political Studies Review* 11 (3): 328–335.

De Ville, Ferdi; Orbie, Jan (2014): The European Commission's Neoliberal Trade Discourse Since the Crisis: Legitimizing Continuity through Subtle Discursive Change: EC's Trade Discourse Since the Crisis. *The British Journal of Politics & International Relations* 16 (1): 149–167.

Entman, Robert M. (2004): *Projections of Power: Framing News, Public Opinion, and U.S. Foreign Policy*. Chicago: University of Chicago Press.

Entman, Robert M. (2007): Framing Bias: Media in the Distribution of Power. *Journal of Communication* 57 (1): 163–173.

English, Patrick; Grasso, Maria T.; Buraczynska, Barbara; Karampampas, Sotiris; Temple, Luke (2016): Convergence on Crisis? Comparing Labour and Conservative

Party Framing of the Economic Crisis in Britain, 2008–14. *Politics & Policy* 44 (3): 577–603.

European Commission (2012): *Industrial Relations in Europe 2012.* Brussels: European Commission.

European Commission (2015): *Industrial Relations in Europe 2014.* Brussels: European Commission.

Fioretos, Orfeo (2001): The Domestic Source of Multilateral Preferences: Varieties of Capitalism in the European Community. In: Hall, Peter A.; Soskice, D. (eds.): *Varieties of Capitalism: The Institutional Foundations of Comparative Advantage.* Oxford: Oxford University Press, 213–244.

Gamson, William A.; Modigliani, Andre (1989): Media Discourse and Public Opinion on Nuclear Power: A Constructionist Approach. *American Journal of Sociology* 95 (1): 1–37.

Gennard, John (2009): The Financial Crisis and Employee Relations. *Employee Relations* 31 (5): 451–454.

Goffman, Erving (1986): *Frame Analysis: An Essay on the Organization of Experience.* Boston: Northeastern.

Hall, Peter A.; Soskice, David (2001): *Varieties Of Capitalism: The Institutional Foundations of Comparative Advantage.* Oxford: Oxford University Press.

Hancké, Bob; Rhodes, Martin; Thatcher, Mark (ed.) (2008): *Beyond Varieties of Capitalism: Conflict, Contradictions, and Complementarities in the European Economy.* Oxford: Oxford University Press.

Hay, Colin (2013): Treating the Symptom Not the Condition: Crisis Definition, Deficit Reduction and the Search for a New British Growth Model: Treating the Symptom Not the Condition. *The British Journal of Politics & International Relations* 15 (1): 23–37.

Hegelich, Simon (2010): Diskurskoalitionen in der Finanzmarktrettung. Das Finanzmarktstabilisierungsgesetz. *der moderne staat – Zeitschrift für Public Policy, Recht und Management* 3 (2): 339–359.

Heinrich, Mathis (2014): Das Transnationale Kapital und die Bearbeitung der Krise(n) der Europäischen Union. *Prokla* 44 (2): 237–254.

Heinrich, Mathis; Kutter, Amelie (2014): A Critical Juncture in EU Integration? The Eurozone Crisis and Its Management 2010–2012. In: Panizza, Francisco; Philip, George (eds.): *Moments of Truth: The Politics of Financial Crises in Comparative Perspective. Conceptualising Change in Comparative Politics: Polities, Peoples, and Markets 1.* New York: Routledge, 120–139.

Heyes, Jason (2013): Flexicurity in Crisis: European Labour Market Policies in a Time of Austerity. *European Journal of Industrial Relations* 19 (1): 71–86.

Holst, Hajo (2013): 'Commodifying Institutions': Vertical Disintegration and Institutional Change in German Labour Relations. *Work, Employment & Society* 28 (1): 3–20.

Howell, Chris (2003): Varieties of Capitalism: And Then There Was One? *Comparative Politics* 36 (1): 103–124.

Johnston, Hank; Noakes, John A. (eds.) (2005): *Frames of Protest: Social Movements and the Framing Perspective.* Lanham: Rowman & Littlefield Publishers.

Kiess, Johannes (2015): Konfligierende Krisenframings deutscher Gewerkschaften und Arbeitgeberverbände. In: Preunkert, Jenny; Vobruba, Georg (eds.): *Krise und Integration. Gesellschaftsbildung in der Eurokrise.* Wiesbaden: Springer, 21–46.

Kiess, Johannes; Norman, Ludvig; Temple, Luke; Uba, Katrin (2017): Path Dependency and Convergence of Three Worlds of Welfare Policy during the Great Recession: UK, Germany and Sweden. *Journal of International and Comparative Social Policy* 33 (1): 1–17.

Knight, Daniel M. (2013): The Greek Economic Crisis as Trope. *Focaal* 2013 (65): 147–159.

Koch-Baumgarten, Sigrid (2010): Verbände Zwischen Öffentlichkeit, Medien Und Politik". In: Hoffjann, Olaf; Stahl, Roland (eds.): *Handbuch Verbandskommunikation*. Wiesbaden: VS, 239–258.

Korpi, Walter (2006): Power Resources and Employer-Centered Approaches in Explanations of Welfare States and Varieties of Capitalism: Protagonists, Consenters, and Antagonists. *World Politics* 58 (2): 167–206.

Kushner, Barry; Kushner, Saville (2013): *Who Needs the Cuts? Myths of the Economic Crisis*. London: Hesperus.

Kutter, Amelie (2013): Zur Analyse von Krisendiskursen. Korpusgestützte Explorationen eer Nordatlantischen Finanzkrise aus Politisch-Ökonomischer Perspektive. In: Wengeler, Martin; Ziem, Alexander (eds.): *Sprachliche Konstruktionen sozial- und wirtschaftspolitischer Krisen in der BRD*. Bremen: Hempen, 242–267.

Lehndorff, Steffen (2011): Before the Crisis, in the Crisis, and beyond: The Upheaval of Collective Bargaining in Germany. *Transfer: European Review of Labour and Research* 17 (3): 341–354.

Lehndorff, Steffen; Dribbusch, Heiner; Schulten, Thorsten (eds.) (2017): *Rough Waters. European Trade Unions in a Time of Crisis*. Brussels: ETUI.

Lévesque, Christian; Murray, Gregor (2013): Gewerkschaftsmacht verstehen: Ressourcen und Fähigkeiten zur Erneuerung strategischen Handlungsvermögens. In: Schmalz, Stefan; Dörre, Klaus (eds.): *Comeback der Gewerkschaften? Machtressourcen, innovative Praktiken, internationale Perspektiven*. Frankfurt a.M.: Campus, 39–56.

Matthes, Jörg (2007): Framing-Effekte: Zum Einfluss der Politikberichterstattung auf die Einstellungen der Rezipienten. Baden-Baden: Nomos.

Matthijs, Matthias (2016): Powerful Rules Governing the Euro: The Perverse Logic of German Ideas. *Journal of European Public Policy* 23 (3): 375–391.

Nagel, Alexander K.; Schipper, Bernd Ulrich; Weymann, Ansgar (2008): Zur religiösen Konstruktion gesellschaftlicher Krise. In: *Apokalypse: Zur Soziologie und Geschichte religiöser Krisenrhetorik*. Frankfurt a.M.: Campus, 303–309.

Pan, Zhongdang; Kosicki, Gerald M. (2001): Framing as a Strategic Action in Public Deliberation. In: Reese, Stephen D.; Gandy, Oscar H.; Grant, August E. (eds.): *Framing Public Life: Perspectives on Media and Our Understanding of the Social World*. London: Taylor & Francis, 35–66.

Pontusson, Jonas; Raess, Damian (2012): How (and Why) Is This Time Different? The Politics of Economic Crisis in Western Europe and the United States. *Annual Review of Political Science* 15 (1): 13–33.

Quiring, Oliver; Kepplinger, Hans Mathias; Weber, Mathias; Geiß, Stefan (2013): *Lehman Brothers und die Folgen: Berichterstattung zu wirtschaftlichen Interventionen des Staates*. Wiesbaden: Springer VS.

Raupp, Juliana (2013): Krisenkommunikation und Media Relations. In: Thießen, Ansgar (ed.): *Handbuch Krisenmanagement*. Wiesbaden: Springer, 175–193.

Roe, Emery (1994): *Narrative Policy Analysis: Theory and Practice*. Durham: Duke University Press.

Scharloth, Joachim; Gerber, Christian; Glättli, Balthasar; Studer, Michel; Bubenhofer, Noah; Ebling, Sarah; Vola, Saskia (2010): Die Schweiz in der Krise: Korpuspragmatische Untersuchungen zur sprachlichen Konstruktion und Diffusion von Krisensemantiken. *Aptum. Zeitschrift für Sprachkritik und Sprachkultur* 6 (2): 99–120.

Scheufele, Bertram; Tewksbury, David (2007): Framing, Agenda Setting, and Priming: The Evolution of Three Media Effects Models. *Journal of Communication* 57 (1): 9–20.

Schmalz, Stefan; Dörre, Klaus (2014): Der Machtressourcenansatz: Ein Instrument Zur Analyse Gewerkschaftlichen Handlungsvermögens. *Industrielle Beziehungen: Zeitschrift für Arbeit, Organisation and Management* 21 (3): 217–237.

Schmidt, Vivien A. (2013): Arguing about the Eurozone Crisis: A Discursive Institutionalist Analysis. *Critical Policy Studies* 7 (4): 455–462.

Schmitter, Philippe C.; Streeck, Wolfgang (1999): *The Organization of Business Interests: Studying the Associative Action of Business in Advanced Industrial Societies*. MPIfG discussion paper 99/1.

Snow, David A.; Rochford, E. Burke; Worden, Steven K.; Benford, Robert D. (1986): Frame Alignment Processes, Micromobilization, and Movement Participation. *American Sociological Review* 51: 464–481.

Sommer, Moritz; Roose, Jochen; Scholl, Franziska; Papanikolopoulos, Dimitris (2016): The Eurozone Crisis and Party Conflicts in Greece and Germany. Discursive Struggles about Responsibility. In: Krieger, Tim; Neumärker, Karl J.B.; Panke, Diana (eds.): *Europe's Crisis: The Conflict-Theoretical Perspective*. Baden-Baden: Nomos, 87–110.

Temple, Luke; Grasso, Maria T.; Buraczynska, Barbara; Karampampas, Sotiris; English, Patrick (2016): Neoliberal Narrative in Times of Economic Crisis: A Political Claims Analysis of the U.K. Press, 2007–14. *Politics & Policy* 44 (3): 553–576.

Thompson, Grahame (2009): What's in the Frame? How the Financial Crisis Is Being Packaged for Public Consumption. *Economy and Society* 38 (3): 520–524.

Urban, Hans-Jürgen. 2012. Crisis Corporatism and Trade Union Revitalisation in Europe. In: Lehndorff, Steffen (ed.): *A Triumph of Failed Ideas European Models of Capitalism in the Crisis*. Brussels: ETUI, 219–242.

Urhammer, Emil; Røpke, Inge (2013): Macroeconomic Narratives in a World of Crises: An Analysis of Stories about Solving the System Crisis. *Ecological Economics* 96: 62–70.

Wodak, Ruth; Angouri, Jo (2014): From Grexit to Grecovery: Euro/Crisis Discourses. *Discourse & Society* 25 (4): 417–423.

Zamponi, Lorenzo; Bosi, Lorenzo (2016): Which Crisis? European Crisis and National Contexts in Public Discourse: The European Crisis and National Contexts. *Politics & Policy* 44 (3): 400–426.

Ziem, Alexander (2010): Kollokationen, Konkordanzen Und Metaphern: Krisenszenarien Im Spiegel. *Aptum. Zeitschrift für Sprachkritik und Sprachkultur* 6 (2): 157–169.

Chapter 17

Comment on "Contention in times of crisis"

Oliver Nachtwey

In taking a perspective on the framing strategies applied by trade unions and employers' associations during the financial and economic crisis after 2008 in Germany and Great Britain, Chapter 16 deals with a topic which is important under empirical (meaning: political) as well as scientific respects. In the debate about trade union power resource theories, strategic choices are especially important. The article thus provides an original perspective for the analysis of industrial relations, since it takes up the concept of framing, which is central to research on social movements, and makes it applicable to the power resource approach. In particular, with regard to the discussed role of communicative power of trade unions (see Brinkmann et al. 2008; Schmalz/Dörre 2013), framing can be a conceptual extension.

The concept is relevant for the analysis of collective actors because it has a cognitive and a strategic dimension. Any strategic choice ultimately depends on the cognitive aspect, i.e. how a situation is interpreted by the actors. The strategic aspect of framing concerns the policy implications that collective actors draw from this interpretation. Framing is not identical to communicative power resources that determine the trade unions' influence on the public. But the process of framing is a prerequisite for developing it.

In the following, I would like to approach this contribution under three aspects. The first aspect concerns the extension of the power resource approach to a more socially constructivist perspective, the second the analysis of the actors' context, in this case German and British associations, and the third the theoretical linkages between the conceptual elements and tools applied in the chapter.

Of course, crises are always socially constructed by the actors themselves. But crises also have their own materiality. The respective narratives of the crisis depend not least on the structural and institutional effects of the crisis. On the one hand, the different positions of the Greek and German economies after the 2008 crisis were not just the result of discursive policies but were based on economic and structural conditions. On the other hand, Germany's ability to enforce its own economic interests and ideas (Ordoliberalism) is sometimes overestimated. The economic and political strength of Germany in Europe is enormous, and in the case of Greece it has made a great contribution to making an ordoliberal example. However, Germany's hegemony in Europe remains limited in terms of, for example, the macro-economic (rescue fund) and monetary policy (quantitative easing), as the other European countries can better correct their debts and national budgets if the ECB massively increases their liquidity.

Media analysis can shed light on many aspects. The paper is very instructive to understand how actors' statements have changed over the post-crisis years and how far they reflect policy preferences. In my opinion, however, the strength of media analyses can only really unfold in connection with the historical political economy of the respective cases. The framing concept with its constructivist perspective is only suitable if it is consistently combined with a materialistic perspective and a concrete policy analysis. What are the respective material interests and traditions of the respective actors, which allow them to fall back on specific frames? What is the relationship to the politics and policies that have been taken?

The reference to the Varieties of Capitalism (VoC) is a good starting point for the question of the paper, but the perspective of institutional complementarity needs more than an extension to an actor's perspective. You need to deepen the historical patterns of the political economy – especially in relation to crisis management (see Gourevitch 1986) and the transmission of neo-corporatist strategies (Streeck/Kenworthy 2005). The different systems of neo-corporatism and the system of industrial relations, liberal volunteerism in Britain and social partnership in Germany, continue to play an important role in shaping the strategy of the specific actors (Berger/Compston 2002).

Above all, the concrete constellations in the political arena play a significant role. In the UK, the Labour Party held the office of prime minister until 2010, and since then, the Conservatives have been in power, having a strong political preference for austerity policies from the outset. In Germany at the beginning of the crisis still the first grand coalition was in office. After the harsh neo-liberalism that she had propagated at the 2003 Leipzig party congress, Chancellor Angela Merkel had already made a pragmatic departure in 2005 and now led a coalition with social democracy. The crisis reaction of the German Federal Government – in particular the special arrangements for short-time work – was in the tradition of German social partnership and the more coordinated model of German capitalism.

It would be interesting to examine the press statements of the Deutscher Gewerkschaftsbund (DGB) and the Trade Union Congress (TUC) additionally with this perspective. This would have explained the different results better than the conceptual perspective of the VoC. For in the UK, the crisis after 2008, unlike in Germany by the DGB, who saw this as a crisis of the market, considered primarily as a labour market crisis and job crisis. Unlike in Germany, unemployment in the UK rose sharply after the 2008 crisis. Also, the fact that the crisis was considered less European than on the European continent can be better understood by looking at the

British economy – the long-lasting deindustrialization, the importance of the financial sector, and the local bubble in the real estate market – rather than the VoC perspective. The finding that TUC and DGB have certain similarities in their demands, both of which aim at a coordinated market economy, is little surprising in that the British unions see continental capitalism ("social market economy") as a better alternative to liberal market economy.

Finally, I would like to draw attention to the combination of theoretical elements within the paper. With their focus on "VoC", Hall and Soskice (2001) are drawing attention to the dynamics of national innovation regimes. These regimes, so they argue, are deriving from a particular interplay between institutions, and thereby create particular socioeconomic models of capitalism in place at the national level. While it can generally be regarded as innovative to transfer this heuristic from Comparative Political Economy to the field of a political sociology of trade union relations, the question arises in how far the institutional settings can be interpreted as explanatory variables for particular "Varieties of Framing". While Hall and Soskice (2001) in their argument are drawing on a theory of comparative advantage to explain the different innovation regimes, it remains an open question whether or not we can transfer this concept to the field of trade unionism.

At the same time, what Kiess does proclaim is a focus on "the interests of actors, their beliefs, strategic aims, and their ability to build coalitions". If we take this ambition one step further and include the formation of these elements, the approach to be taken methodology-wise would have to be one which reconstructs how institutional logics play out "on the ground" (as e.g. in Fligstein 2001). While the chapter does provide sufficient evidence for a story that generally fits well with what we know about labour relations in Germany and the UK, a closer look at the micro-dynamics *inside* the respective associations on what Seeliger (2019) calls "the social construction of organised interest" could provide a microfoundation for connecting the institutionalist VoC-approach with the constructivist meso-level concept of framing.

Guiding hypotheses could then, for example, derive from the assumption that trade unionists who are working on collective bargaining are taking a different position on the crisis and the question of what is an appropriate framing strategy from representatives from the international department of the same organization. Taking this argument yet another step further, one could also take into account the particular character of trade union federations as "meta-organizations" (Ahrne/Brunsson 2008). Because they are themselves consisting of member organizations usually representing workers from different economic sectors that have different backgrounds (and thus also differ in terms of worldviews and interests). Here, for example, one could expect that trade unions from the export sectors are taking a different approach towards international economic organization than do organizations from sheltered sectors (see Hancké 2013; but also Kiess 2015).

While against the background of what we know about the different models of labour relations in the two countries, the theoretical design does leave room for further inquiry of the question, if different "Varieties of Capitalism" do translate into particular "Varieties of Trade Unionism" manifesting themselves, among other things, in particular repertoires of framing strategies. Dealing with such kind of questions in further empirical research does certainly sound like a promising endeavour!

Literature

Ahrne, Göran; Brunsson, Nils (2008): *Meta-Organizations*. Cheltenham: Elgar.
Berger, Stefan; Compston, Hugh (ed.) (2002): *Policy Concertation and Social Partnership in Western Europe*. New York: Berghan.
Brinkmann, Ulrich; Choi, Hae-Lin; Detje, Richard; Dörre, Klaus; Holst, Hajo; Karakayali, Serhat; Schmalstieg, Catharina (2008): *Strategic Unionism: Aus der Krise zur Erneuerung?* Wiesbaden: VS.
Fligstein, Neil (2001). Social Skill and the Theory of Fields. *Sociological Theory* 19 (2): 105–25.
Gourevitch, Peter (1986): *Politics in Hard Times – Comparative Responses to International Economic Crises*. Ithaca: Cornell University Press.
Hall, Peter A.; Soskice, David (2001): *Varieties of Capitalism: Institutional Foundations of Comparative Advantage*. Oxford: Oxford University Press.
Hancké, Bob (2013). *Unions, Central Banks and EMU: Labour Market Institutions and Monetary Integration in Europe*. Oxford: Oxford University Press.
Kiess, Johannes (2015): Konfligierende Krisenframings deutscher Gewerkschaften und Arbeitgeberverbände. In: Vobruba, Georg; Jenny Preunkert (eds.): *Krise und Integration*. Wiesbaden: Springer, 21–46.
Schmalz, Stefan; Dörre, Klaus (ed.) (2013): *Comeback der Gewerkschaften? Machtressourcen, innovative Praktiken, internationale Perspektiven*. Frankfurt a.M.: Campus.
Seeliger, Martin (2019): *Trade Unions in the Course of European Integration. The Social Construction of Organized Interest*. London: Routledge
Streeck, Wolfgang; Kenworthy, Lane (2005): Theories and Practices of Neocorporatism. In: Janoski, Thomas et al. (ed.): *The Handbook of Political Sociology*. Cambridge: Cambridge University Press, 441–460.

Chapter 18

A constant tug of war

Neoliberalism and social unrest in (post)-crisis Europe

Madelaine Moore and Anne Engelhardt

Introduction

> All fixed, fast-frozen relations, with their train of ancient and venerable prejudices and opinions, are swept away, all new-formed ones become antiquated before they can ossify. All that is solid melts into air
>
> (Marx/Engels 1848: 16)

In recent years, European Union (EU) Member States have used the banner of the crisis to push forward a new form of Authoritarian Neoliberalism. However, these processes and transformations of the state have not gone unchallenged, with trade unions and other social movements pushing back. Despite this, many studies of the crisis have tended to: take a top-down approach, exploring how certain fractions of capital have maintained hegemony whilst ignoring the impact of social movements, or have looked solely at social movements and trade unions as independent phenomena, framing the state as a black box, or something acted upon, rather than in relation to. There has been little research that highlights the interrelation between these actors and institutions, seeing them in process, and shaping each other.

In this chapter, we seek to develop a more complex analysis of the state and its relationship with trade unions and movements in the post-crisis period. We seek to introduce a framework that explores the internal relation of such structures and processes answering the following questions: are trade unions state apparatuses or social movements? And, how is this question related to economic and political processes such as crises, and Authoritarian Neoliberalism? In a previous article, we outlined how social movements are not static categories, but rather, as their name suggests, they are dynamic and evolve in relation to time and space (see Engelhardt/Moore 2017). In this chapter, we seek to extend such analysis to trade unions, especially in relation to the state. Our intervention is that most studies isolate such actors and processes, focussing on one and in turn treating the others as static objects. However, to understand subsequent shifts of all three we need a theory that can deal with them in process and relation with one another. This is both a historical and analytical argument. We explore this through two case studies – the role of trade unions in Portugal ("Que se lixe a troika"[1]) and Ireland ("Right2Water" protest) – where each offers a different perspective of these dynamics in an attempt at building a wider state-focussed approach to struggle, concentrating on actors and changes, i.e. the "solid melts into air".

Our chapter is structured as follows: to begin, we outline our theoretical framework and the current gaps in the literature. This leads to a historical analysis of the states under question and how certain institutional forms such as social partnership came into being. From this, we move to the specific state formation that has emerged in the neoliberal and in particular (post)crisis period: namely a more authoritarian state. We then outline the specifics of the cases, and the shifting position of trade unions through anti-austerity protest movements.

Theoretical framework

The material conditions of the (post)crisis period have changed the landscape for trade union activity. We suggest that because of these changing conditions, some unions have aligned with social movements and cannot be considered a state apparatus, although they may retain certain brokerage positions, whilst other unions have maintained their relationship with the state and political parties remaining much closer to the traditional notion of a state apparatus.

Between labour studies and critical political economy

An underlying goal of this research is to further provoke conversation across disciplines. We see an epistemological gap in the study of social movements where movements are segregated from one another as well as the social whole from which they emerge,[2] thus missing the potentialities of struggle (Saraçoğlu 2017).[3] We, following Andreas Bieler's argument (2017: 302), suggest that much social movement literature often ignores the importance of the mode of production and its historical development. Furthermore, shifting global power relations that are mirrored in state institutions must also be addressed (ibid., 301). In contrast, labour studies that focus on the mode of production tend to neglect the state, often seeing it as a black box or neutral mediator.[4, 5]

In a previous article, we outlined in some depth the benefits of a dialectical historical materialist approach to studying social movements. We suggest that a dialectical methodology that prioritises the relationality and processuality based on a deep ontology may have more emancipatory potential, as well as better capture the complexities of our current conjuncture.[6] Studying the social necessitates some level of abstraction, but this cannot occur at the expense of forgetting what we abstract from (Sayer 1992: 59). As Bannerji (2005: 151) concludes, "you cannot tear this live social way of being and its formational journey into component parts and expect it to live and move". Isolating social movements and trade unions from shifts in neoliberal hegemonic practices seems to propose that they are two separate processes or dynamics, potentially interacting or conflicting at certain points, but missing their internal relation. Furthermore, by excluding historical shifts, the process is negated, which is, however, and following Bakker and Gill (2003), important for a social ontology based on process and human agency. There is a blind spot to analysis that seeks to segregate and disaggregate social phenomena from the complex social system that is capitalism. A historical materialist position allows us to understand different power asymmetries and trace how such structural shifts condition institutional changes (Bieler 2017: 303).

The historical materiality of the state

Of particular importance for our analysis of trade unions is the internal processes and relationality of the state. Drawing on a relational materialist state theory, the capitalist state is not a black box or inherently stable; instead, it is marked by contradiction and crisis, and is always re-made reflecting current power constellations (Poulantzas 2014: 144). Although remaining a *capitalist* state, it is not merely an instrument for one class (Clarke 1983: 5) but rather the crystallisation of particular class power relations and past struggles (Poulantzas/Martin 2008). State apparatuses ease, organise, and therefore canalise class struggles. These "canals" (i.e. laws, institutions, public places, etc.) are always contested and due to this are themselves constantly altering. In this way, the capitalist state organises forms of economic, social, and political struggles. At the same time, the state is not a monolithic bloc. Because of struggles (whether from movements or trade unions, for example) it is a heterogeneous ensemble of apparatuses that, although dominated by the interest of capital, have institutionalised some demands of the hegemonic or subaltern classes to varying degrees (Wöhl/Wissel 2008: 9–10).

Despite following this analysis, we do have some issues with Poulantzas, specifically, that he remains top-down, thus can fall into reformist political implications, and does not fully integrate social reproductive concerns into his argument.[7] Not to discount these critiques, his method and understanding of the relational state can be turned around to explore how movements inscribe themselves into apparatuses rather than only how they are hijacked by the state. Conflicts, or even a crisis inside and between the apparatuses, can also be understood as a window of opportunity for social movements. State personnel can utilise struggles for their own institutional interests (Poulantzas 2014: 243). This is a historical argument, where what is taken as

234 Madelaine Moore and Anne Engelhardt

a structure today is not assumed to be the same in the past or will continue in the same form in the future (Bannerji 2005: 151).

Trade unions as a state apparatus?
A historical development

To return to our original question, trade unions have an uneasy character, moving between social movement and apparatus. In times of growing authoritarianism, Poulantzas argues that trade unions are increasingly reformist apparatuses, directly inserted in the administrative structure and reflecting the state's material institutionality (Poulantzas 2014: 225); trade unions will be fully swallowed into state administrational processes, i.e. social partnership (ibid.: 144). This analysis is somewhat limited as it misses the internal struggle within unions, or that unions – like states – could be understood as relational fields of struggle between branches of the working classes. We suggest that when Poulantzas proposes that (ibid.: 155) "the struggles of the popular masses constantly call into question the unity of the state personnel as category in the service of existing power and hegemonic fraction of the dominant classes", this could also be applied to trade unions and their administration as potential or half-state personnel and their relation to social movements.

Josef Esser (1981) also used a materialist state theory to observe how trade union leaderships were operating like state personnel. Although he takes his examples from the West-German trade union landscape, such observations also apply to the development of the trade union movements in Ireland and Portugal. Esser describes how after the economic crisis of 1973 the opportunities for negotiation seemed to have been limited with the subsequent results:

1   Companies emerged from the crisis in a stronger position compared to trade unions, witnessed through weak bargaining contracts and the dismissal of workers (ibid.: 367).
2   Alliances between political parties and trade unions segregated the working classes, concentrating on the interests of particular groups, primarily the industrialised, export-orientated sectors, rather than precarious or atypical labour (ibid.: 368).[8]
3   Trade unions took a defensive position negotiating the terms of lay-offs and wage cuts rather than fighting against them. As such, trade union interests became aligned to the "national interest" pursuing competitive policies on the world market (ibid.: 369).
4   The state becomes critical in "solving" conflicts,[9] especially when parties traditionally linked to the main trade union federations were part of the government, whereas the interests of rank and file members were side-lined (ibid.: 371).
5   This undermined their own bargaining position and resulted in a loss of membership.

Within social partnership, the closer trade unions became to the state and the "national interest" the further they shut themselves off from their membership reflecting a state bureaucracy that it "has shut itself up in a water tight container" (Poulantzas 2014: 223). Through such institutional shifts, their concerns and membership become more exclusionary, rather than promoting alliances with other social movements such as migrant rights women's, environmental, or Lesbian, Gay, Bi and Trans*(LGBT) movements. In moving closer to the state, the social reproductive politics that unions had been a part of by being situated in communities is cut off. In both the case of Portugal and Ireland it is interesting to see how the social partnership model came into being through the particular fragility of the state and character of social struggles.

The political development of the Irish state

The Irish State has remained fairly conservative since independence, with 80–90% of the electorate voting for the two big centre right (nationalist and catholic) parties, Fine Gael or Fianna Fail (Dunphy 2017: 267). As such, there has been little left/right divide (Naughton 2015: 292).[10] Some authors have argued that change has been limited because of the political cultural tendency towards localism and personality politics (Dunphy 2017: 268).[11] Furthermore, Ireland's political culture has been described as cliental, populist, and nationalist (Naughton 2015: 292). However, saying this, working-class community activism has always played a role in Ireland balancing a complex relationship between "disruption and apparent subsumption within the state" (Cox 2017: 10). This history can be partly explained by its colonial past and the impact of imperialism on the development of a working-class identity (ibid.: 11).

Up until the Celtic Tiger period of the 1990s, the Irish economy was underdeveloped, with little industrial revolution and high levels of emigration (Dunphy 2017: 267). The industrialisation policy pursued was dependent on Foreign Direct Investment (FDI) and financial capital, a dependence that continues today (Roche 2007: 397). As a result, Ireland has been the low tax destination for (especially American) multinationals since the 1990s, which fed into the credit fuelled construction boom of the early 2000s.[12] Citing Hardiman's work on the Irish economy, Murphy and Cannon argue that from the 1980s onwards Ireland was a low tax and service-orientated economy, which were the drivers of economic growth and employment (Cannon/ Murphy 2015: 6).

Social partnership in Ireland: context, co-optation, and links to political parties

Social partnership became official in 1987 and continued until 2009. It included the state, trade unions, business groups, and from 1995 civil society organisations. There had been attempts at centralised tripartite pay bargaining in Ireland during the 1970s "with governments trading budgetary commitments and commitments on inflation and jobs for concessions from employers and unions with respect to pay restraint and industrial peace" (Roche 2007: 396). By the 1980s many discredited this process due to poor economic performance and job creation and increasing industrial unrest (ibid.). However, in 1987 the tripartite, formalised social partnership model of three-year national economic and social agreements came into being.[13] As part of the agreements, social policies were designed that targeted unemployment and inequality including the establishment of a minimum wage, fitting into a broader social welfare model. Despite this, wage inequality and the low pay sector grew rapidly, increasing relative poverty levels (ibid., 400). There was a general consensus between the parties to pursue policies aimed at competitiveness and economic prosperity.

Social partnership emerged from a period of intense social and economic crisis, years of free collective bargaining, and an increasingly hostile employer attitude (Geary 2016: 2). Roche expands on this, stating that unemployment was at 19%, and there was increasing public debt and an unsustainable tax burden, and – in part because of institutionalised tax evasion – this was an acute economic crisis but also an acute social crisis reflected in the high levels of emigration (Roche 2007: 397). Thus, in a shift away from Keynesian policies, the state sought to gain control over its public finances and squeeze public spending. Yet, to do so they required political backing, including tempering possible protest from strong public service unions (ibid.).[14] The unions were disposed to enter the agreement because the 1980s had seen the biggest decline in density since the 1920s, falling to 57%, as well as a fear that Thatcherism could be imported from the UK; the social partnership model appeared as a more palatable alternative (ibid.).

For the union movement, social partnership signalled a much closer relationship to the state. As Roche describes (2007: 408), it:

> Provided a statutory basis for the strategic and deliberative agencies of social partnership, essentially formalizing their status as agencies of state, operating under governance arrangements in which representatives of the social partners hold pivotal positions.

For most of the 20th century business unionism had dominated Ireland, with a more politicised approach emerging in the 1980s in the face of crisis and employer hostility from American Multinational Corporations (MNCs). Under social partnership, trade unions moved towards social-democratic ideals in exchange for extensive access to government and some influence in social policy. Critically, many benefits negotiated through the agreements occurred through tax cuts, resulting in a decreased welfare state, and union organisation was undermined with density falling from 45.5% in 1996 to 34% by 2009 where unions were only strong in the public sector and the balance of power had shifted towards employers (Geary 2016: 2). Once social partnership came into force, the way that civil society and trade unions interacted with the state changed, with the interests of workers now linked to Irish capital, under the proviso of stability and growth. Many claim that through this model the union movement had lost its ability to act independently (Erne 2013: 428). Geary's (2016: 2) description of social partnership unions as "co-managers of retrenchment" during times of crisis proved particularly prescient in recent years.

Interestingly, these agreements and the general shift towards the state were also reflected in broader community activism. Laurence Cox (2017: 11) argues that the Irish government has often responded to social movements by including them into policy – such as in the anti-nuclear and feminist movements. Under social partnership this became more pronounced when such groups were officially included (Roche 2007: 405). This gave many community activists a voice in policy development but also locked them to the state and employers.[15] There had, argues Royall (2017: 8), been a long period of co-optation where dialogue was the priority. The dependence of such groups on state funding further limited debate and opposition, but they could now act as service providers (Naughton 2015: 293). Co-optation of civil society organisations and trade unions by the state had become the norm. Community groups, in exchange for funding, became providers of services rather than claimants against the state, channelling energy away from disruptive action to service provision; as such, when funding was cut during the recession, they no longer had the repertoires of protest that had previously existed (Landy 2017).

The development of the Portuguese state

The Portuguese state was crystallised during the social revolution, and since then has been in a constant state of flux. Under the 48 years of right-wing dictatorship the country's economy depended on the continued exploitation of its colonies, and by the end of the 1960s its belated industrial development had resulted in an export-led economy; the annual income per head rose 6.5% a year (Küpeli 2013: 13). International companies, such as West-German and US industries, grew in the low-wage country. Following on from the increasing weariness and resistance to the colonial wars, and a growth in strikes in the emerging industrial workforce,[16] the Portuguese Revolution in 1974 brought the social, economic, and cultural contradictions to the fore (Sperling 2014). During the revolution, a multiplicity of actors, including the anti-colonial forces in Guinea-Bissau, Angola, and Mozambique; a war-tired army; students; women; and labour movements, occupied land and industries, and developed a new education, health, legal, and industrial relations system (Accornero 2015). As such, the Portuguese Constitution is a tessellation of different class demands. While it was one of the most progressive legal frameworks in terms of labour and reproductive rights (Esposito 2014), the capitalist mode of production remained somewhat intact (Varela 2014: 15), tamed by paragraphs that prohibited privatisations (Fonseca/Domingos 1998). Eighty percent of banks and 25% of the land were nationalised;[17] however these processes were wound back in the 1980s when the PS[18] and PSD[19] tried to attract foreign investments and access to the European market. By the 1990s most of the public industries had been privatised (Küpeli 2013: 22).

Portugal has remained a low-wage country with a minimum wage 25% below the European average (Accornero 2015: 36), and a high level of emigration. Although there was a small economic upswing during the 1990s, since the beginning of 2000 and becoming more pronounced during the economic crisis in 2007/2008 Portugal has been struggling to receive government bonds (Rodrigues/Reis 2012). Recent economic growth has some similarities to the Celtic Tiger of Ireland of the 1990s: due to extreme flexibilisation of the labour market in the past five years and low wages and taxes, the often highly educated workforce that remains in the country is now concentrated in outsourced call centres of German, French, and Spanish companies (Costa 2017), or in the booming but fragile tourism sector.

Social Partnership in Portugal: the division of the trade union landscape

According to Hermes Costa (1994: 121) the first step towards the development of social partnership was the foundation of the UGT[20] in 1978. After the revolution, independent parties and trade unions were legalised; and in particular, the orthodox Communist Party (PCP) and its affiliated trade union federation CGTP-IN[21] had a very strong influence in the movements and the workforce, while the PS was instead able to gain electoral support but had little roots in the labour and social movements. The PS and later the UGT were built up and influenced by financial and political interventions from the socialdemocratic parties from West Germany and other countries during the transformation-period. In contrast to the more left-wing structures, the UGT and the PS attempted to canalise the development of the revolution into a parliamentary democracy (Küpeli 2013).

The path was unstable: in 1984, inflation reached almost 30%, and while the state had become a huge employer through state-owned companies, the return of thousands of Portuguese from political exile and the colonies happened in a time of severe economic instability and increasing unemployment. A political crisis ensued with ten government changes within nine years, following on from six provisional governments in the year after the revolution (Barreto 1993: 446). In order to access credit and the European market, the political and social situation needed to be stabilised; thus in 1984, the "Standing Committee for Social Concertation" (CPCS) was created: a tripartite committee including the government, the main trade union federations (CGTP and UGT), and the federations of the employers (CIP, CCP CAP, and later CTP[22]). This "has constituted a permanent forum facilitating social pacts" (Campos Lima/Naumann 2000: 391).

Until 1987, the CGTP had refused to participate in the committee and also campaigned against the European Economic Community (EEC) membership of Portugal (Barreto 1993: 463). Although due to decreased mobilisation, their inability to stop privatisations, and opening towards the European market, the CGTP entered the arena of negotiations (ibid.: 327). From the 17 social pacts signed up to 2008, the CGTP has only signed six, which concerned the education and health and safety plans for the workforce (ibid.: 391). Thus, the trade union landscape has been largely limited to the two politically aligned trade union federations, and while the UGT represents less than 30% of the unionised workforce and the CGTP more than 60%, the UGT has remained a social partner to its affiliated parties, PS and PSD, which have each held governmental positions since the revolution. While the UGT signed all social pacts, the CGTP turned to mobilising strikes and mass demonstrations. Rather than seeing these as contradictory strategies (Campos Lima/Artiles 2011: 392), they could be analysed as a complementary way of "boxing and dancing", where the UGT as a state apparatus profited during negotiations from the pressure on the street, and the CGTP trade unions also had the UGT as a link to the state to negotiate such deals.

This type of labour division between a struggle-orientated, left leaning CGTP and a state-orientated, social partnership UGT was interrupted in 1988, when privatisation and austerity measures were instituted by the first PSD government. In response, both federations organised a general strike together to combat these attacks and the CGTP managed to sign two bargaining contracts locking-in many working-class interests. A joint strategy of both federations did not occur again until the economic crisis and the new wave of austerity measure from 2010 onwards.

As both Ireland and Portugal show, social partnership became the dominant model by the late 1980s with some trade unions acting as a form of state apparatus – balancing the role of negotiation and mobilisation – yet conversely the state required union support due to its fragility in times of crisis. When leaning towards social partnership, trade unions blocked off channels for protest and alternatives to the "national interest", playing the role of a state apparatus. However, although this was true for the beginning of the neoliberal period, with shifts in economy and state, such institutional formations have altered, in turn reformulating the role of trade unions moving on the continuum away from the state and towards movements.

(Post)crisis social movements and trade unions

Returning to the (post)crisis period in both states, we can see that there have been marked structural and institutional changes that have in turn altered the trade union landscape. To explain these shifts more concretely, we draw on the concept Authoritarian Neoliberalism developed by Ian Bruff (2014), as well as insights from Social Reproduction Theory. These, we argue, highlight specific shifts in state form as well as contradictions that are becoming more prescient under neoliberalism. (Post)crisis neoliberalism has two interrelated facets: increasing control and infiltration of social reproduction on the one hand and increasing authoritarianism on the other. Underpinning both is a re-purposing of the state, its policies, and institutions to service the market. This has a tendency to push trade unions out of the state; the institutional rug is being pulled from under them, forcing some to look for alternatives.

The term "Authoritarian Neoliberalism" captures the shift in state towards a more authoritarian character but is linked to certain accumulation strategies that have closed down democratic avenues; spaces for dialogue; and, we would add, increased the social reproductive contradiction. The term rejects the narrow understanding of neoliberalism as a winding back of the state and problematises the separation of so-called market and non-market spaces. Bruff proposes that neoliberalism, far from being about the disembedding of the free market from the state, is instead the re-purposing of non-market institutions, relations, and spaces to serve the market (2014: 114). This can include forms of mobilisation, for example, the use of collective bargaining as a means to discipline labour rather than see them as equal partners, shifts in welfare to workfare, and the decline of socialdemocratic parties.

There is a particular focus on privatisation. The state (public) becomes part of the problem rather than relied upon to deliver public or social goods, and the market takes its place (Bruff 2017). This is a dual process where the public sphere is commodified, turning citizens into consumers of services, but also a political need to outsource labour struggles within the state through the privatisation of (often militant) public services, resulting in a double attack on workers – through spaces of production and reproduction. What needs to be accentuated is the breakdown of the reproduction of communities.[23, 24] It is important to remember that the attacks on workers in the productive sphere under neoliberalism (trade union and collective bargaining rights, strike breaking, etc.) were just as violent in the social reproductive sphere and included a simultaneous expansion and retrenchment of the state through attacks on working-class social reproduction, the shift from workfare to welfare, and final enclosures of communal land and knowledge (Mohandesi/Teitelman 2017). Neoliberalism is deeply embedded in the social reproduction contradiction. Critically, these community-based issues were no longer central to trade union activities in the social partnership period as they were understood as private rather than workplace concerns.

The tendency within neoliberalism to infiltrate non-market spaces with the logic or common sense of neoliberal accumulation strategies has strained the necessary (for the reproduction of capitalism) division between political and economic power. This, linking concretely back to Bruff's term, has resulted in increased authoritarianism and certain contradictory processes of legitimation and democratic crises. Authoritarianism in general should be thought of as more than just brute coercive force (although this is obviously a factor) but also the way that state and institutional power is reconfigured to insulate certain policies and practices from political and social unrest (Bruff 2014: 115). For our neoliberal era, this comes in the form of removal of the social safety nets that limit the ability of society to absorb the effects of socio-economic restructuring, in turn increasing the insecurity and vulnerability of potential political subjects, and thus creating the conditions that allow for more coercive neoliberal practices to be introduced. This produces, and is reproduced by, the growing neoliberal content of non-market institutions – the infiltration of previously immune spaces and weakening of forums where social compromise could take place (for example, trade unions).

Yet, what is missing in such analysis is the *effects* of such shifts and *struggles* these developments can provoke. Linked to such protests and the closing down of alternative models, trade unions have also had to re-address their positions. The sharpened social reproduction contradiction has created a fruitful ground for solidarity across struggles, as well as clarified the capitalist character of the state. This is what has occurred – in different ways – with trade unions in both Ireland and Portugal. Our argument is that after this protest cycle, and the attacks through Authoritarian Neoliberalism, we cannot talk of a union movement, but rather movements, as the unions are themselves facing a moment of decision-making about where they position themselves.

Irish crisis, austerity, and unions

Leading up to the crisis, Ireland had been tethered to a particular model of laissez faire finance capitalism based on financial speculation, a construction boom, and high personal indebtedness (Geary 2016: 1). This model made it particularly vulnerable to the financial crisis (Bach/Stroleny 2013, 342). When the crisis hit, house prices tumbled, the banking sector threatened collapse, and the subsequent bank bailout became sovereign debt.[25] Due to debt escalation the government sought an emergency bailout from the Troika in November 2010. The 2011 European Fiscal Compact Treaty Referendum locked Ireland into strict fiscal targets set by the European

Commission (EC) (Cannon/Murphy 2015: 7), and in order to recover the debt a series of drastic cuts to social spending rather than tax increases were implemented (ibid.). The state continued many of the same privatisation and FDI-orientated policies that lead to the crisis, but now with less democratic oversight. This isolated economic decision-making from public scrutiny saw a rise in executive power. On 15 December 2013, Ireland became the first country to exit the bailout process (Ogle 2016: 83). Many argued that Ireland was now "post-crisis", recording falling unemployment[26] and some growth; the ruling Fine Gael party claimed that austerity "had worked" (Dunphy 2017: 273).[27]

The effects of austerity on the population were huge provoking multiple scales of protest – although not to the same degree as other "PIIGS" (Portugal, Italy, Ireland, Greece, Spain) states. Irish people paid the highest cost per capita of bailing out the financial institutions in Europe (Hearne 2015: 309). Cox argues that austerity in Ireland through linking the tax increases with welfare state cuts equalled one-fifth of GDP and is the single biggest cut to living standards in a developed country since wartime (Cox 2017: 9). As a result, Ireland has seen increased inequality (30.7 on the Gini coefficient in 2008 to 31.2 in 2012), increased income distribution, and poverty levels rising.[28] Missing the multiple scales of protests that did occur, some argued that Ireland had come out of the crisis with few protests (Cannon/Murphy 2015: 1). However, and not neglecting the multiple protests that had occurred (i.e. over public service cuts, bin charges, and the household tax), it was not until 2014 that Ireland really took to the streets – over the introduction of Water Charges. This protest movement dramatically changed the political landscape and pushed the union movement away from the state and social dialogue model.

Although Social Partnership officially ended in 2009, social dialogue and party alliances remained the preferable model for many of the major unions in the ICTU. Social Partnership broke down in 2009 after the government unilaterally imposed a pension levy, a supplementary budget that included pay reductions for public sector workers, and further cuts in public spending (O'Kelly 2010: 426; Geary 2016: 2).[29] Despite this, social dialogue between unions and employers and especially unions and the state continued with the Croke Park (I and II) and Haddington Rd Agreements (CPA and HRA).[30] Bach and Stroleny (2013: 353) point out that these public sector agreements are not a return to social partnership, but rather a framework for *implementing* government cuts rather than negotiation over their content. It was in the interest of the government to continue dialogue during the crisis to avoid industrial strife that could have scared away critical FDI and foreign MNCs (Royall 2017: 10).

The ICTU also held on to their role as social partner, holding only four major protest days between 2008 and 2013.[31] They did not participate in the European Confederation of Trade Union coordinated day of action and solidarity against austerity in 2012, due to claims it might destroy the social peace (Hearne 2015: 310).[32] Furthermore, as the ICTU received some funding from the government, this limited their freedom to protest against it (Geary 2016: 9). Cox argues (2017) that the goal of the ICTU and especially SIPTU[33] – which had a very close relationship with the Labour Party and commitment to social partnership – was to keep protest within controllable bounds and negotiate concessions with the Labour Party. Whatever their intentions, continued dialogue incorporated "trade unions into policies of austerity and creat(ed) top-down rather than bottom up mobilization strategies" (Bach/Stroleny 2013: 352). This was a problematic position, as they now faced a state less willing to accommodate their concerns pushing unpalatable austerity measures that they were required to sell to their members.[34] For, as Cox (2017: 29) describes, "When the state attacked partnership, the core legitimation strategy was undermined, but those organizations had no alternative strategy than hoping for a return to the previous unhappy marriage".

The close relationship between many trade unions and the Labour Party further complicated protest after the Labour Party became a junior government partner following the 2011 election. In the lead up to the 2011 election, Labour had campaigned on a platform of "Labour's way or Frankfurt's way" against austerity (Ogle 2016: 44). Despite campaign rhetoric, once in power, policy became more regressive with the lowest earners facing the highest cuts in the 2012 and 2014 budgets (Finn 2015: 52). In Geary's interviews (2016: 6), most union leaders reported that it was not in their interest to publicly criticise Labour: "Thus any turn to mobilization was hedged with the reservation that to do so would strain union relations with labour and risked jeopardizing any possible gains Labour might achieve". The unions had locked themselves to dialogue with a state and political party that was increasingly turning away from them. They walked a tightrope between their role as state partner and protest, a tension exacerbated by the Water Charges protests, and the further closing down of spaces for negotiation within the state.

As background, the introduction of Water Charges was part of the Memorandum of Understanding dictated by the Troika. The proposed charges were seen by many as a form of regressive taxation and the first step towards privatisation (Muehlebach 2017).[35] In response, one of Ireland's biggest and most inclusive social movements emerged – including huge protests,[36] direct actions; including blockading estates and water meter installations, as well as refusal to pay.[37] Fundamental to the Water Charges protest was the increasingly authoritarian environmental dynamic centred on the regressive nature of the austerity measures between 2012 and 2014 as well as the cognitive and organisational lessons learned from previous campaigns.[38] One survey (Hearne 2015) found that 54.5% of protestors who responded had never protested before.[39] Many were women, the elderly, and unemployed – those who were home during the day and could monitor and blockade the installation of water meters (Muehlebach 2017). The length of the blockades meant that communities needed to organise shifts and held nightly meetings about the logistics and social reproduction of the protest (i.e. school collections, food, and clothing). As one protester stated (ibid.):

> People had each others' backs. Many of the working-class estates, not just in Cobh but all over the country, were in complete lockdown. We simply wouldn't let Irish Water in. Communities, so alienated from each other and broken by poverty, evictions, unemployment, came together. It was magic.

Hearne argues that because of the closing down of alternatives spaces, such as trade unions or electoral politics (with the Labour Party now enforcing austerity), people had to be more creative with their protests to get their message heard (Hearne 2015: 310). As Dunphy asserts, water "charges has proven to be the issue that has acted as a focal point for the entire anti-austerity movement in Ireland" (Dunphy 2017: 273). Water Charges became a concrete way to attack austerity and defend their communities. This move-ment resulted not only in the stopping of charges and a shift leftwards in electoral politics but also in the politicising of ordinary people after a period of professionalisation of politics in such neighbourhoods (Cox 2017: 24).[40] The authoritarian state response to the protests further pushed communi-ties against Irish Water and the state.[41]

Alongside the local actions outlined earlier, the Right2Water (R2W) plat-form played a critical role in organising the movement and represented a break for some of the ICTU unions with the established model. In October 2014, Unite the Union, the Communication Workers Union (CWU), the re-tail union Mandate, the civil service union CPSU, and the plasterers' union OPATSI broke with the other unions to form the R2W platform, alongside community activist groups, some left parties, Sinn Fein, and left independ-ents (Cox 2017: 13).[42] The trade unions and community groups were instru-mental in the alliance, mediating between the different political parties and "ensuring the emphasis has been on building the campaign rather than po-litical rivalries"; furthermore, unions and political parties were forced to be more creative because communities had been activated from the ground up (Hearne 2015: 318). Such an organisational alliance was unprecedented (Cox 2017: 17; Landy 2017).[43]

The water movement and ICTU policy came to a head on 8 July 2015 at the ICTU conference, forcing the ICTU to reassess their position in the shifting institutional and environmental context. Out of a possible 50 ICTU affiliates only five unions were affiliated to R2W, yet a motion was put for-ward against the charges (Ogle 2016: 189). SIPTU and IMPACT, the two largest affiliates that had never lost a vote when voting together, put forward a much-watered down amendment amenable to Labour Party policy.[44] The amendment was narrowly voted down by nine votes, 194 to 203, meaning that the official position of the ICTU was now against Water Charges. This broke with the state and Labour Party position, signalling a cognitive and organisational shift towards the movement and working-class communities that were behind it.[45] In the eyes of many in the left, the ICTU had, up until then, not been a particularly progressive political force, and social partnership had led "to their virtual cooption as part of the state apparatus" (Dunphy 2017: 277). This clear position, forced on the ICTU by the R2W movement, pulled them away from the state. This was a needed institutional shift to regain the trust of working-class communities, for many had:

> Stated that they didn't trust trade unions. They explained that, in their community and to them, trade unions were something they associated with the establishment, with government, and that they had betrayed the working class...they had felt this betrayal in their homes, in their streets and in their lives.
>
> (Ogle 2016: 69–70)

The movement, pushed onto the streets by increasingly regressive environmental dynamics and the closing down of alternative protest channels, forced a cognitive and organisational shift within the trade unions.[46]

Coming out of, and following up on, the success of R2W, the unions alongside some political parties and community activists have established a policy platform called Right2Change (R2C). R2C is a broad electoral policy platform spanning housing, jobs, water, public services, traveller and migrant rights, education, media, and democratic rights, as well as an overhaul of the financial-led economy and tax system (Ogle 2016: 164–165). One hundred and six candidates ran under the R2C platform in the 2016 election (ibid.: 218). The election saw Fine Gael and Labour kicked out of office,[47] and almost 100 out of the 158 seats were filled by people who had campaigned on an anti-Water Charges (if not R2C) platform (ibid.: 235). Although Fine Gael and Fianna Fail still dominate the electoral landscape, 2016 showed a marked shift leftwards and towards independents (Cox 2017: 16).

Portugal between Authoritarian Neoliberalism and anti-austerity movement(s)

In comparison to Ireland, which saw an economic upswing before the crisis in 2007/2008, Portugal's economic growth had remained stagnant.[48] The Portuguese minority government of the PS first sought to stabilise the national economy without external support. In 2003, the right-wing PSD government had adopted a "Labour Code" which in 2009 paved the way for the socialdemocratic PS to change collective bargaining negotiations in several sectors to individual negotiation of working conditions and salaries (Martins 2014: 2), restricted employment in the public sector, as well as closed many public schools, courts, hospitals, and other services (Stoleroff 2013: 311; Dias 2016). Due to the nationalisation of many industries, the number of public workers had increased since 1979 from about 300,000 to 737,774 by 2005; however, in 2012, the figure had declined to 583,812 (ibid.: 311–314). This was due to dismissals of public servants but also – and reflecting Bruff's analysis – due to the huge amount of outsourcing and privatisation processes. Such processes further decreased trade union coverage of workers, weakening the position of trade unions in negotiations whilst at the same time de-stabilising the state politically through increased protest.[49] Another shift towards Authoritarian Neoliberalism has been the implementation of a new comprehensive law which paved the way for a split between civil servants: "Magistrates, judges, diplomatic corps, police and criminal investigation and armed services" maintained their "traditional civil service status" (ibid.: 312), while the working conditions in other sectors, like education and health, were radically restructured. New sanctions and disciplinary dismissals against employees were implemented to reduce the public sector (ibid.).[50]

From March 2010 until March 2011, the PS minority government developed four versions of a Programme for Stability and Growth (PEC) in an attempt to control the national debts.[51] Following this development, and for the first time in 20 years, the two trade union federations decided to oppose these measures and organised a joint strike on 24 November 2010, where three million workers participated. Despite the size, the impact of the strike was not felt beyond Lisbon and Oporto and it had been primarily organised through pressure from different trade unions rather than rank and file members (Stoleroff 2015: 2). Still it led to a unique situation, as in the past the UGT had usually refrained from striking when the PS was in government. Thus, the first break in the social partnership alliance became visible (ibid.). However, despite the severe attacks on labour and its profound change in tactics, the UGT signed the tripartite social pact on employment and competitiveness in March 2011 (Campos Lima/Artiles 2011: 396).

The revision of the Labour Code in 2009 led to the emergence of a new, young, non-unionised, and precarious workforce,[52] yet the impact of the first three PECs were not felt until 2011. On 12 March, the mass demonstrations of Geração à Rasca highlighted the existing anger about precarious jobs and austerity measures, bringing between 300,000 and 500,000 people to the street (Baumgarten 2013). In the same month, PEC-IV was defeated in parliament, as the PSD refrained from supporting it and the Prime Minister José Socrates resigned (Freire 2014). The "intervention" of the Troika began in May 2011: whilst the PS held a caretaker government from April until the next general election in June they signed the Memorandum of Understanding (Martins 2014: 3), obtaining 78 billion euros of financial assistance for the country (Stoleroff 2013: 313–314).

The Troika did not replace the three PEC packages but rather deepened their scope. After the elections, the newly built conservative right-wing government of the PSD and CSD/PP proceeded – now with the external backing of the European financial apparatuses – to implement further austerity measures, targeting labour.[53] The public sector faces massive cuts,[54,55] but as the Constitutional Court reversed some of those decisions the government tried to find another way to enforce the savings. This was through targeting the Taxa Social Única (TSÚ) – the contribution that workers and employers pay for social security.[56] This was the period when the "Que se lixe a Troika!" (QSLT) movement developed. Contrary to the development of social movements in Ireland, the collective activity did not emerge from the communities but rather from left-wing networks and platforms of friends, local organisers, and members of parties or left groups. QSLT became the biggest and most influential platform that emerged between 2011 and 2013. At its peak, the platform was able to mobilise between 1 million (15 September 2015) and 1.5 million (2 March 2013) people to oppose austerity (Engelhardt 2017a).

As a backdrop to austerity, union density had declined from 60.8% in 1978 to about 19% in 2013. Part of the reason for the decline is that due to privatisations many unionised public employees lost their job or were re-employed in a private or self-employed contract and thus not covered by trade union bargaining and activity anymore.[57] This development stresses the thesis that privatisations are also politically important for the government to minimise the number of militant and unionised public workers and hence "outsource" struggle from state apparatuses to the private industry in order to reduce the tensions of political crisis, while this policy creates struggle at the same time. The impressive study carried out by Costa et al. (2015) also highlights how the trade unions as social partners were pushed out of the state apparatuses during the economic and political crisis, where the state took on a more authoritarian character. Interestingly, in 2010 under the PS government, 10.1% of trade union demands were totally accepted and 20.3% were partially integrated in the social pact (ibid.: 61). However, in 2013, under the PSD government, 2.4% were totally accepted, and 9.5% partially (ibid.), showing a drastic decline in trade union influence.

These dynamics illustrate how the trade unions had lost ground with the government and employers, and at the same time were watching social movement networks taking their place and mobilising workers, students, and the poor to mass demonstrations. In order to survive, their turn towards social movement unionism was inevitable. It was a move pushed by the movements and the state alike, shifting towards closer relations between trade unions and social movement platforms. While strikes were at a historical low with 99 in 2007, the figure nearly doubled in 2013,[58] and in that year alone, two general strikes (one co-organised by both federations) were organised in March and June. While QSLT activists had begun to support trade union picket lines, they also pushed the trade union leadership towards joint demonstrations during strike days. By supporting the logistics and organisation of the actions, including food supply, they connected the reproductive and productive issues and actors.

In June 2013, the government was on the brink of collapse. They were unable to implement the TSÚ, following mass protests, strikes, and the judicial crisis in which the Constitutional Court declared several austerity measures as unconstitutional, meaning that 1.3 billion Euros in public spending cuts could not be found (Engelhardt 2017b: 424). After the general strike on 27 June, the trade unions stopped all strikes and protest activity. The unions, alongside the social movement platform QSLT, had no clear strategy of what to expect when the government, instead of giving in to the demands, stepped down. While the trade union federations were not a state apparatus, they also did not act as a social movement, remaining instead silently in the middle. This, however, opened up space for new trade union activists, such as the dockworkers of the Lisbon port and the call centre workers from the health hotline Saúde24 (Costa et al. 2015: 64). These trade unionists developed links and joint strategies with social movement platforms, playing a critical role in the strike of Saúde24 in 2014 and the successful Lisbon dockworkers' strike in 2016.

Although the Troika left Portugal in May 2014, new budgets still have to be accepted by the European Commission. In October 2015, the general elections brought in a new political formation: a minority PS government, tolerated by the left-wing parties Left Bloc and the Communist Party. The result was clearly brought by the anti-austerity movements, which encouraged the majority of voters to opt for anti-austerity parties. For the first time, both trade union federations CGTP and UGT are presented in a semi-government or government position, meaning social partnership has been re-integrated through the already remaining institutional framework of the CPCS. This led to strikes decreasing during the first year of the new government, with trade unions instead concentrating on negotiations. As the economy stabilises, new strikes have emerged, demanding a rollback of the pay-freeze in the public sector and privatisations, reduction of the working week, and increased investments in public infrastructure.

It is unclear how long the upswing can remain and when the next economic meltdown can be expected. In this period, the trade union federations are now divided between their newly gained influence in the government and pressure from below. New labour activists have come to the fore, such as the dockworkers who do not belong to any federation but have won major success in combating precarious labour contracts at the ports,[59] and the call centre trade union, which is growing in a booming, but precarious industry.

Conclusion

This chapter aimed to highlight how trade unions, especially in the (post) crisis period, are neither homogenous nor static actors, but rather reflect and respond to the environmental and institutional dynamics or context they find themselves in. This is both a historical and analytical argument, meaning that we do not just use the historical analysis to undermine our case, but our analysis is developed out of the historical changes we perceive. A historical and relational approach to the state highlights how, although remaining capitalist, it is a field of struggle and in times of crisis can close or open certain channels to trade unions. Furthermore, the turn towards authoritarianism shows a fragility of the state in times of crisis. This shift has transformed, in particular, previous socialdemocratic partnership models that many trade unions had relied upon. It has also provoked multiple struggles, as have multiple struggles provoked some of these shifts, i.e. increased policing, fines, and executive control; it is a dialectic of structure and agency and space needs to be given to both.

Our examples of Ireland and Portugal stress how the relationships between the state, trade unions, and movements unfold as a tug of war; the neoliberal state is continually trying to expand to different fields in the same way that social movements push back and challenge power relations pulling trade unions into the realm of struggle and fragmenting trade union strategies. Thus, trade unions, even if often seen as the mediator of state policies and acting somewhat as a state apparatus, can also form alliances with movements turning the state into an antagonist. This tension is captured by the shifting role and position of trade unions in neoliberal (post)crisis states, where spaces of social partnership are pulled from under them, forcing unions to position themselves as either social movements or a (increasingly ostracised) state apparatus. However, these subsumption processes are never fully subsumed; they are always in process, where reactions to movements in one space provoke movements in another.

What we underline is the incoherence of social partnership in the (post) crisis period of neoliberalism. In the beginning stages of neoliberalism, partnership was (problematically) attractive to unions and the state as a way of issuing in such economic shifts, maintaining policy space, and keeping the peace. Yet, as neoliberalism becomes more crisis prone and authoritarian as a response, such models have become untenable as labour and capital cannot reach a social peace, or social pact within the *capitalist* state. The crisis has shifted from a debt crisis on the books of the Troika to a social and growing political crisis, of limited legitimacy where the burden of austerity has fallen to those at the bottom. In such times, it is necessary more than ever that trade unions take a combative role, aligning with working-class communities against the state and capital.

Notes

1 Engl. "to hell with the troika".
2 "The social is thus a historically changing, open-ended totality, whose reproductive logic resides in all its parts, even if its parts are not necessarily or purely functional or reducible to the whole" (Ferguson 2016: 47).
3 As Cenk Saraçoğlu points out, "In none of these approaches can one find a profound analysis of the connection between the internal contradictions of the social order in general, capitalism in particular, and the emergence of the movements and revolts" (Saraçoğlu 2017: 17).
4 For example, Richard Hyman (2001: 4) developed his influential triangle "the geometry of trade unionism" of society, market, and class, to analyse different characteristics of trade union activity, leaving out the state as a decisive actor and field of struggle. Also, in Beverly Silver's work (2003, 2013) we see a long historical analysis of labour struggles mediated through labour power resources and Karl Polanyi's concept of dual transformation, and although she engages with institutional developments like the labour market, the state, as such, does not appear.
5 For a detailed reflection on labour studies through a materialist state analysis see Alexander Gallas, Vom "Nachlaufspiel" zum multiskalaren Internationalismus (2016a) and "'There is power in a union': A strategic-relational perspective on power resources" (Gallas 2016b).
6 From a dialectical position, it is not a question of how structure influences agency and vice versa (with each seen as exteriorities) but how they inform each other in the process of becoming. Structures are instantiated through human beings – through sensuous human activity, meaning they are historically contingent, yet they also constrain, enable, or channel agency and may also be changed by collective activity.
7 We argue that any analysis of capitalism as a relation and process, that does not fully integrate social reproduction – including the home, institutions, and caring relations – misses half the story and thus potential for emancipatory struggle.
8 This was not just reflected in the sphere of labour struggles but, as Varda Burstyn describes, was also present in the women's currencies in the Canadian Democratic Party. When the struggles intensified in the 1970s, sexism inside the structures intensified over the 1970s and eventually even led to the exclusion of the more radical parts of the feminist movement from the party (Burstyn 1990).
9 For example, as part of the partnership models "neutral" state mediators such as designated labour courts are often established.
10 Before 2015, Fianna Fail held power for the last 69 out of 89 years; it is largely a populist rather than programmatic party, dominated by a strategy of co-optation in the face of disputes (Naughton 2015: 292).
11 Reflected in the important role that independents play in elections (Dunphy 2017: 268).
12 This continues today; for example, in September 2016 the EU Commission announced that the Apple Corporation had avoided taxes of around 13 billion euros, and Apple was told to pay these taxes. However, the Irish government refused to collect stating that the commission was bullying Ireland into accepting the unpaid taxes. This formed the backdrop of the 17th September protests in 2016 (Ogle 2016: 244–245).
13 There were six national Social Partnership Programs, and in 2006 a ten-year agreement called Towards 2016 was concluded with initial pay terms to run until 2008; in 2009 the model collapsed (O'Kelly 2010: 425).

14 As Roche describes (2007: 397),

> the balance of political advantage seemed to lie in brokering a national agreement through which unions might be persuaded to consent to government plans in return for concessions on the shape and focus of sending cuts, as well as modest gains in the areas of pay and income tax reduction.

15 This, one member of the unemployed workers' union stated, could be linked to how militant activities couldn't be carried out if they were against the main funding partners (i.e. the state) (Royall 2017: 9).

16 Even though the number of strikes during the dictatorship was very low: between 1871 and 1920 about 4,636 strikes were registered (Costa and Dias 2016: 148), whereas between 1934 and 1974 the number is very small. The strong cooperation of workers' councils in the "Estado Novo" shows how trade unions as state apparatuses cut themselves off from struggles of the subalterns and were cut off by the rest of the state apparatuses (i.e. the legislation) as strikes were declared a "criminal offence" (ibid.).

17 According to Barreto (1993: 461–462), the nationalisation process mainly targeted the seven big national companies involved in the financial industry and colonial trade; however the multinational enterprises from France, the USA, or West Germany "were not directly affected by the nationalizations and only a few closed their Portuguese subsidiaries following the large pay rises of 1974–75".

18 Partido Socialismo – Socialist Party – part of the social democratic parties/ Second International.

19 Partido Social Democrata – Social Democratic Party – conservative – liberal programme.

20 União Geral de Trabalhadores – General Union of the Workers – trade union federation partly affiliated to the PS and to the PSD.

21 Confederação Geral dos Trabalhadores Portugueses – General Confederation of the Portuguese Workers with which the Intersindical eventually merged; thus today it is called CGTP-IN.

22 CIP – Confederação Empresarial de Portugal – Business Federation of Portugal; CCP – Confederação do Comércio e Serviços de Portugal – Federation of Trade and Service of Portugal; CAP – Confederação dos Agricultores de Portugal – Agricultural Federation of Portugal; CTP – Confederação do Turismo Português – Federation of Portuguese Tourism.

23 This subsumption process is uneven and contradictory, so that waged social reproduction has not supplanted unwaged reproduction, and neither have all these processes been wholly turned into commodities, but it is becoming more correlative with capitalist relations.

24 In each historical epoch this contradiction takes a particular form, as such neoliberal or financialised capital has its own particularities (Fraser 2016: 100). In the drive for increased profit, capital destroys the commodity – labour – that can realise it. "In short, the need to secure the material reproduction of society contradicts the need to secure its social reproduction" (Clarke 1983: 12). The push for increased surplus value, through either expansion of absolute surplus value (expansion of the working day) or relative surplus value (productivity, wage decreases, or privatising the cost of reproduction), as well as the expansion into the remaining sites of subsistence through the enclosure of common land, knowledge, or support networks, threatens the (inter-generational) reproduction of labour power – social reproduction (see also Harvey 2010: 304–308;

Marx/Mandel 1992, in particular see Chapter 10. The Working Day and Chapters 11 and 12 that outline the concepts of relative and absolute surplus value).

25 The debt to GDP ratio increased from 24% in 2007 to 123% in 2013 and the deficit to GDP ratio increased from a small surplus in 2007 to a deficit of 32.4% in 2010 (Geary 2016: 1).

26 Writing in 2015, Daniel Finn points out that unemployment has fallen since the peak of 15% in 2012, to 10%, largely because of mass emigration (475,000 left between 2008 and 2014 from a total working population of 2 million). 17.5% of Irish-born people over the age of 15 currently live abroad (Finn 2015: 50).

27 The bounce back of GDP is misleading as it is used as a tax haven; for example, in 2012, 91 billion euros were counted as service-related exports from these companies, and 40 billion were actually transfer pricing (Finn 2015: 50).

28 The deprivation rate has risen from 11% in 2007 to 25% in 2011, and in 2014 31% equalling 1.9 million people (Hearne 2015: 309). Annual disposable income fell from 24,380 euros to 20,856 between 2008 and 2012.

29 There is now a return to enterprise level bargaining (O'Kelly 2010: 428). In the private sector, they established a protocol after the end of social partnership and in manufacturing, unions tried to maintain wage levels by agreeing to enhance productivity measures. With the end of social partnership the ICTU and IBEC agreed to a protocol that could inform the conduct of local pay bargaining in the private sector and dictated that if disputes continued it could use the state dispute resolution agency (Geary 2016: 7).

30 The Croke Park and Croke Park II agreements were critical in developing opposition within the public service unions to further austerity measures. Public service workers had faced a 25% cut in earnings between 2009 and 2013; importantly, SIPTU and IMPACT had been campaigning for a yes ballot for the new agreement (Erne 2013: 425). CPSU and Unite claimed that an approval of Croke Park II could lead to a split in the ICTU (ibid.: 427). SIPTU and IMPACT claimed that their members should accept this if they wanted to maintain a centralised collective agreement that would prevent further compulsory redundancies, redeployment, and outsourcing. Support for Croke Park I and II was very divided and threatened to split the ICTU, perhaps hinting at the divisions that would occur in the union movement following the water charges protests.

31 These included a protest of around 120,000 in 2009 in Dublin, a 250,000 public sector strike in November 2009, 100,000 marching in November 2010 in Dublin where union leaders were heckled, and in February 2013 110,000 marching across six cities (Cox 2017: 12). Although few in number, these were among the largest protests in living memory in Ireland (ibid.).

32 One union leader stated "political strikes are not part of our DNA" (Geary 2016: 5).

33 The Services, Industrial, Professional and Technical Union – one of the ICTU's largest affiliates, as well as being affiliated to the Labour Party.

34 As an alternative to further cuts, the ICTU put forward their Social Solidarity Pact in 2009 calling for increased corporate and high income tax rates, more training, and a strategic investment fund; this gained little attention in media or government and instead the unions were portrayed as a privileged sectional interest (Geary 2016: 4).

35 This was agreed to by the Fianna Fail-led government (alongside the greens) in negotiation with the Troika in the letter of intent, Memorandum of Economic and Financial Policies, and Technical Memorandum of Understanding in late 2010, with a view to start charging in 2012 (Admin 2014). Up until 2014, water had been financed by the general taxation system with no extra use charges for households. Irish Water, a new (but autonomous) state institution, was set up

and would be in charge of all water services including the installation of water meters and the payment of bills.

36 This included multiple days of action that got over 100,000 people on the streets, some of the biggest protests in Irish history. It was one of the largest and most sustained movements in Ireland since independence (Hearne 2015: 312).

37 By December 2014 over half of households had signalled that they would boycott the charges in a poll carried out by the Irish Times (Finn 2015: 57).

38 The use of Dennis O'Brien's company to install the water meters, a long time Fianna Fail and Fine Gael donor, reflects the corruption of the boom period, helped shift the external cognitive dynamic against Irish Water. Furthermore, there had been a successful water charges movement in the 1990s that fed into the current protest. Organisationally, the bin charges and household charges protest that had been lost in the early years of the crisis highlighted to many the importance of alliances, and setting up organizational processes that could foster solidarity across the political parties, trade unions, and community groups (Ogle 2016).

39 As one protester quoted stated "when politics becomes personal you have no other choice but to get out and protest" (Lynch 2015 quoted in Cox 2017: 24).

40 Following the protests a revised water plan was put in place, which offered a 100-euro conservation grant for everyone who signed up (seen by many as bribery) the promise that it would no longer be administered by the Department of Social Protection resulted in a cut to proposed profits of 80% and a capping of bills until 2018, which turned out to contravene the EU Directive and Eurostat:

> Most thought that he was basically offering a 'bribe' of 100euros as a 'conservation grant' to get as many people as possible on the hook into an Irish Water contract, and that he would then allow the bills to spiral again in 2018 after the next general election.
>
> (Ogle 2016: 87)

Interestingly, the introduction of the conservation grant contravened EU policy, and in July 2015 the European Commission Directorate-General Eurostat ruled that Irish water was "a non-market entity controlled by government" (Eurostat 2015: 12). Irish Water could not be considered a private entity and thus its borrowings would need to be included on the public balance sheet. This destroyed one of the main reasons for introducing water charges put forward by the government around savings (Finn 2015: 63).

41 Jobstown signalled a particular turning point in the relations between the state and the movement. The reaction from the judicial system, government, and gardai to the protest in the working-class community of Jobstown was a crackdown. This period also saw increased policing and the use of the court system as a tool of coercion. Paul Murphy TD described the shift as "political policing" (Ogle 2016: 92).

42 Right2Water was the first attempt by MANDATE and UNITE – two unions that had no Labour Party affiliation – to organise outside the ICTU framework. In particular, in opposition to SIPTU and IMPACT the most important ICTU affiliates those who are close to the Labour Party and had tried to limit dissent with the party since 2011 (Finn 2015: 56).

43 A key question of R2W was "could a campaign be developed that wasn't trade union, political or community-focussed, but that could bring all three together? The concept of the 'three pillars' of Right2Water was born" (Ogle 2016: 64).

44 IMPACT President Gerry King argued for the need to protect their members in water sanitation against outsourcing and privatisation; SIPTU also argued this

stating that the extra money (to be gained from Irish Water) was currently spent on public services (Ogle 2016).

45 As Brendan Ogle describes in his reflection on the conference:

> This was a victory for the Right2Water unions on behalf to the thousands of water warriors nationwide. In that room we were David struggling not to be emasculated by Goliath whereas we knew outside the room that the working class movement was what most trade union members actually supported.

He goes on to state that

> the cheering and congratulations that took over the hall after the vote was a spontaneous manifestation that a people's movement was fighting back within a Congress that many thought had abandoned the working class in the social partnership era. But now we were fighting to claim our movement back.
>
> (Ogle 2016: 194).

46 As Unite spokesperson, Simon Dubbins, stated,

> unions have been slow to engage with the Occupy movement and are accustomed to dealing with formal structures and leadership elites – and so are sometimes uneasy with informal, grass roots-led movements. Learning different methods and different ways of 'doing' democracy is often a steep learning curve for those from this tradition.
>
> (Massey 2015: 25)

47 Labour was reduced to 7 out of their previous 37 seats, and Fine Gael lost 26 out of the 76 seats won in 2011; Right2Change candidates won 36 seats, resulting in a Fianna Fail-led minority government, signalling a shift away from electoral politics over 35% of people did not vote (Ogle 2016).

48 Between 1999 and 2008, the annual GDP increase remained below 1% (Rodrigues/Reis 2012); hence, in "Portugal the global crisis deepened the already critical economic situation" (Campos Lima/Artiles 2011: 394).

49 Elements of the weakening of the state are the pushing out of trade unions from a state apparatus role into a social movement actor, which in turn strengthened the anti-austerity movement. Furthermore, the overall mistrust in the Portuguese political system increased from 17.2% in 2002 to 29.4% in 2008 and "therefore remaining about 10% above the average" (Estanque/Costa 2012: 267). Also telling is the level of abstention in national elections that remains around 40%.

50 In 2011, "public sector workers had their salaries cut by up to 10% and saw their Christmas subsidy reduced by 50%" (Estanque/Costa 2012: 263).

51 The austerity measures included:

> A 5 percent reduction on all expenditure on public sector wages, including a wage cut of between 3.5 percent and 10 percent for wages above €1 500 a month; the freezing of all promotions; reduction in spending on pensions, allowances and other social benefits, including family allowances; raising value-added tax (VAT) from 21 percent to 23 percent; freezing public investment; and privatizations in the transport sector.
>
> (Campos Lima/Artiles 2011: 397)

52 One in every two employees between the ages of 15 and 34 works in precarious employment (Costa et al. 2015: 46).

53 The MoU "established a broad set of structural measures. With regard to the labour market it envisaged measures relating to protection in case of unemployment, protection of employment, working time, setting of wages and active labour market policies" (Martins 2014).

54 Among the measures have been the reduction of the unemployment insurance benefits to "no more than 18 months" (Stoleroff 2014: 8), 27% of cuts of directorships, and the reduction of the overtime payment by 50% (Stoleroff 2013: 311–312).

55 This was especially problematic for the lower paid sectors as many of public employees had accrued debts over the year, with the intention to pay them back with the 13th and 14th "instalment of their annual wages" (Stoleroff 2013: 314).

56 The aim was to reduce the amount that employers contributed from 23.75% to 18% and increase the share of the workers from 11% to 18% (ibid.).

57 For instance, in 2010, about 425,877 workers were still covered by trade union activity and bargaining; in 2013 the number dropped to only 292,005 of workers who could be legally called for strike activity (Costa et al. 2015: 60).

58 The highest number of strikes occurred in 1981 with 756 strikes during that year (Costa et al. 2015: 55).

59 The dockworkers have become especially active across social movements; they were the only trade union which openly supported the anti-austerity movement and the precarious networks from 2012 onwards. And in response, when they went on strike in 2016, LGBT networks, students, unemployed, and feminist groups were active in turning public opinion in support of the dockworkers, supporting their picket lines, and mobilising for a joint national demonstration against precarious labour.

Literature

Accornero, Guya (2015): Back to the Revolution: The 1974 Portuguese Spring and Its "Austere Anniversary". *Historein* 15 (1): 32–48.

Admin (2014): *Thicker Than Uisce*. Broadsheet.ie.

Bach, Stephen; Stroleny, Alexandra (2013): Public Service Employment Restructuring in the Crisis in the UK and Ireland: Social Partnership in Retreat. *European Journal Industrial Relations* 19 (4): 341–357.

Bakker, Isabella; Gill, Stephen (eds.) (2003): *Power Production and Social Reproduction: Human In/Security in the Global Political Economy*. London: Palgrave.

Bannerji, Himani (2005): Building from Marx: Reflections on Class and Race. *Social Justice* 32 (4): 144–160.

Barreto, José (1993): Portugal: Political Relations Under Democracy. In: Ferner, Anthony; Hyman, Richard (eds.): *Industrial Relations in the New Europe*. Oxford: Blackwell Publishing, 445–481.

Baumgarten, Britta (2013): Geracao a Rasca and Beyond: Mobilizations in Portugal after 12 March 2011. *Current Sociology* 61 (4): 457–473.

Bieler, Andreas (2017): Fighting for Public Water: The First Successful European Citizens' Initiative "Water and Sanitation Are a Human Right". *Interface* 9 (1): 300–326.

Bruff, Ian (2014): The Rise of Authoritarian Neoliberalism. *Rethinking Marx* 26 (1): 113–129.

Bruff, Ian (2017): Authoritarian Neoliberalism and the Myth of Free Markets. *Progress in Political Economy (PPE)*. http://ppesydney.net/authoritarian-neoliberalism-myth-free-markets/.

Burstyn, Varda (1990): The Waffle and the Women's Movement. *Studies in Political Economy* 33 (1): 175–184.

Campos Lima, Maria da Paz; Artiles, Antonio M. (2011): Crisis and Trade Union Challenges in Portugal and Spain: Between General Strikes and Social Pacts. *Transfer* 17 (3): 387–402.

Campos Lima, Maria da Paz; Naumann, Reinhard (2000): Social Pacts in Portugal: From Comprehensive Policy Programmes to the Negotiation of Concrete Industrial Relations Reforms? In: Fajertag, Guiseppe; Pochet, Philippe (eds.): *Social Pacts in Europe New Dynamics*. Brussels: ETUI, 321–341.

Cannon, Barry; Murphy, Mary P. (2015): Where Are the Pots and Pans? Collective Responses in Ireland to Neoliberalization in a Time of Crisis: Learning from Latin America. *Irish Political Studies* 30 (1): 1–19.

Clarke, Simon (1983): State, Class Struggle, and the Reproduction of Capital. *Kapitalstate* 10: 113–130.

Costa, Hermes A. (1994): A construção do pacto social em Portugal. *Revista Crítica Ciências Sociais* 39 (5): 119–146.

Costa, Hermes A. (2017): Opinião. "Call centers" entre a fatalidade e a utopia. *PÚBLICO*. www.publico.pt/2017/07/07/economia/opiniao/call-centersi-entre-a-fatalidade-e-a-utopia-1778052 (checked 12.13.17).

Costa, Hermes A.; Dias, Hugo (2016): The Strike as a Challenge to the North and to the South. *Workers of the World* 8 (1): 143–159.

Costa, Hermes A.; Dias, Hugo; Soero, José (2015): Strikes and Austerity in Portugal: Perspectives, Expression and Recomposition. *RCCS Annual Review* 7: 45–73.

Cox, Laurence (2017): The Irish Water Charges Movement: Theorising 'the Social Movement in General'. *Interface* 9 (1): 161–203.

Dias, Joao P. (2016): The Transition to a Democratic Portuguese Judicial System: (Delaying) Changes in the Legal Culture. *International Journal of Law in Context* 12 (1): 24–41.

Dunphy, Richard (2017): Beyond Nationalism? The Anti-Austerity Social Movement in Ireland: Between Domestic Constraints and Lessons from Abroad. *Journal of Civil Society* 13 (3): 267–283.

Engelhardt, Anne (2017a): *Anti-Austerity Movements and Authoritarian Statism in Portugal: Integrating Social Movement Research into Poulantzas's Theory of the Capitalist State*. New Research in GPE Working Paper 04/2017, University of Kassel.

Engelhardt, Anne (2017b): Know Your Rights: Portugal zwischen Verfassungsaktivismus und sozialen Bewegungen. Die Staatskrise 2013 aus der Sicht materialistischer Bewegungsforschung. *Kritische Justiz* 50 (4): 417–433.

Engelhardt, Anne; Moore, Madelaine (2017): Moving Beyond the Toolbox: Providing Social Movement Studies with a Materialist Dialectical Lens. *Momentum Quarterly. Zeitschrift für Sozialen Fortschritt* 6 (4): 270–288.

Erne, Roland (2013): Let's Accept a Smaller Slice of a Shrinking Cake. The Irish Congress of Trade Unions and Irish Public Sector Unions in Crisis. *Transfer* 19 (3): 425–430.

Esposito, Vincent L. (2014): *Constitutions Through the Lens of the Global Financial Crisis: Considering the Experience of the United States, Portugal, and Greece*. Law School Student Scholarship. Paper 461.

Esser, Josef (1981): Staatsfixierung oder 'Stärkung der eigenen Kraft?': Überlegungen zum aktuellen Verhältnis Staat – Gewerkschaften in der Bundesrepublik. *Gewerkschaftliche Monatshefte* 32: 366–375.

Estanque, Elisio; Costa, Hermes A. (2012): Labour Relations and Social Movements in the 21st Century. In: Erasga, Dennis (ed.): *Sociological Landscape – Theories, Realities and Trends.* Rijeka: InTech, 257–282.

Eurostat (2015): Sector Classification of Irish Water. *Directorate D: Government Finance Statistics and quality.* http://ec.europa.eu/eurostat/documents/1015035/6761701/Advice-2015-IE-Classification-of-Irish-Water-UpdateIII.pdf   (checked 12.13.17).

Ferguson, Susan (2016): Intersectionality and Social-Reproduction Feminisms: Toward an Integrative Ontology. *Historical Materialism* 24 (2): 38–60.

Finn, Daniel (2015): Ireland's Water Wars. *New Left Review 95.*

Fonseca, Guilherme Da; Domingos, Ines (1998): Constitutional Limitations on Privatisation. The Constitution of the Portuguese Republic and the Constitutional Case-Law. A few notes. *Documentacao e Direito Comparado* 73/74: 129–140.

Fraser, Nancy (2016): Contradictions of Capital and Care. *New Left Review* II: 99–117.

Freire, A. (2014): *The Condition of Portuguese Democracy during the Troika's Intervention.* ECPR Conference Paper: Crisis politics in Southern Europe: Challenges to Democratic Governance.

Gallas, Alexander (2016a): Vom "Nachlaufspiel" zum multiskalaren Internationalismus. In: Brand, Ulrich; Schwenken, Helen; Wullweber, Joscha (ed.): *Globalisierung Analysieren, Kritisieren und Verändern. Das Projekt Kritische Wissenschaft. Christoph Scherrer zum 60. Geburtstag.* Hamburg: VSA, 145–162.

Gallas, Alexander (2016b): "There Is Power in a Union": A Strategic-Relational Perspective on Power Resources. In: Truger, Achim; Hein, Eckhard; Heine, Michael; Hoffer, Frank (eds.): *Monetäre Makroökonomie, Arbeitsmärkte und Entwicklung. Festschrift für Hansjörg Herr.* Metropolis-Verlag: Marburg, 195–210.

Geary, John (2016): Economic Crisis, Austerity and Trade Union Responses: The Irish Case in Comparative Perspective. *European Journal of Industrial Relations* 22 (2): 131–147.

Harvey, David (2010): *A Companion to Marx's Capital.* London; New York: Verso.

Hearne, Rory (2015): The Irish Water War. *Interface* 7 (1): 309–321.

Hyman, Richard (2001): Understanding European Trade Unionism: Between Market, Class and Society. London: SAGE.

Küpeli, Ismail (2013): *Nelkenrevolution Reloaded? Krise und soziale Kämpfe in Portugal, Systemfehler.* Münster: Edition Assemblage.

Landy, David (2017): *How we won the Irish Water War – The Fight Over Interpretation.* Paper presented at the Alternative Futures 2017, Manchester.

Martins, D.C., 2014. *Labour Law in Portugal between 2011 and 2014.* Paper for the "Young Scholars Meeting" of the "XI European Regional Congress 2014".

Marx, Karl; Engels, Friedrich (1848): Man*ifesto of the Communist Party.* Marxists Internet Archive (marxists.org).

Marx, Karl; Mandel, Ernest (1992): *Capital: Volume 1: A Critique of Political Economy.* Reprint edition. New York: Penguin.

Massey, Doreen (2015): European Alternatives: A Roundtable Discussion with Marina Prentoulis, Sirio Canos and Simon Dubbins. *Soundings* 60: 13–28.

Mohandesi, Salar; Teitelman, Emma (2017): Without Reserves. In: Bhattacharya, Tithi (ed.): *Social Reproduction Theory.* London: Pluto Press, 37–66.

Muehlebach, Andrea (2017): The Irish Water Insurgency: No More Blood from These Stones. *ROAR Magazine.* https://roarmag.org/essays/ireland-anti-austerity-water-protests/ (accessed 8.10.17).

Naughton, Mary (2015): An Interrogation of the Character of Protest in Ireland since the Bailout. *Interface* 7 (1): 289–308.

Ogle, Brendan (2016): *From Bended Knee to a New Republic: How the Fight for Water Is Changing Ireland*. Dublin: The Liffey Press.

O'Kelly, Kevin P. (2010): The End of Social Partnership in Ireland? *Transfer* 16 (3): 425–429.

Poulantzas, Nicos A. (2014): *State, Power, Socialism, Radical Thinkers*. London: Verso.

Poulantzas, Nicos A.; Martin, James (2008): *The Poulantzas Reader: Marxism, Law, and the State*. London: Verso.

Roche, William K. (2007): Social Partnership in Ireland and New Social Pacts. *Industrial Relations* 46 (3): 395–425.

Rodrigues, Joao; Reis, José (2012): The Asymmetries of European Integration and the Crisis of Capitalism in Portugal. *Competition & Change* 16 (3): 188–205.

Royall, Frédéric (2017): Resisting Austerity? The Case of the Irish National Organisation of the Unemployed. *Journal of Contemporary European Studies* 25 (1): 73–87.

Saraçoğlu, Cenk (2017): Building an Alternative to Mainstream Social Movement Theories: Totality and Antagonism. In: Balashova, Oksana; Karatepe, Ismail D.; Namukasa, Aishah (eds.): *Where Have All the Classes Gone? A Critical Perspective on Struggles and Collective Action, Labour and Globalization*. München: Rainer Hampp, 12–28.

Sayer, Andrew (1992): *Method in Social Science: A Realist Approach*. London: Routledge.

Silver, Beverly (2013): Theorising the Working Class in Twenty-First-Century Global Capitalism. In: Atzeni, Maurizio (ed.): *Workers and Labour in a Globalised Capitalism. Contemporary Themes and Theoretical Issues*. London: Palgrave, 46–69.

Silver, Beverly (2003): *Forces of Labor: Workers' Movements and Globalization since 1870*. Cambridge: Cambridge University Press.

Sperling, Urte (2014): *Die Nelkenrevolution in Portugal*. Köln: PapyRossa.

Stoleroff, Alan (2013): Employment Relations and Unions in Public Administration in Portugal and Spain: From Reform to Austerity. *European Journal of Industrial Relations* 19 (4): 309–323.

Stoleroff, Alain. (2014): *Towards an Assessment of Portuguese Union Strategies in the Context of Austerity and Adjustment: Union Leaders' Discourse Meets Sociological and Political Analysis*. Working Paper, ISCTE-Lisbon University Institute.

Stoleroff, Alan (2015): *Interview*.

Varela, Raquel (2014): *História do povo na Revolução Portuguesa 1974–75*. Lisboa: Bertrand.

Wöhl, Stefanie; Wissel, Jens (2008): Staatstheorie vor neuen Herausforderungen. Einleitung. In: Wissel, Jens; Wöhl, Stefanie (eds.): *Staatstheorie vor neuen Herausforderungen: Analyse und Kritik*. Münster: Westfälisches Dampfboot, 7–22.

Chapter 19

Social movements or state apparatus?

Roland Erne

Madeleine Moore and Anne Engelhardt are proposing a strong thesis: "The shifting role and position of trade unions in neoliberal (post)crisis states, where spaces of social partnership are pulled from under them, [are] forcing unions to position themselves as either social movements or a (increasingly ostracised) state apparatus" (2018: xx). And yet, the empirical material on the cycles of union protest and accommodation in Ireland and Portugal presented in their chapter also allows less Manichean conclusions. At different points in time, the very same unions responded quite differently to the shift to more vertical modes of economic governance after the crisis. Periods of accommodation followed periods of contestation, and vice versa.

On the use of typologies

The distinction of unions as social movements and as part of the state apparatus is meaningful. Nevertheless, I would like to add some words of caution on the use of typologies in comparative research. Sure, in comparison to their Southern European counterparts, most Irish union leaders have pursued less contentious strategies in response to the imposition of wage and austerity cuts. And yet, it is misleading to describe the Irish union movement as a whole – or Services Industrial Professional and Technical Union (SIPTU) or IMPACT in particular – as an extension of an (increasingly ostracised) state apparatus. If that description were true, IMPACT (now called Fórsa) would hardly have been able to force Ryanair to recognise trade unions in December 2017, as the result of a concerted union effort in conjunction with other unions across Europe, which included the threat of coordinated, transnational strike action of Ryanair pilots (Golden and Burtenshaw 2017).

Union movements and individual unions have always included both contentious and partnership-oriented sections. Whereas these intra-union differences at times impeded the conclusion of corporatist arrangements, governments and employers' associations would hardly have an interest in corporatist arrangements in the absence of any threat of contentious collective action. The reformist Portuguese union confederation UGT, for example, would hardly have been able to conclude any social partnership agreements with Portuguese governments and employers without the "street pressures" applied by the more radical union federation CGTP-IN. Union movements should therefore not be put in different boxes, based on their alleged partnership-oriented or contentious union strategies. We also do not need to create a middle category to which union, that are neither social movements nor part of the state apparatus, could be assigned to. What we need instead is a different use of analytical typologies.

Real-life actors can hardly afford to pursue a clear-cut strategy because real situations are hardly ever clear-cut (Crouch 2005). It follows that one should not aim to put particular unions into specific boxes, as this must entail the use of stylised evidence to ensure that a specific real-life case fits into a box. And yet, acknowledging these practical incongruencies does not imply the end of clear-cut typologies. On the contrary, clear-cut frameworks do help us with explaining unions' varying strategic choices, but only if one uses them as a heuristic tool. Such tool helps us capture the "double character" of unionism, which is at work within each union and union movement (Zoll 1976). The use of typologies as a heuristic tool differs from the recurrent use of typologies in much of industrial relations and political economy research, which likes to put different varieties of unions, countries, growth models, or capitalisms into specific boxes. Heuristic typologies, however, serve another purpose. They help us capture the tensions and latent features present in each singular case. This may help us get a better understanding of the factors that trigger institutional change (Crouch and Farrell 2004).

The power of a union to conclude exchanges with employers and/or political leaders implies a (partial) renunciation of its political and/or industrial mobilisation powers, i.e. the capacity to wage industrial action and political mobilisations. Conversely, a union's exchange power remains dependent on its capacity to threaten the social consensus. The exchange power of a union depends on its mobilisation power. In consequence, exchange power uses – but does not reproduce – mobilisation power (Erne 2008: 33). This may explain why union responses to the crisis, and the vertical policy interventions it triggered, very much oscillated between phases of protest and accommodation (Stan et al. 2015).

In the Irish public sector, for example, most union members went on a national strike in 2009 and subsequently engaged in a prolonged period of "work-to-rule" against pay cuts proposed by the Irish government. These industrial actions were not able to stop the proposed pay cuts, not least because the government did not apply any of the proposed wage cuts to the so-called "semi-state" sector. By contrast to their counterparts in Southern Europe, this meant that the most militant Irish union members in the public transport sector, which incidentally also retain the highest amount of structural power (Silver 2003), could not enter the pay dispute.

In June 2010, most union members in public education, healthcare, and the civil service accepted a national public-sector agreement (Croke Park 1). This agreement reflects a lack of industrial strength and political pressures from Labour as well as from the centre-right parties Fine Gael and Fianna Fail (Allen and O'Boyle 2013; Culpepper and Regan 2014). In addition, the neoliberal media bias applied significant pressure on union leaders (Mercille 2013). Whereas unions and their members agreed to cooperate on wide-scale reforms of the public sector, the government promised not to impose layoffs or further pay cuts.

When the government demanded further pay cuts in 2013, however, the members of SIPTU and most other unions rebelled once again and voted against the Croke Park 2 Agreement, in defiance of their union leadership (Erne 2013). In turn, this revolt led to the adoption of the Financial Emergency Measures in the Public Interest Act by the Fine Gael – Labour Party government, which gave the Minister for Public Expenditure and Reform the power to determinate pay and conditions of public sector workers unilaterally. Thus, after having been confronted with the "sovereign power of the state" (Szabó 2018), most of union members supported a new public pay agreement (Haddington Road Agreement) as the lesser evil. The new agreement included further wage cuts and working time increases, which were, nonetheless, not as severe as those of the Croke Park 2 Agreement (Maccarrone et al. forthcoming).

The portrayal of Ireland as the poster child of austerity is yet hardly warranted, as shown by Roche, O'Connell, and Prothero (2016). The setbacks Irish unions suffered in the field of public collective bargaining did not lead to the end of contentious union action, as nicely shown in Moore and Engelhardt's discussion of the *right2water* campaign. Contentious union action just moved from the area of collective bargaining to struggles about access rights to public services. Similar shifts also occurred elsewhere, as shown, for example, by the *right2water* struggles in Greece, Portugal, Italy, Berlin, and at the European Union (EU) level (Bieler 2017; Bieler and Jordan 2017; Erne and Blaser 2018).

Nevertheless, it is not yet clear to what extent the analytical distinctions between a social partnership and contentious union orientations may help us explain the shift of contentious union action from the area of collective bargaining to the sphere of social reproduction. Irish community organisations had been incorporated into the state's social partnership machinery during the Celtic Tiger years to an even higher degree than the unions. Whereas unions preserved a certain degree of financial autonomy, despite their dependence on the state's cooperation in the collection of union dues at source, community organisations became very dependent on state funding (Visser 2018). Accordingly, the Irish *right2water* demonstrations would have hardly been possible without considerable union funding for the campaign.

Thus, Moore and Engelhardt's chapter (Chapter 18) calls for further research: what explains the increased salience of disputes over public service provisions in labour mobilisations? And why are unions much more successful in "right2publicservice" campaigns in comparison to more traditional actions in defence of workers' terms and conditions? Whereas answers to the second question may be found relatively easily, by studying in more detail the complementary dynamics between unions and social movements identified by Moore and Engelhardt, answers to the first question are more difficult to find. This is true especially if we are limiting our attention to "the state" and the related dynamics between national political and socio-economic actors.

Problematising the state

Moore and Engelhardt's focus on state structures is very warranted. The more vertical governance structures transcend national boundaries, however, the more one must move beyond a Weberian or Gramscian focus on the nation-state (Jessop 2016). We have therefore set out an ERC research project that aims to go beyond the methodological nationalism that is still dominating much of industrial relations and political economy research. We need not only a better understanding of the interplay between the old and new social movements and the state, but there is also an imperative to problematise the nation-state and the emerging EU state structures that are reconfiguring it (Erne 2015, 2018a).

Until the advent of the Euro crisis, the EU's political and business leaders had believed that the horizontal market pressures would lead to an automatic convergence of the European economy, hence, their resistance to any idea of an EU governance system, especially in industrial relations and social policy (Léonard et al. 2007). When the Euro crisis, however, demonstrated that horizontal market pressures had not led to the desired convergence but rather to severe economic imbalances, the tune changed substantially. In 2011, the European Parliament and Council adopted the so-called Six-Pack of EU laws on EU economic governance, which made the social and economic policies of Member States subject to binding EU recommendations. These vertical EU interventions also affect policy areas that have hitherto been largely shielded from EU interventions, namely industrial relations and social policy (Erne 2015).

The pertinent question can therefore hardly be *if* there will be any European coordination of national wage and social policies, as suggested by Höpner and Seeliger (2017), as there already is one. In fact, since 2011, the EU's new economic governance (NEG) regime has already been coordinating national wage and social policies. Since the macroeconomic imbalance procedure came into force as part of the six-pack of EU laws in 2011, nominal unit labour costs (ULC) have not risen above the allowed scoreboard ceiling of plus 9% over a period of three years in almost any eurozone state. Nonetheless, the EU's country-specific recommendations continue to outline measures that depress ULC, apart from the recommendations for Germany. Likewise, the modes and scope of public service provisions have also become an issue for EU coordination. EU country-specific recommendations are also targeting public transport, water, and health services.

This form of European coordination is operating in a way that is not labour-friendly: rendering past distinctions between optimists and pessimists on the European coordination of wage policies meaningless, which had assumed that a European coordination would always favour labour. Even so, our preliminary analyses of the EU's NEG regime have also uncovered internal contradictions that may be exploited by labour movements.

National and EU policymakers recurrently refer to the "fiscal space", i.e. the budgetary room given to a national government to provide resources for public purposes without breaching fiscal benchmarks set in the NEG scoreboards. Contrariwise, unions could refer to the vast, yet unused "wage bargaining space", i.e. the room for additional wage increases given the huge differences between ULC ceilings set by the NEG scoreboard and the actual ULC developments. In the 2010–2012 period, the nominal ULC figure for Ireland was −10.4%. In the 2014–2016 period, this figure had declined further to −20.5%, even if an increase of up to +9.0% would have been acceptable, according to the NEG scoreboard. The figures for other countries are pointing in the same direction. The figures of Germany, for example, had also remained significantly below the +9.0% MIP thresholds, with +3.0% (2010–2012) and +5.2% (2014–2016) (European Commission 2013: 30; 2018: 45).

The difference between the reported ULC figures that show that there are no excessive wage increases and NEG interventions that imply the contrary is just one contradiction of the NEG regime that the labour movement could politicise. Another politicisation strategy is dependent on unions' capacity to highlight the similar patterns behind NEG recommendations that aim to further commodify public services across countries. The success or failure of such a strategy, however, can only be assessed if our analytical lenses are transcending the nation-state; hence, our commitment to multi-sited fieldwork (Erne 2018a).

The increasing salience of EU interventions in industrial relations and social policy is politicising the EU integration process, as it is easier for social and political actors to politicise vertical EU governance interventions in comparison to abstract horizontal market forces (Erne 2008). What remains to be seen is to what extent the concomitant politicisation processes will restructure the political space along class or national divides. Whereas Hooghe and Marks (2006) have stressed workers' alleged primordial attachment to the nation-state, our analysis of the recent EU referendum debates in Ireland and France has shown that class politics explains workers' and unions' growing Euroscepticism better than cultural politics (Béthoux et al. 2018). The formation of vertical EU state structures may paradoxically favour the creation of a transnational democracy. Democracy requires not only people (demos) but also political power (kratos). Furthermore, democratisation has historically occurred due to struggles that politicised class conflict around tangible social demands. In our current research, we are therefore exploring to what extent European anti-austerity protest movements are politicising the NEG along class and national divides (Erne 2018b).

Acknowledgements

I would like to acknowledge the comments provided by Bianca Föhrer, Darragh Golden, Jamie Jordan, Sabina Stan, and Imre Szabó on an earlier draft of this chapter. This work was supported by the EU's Jean Monnet Chair programme [grant agreement 2016–2391] and the European Research Council grant "Labour Politics and the EU's New Economic Governance Regime (European Unions)" [grant agreement 725240].

Literature

Allen, Kieran; O'Boyle, Brian (2013). *Austerity Ireland. The Failure of Irish Capitalism*. London: Pluto Press.
Béthoux, Élodie; Erne, Roland; Golden, Darragh (2018). A Primordial Attachment to the Nation? *British Journal of Industrial Relations*. Online First.
Bieler, Andreas (2017). Fighting for Public Water. *Interface* 9 (1): 300–326.
Bieler, Andreas; Jordan, Jamie (2017). Commodification and 'The Commons'. *European Journal of International Relations*, Online First.
Crouch, Colin (2005). *Capitalist Diversity and Change*. Oxford: OUP.
Crouch, Colin; Farrell, Henry (2004). Breaking the Path of Institutional Development? Alternatives to the New Determinism. *Rationality and Society* 16 (1): 5–43.
Culpepper, Pepper D.; Regan, Aidan (2014). Why Don't Governments Need Trade Unions Anymore? *Socio-Economic Review* 12 (4): 723–745.
Erne, Roland (2008). *European Unions*. Ithaca: Cornell University Press.
Erne, Roland (2013). Let's Accept a Smaller Slice of a Shrinking Cake. *Transfer* 19 (3): 425–430.
Erne, Roland (2015). A Supranational Regime that Nationalizes Social Conflict. *Labor History* 56 (3): 345–368.
Erne, Roland (2018a). Labour Politics and the EU's New Economic Governance Regime (European Unions). *Transfer* 24 (2): 237–247.
Erne, Roland (2018b). How to Analyse a Supranational Regime that Nationalises Social Conflict? In: Nanopoulos, Eva; Vergis, Fotis (eds.): *The Crisis Behind the Euro-Crisis*. Cambridge: CUP.
Erne, Roland; Blaser, Markus (2018): Direct Democracy and Trade Union Action. *Transfer* 24 (2): 217–232.

European Commission (2013). *Alert Mechanism Report 2014*. COM/2013/0790 Final. https://eur-lex.europa.eu/legal-content/EN/TXT/?qid=1476351226272&uri=CELEX:52013DC0790.

European Commission (2018). *Alert Mechanism Report 2018*. COM/2017/771 final/2. https://eur-lex.europa.eu/legal-content/EN/TXT/PDF/?uri=CELEX:52017DC0771R(01)&qid=1529498023761&from=EN.

Golden, Darragh; Burtenshaw, Ronan (2017). Ryanair's Humble Pie. *Jacobin*, 12th December. www.jacobinmag.com/2017/12/ryanairs-humble-pie.

Hooghe, Lisbet; Marks, Gary (2004). 'Europe's blues'. *PS* 39 (2): 247–250.

Höpner, Martin; Seeliger, Martin (2017). *Transnationale Lohnkoordination zur Stabilisierung des Euro?* Discussion Paper 17/13. Köln: MPIfG.

Jessop, Bob (2016). *The State: Past, Present, Future*. Cambridge: Polity.

Léonard, Evelyn; Erne, Roland; Smismans, Stijn; Marginson, Paul (2007). *New Structures, Forms and Processes of Governance in European Industrial Relations*. Luxembourg: Official Publication of the European Communities.

Maccarrone, Vincenzo; Erne, Roland; Regan, Aidan (2019). Ireland: The Trajectory of Collective Bargaining and Industrial Relations Reform. In: Müller, Torsten; Vandaele, Kurt; Waddington, Jamie (eds.), *Collective Bargaining in Europe*. Brussels: ETUI.

Mercille, Julien (2013). The Role of the Media in Fiscal Consolidation Programmes. *Cambridge Journal of Economics* 38 (2): 281–300.

Roche, William K.; O'Connell, Philip J.; Prothero, Andrea (eds.) (2016). *Austerity and Recovery in Ireland*. Oxford: OUP.

Silver, Beverly J. (2003). *Forces of Labor*. Cambridge: Cambridge University Press.

Stan, Sabina; Helle, Idar; Erne, Roland (2015). European Collective Action in Times of Crisis. *Transfer* 21 (2): 131–139.

Szabó, Imre (2018). Trade Unions and the Sovereign Power of the State. *Transfer* 24 (2): 163–178.

Visser, Anna M. (2018). Democracy, CSOs, and State Funding: The Ways in Which the State Funding Influenced the Democratic Roles of Anti-Poverty Networks in Ireland from 2004 to 2011. PhD Thesis. UCD: Dublin.

Zoll, Rainer (1976). *Der Doppelcharakter der Gewerkschaften*. Frankfurt: Suhrkamp.

Index

Note: **Bold** page numbers refer to tables; *italic* page numbers refer to figures and page numbers followed by "n" denote endnotes.